CIM

STUDY TEXT

Diploma

International Marketing Strategy

First edition June 1999
Second edition May 2000

ISBN 0 7517 4109 4(previous edition 0 7517 4089 6)

British Library Cataloguing-in-Publication Data
A catalogue record for this book
is available from the British Library

Published by

BPP Publishing Limited
Aldine House, Aldine Place
London W12 8AW

www.bpp.com

Printed in England by DACOSTA PRINT,
35/37 Queensland Road, London
N7 7AH (0207 7700 1000)

We are grateful to the Chartered Institute of Marketing for permission to reproduce in this text the syllabus, tutor's guidance notes, and past examination questions.

Contents

BPP
PUBLISHING

Contents

Page

HOW TO USE THIS STUDY TEXT

Aims of this Study Text

To provide you with the knowledge and understanding, skills and applied techniques required for passing the exam

The Study Text has been written around the CIM syllabus (reproduced below, and cross-referenced to where in the text each topic is covered) and the CIM's Tutor's Manual.

- It is **comprehensive**. We do not omit sections of the syllabus as the examiner is liable to examine any angle of any part of the syllabus - and you do not want to be left high and dry.

- It is **on-target** - we do not include any material which is not examinable. You can therefore rely on the BPP Study Text as the stand-alone source of all your information for the exam.

To allow you to study in the way that best suits your learning style and the time you have available, by following your personal Study Plan (see below)

You may be studying at home on your own until the date of the exam, or you may be attending a full-time course. You may like to (and have time to) read every word, or you may prefer to (or only have time to) skim-read and devote the remainder of your time to question practice. Wherever you fall in the spectrum, you will find the BPP Study Text meets your needs in designing and following your personal Study Plan.

To tie in with the other components of the BPP Effective Study Package to ensure you have the best possible chance of passing the exam

Recommended period of use	Elements of BPP Effective Study Package
3-12 months before exam	**Study Text** Acquisition of knowledge, understanding, skills and applied techniques
1-6 months before exam	**Practice and Revision Kit (9/2000)** Tutorial questions and helpful checklists of the key points lead you into each area. There are then numerous examination questions to try, graded by topic area along with realistic suggested solutions prepared by marketing professionals in the light of the Examiner's Reports. The September 2000 edition will include the December 1999 and June 2000 papers.
1–6 months before exam	**Success Tapes** Audio cassettes covering the vital elements of your syllabus in less than 90 minutes per subject. Each tape also contains exam hints to help you fine tune your strategy.

BPP
PUBLISHING

Settling down to study

By this stage in your career you may be a very experienced learner and taker of exams. But have you ever thought about *how* you learn? Let's have a quick look at the key elements required for effective learning. You can then identify your learning style and go on to design your own approach to how you are going to study this text - your personal Study Plan.

Key element of learning	Using the BPP Study Text
Motivation	You can rely on the comprehensiveness and technical quality of BPP. You've chosen the right Study Text - so you're in pole position to pass your exam!
Clear objectives and standards	Do you want to be a prizewinner or simply achieve a moderate pass? Decide.
Feedback	Follow through the examples in this text and do the Action Programme and the Quick quizzes. Evaluate your efforts critically - how are you doing?
Study Plan	You need to be honest about your progress to yourself - do not be over-confident, but don't be negative either. Make your Study Plan (see below) and try to stick to it. Focus on the short-term objectives – completing two chapters a night, say - but beware of losing sight of your study objectives
Practice	Use the Quick quizzes and Chapter roundups to refresh your memory regularly after you have completed your initial study of each chapter

These introductory pages let you see exactly what you are up against. However you study, you should:

- **read through the syllabus and teaching guide** - this will help you to identify areas you have already covered, perhaps at a lower level of detail, and areas that are totally new to you

- **study the examination paper section,** where we show you the format of the exam (how many and what kind of questions etc).

Key study steps

The following steps are, in our experience, the ideal way to study for professional exams. You can of course adapt it for your particular learning style (see below).

Tackle the chapters in the order you find them in the Study Text. Taking into account your individual learning style, follow these key study steps for each chapter.

Key study steps	Activity
Step 1 *Chapter Topic List*	Study the list. Each numbered topic denotes a **numbered section** in the chapter.
Step 2 *Setting the Scene*	Read it through. It is designed to show you **why the topics in the chapter need to be studied** - how they lead on from previous topics, and how they lead into subsequent ones.
Step 3 *Explanations*	Proceed **methodically** through the chapter, reading each section thoroughly and making sure you understand.
Step 4 *Key Concepts*	**Key Concepts** can often earn you **easy marks** if you state them clearly and correctly in an appropriate exam.
Step 5 *Exam Tips*	These give you a good idea of how the examiner tends to examine certain topics – pinpointing **easy marks** and highlighting **pitfalls**.
Step 6 *Note taking*	Take **brief notes** if you wish, avoiding the temptation to copy out too much.
Step 7 *Marketing at Work*	Study each one, and try if you can to add flesh to them from your **own experience** - they are designed to show how the topics you are studying come alive (and often come unstuck) in the **real world**.
Step 8 *Action Programme*	Make a very good attempt at each one in each chapter. These are designed to put your **knowledge into practice** in much the same way as you will be required to do in the exam. Check the answer at the end of the chapter in the **Action Programme review**, and make sure you understand the reasons why yours may be different.
Step 9 *Chapter Roundup*	Check through it very carefully, to make sure you have grasped the **major points** it is highlighting
Step 10 *Quick Quiz*	When you are happy that you have covered the chapter, use the **Quick Quiz** to check your recall of the topics covered. The answers are in the paragraphs in the chapter that we refer you to.
Step 11 *Illustrative questions*	Either at this point, or later when you are thinking about revising, make a full attempt at the **illustrative questions**. You can find these at the end of the Study Text, along with the **answers** so you can see how you did.

BPP
PUBLISHING

Developing your personal Study Plan

Preparing a Study Plan (and sticking closely to it) is one of the key elements in learning success.

First you need to be aware of your style of learning. There are four typical learning styles. Consider yourself in the light of the following descriptions. and work out which you fit most closely. You can then plan to follow the key study steps in the sequence suggested.

Learning styles	Characteristics	Sequence of key study steps in the BPP Study Text
Theorist	Seeks to understand principles before applying them in practice	1, 2, 3, 7, 4, 5, 8, 9, 10, 11 (6 continuous)
Reflector	Seeks to observe phenomena, thinks about them and then chooses to act	
Activist	Prefers to deal with practical, active problems; does not have much patience with theory	1, 2, 8 (read through), 7, 4, 5, 9, 3, 8 (full attempt), 10, 11 (6 continuous)
Pragmatist	Prefers to study only if a direct link to practical problems can be seen; not interested in theory for its own sake	8 (read through), 2, 4, 5, 7, 9, 1, 3, 8 (full attempt), 10, 11 (6 continuous)

Next you should complete the following checklist.

Am I motivated? (a) ☐

Do I have an objective and a standard that I want to achieve? (b) ☐

Am I a theorist, a reflector, an activist or a pragmatist? (c) ☐

How much time do I have available per week, given: (d) ☐

- the standard I have set myself
- the time I need to set aside later for work on the Practice and Revision Kit and Passcards
- the other exam(s) I am sitting, and (of course)
- practical matters such as work, travel, exercise, sleep and social life?

Now:

- take the time you have available per week for this Study Text (d), (e) ☐ and multiply it by the number of weeks available to give (e).
- divide (e) by the number of chapters to give (f) (f) ☐
- set about studying each chapter in the time represented by (f), following the key study steps in the order suggested by your particular learning style.

This is your personal **Study Plan**.

Short of time?

Whatever your objectives, standards or style, you may find you simply do not have the time available to follow all the key study steps for each chapter, however you adapt them for your particular learning style. If this is the case, follow the Skim Study technique below (the icons in the Study Text will help you to do this).

Skim Study technique

Study the chapters in the order you find them in the Study Text. For each chapter, follow the key study steps 1-2, and then skim-read through step 3. Jump to step 9, and then go back to steps 4-5. Follow through step 7, and prepare outline Answers to the Action Programme (step 8). Try the Quick Quiz (step 10), following up any items you can't answer, then do a plan for the illustrative question (step 11), comparing it against our answers. You should probably still follow step 6 (note-taking).

Moving on...

However you study, when you are ready to embark on the practice and revision phase of the BPP Effective Study Package, you should still refer back to this Study Text:

- as a source of **reference** (you should find the list of Key Concepts and the index particularly helpful for this)

- as a **refresher** (the Chapter Roundups and Quick Quizzes help you here).

A note on pronouns

On occasions in this Study Text, 'he' is used for 'he or she', 'him' for 'him or her' and so forth. Whilst we try to avoid this practice it is sometimes necessary for reasons of style. No prejudice or stereotyping according to sex is intended or assumed.

BPP PUBLISHING

SYLLABUS

Aims and objectives

- To enable students to develop a thorough understanding of international marketing theory and key concepts

- To develop a knowledge and understanding of vocabulary associated with international/global marketing strategy in different types of economies, organisations and market situations

- To appreciate the complexities of international and global marketing in a mix of economies

- To create an awareness of processes, context and influences associated with international and global marketing strategies in a range of economies

- To develop students' appreciation of strategies and plans for a mix of international and global economies

- To develop an understanding of the implications for implementation, monitoring and control of the international marketing planning process.

Learning outcomes

On successful completion of this unit students will be able to:

- Demonstrate an understanding of the changing nature of the international trading environment, the major trends, strategic and contextual, affecting the global decision, and the different business and social/cultural conventions which affect buying behaviour and marketing approaches in international markets

- Determine marketing strategies appropriate to industrialised, developing and lesser developed economies, and identify and explain the relevant sources of information and analysis necessary to support the appropriate strategy

- Formulate strategies for export, international, multi-national, transnational and global marketing operations and evaluate the relevant organisational changes as an organisation moves through the export to global spectrum

- Select and justify an appropriate marketing strategy, marketing mix and evaluate the financial, human resource, operational and logistical implications of different international strategies

- Determine the appropriate control measures in international operations

Indicative content and weighting

Covered in Chapter

1 International strategic analysis (30%)

1.1 Identifying and analysing opportunities in the international trading environment. Changing patterns of trade globally and types of markets (product/service/commodity/not for profit).   1, 3, 9

1.2 The strategic and contextual elements of global operations – organisational and external. Global and multinational marketing as a strategic decision. Strategic networking and the international supply chain.   1, 3, 12

2   International strategic planning (30%)

BPP PUBLISHING

TUTOR'S GUIDANCE NOTES

The following is BPP's summary of the Tutor Manual produced by the CIM for this subject.

The syllabus is designed to reflect the need to look at the international and global environment when devising marketing strategies. The paper therefore contains elements of the other Diploma, Advanced Certificate and Certificate papers all couched in the International context. The need to differentiate between appropriate marketing strategies for industrialised, developing and less developed countries is also emphasised.

This paper is not just about the marketing mix applied overseas. It requires sound understanding of international business and an understanding of how marketing relates to other business functions against the background of an ever changing world economy.

The aims of the paper are for students to be able to develop marketing strategies for countries other than their own, to understand the impact of international competitors on the domestic market, and also to promote understanding of the extent to which standardisation or adaptation of the marketing mix is appropriate in international markets.

In the examinations, the examiners will be looking for the following:

- Appropriate theory and concepts
- Analysis and synthesis
- Application of knowledge/theories/concepts in practice
- Relevant examples
- Evidence of wide reading

Students should, above all, answer questions in an International context, in an imaginative yet realistic manner.

BPP PUBLISHING

THE EXAM PAPER

Assessment methods and format of the paper

	Number of marks
Part A: one compulsory case study, with two questions	40
Part B: three questions from six (equal marks)	60
	100

Time allowed: 3 hours

Section A is a mini-case scenario against which students should recommend action, or alternatively an extract from an article on International issues to be commented on and action recommended. Generally the answer will need to be written in a report format.

Section B will contain questions testing across the whole syllabus range, and knowledge will need to be applied to the context of the question set.

Analysis of past papers

The analysis below shows the topics which have featured in papers set under the old and new syllabus since 1997. The Specimen Paper for the new syllabus consisted of the December 1998 paper with some additional question options.

Until the December 1997 sitting, the compulsory case study was worth 50 marks.

December 1999 (first new syllabus sitting)

Part A

1   International marketer and manufacturer of jeans facing competition and reversal of fortune.

    (a)   Environmental variables - use of marketing information system
    (b)   Strategic 10 year international marketing plan.

Part B

2   Marketing to developed and less developed countries
3   Internal factors when deciding to go global
4   *Either:*   Knowledge based organisations
    or: Use of databases in gaining competitive advantage
5   Cultural differences and the international marketing mix
6   Motivation of a global workforce
7   Global standardisation strategy

June 1999

Part A

Zimbabwe flower growing industry seeking new markets
1   (a)   Factors to consider when entering the European or ASEAN market
    (b)   Design a generic marketing strategy

Part B

2   Risk and revenue as a form of global partnering
3   Satellite broadcasting and global advertising
4   Market and distribution channel development in young economies
5   Electronic commerce: impact, dangers and opportunities
6   The pricing decision in the international market
7   Organisational change from domestic to global operator

December 1998 / New syllabus specimen paper

Part A

1   Sri Lankan tea production and international marketing

    (a)   Preparation of a UK market entry plan

    (b)   Operational, human resource, production and financial considerations

Part B

2   *Either:*   Segmentation of international markets
    or: Use of internet in segment identification
3   Developments in distribution and logistics
4   Use of expatriates rather than locals in overseas branches
5   *Either:*   Global positioning, planning and control
    or: Intelligence bases
6   Macro influences on world trade and the effect on marketing strategies
7   *Either:*   Effective control systems for international planning
    or: Knowledge based control systems

June 1998

Part A

1   International marketing strategy of Harley Davidson

    (a)   Strategic issues to be faced when planning overseas expansion

    (b)   Options for a market entry strategy in a chosen area

Part B

2   Limits to product standardisation
3   Globalisation process and market entry methods
4   International marketing research and its problems
5   Planning, executing and controlling an international advertising campaign
6   Retailers in developing v. developed countries; impact on marketing plan
7   Definition and development of 'globalisation'

December 1997

Part A

Global fast food chain faces competitors.

1   (a)   Market analysis
    (b)   Planning, implementation and control of a response to competitors

Part B

2   Market entry criteria
3   Communications
4   Distribution
5   Financial risk
6   Self reference criteria
7   Underdeveloped country markets

BPP PUBLISHING

The exam paper

June 1997

Part A

Californian-based carpet firm is seeking to enter Europe via a franchise agreement.

1   (a)   Research programme to underpin launch
    (b)   Planning and control issues

Part B

2   Marketing services internationally
3   Managing the transition from domestic to global operations
4   Adapting global brands to local/regional cultures
5   New product development
6   Emerging markets research
7   Organisational issues of globalisation and localisation

STUDY CHECKLIST

This page is designed to help you chart your progress through the Study Text, including the Action Programme and illustrative questions. You can tick off each topic as you study and try questions on it. Insert the dates you complete the chapters Action Programme and questions in the relevant boxes. You will thus ensure that you are on track to complete your study before the exam.

	Text chapters	Action Programme		Illustrative questions	
	Date completed	*Number*	*Date completed*	*Number*	*Date completed*

PART A: INTERNATIONAL STRATEGIC ANALYSIS

	Text chapters Date completed	Action Programme Number	Date completed	Illustrative questions Number	Date completed
1 The development of international trade		1, 2		1	
2 The environment of international trade		1,2,3,4, 5,6,7		2	
3 Competing in the global market		1		3	
4 Culture: buyer and organisational behaviour		1, 2		4	
5 Researching and analysing overseas markets		1, 2		5	

PART B: INTERNATIONAL STRATEGIC PLANNING

	Text chapters Date completed	Action Programme Number	Date completed	Illustrative questions Number	Date completed
6 Going international: planning for international marketing		1, 2, 3		6	
7 Market entry methods		1		7	
8 Organising for international marketing		1, 2, 3		8	

PART C: INTERNATIONAL STRATEGY IMPLEMENTATION AND CONTROL

	Text chapters Date completed	Action Programme Number	Date completed	Illustrative questions Number	Date completed
9 International product management. Standardisation and differentiation		1, 2		9	
10 International pricing decisions		1, 2		10	
11 International marketing communications		1, 2		11	
12 International distribution and logistics		1, 2		12	
13 International marketing of services		1, 2, 3		13	
14 Control issues in international marketing		1		14	

Part A
International strategic analysis

1

The Development of International Trade

Chapter Topic List	Syllabus Reference
1 Setting the scene	-
2 Why do companies and countries trade?	1.1
3 International marketing	1.2
4 The principle of comparative advantage	1.8
5 The global market	1.1
6 The context of world trade	1.2, 1.3, 2.8

Learning Outcomes

Upon completion of this chapter you will have a good understanding of the background to and context of world trade. You will be able to answer these questions.

- Why do companies and countries trade?

- What is international marketing?

- What factors influence the world trading environment?

This will be a good foundation for the detail to follow regarding analysis of the international environment, planning the IM strategy and implementing and controlling it.

Key Concepts Introduced

- International marketing
- Comparative advantage
- Terms of trade
- Competitive advantage

- Globalisation
- Global company
- Commodity

Examples of Marketing at Work

- Smaller businesses and exporting
- Satellites
- Japanese firms
- Buying power of the West

- Guinness
- Cut glass
- The IMF
- The Welsh Development Agency

BPP PUBLISHING

1 SETTING THE SCENE

1.1 Without international trade, there would be no international marketing. The conditions of international trade mean that you can only very rarely regard international marketing as an extension of domestic marketing. This chapter looks at the development of international trade and the environment within which it operates. International trade affects the global economy and represents an opportunity for firms to exploit segmentation. It is also a source of huge complexity.

1.2 At one time it was felt that countries were independent economic units and that trade did not affect the whole economy. Comparative advantage (Section 3) offers reasons why it is in countries' best interests to encourage international trade, as it has the potential to make all parties better off for the same amount of effort. Recent international agreements (Section 4) have prodded the world towards freer trade but there is still some way to go to a genuinely global market in every sector.

1.3 This chapter forms a base underpinning the rest of the study text. Bear its points in mind as you work your way through the chapters.

2 WHY DO COMPANIES AND COUNTRIES TRADE?

The importance of trade for companies

2.1 Any business pursues **profits**. An overseas market or the global market offers larger profits.

- Increased **volume sales** overall
- The ability to **specialise** more
- The ability to **segment a wider market**
- The ability to **draw resources** from a wider market

2.2 For example, the UK domestic market for aircraft (both civilian and military) could not support an aerospace industry as the demand would not be big enough, but exports enable such companies to be profitable.

2.3 Small businesses, too, can benefit from export markets, as the following reports show.

Marketing at Work

- A European Business Survey conducted by Grant Thornton and Business Strategy suggested that 'smaller businesses that pursue export opportunities are better equipped to ensure their domestic growth and to disseminate the lessons of success'. The EU is the dominant destination but small exporters from the UK export to the US and to the Asia Pacific region.

- Small and medium sized firms cannot afford to ignore export opportunities (*The Times*, March 30 1999). Even though the recent strength of sterling has meant that export levels have fallen, such businesses are working hard to grab sales outside the UK. M4 Data, a designer and manufacturer of computer hardware with a turnover of £15 million (70% coming from export sales) has been hit by the slump in the Far East, but is looking to diversify by increasing exports to India by 50%.

2.4 Many firms could not survive at all without international trade. Volvo and Saab, the Swedish car manufacturers, sell by far the majority of their output in overseas markets, as Sweden would be too small to support them. Some of the world's largest chemicals companies are Swiss, yet Switzerland is hardly big enough for them.

The company in the international trading environment

2.5 All companies are affected by **economic forces**. Different firms respond in a variety of ways to these forces.

- Some **ignore overseas markets** and concentrate on their domestic market
- Some **export** to overseas markets
- Some **internationalise** their marketing and their production

2.6 This is because overseas markets are not only a place where **customers** can be found. They are a source of **resources** with which customers can be satisfied. A firm based abroad, acting as an international business, has many more sources of supply than one trading only at home.

2.7 Some commentators believe that some companies have become **independent of their national origins** - but we return to this debate in a later chapter. The point is to understand that international business involves a lot more than **marketing activities**.

The importance of international trade for countries

2.8 The environment of **international trade is controlled and policed** by national governments directly or as a result of treaties. Most governments believe that international trade is beneficial.

(a) A country normally **exports** goods which it can produce most efficiently, that is, at lowest cost relative to other countries, and it normally imports goods in which other countries are relatively more efficient. This is called the principle of **comparative advantage**. World output is larger when each country **specialises** in goods it can produce most efficiently.

(b) The goods in which a country will have comparative advantage depend partly on supplies of the **factors of production**. A country with much richer agricultural land will tend to export agricultural products.

(c) Comparative advantage is influenced by **research and development** both in technology and work organisation. The United States, because of the scale of its expenditure on research and development over many years, tends to have comparative advantage in goods embodying advanced technology.

(d) A country should expect the **make-up of its exports and imports to change** over time. Thus the UK has moved from being the leading country for manufactured goods to a situation where service industries now play a leading role.

2.9 International trade

- Enables countries to '**specialise**'
- Serves as a means of developing **political links** with other countries
- **Increases competition** and possibly **efficiency of production**
- Creates **larger markets,** with the potential for **economies of scale** in production

2.10 As we shall see later, the principles of free international trade are not universally accepted. Free trade brings greater competition and a threat to existing producers.

BPP PUBLISHING

3 INTERNATIONAL MARKETING

> **Key Concept**
>
> **International marketing (IM)** refers to the marketing of goods and services in two or more countries.

3.1 New markets may be sought for the following reasons.

(a) A firm might want to extend the product life cycle.

(b) Where there is intense competition in the home market, a firm might want to escape to less competitive markets.

(c) The domestic market might offer low growth prospects.

(d) The domestic market might offer significant risk.

3.2 In terms of **competitive strategy**, international activities can be justified on the following grounds as outlined by Michael Porter.

(a) **Cost leadership**. The domestic market may be too small for the firm to reap the economies of scale which may be necessary for a cost leadership strategy.

(b) **Differentiation**. A differentiated product may appeal to a number of different overseas markets.

(c) **Focus**. Oddly enough, international marketing can be used to implement a focus strategy, which is a concentration on a core segment of consumers. The segment does not have to be defined in national or ethnic terms, but in terms of wealth, life-style and so forth. Haute couture fashion, perfumes and other luxury goods may appeal to people of a similar income bracket the world over.

(d) To **pre-empt competition** from overseas producers. World trade is becoming liberalised. Firms can expect incoming competition. They might have no alternative to competing abroad.

3.3 Other reasons to market overseas are these.

(a) The market for a product is **unquestionably a global one**.

Marketing at Work

Many countries are seeking to put satellites into orbit. They can choose between Europe's Ariane programme, China's Long March rocket, Russia's Proton programme, and the US space shuttle.

(b) Overseas operations might be **cheaper than manufacturing at home**. However, differences in labour costs are exaggerated. Labour rates in South Korea have caught up with wage rates in some Western countries.

(c) Competitors are entering the overseas market.

(d) A company executive may recognise a **chance opportunity** while on a foreign trip. The firm may receive orders or requests for information from potential overseas customers.

(e) **Profit margins** may be higher abroad.

(f) **Seasonal fluctuations** may be levelled out (peak periods in some countries, for example those related to the weather coincide with troughs in others).

(g) It offers an opportunity of disposing of **excess production** in times of low domestic demand.

(h) The firm's prestige may be enhanced by portraying a global image.

(i) **Stakeholder expectations** (eg a specified return on capital employed) may drive the decision.

3.4 Reasons for **avoiding involvement** in international marketing are these.

(a) Profits may be affected by **factors outside the firm's control** (eg due to fluctuation of exchange rates and foreign government actions).

(b) The necessary **adaptations** to the product will diminish the effects of economies of scale.

(c) **Anti-dumping duties** are more quickly imposed now than in the past, so overseas markets are less available as convenient places to sell excess stock at marginal cost.

3.5 Some **key factors** differentiating domestic and international marketing are outlined in the table below.

	Domestic	International
Social and cultural factors	Relatively homogeneous market 'Rules of the game' understood Similar purchasing habits	Fragmented, diverse markets Rules diverse, changeable and unclear Diverse purchasing habits
Economic factors	National price Uniform financial climate Stable business environment	Diverse national prices Variety of financial climates, ranging from very conservative to highly inflationary Multiple business environments, some unstable
Competitive factors	Competitors' products, prices, costs and plans usually known	Many more competitors, but little information about their strategies
Political legal factors	Relative freedom from government interference Political factors relatively unimportant	Involvement in national economic plans Political factors often significant
Technological factors	Use of standard production and measurement systems	Training of foreign personnel to operate and maintain equipment

3.6 Before getting involved in international marketing, the company must consider both **strategic** and **tactical** issues.

(a) **Strategic issues**

(i) Does the decision to get involved in IM fit with the company's overall **mission and objectives?**

(ii) Does the organisation have the **resources** to exploit **effectively** the opportunities overseas?

(b) **Tactical issues**

(i) How can the company get to understand **customers' needs and preferences** in foreign markets?

(ii) Does the company know how to **conduct business** abroad, and deal effectively with **foreign nationals?**

BPP
PUBLISHING

(iii)   Are there **foreign regulations** and associated **hidden costs?**

(iv)   Does the company have the necessary **management skills?**

Marketing at Work

Japanese firms

A little while ago, it was assumed that, following the success of Japanese firms worldwide in motor vehicles (Nissan, Honda, Toyota) and consumer electronics (eg Sony, JVC, Matsushita), no Western companies were safe from Japanese competition. Kao (household goods), Suntory (drinks), Nomura (banking and securities) were seen as successors to firms such as Procter and Gamble, Heineken etc.

This has not happened: for example, Japanese pharmaceutical firms, such as Green Cross, have not achieved the world domination anticipated in 1982. US and European firms are still dominant in this industry.

Perhaps cars and consumer electronics are the exception rather than the rule. The reason for this might be distribution. Normally, outsiders do not find it easy to break into established distribution patterns. However distribution channels in cars and consumer electronics offered outsiders an easy way in.

(a)   The car industry is vertically integrated, with a network of exclusive dealerships. Given time and money, the Japanese firms could simply build their own dealerships and run them as they liked, with the help of local partners. This barrier to entry was not inherently complex.

(b)   Consumer electronics

(i)   In the early years, the consumer electronics market was driven by technology, so innovative firms such as Sony and Matsushita could overcome distribution weaknesses.

(ii)   Falling prices changed the distribution of hifi goods from small specialist shops to large cut-price outlets, such as Comet. Newcomers to a market are the natural allies of such new outlets: existing suppliers prefer to shun 'discount' retailers to protect margins in their current distribution network.

Japanese firms have not established dominant positions:

(a)   in healthcare, where national pharmaceuticals wholesalers are active as 'gatekeepers';

(b)   in household products, where there are strong supermarket chains;

(c)   in cosmetics, where department stores and specialist shops offer a wide choice.

---

4   THE PRINCIPLE OF COMPARATIVE ADVANTAGE

4.1   Predating the principle of **comparative advantage** (which we will discuss shortly) is the theory of **absolute advantage,** developed by Adam Smith in his book *The Wealth of Nations*, published in the late eighteenth century. Smith argued that the wealth of a country is decided by the **level of goods and services** enjoyed by its people. Different countries can produce some goods more **efficiently**, using fewer resources, than others, because of factors including **natural resources, technology** and **labour supply** and **skills**. Each country should therefore develop those areas where it holds absolute advantage.

4.2   However, this theory when taken to its extreme could mean that a country did not trade at all because it had all the resources it needed, at the lowest cost, at home. At the other end of the spectrum, citizens of a country should never buy domestically produced goods if they could all be obtained more cheaply from overseas. In practice these situations do not occur. It is generally agreed that **trade is beneficial** for all countries.

4.3   So why is this? Why do nations **export** certain goods and **import** others?

(a)   In some cases the reason is clear.

(i)   It would not be **practical** (or possible!) for Britain to grow bananas and coffee to meet its needs, so it buys them from abroad.

(ii) The UK's own supply of raw material is **insufficient for its needs,** so it imports a wide range of these from countries around the world.

(b) But why does Britain buy large amounts of manufactured goods from the USA, the rest of Western Europe and Japan? Britain still undertakes manufacturing (although it is becoming a largely service-driven economy). Why does Switzerland export large amounts of chocolate and Japan export electronic goods?

This kind of trade is explained by the principle of **comparative advantage** which demonstrates that international trade without barriers is beneficial for all countries that engage in it. (It was developed by David Ricardo, an English economist, early in the last century.)

Key Concept

Comparative advantage is the principle that economic agents are best employed in activities which countries carry out relatively better than they do other activities. A country has a comparative advantage in producing good X over good Y if it can produce good X at a low opportunity cost relative to good Y. Applied to international trade, a country will gain from specialising in producing goods in which it has a comparative advantage.

4.4 Let us develop a simple example.

	UK	Spain	Ratio *Spain:UK*
Labour hours needed to make one car	100	500	5:1
Labour hours needed to make a pair of shoes	2	5	5:2

In this example, the UK is more efficient at producing **both** cars and shoes. The UK clearly has an **absolute advantage** in the production of both cars and shoes. So can each country gain by trading? The answer is yes, if each follows the principle of comparative advantage.

4.5 Which country has the comparative advantage in which product?

(a) Consider cars first.

(i) Under UK conditions, shifting enough labour from shoe production to produce one more car (100 man hours) requires giving up the opportunity to produce 50 pairs of shoes.

(ii) In Spain, shifting enough labour from shoes to produce one more car (500 hours) means giving up 100 pairs of shoes.

Thus, the opportunity cost of cars in terms of shoes is lower in the UK than in Spain. Hence, the UK has a comparative advantage in car production.

(b) Similarly, shifting enough labour from cars to make 100 pairs of shoes (200 hours) will 'cost' two cars not produced in the UK. In Spain, 100 pairs of shoes will 'cost' only one car (500 man hours). Hence, Spain has a comparative advantage in shoe production.

4.6 The significance of this can be seen if we look at what happens when the UK and Spain **shift production** from one good to another.

(a) **Year 1**

	UK	Spain	Total
Cars produced	1,000	1,000	2,000
Shoes produced	100,000	100,000	200,000

(b) The UK adds, say, 100 cars to its output by shifting 10,000 labour hours from shoes, reducing shoe output in the UK by 5,000 pairs (since one car = 50 pairs of shoes = 100 labour hours). Spain steps up its shoe output by 7,000 pairs by shifting 35,000 labour hours from car to shoe production, reducing its car output by 70 (since one car = 100 pairs of shoes = 500 labour hours).

Year 2

	UK	Spain	Total
Cars produced	1,100	930	2,030
Shoes produced	95,000	107,000	202,000

As a result of these production changes, world output of both cars and shoes will have increased. Car output is up 100 in the UK but down only 70 in Spain; there is a net gain of 30 cars. Shoe output is up 7,000 pairs in Spain and down only 5,000 pairs in the UK.

4.7 Of course, the production levels in each country may not be what each requires to satisfy **domestic consumption demand**.

   (i)   The UK may now have too many cars and not enough shoes while Spain may be flooded with shoes but not enough cars.

   (ii) In order to benefit from the increase in world output, the gains in productive efficiency must be **redistributed by trade**. The UK must export some of its cars in exchange for some of Spain's shoes.

   (iii) Suppose the UK agrees to export 85 cars to Spain in exchange for 6,000 pairs of shoes. This is clearly beneficial to the UK since the switching of domestic production from 85 cars would have only produced 4,250 pairs of shoes. There is a net gain to the UK of 1,750 pairs of shoes. This exchange is also beneficial to Spain since the production of 6,000 pairs of shoes is only equivalent to 60 cars; there is a net gain of 25 cars to Spain through trade.

The significance of the principle of comparative advantage

4.8 Comparative advantage underpins the following two beliefs.

   (a) **Countries should specialise in what they produce best**, even when they are less efficient than other countries in producing every type of good. Increased specialisation in the production of a good may also lower the opportunity cost of producing that good.

   (i)   **Scale economies.** Increased production of a good by one country may justify building larger plants such that average unit costs fall as production rates increase.

   (ii) **Learning by doing.** The knowledge and expertise gained through specialisation may lead to greater efficiency and reduced production costs.

   (b) **International trade should be allowed to take place without restrictions.** Free trade plus specialisation will result in an increase in the world's output, and all countries will share in the benefits.

Does the principle apply in practice?

4.9 Countries do specialise in the production of certain goods for trade. For example, the UK imports most of the wine it consumes, and 'pays' for this with exports of other goods (whisky, for example).

4.10 However, there are certain restrictions on how the principle operates.

(a) **Free trade does not always exist.** Some countries take action to protect or promote domestic industries and to discourage imports. This means that a country might produce goods in which it does not have a comparative advantage.

(b) **Transportation and transaction costs** can be very high in international trade so that it may be cheaper to produce goods in the home country. The costs of such tasks as locating goods, negotiating agreements, shipping and insurance, may preclude profitable trade.

(c) **Differentiation.** Countries might produce similar goods, but give them **sufficiently unique characteristics** to make them competitive in any country of the world. For example, Italy, Spain, West Germany and the UK all manufacture cars, but there are sufficient varieties of design that each country can export cars to the other countries. Some Ford models are imported to the UK from plants in continental Europe, whereas other Ford models are made in the UK for export elsewhere.

Action Programme 1

Can a country have a comparative advantage in all goods?

Terms of trade

4.11 In the example earlier we assumed only two countries, each trading a single product. It was a simple task, therefore, to identify the range for the **terms of trade** which would make trade beneficial for both countries.

Key Concept

Terms of trade: the ratio of export prices to import prices.

4.12 In the real world many countries trade many different goods, so it is not so easy to estimate the terms of trade. The prices of commodities traded are measured by an **index of prices**, appropriately weighted to reflect relative importance in the volume of trade. The terms of trade facing a country are expressed as a percentage:

$$\text{Terms of trade} = \frac{\text{Index of export prices}}{\text{Index of import prices}} \times 100$$

In the base year the value of the terms of trade index will be 100.

4.13 If the index **increases,** compared to the base year, the terms of trade are said to have improved; in other words, a given quantity of exports will purchase **more** imports than before. If the index falls, then the terms of trade have worsened.

Marketing at Work

The behaviour of producers and buyers can have serious consequences for world trade and especially for those countries which are least able to retaliate. Consider the extent to which the major western nations have, at various times in the past, been able to improve their terms of trade at the expense of producers of primary products (bananas or coffee spring to mind). As the primary producing countries of South America and Africa have weakened economically, so too has their ability to counteract the buying power of the West. Monopoly power and its impact on terms of trade was also visibly demonstrated by the oil-producing and exporting (OPEC) nations in the 1970s, when the real price of oil rose dramatically.

The advantages of free international trade

4.14 There are other advantages to the countries of the world in encouraging free international trade.

(a) Some countries have **raw materials** surplus to their needs and others have a deficit. A country with a surplus can export them. A country with a deficit must either import them or accept restrictions on its economic prosperity and standard of living.

(b) International trade **increases competition** amongst suppliers in the world's markets, which benefits consumers, undermining monopolies and promoting the pressure to be efficient.

(c) International trade creates **larger markets** for a firm's output and so some firms can benefit from **economies of scale**.

(d) There are **political advantages** because the development of trading links provides a foundation for economic and political links. An example is the European Union and its single market programme.

(e) From the consumer's point of view, international trade should provide **greater choice, lower prices** and **better quality** products.

Why do countries often try to avoid specialisation?

4.15 In practice many countries try to avoid **specialisation**. Where there is a major export industry already in existence, the country's government might actively encourage the growth of other unrelated industries.

4.16 The reasons for not wanting to specialise may be as follows.

(a) **Comparative advantage is never stable.** Technological change might mean that other countries can begin to compete successfully. To take our earlier example, investment might make Spain better at producing cars over a very short time period.

(b) **Diversity** protects against the consequences of a **fall in world demand** for the product in which the country specialises.

(c) Crops are subject to the **uncertainties of climate**. A poor harvest or a crop disease might be disastrous if the country relies on that product alone. The economic history of many countries in Latin America and Africa, reliant on commodity crops, bears out this view.

(d) **Market segmentation** and **product differentiation** have enabled suppliers to develop markets so that countries producing variants of the same product are able to sell their goods to each other.

(e) Multinational companies may choose to site some **manufacturing or assembly activity** in each country in which they operate and these decisions are not necessarily consistent with the principle of comparative advantage.

(f) A country may find itself a victim of **import restrictions** in the rest of the world and this may make it cautious about over specialisation.

(g) Governments might wish to develop a **self sufficient economy** for developing 'home' industries. An example would be the defence industry in some countries.

(h) **Special interest groups** can influence the government to restrict imports, which is often in the interest of industries which are subject to import competition and are able to exert political pressure. Arguments for trade restriction are easily intermingled with patriotic sentiment.

> ### Action Programme 2
>
> You work for Mega plc, a multinational corporation with production in a number of countries, and sales in a number of markets. What relevance do you think that the concept of comparative advantage would have for strategic decisions such as whether to export or to manufacture overseas?

4.17 To the theories of absolute and comparative advantage must be added a brief consideration of **competitive advantage**. The question to ask is why some nations succeed and others fail in competition in the international arena. For example the UK, although prosperous, has been in relative decline. This question has been addressed by Michael Porter in his book *The Competitive Advantage of Nations*.

4.18 A **competitive nation**, Porter assumes, does not exist. The only meaningful measure of national competitiveness is the productivity and effectiveness of its **industries**. We discuss this in more detail in Chapter 3 when we think about the global market.

> ### Key Concept
> **Competitive advantage** denotes those factors which enable a firm to compete successfully with competitors on a sustained basis.

5 THE GLOBAL MARKET

5.1 Since 1945, the volume of world trade has increased. There have been two routes.

(a) **Import substitution.** A country aims to produce manufactured goods which it previously imported, by protecting local producers. This has had limited success.

(b) **Export-led growth.** The success of this particular strategy has depended on the existence of open markets elsewhere. Japan, South Korea and the other Asian 'tiger' economies (eg Taiwan) have chosen this route.

5.2 This has meant a proliferation of suppliers exporting to, or trading in, a wider variety of places. However, the existence of global markets should not be taken for granted in terms of **all** products and services, or indeed in **all** territories.

(a) Some **services** are still subject to managed trade (e.g. some countries prohibit firms from other countries from selling insurance). Trade in services has been liberalised under the auspices of the WTO.

(b) **Immigration.** There is unlikely ever to be a global market for labour, given the disparity in skills between different countries, and restrictions on immigration.

(c) The market for some goods is much more 'globalised' than for others.

(i) Upmarket luxury goods may not be required or afforded by people in developing nations.

(ii) Some goods can be sold almost anywhere, but to limited degrees. Television sets are consumer durables in some countries, but still luxury or relatively expensive items in other ones.

(iii) Other goods are needed almost everywhere. In oil a truly global industry exists in both production (e.g. North Sea, Venezuela, Russia, Azerbaijan, Gulf states) and consumption (any country using cars and buses, not to mention those with chemical industries based on oil).

Marketing at Work

Guinness

Guinness stout has been in some Asia-Pacific markets for over a hundred years as the expatriate's drink of choice. The export was stronger than its UK counterpart and was even sold as a tonic. Growth in Asia has expanded the beer market. Excluding Australia there are now twenty beer brands as opposed to five.

The current strategy is to maintain the appearance of the beer in a consistent communication method. Promotions are varied for particular markets.

In Asia-Pacific Guinness decided to work with individuals and entrepreneurs prepared to put up their own cash.

The Irish Pub Company, which designs and builds the pubs in Ireland, kits them out with Irish bric-a-brac and then flat-packs them to the destination where they are reassembled. Buyers choose from a number of different styles, including the Irish Country Cottage Pub, the Traditional Irish Pub-shop, the Victorian Dublin pub, the Gaelic Pub and the Irish Brewery Pub.

The Irish Pub Company has a team permanently in Ireland buying genuine fixtures and fittings, and Guinness works with a recruitment firm to find Irish bar and catering staff prepared to decamp to far-flung locations.

The investor typically invests up to $1.5 million, and owns the pub, but so successful is the concept that they make a return within two years.

Extracts from Marketing Business, March 1998

Global production

5.3 Global production implies that a firm's production planning is considered on a global scale.

(a) **Global manufacture**. A company can **manufacture** components for a product in a number of different countries. Japanese companies sometimes ship components for assembly to their factories overseas.

(b) **Global sourcing**. Sub-components may be purchased from countries overseas. As the case example below demonstrates, companies can exploit the comparative advantages of different countries.

Marketing at Work

Cut glass

Global competition might in theory lead to low added value work being done in some countries and high added value work being done in other countries.

In the UK cut glass industry there are very few manufacturers making all their glass only in the UK. 'It is common practice to buy plain crystal glasses, called blanks, from say, the Czech Republic or Slovenia, and decorate them'.

In practice this has led to consolidation, with the Irish company Waterford Wedgwood being one of the few crystal glass companies straddling two or more markets.

5.4 The extreme form of global 'production' has been referred to by Kenichi Ohmae as **insiderisation**. In other words, in each of your markets you build up a production and distribution organisation from scratch or in conjunction with local suppliers, even though there may be few variants to the product from market to market. (Coca-Cola has done this in Japan.)

Exam Tip

The global market may not feature on its own as part of a question, but it underpins many of the other questions (eg how a global company should respond to a strong local competitor).

Conflicting forces

5.5   Any discussion of international business is fraught with uncertainty, simply because there is such a variety of **conflicting forces**.

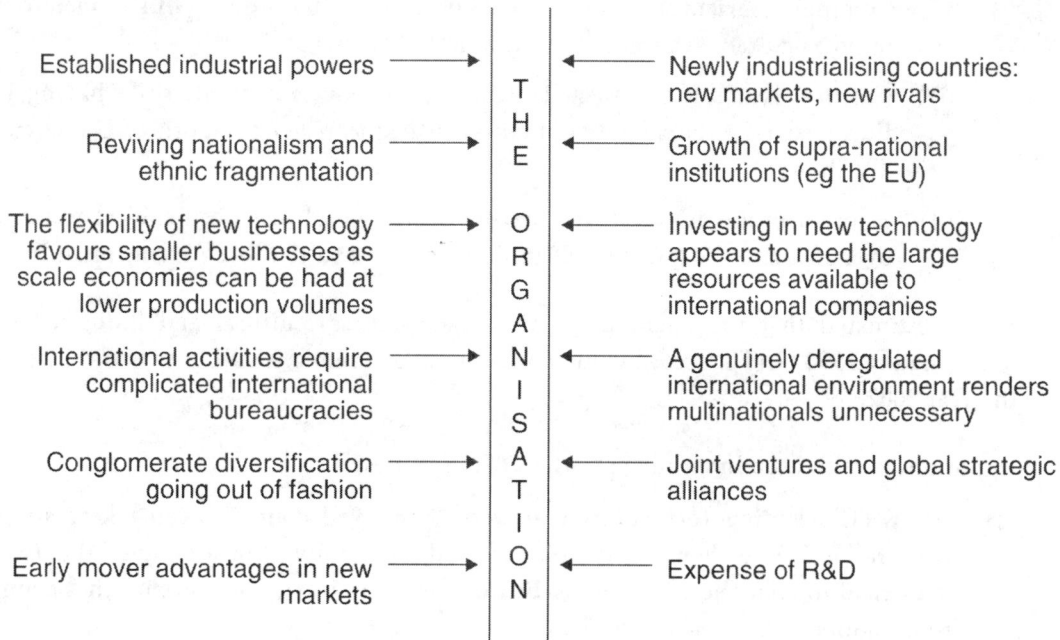

	THE ORGANISATION	
Established industrial powers →		← Newly industrialising countries: new markets, new rivals
Reviving nationalism and ethnic fragmentation →		← Growth of supra-national institutions (eg the EU)
The flexibility of new technology favours smaller businesses as scale economies can be had at lower production volumes →		← Investing in new technology appears to need the large resources available to international companies
International activities require complicated international bureaucracies →		← A genuinely deregulated international environment renders multinationals unnecessary
Conglomerate diversification going out of fashion →		← Joint ventures and global strategic alliances
Early mover advantages in new markets →		← Expense of R&D

International institutions and agreements

5.6   International trade is of such significance that **rules and regulations** governing its performance have to be established. The experience of the 1930s where protectionism led to depression on a worldwide scale, and the subsequent second World War partly brought about by the depression, led the major economic powers to consider the necessity of regulating government intervention in the world market.

The World Trade Organisation (WTO)

5.7   The **WTO** was formed in 1995 as successor to the former **General Agreement on Tariffs and Trade** (GATT). The GATT was originally signed by 23 countries in 1947 as an attempt to promote free trade (its membership increased to 128 countries).

- To **reduce existing barriers** to free trade

- To **eliminate discrimination** in international trade

- To **prevent the growth of protectionism**

5.8   GATT succeeded in reducing world tariffs substantially, after a series of 'rounds' of negotiation.

(a)   The 'Kennedy round' of the 1960s led to tariff cuts of about 30%, bringing the average duty on manufactured goods down to about 10% by 1972.

(b)   The 'Tokyo round' of the late 1970s led to further tariff reductions of approximately 30%. Trade between advanced industrialised nations in particular was favoured, with tariff cuts of 38%. The cut was a lower 25% in the case of trade between advanced industrialised and newly industrialised countries.

BPP PUBLISHING

(c) The talks in the '**Uruguay round**' which were concluded in December 1993 represented the culmination of seven years of work on a very ambitious programme for the liberalisation of world trade.

    (i) A major sticking point was in the area of **agriculture**. The European Union's Common Agricultural Policy has been seen by other GATT members as providing excessive trade protection to EU farmers.

    (ii) **Cultural** issues were affected. The French government (despite having lured EuroDisney to the outskirts of Paris) wished to restrict imports of US movie and TV shows.

    (iii) Another problem was in the **textiles** sector which has been subject to tariffs of over 15% and the quota levels imposed by the Multi-Fibre Arrangement.

5.9 It was estimated that the opening up of markets for agricultural and industrial goods following the 1993 GATT accord could add around US$200-300 billion to world income by the year 2002.

5.10 Important facts to keep in mind about the WTO are these.

(a) The WTO has **dispute resolution** powers. Aggrieved countries can take matters up with the WTO if they cannot be resolved bilaterally. For example, the EU has threatened to refer the US's **Helms-Burton** law, which tries to prevent other countries from trading with Cuba, to the WTO.

(b) Membership of the WTO requires adherence to certain conditions regarding **competition** in the home market etc.

(c) Membership is **restricted**. China, for example, has applied to join but there are doubts as to the genuine commitment to its markets.

United Nations Conference on Trade and Development (UNCTAD)

5.11 Dissatisfaction by underdeveloped and developing countries with GATT, due to the dominance of the rich nations, led to the formation of UNCTAD, under the aegis of the United Nations in 1964. Its influence has been modest in direct terms, but it has acted as a focus and pressure group for the less rich countries to influence other trade groups to provide special and favourable terms for underprivileged economies.

Organisation for Economic Co-operation and Development (OECD)

5.12 Known as the 'rich man's club', the **OECD** now constitutes the 24 leading industrialised nations in the world. Its role is consultative, and was primarily formed as an economic response to the then eastern bloc. Nowadays it performs a significant role in providing statistical information and economic reports to member nations.

The World Bank

5.13 The **World Bank** (properly called the International Bank for Reconstruction and Development) emerged in 1944 to provide **economic aid** for the rebuilding of Europe and the Far East, damaged by five years of war. Through its member countries the World Bank supplies **capital** on favourable terms (soft loans) to aid economic reconstruction of an economy. Where the economic failure is as a result of political negligence, strict conditions may be associated with the loan (e.g. control of money supply).

International Monetary Fund (IMF)

5.14 An offshoot of the same 1944 agreement, the IMF attempts to **regulate and stabilise currency exchange rates**. It is basically a forum for international negotiation on fiscal policy, but since the 1970s the power of multinational institutions to move funds around the world has eroded the influence of the IMF. In Europe the role of currency stabilisation has been largely assumed by the EU.

Marketing at Work

The IMF has been critical in organising financial assistance to the troubled economies of South East Asia. As a price for its aid, recipient countries have been required to reform their financial systems.

Group of Seven (G7)

5.15 Another 'grouping' you may read about is **G7**. G7 is not an organisation but an **informal** group of seven major industrial powers (the US, Japan, Germany, France, the UK, Italy and Canada) who meet regularly to discuss matters of mutual economic interest. The summit meetings have become more elaborate over the years with head of state involvement. Russia was recently invited to joint and so form the **G8**, but there is currently little faith in the Russian economy so its membership is, at least presently, of less significance.

Effect of trade organisations on the exporter

5.16 Freer trade between developed countries has allowed freer movement of goods and some services.

(a) For a time the third world has been able to introduce barriers such as licensing of imports, currency controls, and limits on ownership of businesses, as well as the normal tariff restrictions.

(b) More recently, much of the impetus for protectionism has come from the **developed** world. The EU wishes to protect its farmers from cheap imports. The US wishes to restrict access to some of its markets.

5.17 Over the last four decades the World Bank and the International Monetary Fund have arguably introduced a degree of stability into the world economy, and in particular have advised developing nations thus providing many opportunities to **developed nations** for exports tied to loans (**tied aid**).

6 THE CONTEXT OF WORLD TRADE   Specimen paper

6.1 This section explores some of the factors behind world trade and where relevant, points out where you can read more elsewhere in the text.

6.2 Some years ago, Harvard Business School professor Ted Levitt predicted the development of a '**global village**' in which consumers around the world would have the same needs and attitudes and use the same products. The whole debate about **globalisation** still goes on, with the attendant question of whether to **standardise** or **adapt** the marketing mix. We discuss the standardisation v adaptation debate further in Chapter 9.

BPP PUBLISHING

Key Concept

'**Globalisation** of markets' (Levitt 1983) is an expression which relates first to demand: tastes, preferences and price-mindedness are becoming increasingly universal. Second, it relates to the supply side: profits and services tend to become more standardised and competition within industries reaches a world-wide scale. Third, it relates to the way firms, mainly **multinational corporations** (ie those with operations in more than one country), try to design their marketing policies and control systems appropriately so as to remain winners in the global competition of global products for global consumers. (*Usunier*)

6.3 Other writers have developed the globalisation debate and the factors defining **global competitiveness**. They include Kenichi Ohmae, C K Prahalad, Gary Hamel and Michael Porter. We outline their contributions in Chapter 3.

Key Concept

A **global company** is 'an organisation that makes no distinction between domestic and international business' (Terpstra). Few such organisations genuinely exist.

6.4 Some would say that **global marketing organisations** are rare. Industry structures change, foreign markets are culturally diverse, and the transformations brought about by developments in information technology mean that the world market is in a state of **turbulence**. The **financial crisis in Asia** caused significant political and economic unrest, for example. We look at its '**contagion effect**' in more detail in Chapter 2. Continuing to follow the same marketing strategy can be risky. Global players must always seek new **low cost production areas**.

6.5 In an article in the *Financial Times*, Jerry Wind points out some of the changes that have happened in the world market place:

   (a) **Globalisation of business** - increased competition and global customers

   (b) **Science and technology** developments (computing, telecommunications and information science)

   (c) Mergers, acquisitions and **strategic alliances**

   (d) Changing **customer values** and behaviour

   (e) Increased **scrutiny** of business decisions by government and the public, with greater focus on ethical dimensions (we look at these in Chapter 14)

   (f) increased **deregulation**, privatisation and co-operation between business and government

   (g) Changes in **business practices** - downsizing, outsourcing and re-engineering

   (h) Changes in the **social and business** relationships between companies and their employees, customers and other stakeholders

6.6 While more and more companies are competing in the world market place, most of them tend to focus on the developed markets of North America, Europe and Japan. A vast majority (86%) of the world's population resides in countries where GDP is less than $10,000 per head. Such countries offer tremendous marketing opportunities if the offering is presented correctly. Different stages of country development may be analysed using the **international trade life cycle model**. (Chapter 9)

6.7 This leads on to the question of **market convergence** - how likely is it that consumers' tastes and preferences may converge? On the face of it, there is no reason why they should not, but in practice this is unlikely. Someone who lives in a very hot country is never going to want many sweaters, or be likely to go cycling in the midday sun just for the sake of getting some exercise.

6.8 **Convergence theories** do have strong anecdotal support. The average French high school student appears very similar to American students of the same age (clothing, eating and entertainment preferences). Take a student from Nigeria and compare him to one from Finland, however, and the story is likely to be different.

6.9 Going international can add to the **value chain**. Integrating the supply chain across several countries can lead to considerable cost savings. Increased levels of customer service allied with these cost savings can lead to a dominant market position. This needs an organisational culture that is aware of the supply chain and customer service whatever the country (or countries) of operation.

6.10 Li and Fung, the Hong Kong based export trade company, has a highly developed **international supply chain** that makes the most of production facilities and cost structures in its various spheres of operation. For an example of its country-hopping activities, see page 306.

Different products

6.11 You should not forget that world trade is comprised of **different types of product market** and each one has different marketing processes. Commodities, semi-processed goods, services, government procurement, consumer products, business to business and not-for-profit markets are some examples. We consider some of the differences between them in discussion of buyer behaviour and product marketing in Chapters 4 and 9.

Original equipment manufacturers (OEM) agreements

6.12 This occurs when an international producer supplies products to a local firm who then sells the products under the local brand. This is basically about distribution and volume advantages for the supplier and expansion of product range for the local firm. Japanese companies provide examples, for example selling Japanese VCRs through American companies.

6.13 Disadvantages of OEM

- No brand identity for producer
- Producer forgoes control
- Success depends on efforts of the local firm

Commodities

6.14 A **commodity** is a primary product such as coffee, copper, cotton, tin or agricultural produce such as apples. Some of these are branded in their own right, such as Cape apples, Geest bananas or even De Beers diamonds. We look at them in more detail in Chapter 4 in the context of buyer behaviour.

BPP PUBLISHING

Government buying

6.15 The government offers a huge opportunity for many companies, many of whom rely on the **government market** for a large portion of their sales. Defence contractors are a key example, but governments also buy for schools, highways, hospitals and housing projects.

6.16 Government buyers are accountable to the public and perhaps as a result of this there is a lot of red tape to be cut through, and often there is an emphasis on getting a low bid to make the best use of available **resources.** Total government spending is determined by **budget considerations** rather than commercial pressures or marketing decisions. Some companies (such as Eastman Kodak in the US) have set up separate departments to handle marketing to the government.

6.17 **World institutions** such as the IMF and World Bank have significant influence on development of world trade and the restructuring of struggling economies. We talk about World Bank structural adjustment programmes in Chapter 2. **Regional organisations** also drive global trade.

Marketing at Work

The Welsh Development Agency has managed to secure significant levels of investment from foreign and hi-tech companies in Wales. £11 billion pounds worth of investment has flowed into the country the past 23 years. Wales has the largest concentration of Japanese companies in Europe. A Chinese shoe manufacturing company is soon to follow

---

6.18 Other **global drivers** (factors encouraging the globalisation of world trade) include the following.

(a) **Financial factors** eg Third world debt. Often the lenders require the initiation of economic reforms as a condition of the loan.

(b) **Country/continent** alliances, such as that between the UK and USA, which fosters trade and other phenomena such as tourism.

(c) **Legal factors** such as patents and trade marks, which encourage the development of technology and design.

(d) **Stock markets** trading in international commodities. Commodities are not physically exchanged, only the rights to ownership. A buyer can, thanks to efficient systems of grading and modern communications, buy a commodity in its country of origin for delivery to a specific port. There is also a market in **futures,** enabling buyers to avoid the effect of price changes by buying for future delivery at a set price. This smoothes the process of international trade and lowers risk.

Key Concept
A **commodity** is a tangible good or service resulting from the process of production, but Is generally taken to mean a primary product such as coffee, rubber or tin.

(e) The level of **protectionist** measures. We look at these in Chapter 3.

6.19 This, of course, is not an exhaustive list. Just be aware as you are reading through the text that world trade has **strategic** and **contextual** elements. That is, any company seeking to expand its operations overseas (or an already global player seeking to extend them) must make sure that going international fits with its strategy, and must have regard to a host of factors in the world trading environment.

Chapter Roundup

- The economic justification for overseas trade is the principle of **comparative advantage**. This suggests that overall production increases if countries specialise at what they do best, and trade with each other.

- International marketing can be differentiated from domestic marketing and comprises **strategic decisions**. New markets may be sought for a variety of reasons.

- **Companies** also benefit from trade. Some would not have a market large enough for their products without exports. Others depend on trade to secure inputs of materials.

- **Free trade** is accepted amongst the industrial and now most of the developing world as necessary for prosperity.

- Various **international organisations**, including the WTO, monitor world trade.

- Do these developments lead to **globalisation** - a single market for the world in which borders do not matter? Yes and no. A few products and industries are genuinely global. Many are not and national borders are still very relevant.

- It is important to view international trade in its context.

Quick Quiz

1   How can companies benefit from international trade? (see paras 2.1-2.4)
2   What are the benefits of international trade for countries? (2.8)
3   What is international marketing? (3)
4   Why might new markets be sought? (3.1)
5   What are the implications of the principle of comparative advantage? (4.8)
6   What do you understand by terms of trade? (4.11, 4.12)
7   Why might countries avoid specialisation? (4.16)
8   What is a competitive nation, according to Porter? (4.18)
9   Name some international institutions and agreements governing world trade (5.6 - 5.15)
10   What is the role of the World Bank? (5.13)
11   What is globalisation? (6.2)
12   What is market convergence? (6.7)

Action Programme Review

1   No, because the opportunity cost for one good is always the inverse of another. If a country has a comparative advantage in one good, it must have a comparative disadvantage in at least one other. The opportunity for mutually beneficial trade exists wherever a comparative advantage exists.

2   This is a hard question, as there are so many factors involved in the overseas investment decisions. Furthermore, the principle of comparative advantage applies to countries not companies. However, if a company has a wide spread of production activities, it might end up locating them in those countries which have a comparative advantage in the various activities, but this would be subject to other considerations. The principle has some effect, but will be only one among many influences.

Now try illustrative question 1 at the end of the Study Text

2 The Environment of International Trade

Chapter Topic List	Syllabus Reference
1 Setting the scene	-
2 Understanding international markets	1.4
3 The political and legal framework	1.4
4 Protectionism in international trade	1.4
5 Economic structure and development	1.4
6 Regional trading groups	1.3
7 The single European market	1.3
8 Social and cultural behaviour	1.4
9 Technology	1.4, 3.4
10 E-commerce and the Internet	3.5
11 Geography	1.4
12 A key pitfall: self reference	1.4
13 Coping with currency fluctuations: exchange rates	1.5
14 European economic and monetary union	1.3

Learning Outcomes

After studying this chapter you will have an understanding of the following:

- changes in the world trading environment: countries and regional groups
- major international bodies influencing world trade
- the SLEPT factors affecting international trade
- foreign currency considerations in international trade

Key Concepts Introduced

- Political risk
- Protectionism
- Classifications of economic development
- Structural adjustment programmes
- Balance of payments

- Demography
- Electronic commerce
- Exchange rate
- EMU

Examples of Marketing at Work

- Oil in the Caspian Sea
- Internet services
- The Euro
- Country statistics
- The IMF and Russia
- India and China
- European aviation
- Socio-economic status

- Cinema
- Telephones
- E-commerce
- Peapod.com
- Hullachan
- Marks and Spencer
- Pricing in Euros

1 SETTING THE SCENE

1.1 This chapter narrows the focus to the individual firm and industry and the complexities faced in competing internationally which do not exist in the domestic market. International companies need to understand the marketing environment clearly in order to do well.

1.2 In section 2, we offer an overview of some of the issues a firm faces when competing overseas. A huge variety of SLEPT factors have to be dealt with. In sections 3 - 9 we go over the PEST or SLEPT factors with a focus on some examples. Some of these will be familiar to you from other CIM syllabuses you have studied or are currently studying, but we give a slant of particular relevance to international marketing. For example, the importance of new technology is without doubt - but technology is influential in different ways, depending on the economic development of each market. Cultural issues also feature very significantly in the difficulties facing firms seeking to do International business.

1.3 Geography and the problems of the self-reference criterion appear briefly as sections 10 & 11.

1.4 Another 'uncontrollable' factor which affects the individual firm is **exchange rates** (Section 12). This section covers, in some detail, the complexities of dealing with currency exchange rates.

1.5 This is followed by a section which deals with the current debates surrounding the European Exchange Rate Mechanism (ERM) and the issue of the Single Currency - the Euro. If you read through the debate on the merits and demerits of the single European currency, those business people who support it do so because it will reduce transaction costs and inconvenience of coping with many foreign currencies. Others oppose it as it reduces the government's apparent autonomy, though how real this autonomy is, in the light of the vast amount of money shooting around the foreign exchange markets, is open to question.

2 UNDERSTANDING INTERNATIONAL MARKETS   12/99

2.1 **SLEPT** (social, legal, economic, political and technological) factors are all key issues in a firm's **domestic** environment. The same factors apply when we are discussing a firm's international exposure - they just become more complex.

2.2 An organisation is subject to the following international influences.

  (a) In times of increasing free trade, firms can expect **incoming competition**. That said, the possibility of competing abroad is also available.

BPP PUBLISHING

(b) A firm can **attract investment** from overseas institutions. Competing firms from overseas can receive investments from domestic institutions. For example, non-UK banks paid large sums to acquire UK stock brokers and investment firms.

(c) The **barrier** between the domestic and international environment is relatively **permeable**.

(d) **Political factors** and **legal factors**

    (i) **Political conditions** in individual foreign markets (eg package tour firms and Egypt after terrorist shootings of tourists) or sources of supply (eg risk of nationalisation)

    (ii) **Relationships between governments** (eg UK exporters and investors were worried that Anglo-Chinese disputes over Hong Kong would damage their trade with China)

    (iii) Activities of **supra-national** institutions (eg EU regulations on packaging/ recycling)

    (iv) **Laws and regulations** (eg California's new tough emission standards for cars)

(e) **Economic factors** include the following.

- The overall level of **economic activity**
- The relative levels of **inflation** in the domestic and overseas market
- The **exchange rate**
- The **relative prosperity** of individual overseas markets
- **Economic growth** in newly industrialised countries
- A shift towards **market economies**

(f) **Social and cultural factors** include the following.

- The **cultures and practices** of customers and consumers in individual markets.
- The **media and distribution** systems in overseas markets.
- The differences of **ways of doing business**.
- The degree to which **national** cultural differences matter.
- The degree to which a firm can use its own **national culture as a selling point**.

(g) **Technological** factors

- The degree to which a firm can **imitate** the technology of its competitors
- A firm's access to domestic and overseas **patents**
- **Intellectual property** protection
- **Technology transfer** requirements
- The relative **cost** of technology compared to labour
- The competence of potential service contractors in the target country

---

Marketing at Work

An example of the intermingling of political and environmental factors is the development of oil in the Caspian Sea and its distribution to the West.

(a) The legal status and authority over the Caspian Sea has been disputed. The various states (Russia, Azerbaijan, Turkmenistan and Iran) that now border it have not always seen eye to eye. The seabed is to be divided entirely into national sectors, an important issue where oil distribution is concerned.

(b) A number of oil companies want to build a pipeline from Azerbaijan to the West.

    (i) Russia wants the pipeline to go through Russia for loading on to boats.

(ii) A problem is that this would take the pipeline through Chechnya, where there has been warfare. The Western oil countries favoured a pipeline direct through Turkey. As the main inheritor of the former USSR, Russia still takes a 'proprietary' interest. Eventually, Lukoil, the major Russian oil company was offered a substantial stake in the project

(iii) The US was keen to prevent central Asian oil from passing through Iran, which is also building a pipeline.

Exam Tip

In almost any question in this syllabus, SLEPT factors can be brought in somehow. Arguably they are the defining factors which make international markets different from the home market. The December 1999 exam contained a question on how environmental variables can contribute to a firm's position.

---

3 THE POLITICAL AND LEGAL FRAMEWORK

3.1 At some time, most companies engaged in international marketing suffer because of the political or legal structure of a country.

Political risk

Key Concept

Political risk is the possibility of turbulence (eg civil war, revolution, changes in government policy) in the political environment.

3.2 The level of risk involved will depend on several factors.

- The attitudes of the country's government
- The product being traded
- The company wishing to trade

Political government of the country

3.3 The development of plans for international marketing will depend on the following factors.

(a) **The stability of the government**. Rapid changes or political unrest make it difficult to estimate reactions to an importer or a foreign business.

(b) **International relations.** The government's attitude to the firm's home government or country may affect trading relations. A recent example was the decision by the government of Malaysia to ban British firms from public sector contracts. This was in response to articles in the UK media. Happily, this ban has been rescinded.

(c) The **ideology** of the government and its **role in the economy** will affect the way in which the company may be allowed to trade, and this might be embodied in legislation.

(d) **Informal relations** between government officials and businesses are important in some countries. Cultivation of the right political contacts may be essential for decisions to be made in your favour.

The product

3.4 The nature of the goods or services being offered may affect the 'degree of interest' which a government takes in a particular trading deal. Generally the more important the goods to the economy or the government, the more interest will be taken.

- Key consumer basics
- Armaments and equipment for forces and police
- Key equipment and raw materials for indigenous industry
- Products significantly affecting employment
- Culturally sensitive goods

Marketing at Work

Firms selling Internet services have to deal with governments that wish, for a variety of moral and political reasons, to censor certain material available over the net.

The company wishing to trade

3.5 The previous relations of the company, and its home country, with the host country can affect the risk to the company. Factors influencing the company's acceptability include the following.

- Relations between the company's home government and the overseas government
- Size of company
- The past relations and reputation of the company in dealing with foreign governments
- The degree of local employment and autonomy of operations generated by the activity

Expropriation and other dangers

3.6 Political risk is still relevant with regard to overseas investment, especially in large infrastructure projects overseas. History contains dismal tales of investment projects that went wrong, and were expropriated (nationalised) by the local government.

(a) Suspicion of foreign ownership is still rife, especially when prices are raised.

(b) Opposition politicians can appeal to nationalism by claiming the government sold out to foreigners.

(c) Governments might want to re-negotiate a deal to get a better bargain, at a later date, thereby affecting return on investment.

3.7 In addition to expropriation, there are other dangers.

- Restrictions on profit repatriation (eg for currency reasons)
- 'Cronyism' and corruption leading to unfair favouring of some companies over others
- Arbitrary changes in taxation
- Pressure group activity

3.8 There are many sources of data. The *Economist Intelligence Unit* offers assessment of risk. Management consultants can also be contacted. Companies should ask the following six questions (according to Jeannet and Hennessey).

1	How stable is the host country's political system?
2	How strong is the host government's commitment to specific rules of the game, such as ownership or contractual rights, given its ideology and power position?
3	How long is the government likely to remain in power?
4	If the present government is succeeded, how would the specific rules of the game change?
5	What would be the effects of any expected changes in the specific rules of the game?
6	In light of those effects, what decisions and actions should be taken now?

Coping with political risk

3.9 The approach taken depends on the degree of risk and the level of involvement.

		Low	High
Level of risk	High	• Keep low profile • Communicate via third parties • High level contacts • Short term deals • Export credit insurance	• Contingency plans • Disinvest? • Act for stability?
	Low	No need to worry	No need to worry - but monitor for increasing riskiness

Level of involvement

3.10 Measures to **reduce political risk** are as follows.

- Use local partners with good contacts
- Vertical integration of activities **over** a number of different countries
- Local borrowing (although not a good idea in high inflation countries)
- Leasing rather than outright purchase of facilities in overseas markets
- Take out insurance

Legal factors

3.11 In international markets we are interested in legislation which may affect a firm's trade with a particular country.

- **Domestic legal system**
- **Structure of company law**
- **Local laws**

3.12 Legal implications extend far beyond the marketing mix. Each country may legislate for example, on the following issues, and these may affect the marketer to a greater or lesser degree.

(a) **Export and import controls** for political, environmental, or health and safety reasons. Such controls may not be overt but instead take the form of bureaucratic procedures designed to discourage international trade or protect home producers.

(b) **Favourable trade status** for particular countries, eg EU membership, former Commonwealth countries.

(c) **Monopolies and merger legislation**, which may be interpreted not only within a country but also across nations. Thus the acquisition of a company in country A, by company B, which both sell in country C may be seen as a monopolistic restraint of trade.

(d) **Law of ownership.** Especially in developing countries, there may be legislation requiring local majority ownership of a firm or its subsidiary in that country, for example.

(e) **Taxation law** may be used to encourage or discourage particular import/export activities. For example, freeports may be set up, or generous tax incentives for inward investment may be offered.

(f) **Acceptance of international trademark, copyright and patent conventions.** Not all countries recognise such international conventions.

(g) Determination of minimum **technical standards** which the goods must meet, eg noise levels, contents and so on.

(h) **Standardisation measures** such as packaging sizes.

(i) **Pricing regulations**, including credit (eg, some countries require importers to deposit payment in advance and may require the price to be no lower than those of domestic competitors).

(j) **Restrictions on promotional messages**, methods and media.

(k) **Product liability.** Different countries have different rules regarding product liability (ie the manufacturer's/retailer's responsibility for defects in the product sold and/or injury caused). US juries are notoriously generous in this respect.

4 PROTECTIONISM IN INTERNATIONAL TRADE

> **Key Concept**
> **Protectionism** is the discouraging of imports by raising tariff barriers, imposing quotas etc in order to favour local producers.

4.1 We will now identify the different forms of **protectionist measures** available to governments. Some governments seek to prevent the influence of international trade by making it harder to import from overseas.

- **Tariffs** or customs duties
- Non tariff **barriers**
- Import **quotas and embargoes**
- **Subsidies** for domestic producers
- Exchange **controls**
- Exchange rate **policy**

Tariffs or customs duties

4.2 A **tariff** is a **tax on imports**.

(a) The importer is required to pay either a percentage of the value of the imported good (an *ad valorem* duty), or per unit of the good imported (a **specific duty**).

(b) The government **raises revenue** and domestic producers may expand sales, but **consumers** pay higher prices if they buy imported goods. They may have to buy domestic goods of a lesser quality.

Non-tariff barriers

4.3 The table on page 32 outlines some of the barriers which exist.

Import quotas

4.4 **Import quotas** are **restrictions** on the quantity of product allowed to be imported into a country.

    (a) The restrictions can be imposed by **import licences** (in which case the government gets additional revenue) or simply by granting the right to import only to certain producers.

    (b) **Prices will rise** because the supply of goods is artificially restricted. The consumer pays more while foreign producers benefit. Japanese firms may have benefited financially from quotas on their goods (eg cars) in the past, imposed by some European countries and the US. Quotas, like tariffs, are also likely to provoke **retaliation**.

Minimum local content rules

4.5 Related to quotas is a requirement that, to avoid tariffs or other restrictions, products should be made **in** the country or region in which they are sold. In the EU the product must be of a specified **minimum local content** (80% in the EU) to qualify as being 'home' or 'EU-made'. This is one of the reasons Japanese and Korean manufacturers have set up factories in Europe.

Minimum prices and anti-dumping action

4.6 **Dumping** is the sale of a product in an overseas market at a price lower than charged in the domestic market. **Anti-dumping measures** include establishing quotas, minimum prices or extra excise duties.

Embargoes

4.7 An embargo on imports from one particular country is a **total ban**, a zero quota. An embargo may have a political motive, and may deprive consumers at home of the supply of an important product.

Subsidies for domestic producers

4.8 An enormous range of government **subsidies** and assistance for exporters is offered, such as **export credit guarantees** (insurance against bad debts for overseas sales), financial help and assistance from government departments in promoting and selling products. The effect of these grants is to make unit production costs lower. These may give the domestic producer a **cost advantage** over foreign producers in export as well as domestic markets.

Exchange controls and exchange rate policy

4.9 Many countries have **exchange control regulations** designed to make it difficult for importers to obtain the currency they need to buy foreign goods.

4.10 If a government allows its currency to depreciate, imports will become more expensive. Importers may cut their profit margins and keep prices at their original levels for a while, but sooner or later prices of imports will rise. A policy of exchange rate depreciation in this context is referred to as a **competitive devaluation**.

Marketing at Work

In the last several years whilst European countries were preparing to meet the criteria to establish a common currency, the Euro, there were considerable changes in the relative valuations of the individual country currencies. In particular, the pound sterling has strengthened making it more difficult for British exporters to sell their products abroad.

BPP PUBLISHING

Unofficial non-tariff barriers

4.11 Some countries are accused of having **unofficial barriers to trade**, perpetrated by government. Here are some examples.

(a) **Quality and inspection procedures** for imported products, adding to time and cost for the companies selling them.

(b) **Packaging and labelling** requirements may be rigorous, **safety and performance** standards difficult to satisfy and **documentation procedures** very laborious.

(c) Standards which are much easier for domestic manufacturers to adhere to.

(d) Restrictions over **physical distribution**.

(e) Toleration of **anti-competitive practices** at home.

Action Programme 1

Why might a US car manufacturer support protectionist policies, despite the effects of restraining trade, and a Swedish manufacturer choose to oppose protectionist measures?

---

5 ECONOMIC STRUCTURE AND DEVELOPMENT 12/99

5.1 Economic factors affect both the demand and the ability to acquire goods and services. Even in lesser developed countries (see below) there often exists a wealthy elite who provide a significant demand for sophisticated consumer goods.

5.2 Countries generally have larger agricultural sectors in the early stages of economic development (for example India and Africa). As the economy develops, the manufacturing sector increases. The industrialised countries publish detailed statistics - the production of hundreds of industries may be recorded.

5.3 The correct **classification of economic information** is the subject of international standards. Industrial production, imports and exports are classified under standard headings. Many countries now follow the United Nations' international standard industrial classification (**ISIC**).

Level of economic development

5.4 Commonly, economists and marketers categorise countries into five broad types. Each type then exhibits a fairly consistent pattern of demand for goods and services. Commonly used factors in classifying countries include the following.

(a) **Infrastructure** (eg the development of roads, transport, communications and energy distribution).

(b) **Education** and literacy levels.

Non tariff trade barriers in detail

FORMAL TRADE RESTRICTIONS

A Non tariff import restrictions (Price related measures)

Surcharges at border
Port and statistical taxes
Non discriminatory excise
Taxes and registration charges
Discriminatory excise taxes
Government insurance requirements
Non discriminatory turnover taxes
Discriminatory turnover taxes
Import deposit
Variable levies
Consular fees
Stamp taxes

Various special taxes and surcharges

B Quantitative restrictions and similar specific trade limitations (Quantity-related measures)

Licensing regulations
Ceilings and quotas
Embargoes
Export restrictions and prohibitions
Foreign exchange and other monetary or financial controls
Government price setting and surveillance
Purchase and performance requirements
Restrictive business conditions
Discriminatory bilateral arrangements
Discriminatory regulations regarding countries of origin
International cartels
Orderly marketing agreements
Various related regulations

C Discriminatory freight rates

ADMINISTRATIVE TRADE RESTRICTIONS

D State participation in trade

Subsidies and other government support
Government trade, government monopolies and granting of concessions or licences
Laws and ordinances discouraging imports
Problems relating to general government policy
Government procurement
Tax relief, granting of credit and guarantees
Boycott

E Technical norms, standards and consumer protection regulations

Environmental emission standards
Health and safety regulations
Pharmaceutical control regulations
Product design regulations
Industrial standards
Size and weight regulations
Packing and labelling regulations
Package marking regulations
Regulations pertaining to use
Regulations for the protection of intellectual property
Trademark regulations

F Customs processing and other administrative regulations

Antidumping policy
Customs calculations bases
Formalities required by consular officials
Certification regulations
Administrative obstacles
Merchandise classification
Regulations regarding sample shipments return shipments, and re-exports
Countervailing duties and taxes
Appeal law
Emergency law

BPP PUBLISHING

(c) **Ownership of durables** (for example, telephone, TV, fridge, etc as appropriate).

(d) **GDP** (Gross Domestic Product) per head. This, effectively, is the value of goods and services produced within the economy.

5.5 All of the first three may be claimed to be dependent on GDP. GDP on a **per capita** basis, suitably adjusted for purchasing power, is probably the best single indicator of economic development.

5.6 A danger in using GDP is that it considers only the **average**. The **distribution of wealth** is critical in poor countries, where a market may exist amongst above average sections of the population.

Classification of economic development

5.7 Generally each country can be classified under one of five headings.

> **Key Concepts**
>
> **Lesser developed country (LDC).** Relies heavily on primary industries (mining, agriculture, forestry, fishing) with low GDP per capita, and poorly developed infrastructure.
>
> **Early developed country (EDC).** Largely primary industry based, but with developing secondary (manufacturing) industrial sector. Low but growing GDP, developing infrastructure.
>
> **Semi-developed country (SDC).** Significant secondary sector still growing. Rising affluence and education with the emergence of a 'middle class'. Developed infrastructure.
>
> **Fully developed country (FDC).** Primary sector accounts for little of the economy. Secondary sector still dominates, but major growth in tertiary (service) sector. Sophisticated infrastructure.
>
> **Former Eastern Bloc country (EBC).** May be any of the above, but the 'command economy' under communism has left a legacy that defies straightforward classification. For example, Russia, has most of the features of an SDC but lacks a developed infrastructure though it has a well educated middle class.

> **Exam Tip**
>
> The December 1999 exam contained a question on the differences to be encountered in marketing to developed and less developed countries.

Measuring levels of economic development

5.8 Measures that may be used by the international marketer include the following.

- **GDP** per head
- **Source of GDP** (primary, secondary or tertiary sector based economy)
- **Living standards** (ownership of key durables may be used as a surrogate measure)
- **Energy** availability and usage
- **Education** levels
- **Environmental issues** are becoming more important since the Rio Summit

5.9 Data on most of these variables can be found in most international yearbooks such as 'The Economist Book of Vital World Statistics'. Countries do not develop in all sectors equally. Thus a company selling agricultural machinery would look at both GDP and primary sector growth.

Marketing at Work

USA			*India*	
GDP:	£3,767,010m		GDP:	£218,169m
Population:	c263m		Population:	c936m
Illiteracy rate:	0.5%		Illiteracy rate:	48%
Life expectancy:	men 72, women 79		Life expectancy:	men 58, women 58
Germany			*Malaysia*	
GDP:	£1,104,510m		GDP:	£36,838m
Population:	c82m		Population:	c20m
Illiteracy rate:	-		Illiteracy rate:	16.5%
Life expectancy:	men 73, women 79		Life expectancy:	men 69, women 73
Hungary			*South Korea*	
GDP:	£19,472m		GDP:	£198,681m
Population:	c10m		Population:	c46m
Illiteracy rate:	0.8%,		Illiteracy rate:	2%
Life expectancy:	men 65, women 74		Life expectancy:	men 68, women 76
Brazil			*Japan*	
GDP:	£327,120m		GDP:	£1,970,128m
Population:	c156m		Population:	c125m
Illiteracy rate:	16.7%		Illiteracy rate:	-
Life expectancy:	men 64, women 70		Life expectancy:	men 77, women 83

Structural adjustment programmes

Key Concept

Structural adjustment programmes have been taken up by some developing countries as a way of helping their economies towards fuller participation in the global market, restoring economic order through a mixture of interventionist and free-market strategies.

5.10 In the early 1980s there was a severe deterioration in commodity prices, affecting many developing countries which depended heavily on the export of primary products. Africa was particularity hard hit. Added to this, an unprecedented jump in interest rates made developing countries' debt burdens increasingly unmanageable.

5.11 Main factors exacerbating the situation

- State subsidies to industry
- Existence of a 'command' economy
- An artificially high domestic currency
- Lack of foreign currency
- Food shortages

5.12 These difficulties led to the espousal of **structural adjustment programmes** by international institutions such as the World Bank and the IMF. Such programmes abandoned inward looking projects and concentrated instead on **unprotected participation** in the international market via certain measures.

- Drastic reduction in trade barriers
- Reduction of subsidies and price controls
- Freer movement of capital
- Privatisation of state-owned firms
- Elimination of control on private foreign investment

BPP PUBLISHING

- Reduction in the role of the state
- Devaluation of currencies

5.13 Many countries of Africa and Latin America, as well as some in Asia and the Arab world, embarked on such programmes in the 1980s, especially when lenders were insisting upon economic reforms. They were often slow to implement, however, and it became obvious that the adjustment to a free market could not happen all at once.

5.14 By the early 1990s, most African economies were still stuck in recession. Adjustment programmes based upon trusting to free market forces were generally not working. The majority of the adjustment programmes regarded as relatively 'successful' (small in number) have restored economic order through a contribution of **macro** and **micro** strategies of defending exchange rates, imposing price controls on key goods and services, fixing interest rates and guaranteeing relative stability of wages and profit margins, rather than complete abandonment of the economy to sink or swim.

5.15 The debt crisis is not over, however. Between 1982 and 1997, the total foreign debt of sub-Saharan Africa grew from $57 billion to $144 billion. The standard of living of the majority of the population has also declined. Workers and civil servants in Africa, for example, are increasingly devoting some of their time to farming on the outskirts of their towns. There has been pressure to rethink these programmes, and pay heed to social as well as economic policy.

5.16 The need to define a new approach became even more urgent in the early 1990s following the collapse of communism in Eastern Europe and disintegration of the Soviet Union. The collapse of communism created institutional chaos. Basic institutions underpinning the market in a developed capitalist society were non-existent.

5.17 The last few years has witnessed profound restructuring of former Eastern bloc countries. Attention was focused on price liberalisation, setting up a convertible currency and the privatisation process.

5.18 Since the collapse of the Soviet Union, Western leaders have found it difficult to help Russia's economy into the free market. The IMF gave Russia billions of dollars under much looser terms than those given to other borrowers. Russia was invited to joint the G7 (and make it the G8) despite Russia's tiny economy and weak links to the developed world. Recent devaluations of the rouble and political change have meant that there is not much faith in the Russian economy. It is too much to expect that a transition from 70 years of communist central economic planning (a 'command economy') to a free market can happen overnight.

Marketing at Work

The IMF promised Russia as much as $4.8bn in new loans to prevent the threat of national bankruptcy. The parties agreed on targeting a 2% primary budget surplus as a condition of the loan.

Identifying market size

5.19 The economic worth of a consumer market is based on some general factors.

- The number of people in the market
- Their desire to own the goods
- Their ability to purchase the goods

5.20 Thus in measuring a market, the marketer will obtain information on the following, although they are often crude measures.

(a) **Population**. Its size, growth and age structure, household composition, urban vs. rural distribution. Household size and spatial distribution affect demand for many consumer goods.

(b) **Income**. GDP per head is a crude measure of wealth and account should also be taken of distribution of GDP among various social groups, and their purchasing power.

(c) **Consumption patterns**. The ownership of various goods and the consumption of consumables are indicators of potential demand.

(d) **Debt and inflation**. A high level of debt in a country may indicate import controls (or their possible introduction) or weak currency and currency controls. Inflation may affect purchasing power. In either case ability to pay will be reduced.

(e) **Physical environment**. Physical distance, climate and topography will affect demand in various ways. The availability of natural resources can directly affect demand for equipment and so on to exploit these resources.

(f) **Foreign trade**. The trade relations of a country will affect the attitude towards foreign goods. Factors include economic relations (for example, a member of same economic group such as the EU) and balance of trade.

The balance of payments

> **Key Concept**
>
> The **balance of payments** is the statistical accounting record of all of a country's external transactions in a given period. The balance of payments account of any country records the revenues and payments during the course of a year from all economic transactions between its government, firms and residents, and the corresponding counterparts in those countries with which it trades.

5.21 International trade can present countries with balance of payments problems arising from a persistent mismatch in the flows of exports and imports, resulting in **surpluses** or **deficits** in the value of goods and services exchanged.

5.22 The potential problems arising from **persistent deficits** (as in the case of the UK) are readily identified.

(a) Since a balance of payments deficit represents a **leakage of income** from the national economy, there is a danger that economic growth will be retarded, unless internally generated growth can compensate for this.

(b) A persistent deficit is likely to put **downward pressure on the exchange rate** as confidence in the currency is weakened and a demand for it falls.

(c) A depreciating exchange rate will mean that the **price of imports** in domestic terms will be rising, putting pressure on domestic inflation with consequent knock-on effects for wage demands and unemployment.

5.23 The potential problems arising from **persistent surpluses** (as in the case of Japan) are not so readily identified. Nevertheless, problems can emerge.

(a) A balance of payments surplus represents an injection into the national economy which may result in an **overheating of the economy** if domestic production is already at full capacity.

(b) Overheating will tend to reflect itself in **upward pressure on prices** as total demand for goods exceeds total supply.

(c) Surpluses are likely to put **upward pressure on the exchange rate** which will push up the price of exported goods in foreign countries. This gives rise to the possibility that the surplus will decline.

Goods

5.24 The **visible balance** is sometimes referred to as the **'balance of trade'**, the difference between the value of exported goods from the UK and imported goods to the UK. Prior to the growth in the importance of services, the visible balance was considered to be the major indication of the economic strength of the UK's international trade position.

5.25 Manufactured goods remain the major item of visible external trade. The balance of trade in goods has been negative in the UK for many years, having to be made up from the **'invisible sector'**- see below. Note, too, that UK exports include manufacture by foreign-owned firms (such as Ford and Nissan).

Services

5.26 The **invisible balance** consists of services, interest, profit and dividends, and transfers. Traditionally, the UK's 'invisible' balance has always shown a significant surplus, counteracting to some extent the growing visible deficit.

5.27 **Services** are an important item in the UK's balance of payments.

- **International transport** services (by sea and air, both passengers and cargo)

- **Financial services** (such as banking, insurance, brokerage)

- Earnings from **tourism**

- **Government contributions** to the EU and spending on the **military**

Interest, profits and dividends as an item of invisible trade

5.28 When a country's residents invest heavily in foreign countries, there will initially be an outflow of capital investment from that country but eventually there will be an inflow of interest, profits and dividends on those investments.

(a) **Direct investment earnings**. These are profits of overseas branches, overseas subsidiary companies and overseas associated companies remitted to the UK. Direct investment earnings might bring income into the country (the profits of UK firms operating overseas) or cause outflows (profits of overseas firms from their investments in the UK).

(b) **Portfolio investment earnings** (interest and dividends on stocks and shares held in securities overseas by UK residents, or held in UK securities by overseas residents).

(c) **Interest on borrowing and lending** abroad by banks.

Transfers as an item of invisible trade

5.29 General government transfers are grants to overseas countries, subscriptions and contributions to international organisations such as the EU and other transfers by the UK government overseas or to the UK government from overseas.

6 REGIONAL TRADING GROUPS

Types of trading group

6.1 Currently, a number of **regional trading arrangements** exist, as well as global trading arrangements. These regional trading groups take three forms.

- Free trade areas
- Customs unions
- Common markets

Free trade areas

6.2 Members in these arrangements agree to lower barriers to trade amongst themselves. They enable free movement of **goods** and **services,** but not always the factors of production.

Customs unions

6.3 **Customs unions** provide the advantages of free trade areas and agree a common policy on tariff and non-tariff barriers to **external countries.** Internally they attempt to harmonise tariffs, taxes and duties amongst members.

Economic unions/common markets

6.4 In effect the members become one for economic purposes. There is free movement of the factors of production. The EU has economic union as an aim, although not all members, including the UK, necessarily see this goal as desirable. The EU has a 'rich' market of over 300 million people and could provide a counterweight to countries such as the USA and Japan.

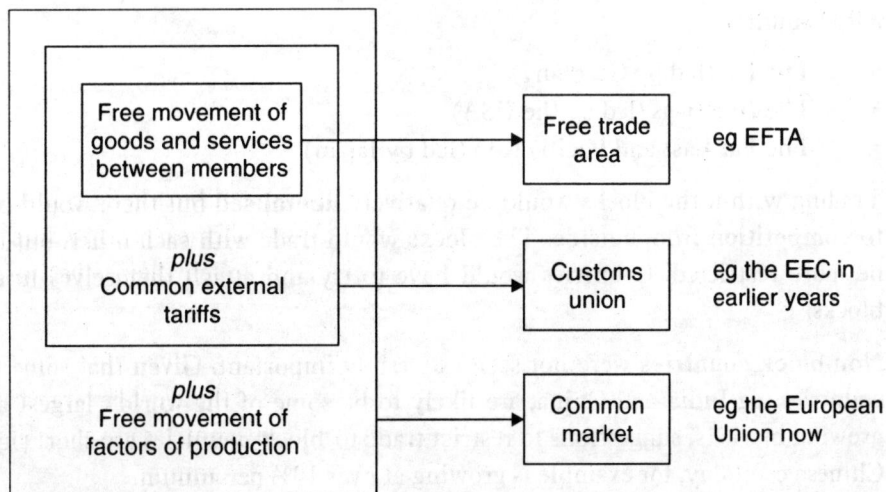

Free movement of goods and services between members	→ Free trade area	eg EFTA
plus Common external tariffs	→ Customs union	eg the EEC in earlier years
plus Free movement of factors of production	→ Common market	eg the European Union now

6.5 The major regional trade organisations are as follows.

(a) North American Free Trade Agreement (**NAFTA**) - US, Canada and Mexico.

(b) European Free Trade Association (**EFTA**) - Norway, Switzerland, Iceland, Liechtenstein.

(c) European Union (**EU**) - Ireland, Britain, France, Germany, Italy, Spain, Portugal, Finland, Sweden, Denmark, Luxembourg, Belgium, the Netherlands, Austria, Greece. A number of other countries have applied to join.

(d) Asean Free Trade Area (**AFTA**) - Brunei, Indonesia, Malaysia, the Philippines, Singapore, Thailand.

(e) Asia-Pacific Economic Co-operation (**APEC**) - Australia, Brunei, Malaysia, Singapore, Thailand, New Zealand, Papua New Guinea, Indonesia, the Philippines, Taiwan, Hong Kong, Japan, South Korea, China, Canada, US, Mexico, Chile.

(f) **Mercosur** - Brazil, Argentina, Paraguay and Uruguay (Chile is an associate).

(g) Southern African Development Community (**SADC**); Angola, Botswana, Lesotho, Malawi, Mozambique, Mauritius, Namibia, South Africa, Swaziland, Tanzania, Swaziland, Zimbabwe.

(h) West African Economic and Monetary Union (**UEMOA**) - Ivory Cost, Burkina Faso, Niger, Togo, Senegal, Benin and Mali.

(i) South Asian Association for Regional Co-operation (**SAARC**) - India, Pakistan, Sri Lanka, Bangladesh, the Maldives, Bhutan and Nepal.

(j) Andean Pact - Venezuela, Colombia, Ecuador, Peru and Bolivia.

(k) Association of Southeast Asian Nations (**ASEAN**) - Indonesia, Malaysia, Philippines, Singapore and Thailand.

Regional trading agreements and the global market

6.6 Regional trading blocks only extend the benefits of free trade to their members. They may distort **global** trading patterns.

6.7 An idea, widely held in the 1980s, described the international business environment in the following way. This was called the '**Triad Theory**'.

(a) The industrial world was supposed to be falling into **three trading blocks**, each led by a lead country.

- The EU (led by Germany)
- The Americas (led by the USA)
- The Far East and Pacific Rim (led by Japan)

(b) Trading within the blocks would be relatively **liberalised** but there would be **barriers to competition** from outside. The blocks would trade with each other, but this would be more restricted. Countries would have to try and attach themselves to one of the blocks.

(c) **Non-block countries** were not seen as terribly important. Given that some non-block countries, eg India and China, are likely to be some of the world's largest and fastest growing markets, suggestions to restrict trade to 'block' countries are short sighted. The Chinese economy, for example is growing at over 10% per annum.

6.8 The theory of trading blocks does not provide a complete analysis of world trade.

(a) The block theory **works better for some industries** than others.

(i) The EU and US have had extensive programmes to protect agriculture, to the outrage of more efficient producers (such as the Cairns Group representing Australia and some other countries).

(ii) Even in sensitive industries like aerospace, there is free trade. (Despite US - EU disputes about subsidies for their respective national champions Boeing and Airbus, British Airways buys Boeings and some US airlines have purchased from Airbus.)

(b) The block theory does not really take **investment flows** into account.

(i) The **fear of protectionism** has encouraged Japanese and Korean companies to invest in Europe and the US. Significant investments in the US economy have been made by UK companies. Even though the bulk of the UK's trade is with EU countries, UK investments overseas are wide ranging.

(ii) Another important component of recent liberalisation is the relatively free **movement of capital** between major centres. Certain financial services industries are global. It is now much easier for companies to tap overseas capital markets. Daimler-Benz for example is quoted on the New York Stock Exchange.

(c) The block theory does not account for all **trade** flows. The US is Japan's most significant **individual** export market, although East Asia as a region has overtaken the US as a market for Japanese's goods.

(d) The **World Trade Organisation** (WTO) regulates world trade.

(e) The three blocks might be **superseded by economic growth** in countries outside them.

(i) In a recent survey of China, the *Economist* predicted that within forty years or so, it will have an economy as large as that of the US. The same might be true of India. Both countries are in the process of deregulation.

(ii) Both these huge countries have a large mix of skills, with poor rural industries, relatively sophisticated industrial and service sectors, and good education systems.

Marketing at Work

Developing countries and technology.

India

Software exports from India are growing at a 'blistering pace'. For eight consecutive years, they have grown by more than 50%, with lots of business coming from year 2000 contracts. The US is the main market (57% of sales), with the EU accounting for 26% and Japan 8%. The top wealth creators in India are now information technology companies, the top three being Satyam Computer, Wipro and Infosys Technologies.

China

China knows exactly how many Internet users it has because everyone has to register with the government before opening an account. The number of users is expected to grow from 600,000 at the end of 1997 to 10 million by 2000. This is a very small proportion of its population of around 1,221 million, and with only 540,000 computers currently connected to the Internet it seems that there will continue to be low penetration rates, but a huge potential market.

Computer Business Review

(f) **Knowledge-based industries** (which many writers such as Drucker believe are the motors of future economic growth) are hard to evaluate and control. **Technology** might make ideas as to trading blocks obsolete.

(g) All trading blocks have extensive economic interactions with **third world countries**. They will have a growing relationship with countries in the former Soviet Union and Eastern Europe, which have recently entered the global market.

6.9 A significant effect of regional trade blocs has been the rush to qualify for **local status** by multinational firms. This has been achieved by the multinationals setting up within one or more member states. Thus France, Germany and the UK have seen considerable inward investment from US and Japanese firms.

7 THE SINGLE EUROPEAN MARKET

7.1 Since 31 December 1992 there has been a 'single European market'.

(a) The **single European market** is supposed to allow for the free movement of **labour, goods and services** between the member states of the EU.

(i) **Physical barriers** (eg customs inspection) on goods and service have been removed for most products. Companies have had to adjust to a new VAT regime as a consequence.

(ii) **Technical standards** (eg for quality and safety) should be harmonised.

(iii) **Governments should not discriminate** between EU companies in awarding public works contracts.

(iv) **Telecommunications** should be subject to greater competition.

(v) It should be possible to provide **financial services** in any country.

(vi) Measures are being taken to rationalise **transport** services.

(vii) There should be **free movement of capital** within the community.

(viii) **Professional qualifications** awarded in one member state should be recognised in the others.

(ix) The EU is taking a co-ordinated stand on matters related to **consumer protection.**

(b) At the same time, there are many areas where harmonisation is some way from being achieved.

(i) **Company taxation**. Tax rates, which can affect the viability of investment plans, vary from country to country within the EU.

(ii) **Indirect taxation (VAT)**. Whilst there have been moves to harmonisation, there are still differences between rates imposed by member states.

(iii) **Differences in prosperity**. There are considerable differences in prosperity between the wealthiest EU economy (Germany), and the poorest (eg Greece). The UK comes somewhere in the middle.

(1) Grants are sometimes available to depressed regions, which might affect investment decisions.

(2) Different marketing strategies are appropriate for different markets.

(iv) **Differences in workforce skills**. Again, this can have a significant effect on investment decisions. The workforce in Germany is perhaps the most highly trained, but also the most highly paid, and so might be suitable for products of a high added value.

(v) **Infrastructure**. Some countries are better provided with road and rail than others. Where accessibility to a market is an important issue, infrastructure can mean significant variations in distribution costs.

(vi) **Delays**. Single market regulation is still being introduced in some industries (insurance).

(vii) **Social differences**. The UK's welfare state is far less generous than Germany's.

7.2 Two other points about the EU are worthy of note.

(a) Bear in mind that the EU is much **more** than a single market and a free trade area. It has its own Parliament, elected from throughout the EU, civil service and courts, and it is one of the many political arrangements in which the countries of Western Europe are involved. It has a political and constitutional dimension largely absent from other free trading arrangements.

(b) The EU is set to **expand** from its current membership. Candidates for membership include Poland, Hungary, the Czech Republic, Cyprus (subject to a political settlement) and Turkey (subject to various economic and political changes). This expansion will have a significant impact on two areas.

(i) The EU's constitutional arrangements.

(ii) The EU's budgetary arrangements. Already the agriculture budget is being cut. Funds also flow from the EU to economically depressed regions (eg parts of Greece, Merseyside). These may change.

Company planning for the single European market

7.3 The Department of Trade and Industry listed seven key questions of business strategy, which UK firms (and other EU firms) should face up to. These are especially pertinent to the single currency.

(a) How has the market changed for our business?

(b) Should we shift from being a UK firm with a UK market, to a European firm with a European market?

(c) If we became a European firm with a European market, would this alter the **scale of our operations**?

(d) In what ways will we become vulnerable in our existing markets to new or greater competition?

(e) Is our management structure suitable for exploiting new opportunities, and taking defensive measures against new threats?

(f) Should we be seeking mergers or takeovers to strengthen our market position, broaden our product range, or spread our financial risk?

(g) Who in the firm is going to be responsible for making the key decisions about how to exploit the single market opportunities?

7.4 These broad strategic questions can be developed in greater detail. Here are just a few possible implications of the changes for marketing and sales related operations.

(a) **Marketing**

- What new customers can be reached?
- Is the wider market attractive?

- What **market information** do we need, and how do we get it?
- Are our products and services suitable for the wider market?
- What will competition be like?

(b) **Sales**

- How can we reach the potential new customers?
- How can we sell into the new market?
- What sales literature, advertising and sales promotions will be needed?

(c) **Distribution.** What will be the distribution organisation for the new markets - eg, transport, warehousing, dealer agreements, delivery times etc.?

(d) **Product development**

- What changes are needed to make our products and services more attractive to the new markets?
- What resources will be needed to develop new products?
- Is there scope for collaborative ventures in product development with other EU firms?

Marketing at Work

Aviation in the EU

On April 2, 1997 the European Union completed the liberalisation of its aviation market. From that day, European airlines saw the removal of the last restrictions on their operations, leaving them free to operate domestic services in countries other than their own. In the past, air transport (including level of fares and services) had been heavily regulated, as many governments chose to support the 'national' airline. The UK was one of the first to privatise air transport. The final stage allows airlines to set their own fares or services within the EU, subject to predatory pricing restrictions.

In 1996 there were 156 carriers offering scheduled services, compared with 99 in 1986. Airlines such as Ryanair, EasyJet and Virgin Express have all introduced low cost flights between a range of EU countries.

However, fares for many European routes are still higher than the equivalent distances in the US. In part this is because airports are still publicly owned, in the main, and landing 'slots' (periods of time available for take off and landing) are hard to come by.

Cross border mergers

7.5 One of the results of the single European market has been a spate of mergers. As we shall see, acquiring an overseas firm is an often-used 'mode of entry' to European markets. Examples are as follows.

(a) Slowly but surely the European **defence industry** will be rationalised.

(b) Many UK water firms and rail firms are owned by French companies.

(c) Some firms, such as General Motors, already operate on a Europe-wide basis, with one model being sourced from one country. This offers the advantage of economies of scale.

(d) Some major UK retailers (eg Tesco) have sought to grow by acquiring retailers in other countries.

8   SOCIAL AND CULTURAL BEHAVIOUR

Demographic issues in overseas markets

> **Key Concept**
> **Demography** is the 'analysis of statistics on birth and death rates, age structures of populations, ethnic groups within communities etc.' (Bennett, *Dictionary of Personnel and Human Resources Management*).

8.1   The adjective **demographic** is sometimes used to denote the population-related aspects of an issue.

8.2   The **purpose** of studying a country's population and trends within it is as follows.

(a)   People create a demand for goods and services.

(b)   If economic growth exceeds population growth you would expect to see enhanced **standards** of living. **Quality of life** measures would also include pollution measures, life expectancy rates, infant mortality and so on.

(c)   Population is a source of labour, one of the **factors of production.**

(d)   Population creates demands on the physical environment and its resources, a source of increased international political concern. (the Kyoto conference in Japan at the end of 1997 agreed reductions in carbon dioxide).

8.3   The higher rate of population growth in **less-developed countries** compared with developed countries has arisen due to a continuing high birth rate and a declining death rate although some populations are being threatened by the HIV virus (for example in South Africa). Social changes (eg attitudes to large families) have not accompanied medical advances imported from developed societies. People are living longer.

(a)   Growing populations

- Require fast economic growth just to maintain living standards
- Result in overcrowding on land and/or cities and a decline in the quality of life
- Require more resources for capital investment
- Stimulate investment (as the market size is increasing)
- Lead to enhanced labour mobility

(b)   Falling populations

- Require more productive techniques to maintain output
- Make some scale economies harder to achieve
- Put a greater burden on a decreasing number of young people
- Exhibit changing consumption patterns

8.4   Here are some statistics, which might help to explain the importance many businesses are placing on overseas markets. The figures are taken from *Social Trends*.

	1997 *Population* *(millions)*	*2025 (est.)* *Population* *(millions)*	*%* *increase* *1997-2025*
World population	5,848.7	8,039.1	37%
European Union	373.3	368.5	(1.2)%
Other European countries	355.9	332.6	6%
Canada and USA	301.7	369.0	22%
Africa	758.4	1,453.9	91%
Asia	3,538.5	4,784.8	35%

BPP PUBLISHING

Latin America and Caribbean	491.9	689.6	40%
Oceania (including Australia)	29.1	40.7	40%

Age structure and distribution

8.5 We should now discuss the **age structure** of the population.

(a) The effect of greater life expectancy is that a larger proportion of the population will be senior citizens and unlikely to be working. These offer significant opportunities to international marketers. The UK, Europe and Japan all face an ageing population.

(b) The proportion of old people is lower in developing countries. In Egypt and Iran, over half the population is below the age of 30.

Geographic distribution

8.6 Where we live is another important feature of demography. The above arguments have taken the individual country as a homogenous unit. In practice, however this is a vast oversimplification. A country may suffer the problems of overpopulation in some areas and underpopulation in others.

Action Programme 2

The Republic of Guarana in Latin America is undergoing a number of major changes. Now a democracy, it has re-established links with Western providers of capital, who are investing in the country, to extract its unique resource of Vrillium. In particular, large numbers of Vrillium mines have been opened in the San Serif valley. This comprises about 10% of the country's land area and is the site of Guarana's elegant capital Bosanova. This new economic activity is welcome. The mines and related industries will spur rapid economic growth. Bosanova has a population of 50,000. 80% of Guarana's population are peasant farmers. The prices of their crops on world markets have plummeted and the government of Guarana is alarmed at the growing rural poverty, especially as the population is increasing and agriculture is primitive and inefficient. The government has little money to invest in the countryside.

Jot down what you think are the consequences of the huge increase in industrial and mining activities in Bosanova?

8.7 Demography also deals with the effect of concentration and dispersal of population in particular areas. Industrialisation has traditionally meant a shift from the countryside to the towns and can be seen in the explosive growth of **mega-cities** in Latin America (Mexico City, Sao Paolo in Brazil), and Asia (eg Bombay, Shanghai, Jakarta).

Sex

8.8 There is often an imbalance in the population between the numbers of men and the numbers of women. This has arisen for a number of reasons.

(a) Males tend to die younger.

(b) In some countries male children are more valued than female children, and female children are more likely to suffer infanticide.

8.9 The **work roles** played by males and females in different societies vary, even within the industrial world. In different societies, women and men have distinct purchasing and social powers. This is a key cultural issue.

Ethnicity

8.10 Only a few societies are homogenous, with populations of one culture and ethnic background. Japan is an example, although the population includes descendants of Koreans. On the other hand, societies like the USA and the UK have populations drawn from a variety of different areas.

Buying patterns

8.11 Buying behaviour is an important aspect of marketing. Many factors influence the buying decisions of individuals and households. Demography and the **class structure** (the distribution of wealth and power in a society) are relevant in that they can be both **behavioural determinants** and **inhibitors**.

(a) **Behavioural determinants** encourage people to buy a product or service. The individual's personality, culture, social class, and the importance of the purchase decision (eg a necessity such as food or water, or a luxury) can predispose a person to purchase something.

(b) **Inhibitors** are factors, such as the individual's income, which will make the person less likely to purchase something.

8.12 **Socio-economic status** can be related to buying patterns in a number of ways, both in the amount people have to spend and what they spend it on. It affects both the quantity of goods and services supplied, and the proportion of their income that households spend on goods and services.

Marketing at Work

(a) India has a large peasantry and an industrial proletariat, but its huge population size means that its wealthy middle class is bigger than the populations of many developed countries. With import liberalisation and economic deregulation, this should be an attractive segment for marketers.

(b) The level of inequality in society also influences its attractiveness to the marketer. Brazil has the greatest degree of inequality in the world. Japan, famously, has low inequality.

   (i) In societies of high inequality, wealth is concentrated, hence the buying power of the majority is limited. This might suggest more success in selling luxury goods.

   (ii) Where equality is higher, there may be a higher demand for mass market goods as more people will have access to them.

Family structure

8.13 The role of the family and family groupings varies from society to society.

(a) In societies such as India, the **caste system** still exists and family structures can be part of this wider network.

(b) **Extended families** are still strong in many countries, especially where the family is to assume most of the burden of looking after the elderly: many countries do not have a welfare state.

(c) Family size varies.

8.14 Marketers have often used the model of the **family life cycle** (FLC) to model purchase and consumption patterns. You will have encountered it before.

- Bachelor - single people
- Newly-weds - household and childcare products
- Full nest
- Empty-nest: children have left home
- Solitary survivor

8.15 This model may not hold.

(a) Quite often, households contain three generations (grand-parents, parents, children).

(b) People leave home later in life. In countries such as Italy and Spain it is common for adult children to live at home.

(c) Purchase and consumption decisions vary.

Culture

8.16 Economic prosperity, in other words the ability to pay, accounts only partially for the demand for goods. The desire to acquire the goods is probably more significant. The importance we attach to the ownership of goods and use of services is determined by the learning process we acquire through **cultural and social education**. We learn how to be consumers by interacting with others and observing their reactions. Thus the comparison of the UK and French attitudes to food may explain why microwave cookers have had less acceptance in France than in the UK.

> ### Exam Tip
> Demography and culture were key issues facing Amway in the December 1996 mini-case. Amway wanted to introduce door-to-door selling to China, a huge market with rapidly rising incomes - but door-to-door cold calling is not part of the culture. (Amway is following Avon, so its choice of strategy may be influenced by the choices of other firms.)

9 TECHNOLOGY

What is technology?

9.1 A simple answer to the question 'what is technology?' would include vague references to advanced machines, computers and so forth, but the word can also denote simple objects like the wheel. Technology can also refer to the ways in which these objects are developed.

9.2 Buchanan and Huczynski, quoting Langdon Winner, note three uses of the word technology.

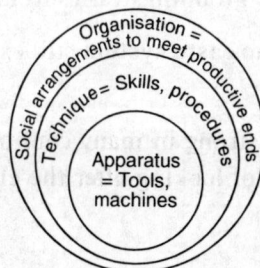

You can see that **apparatus** is in **techniques**, and techniques are co-ordinated by **organisations**. Let us take a simple example.

(a) The **apparatus** in a photographer's studio includes cameras, lighting equipment, a dark room, developing tanks, chemicals, enlargers, light sensitive paper for printing and so forth.

(b) Taking a photograph of, say, a family group involves combining these machines in a particular way. A **technique** might be to shine the lights in a particular way for a desired effect, with the use of a particular shutter speed. This is **purposive**: the photographer knows what he or she is trying to achieve and knows how to use the equipment and chemicals to a desired effect.

(c) The **organisation** would include the whole social and technical structure. For example, it may be that there is a division of labour. One person might be responsible for arranging the lights and taking the picture, which form one set of skills. Another person might be responsible for developing the film and printing it, another set of skills.

9.3 The history of the past 200 years has been one of enormous economic growth. Many countries are able to support populations which in the early 19th century would have been inconceivable.

9.4 Material advances have promoted a large complex of economic, social, political and cultural changes These changes have included the following.

(a) **Industrialisation** (eg movement of labour and resources from agriculture to industry) which has been a feature of many overseas markets.

(b) **Modernisation** (urbanisation, reduction in death rates, centralising government and so forth).

Marketing at Work

An example can be based on the effect that a 'new' technology can have on an old one. Different technologies are adopted at different rates. The cinema ('moving pictures') was once a new medium.

(a) In the UK the fall in cinema attendances has largely been caused by television, a new technology which has fallen in cost since its invention. Television itself has been subject to competition from video. New technology has also increased the number of television channels available.

(b) In India, on the other hand, television penetration might be high in urban areas but less so in the poorer villages. Cinema is still India's principal medium for distributing moving pictures, and the Indian film industry is more prolific than Hollywood.

Technological development and the marketing mix: a cautionary perspective

9.5 Technology, or investment in it, in the narrow sense, cannot on its own promote economic growth. The first use of **steam** power was discovered, not in 18th century England, but almost 2,000 years before: there was, however, no 'use' for it. Societies with large pools of slave labour had little need for 'labour-saving' inventions.

9.6 Steven Yearley (*Science, Technology and Social Change*) mentions the very uneven success that modern apparatus and technique have had in 'modernising' underdeveloped countries.

(a) The **environmental consequences** of introducing western technology to underdeveloped countries have been ill thought out.

(b) The **economic consequences** have not been as beneficial as might at first be supposed. 'The prestigious new production technologies have not worked optimally or even satisfactorily.' The problems are two-fold.

(i) **Technological dependency** leading to a heavy foreign currency payments burdens. The country has to import **spare parts,** and even raw materials, to run machinery. It might have to pay for **expatriate technicians**. This is expensive, and so the costs of the technology might be greater than anticipated, thus reducing any economic benefit.

(ii) The inappropriateness of Western technology. **Climatic** conditions can affect performance. **Infrastructural** deficiencies such as naturally poor roads affect, for example, the 'good design' of a car. The **labour/capital** mix means that in poor countries, with surplus labour, labour intensive industries rather than labour saving capital equipment might be a better use of resources.

Action Programme 3

The Republic of Rukwa is a largely agricultural society. For foreign exchange, it is dependent on the exports of kwat. Kwat is a grain which can only be grown in Rukwa's climate. It is, however, widely in demand in Western markets as a 'health' food. Kwat is grown by peasant farmers on small plots of land on banks of the River Ru. At present, the harvested Kwat is transported by ox-drawn barges down the River Ru to port Ruk for export. The process is slow, owing to bottlenecks on the river. The government is thinking of several alternatives to ease this situation. Rukwa has no other natural resources.

1   Build a high speed road, and use foreign loans to buy lorries and four-wheel drive vehicles for farmers.

2   Build a railway, with imported steel and engines.

3   Widen the River Ru at key points, and purchase outboard motors for the barges.

What do you think is right or wrong with all these alternatives?

9.7   The relevance of this to international marketers is as follows.

(a) **How do you define customer needs?** Elite groups sometimes 'need' products which are not economically beneficial for society.

(b) To what extent do you apply the societal marketing concept to overseas markets?

(c) The marketing mix may presuppose a level of **technological development** which is in fact non-existent for large parts of the population.

Level of technological development

9.8   The level of technological development in a country is important in the marketing of many products.

- Understanding **how the product is used**
- The provision of **support services** for the product
- The existence of an appropriate **distribution network**
- **Communication** with the customer

How to use the product

9.9 Many products are technically sophisticated and require a level of **technological awareness** that may not be widely available. Technologically aware cultures recognise switches and buttons and instructions almost instinctively.

Support services

9.10 Many products require maintenance and spare parts which may be unavailable outside the most technologically advanced economies. The classic solution is known as the 'backward invention' in which the product is simplified to either the level of support available or, ultimately, the point at which the owner can support the product himself.

Distribution network

9.11 Certain products require an **infrastructure for their distribution** and use. Thus a TV requires both electricity and a TV transmission service. Telephones require a carrier network. Distribution of medicines and foodstuffs require careful handling and temperature conditions in transit, necessitating specialised and sophisticated transport.

Communications

9.12 In western countries we accept the ease with which we can communicate. In other countries the availability of the media may be somewhat limited. Telephone ownership may be low. Postal systems may be inadequate. Road and rail transport may be insufficient. TV and radio coverage may be limited. In many underdeveloped countries the use of personal selling either at the retail level, or on a business to business basis, is the only option.

Marketing at Work

(a) *Telephone access.* The world had about 800 million main telephone lines at the end of 1997. The global network has grown nearly tenfold in the past 40 years, according to a new report by the International Telecommunication Union. The world is likely to have almost a billion telephone lines in 2000.

(b) *Teledensity.* Telephone density - the number of lines per 100 people - has quadrupled since 1960. It varies greatly. A quarter of countries still have a teledensity below one. But the experience of countries such as Singapore and South Korea shows that teledensity can grow faster than was once thought. China has moved from fewer than one main line per 100 people to more than five since 1990, accounting for one-fifth of the 300m or so lines added in the period. It takes on average 17 years to go from one line per 100 to ten, but about nine years to go from ten to twenty.

The Economist, 4 April 1998

Action Programme 4

A firm has developed a drug which can cure Alzheimer's disease. What factors do you think would distinguish its export marketing efforts to a country in the EU from its export marketing efforts to a country in the Third World?

---

10   E-COMMERCE AND THE INTERNET

Electronic commerce

10.1   Electronic commerce is the latest example of the impact of technology on global markets.

BPP PUBLISHING

> ## Key Concepts
>
> **Electronic commerce** (e-commerce, e-business, e-biz) can be defined as using an electronic network to speed up all stages of the business process, from design to buying, selling and delivery. The process is fairly familiar between companies, but less so between retailer and customer.
>
> The **internet** is the sum of all the separate networks (or stand-alone computers) run by organisations and individuals alike. (It has been described as an **international telephone service** for computers.)
>
> 'The internet offers efficient, fast and cost effective email, massive information search and retrieval facilities. There is a great deal of financial information available and users can also access publications and news releases issued by the Treasury and other Government departments.
>
> To access the internet you require a microcomputer, a modem and the services of an internet provider.
>
> One of the main uses of the internet is for the sending and receiving of email. This has become a popular method of communication for companies of all sizes.
>
> The main advantage of email is the speed of delivery; messages are delivered within a few seconds and take no longer to travel to Moscow than to Manchester. Messages can be sent to multiple addresses, they can contain images, sound and computer files in addition to the text.'
>
> *Certified Accountant*, August 1997

10.2 Electronic commerce in the sense of customer buying via the Internet has had a slow start, in the UK at least. There are many factors contributing to this, one of the chief ones being people's concern about the **security of on-line transactions**. However, a massive increase in e-commerce is on the way according to some forecasts. Here are some figures on European usage.

	UK	France	Spain	Germany	Sweden
% of companies with web sites	51	25	16	48	54
% of companies selling via the net	9	3	9	9	10
Value of goods sold online 1999 (€m)	5,300	3,400	400	3,600	700
PC penetration at home (% of population)	37.3	26.6	27.4	35	64
Online penetration (% of population)	26.3	8.7	10.5	16.2	41
People with internal access (millions)	12.5	5.21	3.91	11.2	3.63
Mobile phone penetration (% of consumers)	34.8	28.5	31.4	24.5	55.2
% internet users who shop online	25	10	9	36	33

(Source: *Connectis, March 2000*)

10.3 The London Chamber of Commerce predicts that by 2001, e-commerce will account for 5% of all worldwide sales, worth £20 trillion. Cheaper personal computers will help to boost the trend, as have free internet access services, such as Dixons' Freeserve.

Marketing at Work

The travel business is currently the largest e-commerce category, with around 40% of the e-commerce market. International companies are setting up websites to take advantage. America's Travelocity launched its UK home page recently, giving access to the computer system used by 40,000 travel agents around the world. Conventional methods of booking holidays are under threat. High street travel agents who are not in touch may not survive the competition, as the value they provide will be put under scrutiny.

The phenomenon of e-commerce is not just the domain of the large firm. Jack Scaife, a Yorkshire family butcher in the UK, uses the Internet to sell black pudding and bacon all over the world. The Internet can give the smallest business the same global reach as the largest. Indeed it has been found that the best websites belong to small firms. Larger firms such as the big car manufacturers are adopting e-commerce at a much slower pace, with websites that are little more than promotional material rather than venues for direct selling. To quote an example, an article in *PC Week online* found that Exxon's website consisted largely of job advertisements and a download of the Tiger mascot. For now, the leaders in this area remain books, electronics, catalogues, food and CD sellers. Many big companies are, however working on business-to-business e-commerce projects that consumers never see.

10.4 Electronic commerce draws businesses, suppliers and customers closer together, enabling collaboration on **design**, pinpointing of **consumer demand** and sharpening of **marketing strategies**. It opens markets for 24 hours a day.

10.5 Governments are major players in the market for goods and services. Public purchasing accounts for 11% of European GDP. The European Commission has set a target of 25% of public procurement to be done via e-commerce by 2003. The UK government wants 25% of its services available on-line by 2001.

10.6 E-commerce is not restricted to the major industrialised nations represented in the US, Europe and Japan. It is predicted that Latin American countries will spend $8 billion a year on-line by 2003. Sales of computer equipment here in 1998 reached $22 billion. There are still hurdles to be overcome, such as finding secure methods of on-line payment and bureaucratic customs procedures, coupled with expensive Internet access fees. Three quarters of all money spent on the Internet in Latin American countries is currently sent to overseas companies, predominantly in the US. Many UK technology firms are desperate for new markets and the region is therefore vital.

10.7 Companies going on the Internet must have regard to **local culture and tastes**. It has been found that most attempts by Internet retailers in the US to target other countries consist mainly of translating an existing website into the relevant native language. Companies who want to compete more effectively must take account of varying regional characteristics.

10.8 In early 1999 the UK government unveiled a new **legal framework for e-commerce**, designed to boost public confidence in using the Internet. Among other proposals, the courts are to be allowed to recognise **electronic signatures** as legally binding. The aim is to make the UK one of the easiest places to do 'e-biz' in the world. The US administration is also seeking to encourage the development of the 'digital company', pushing for greater access to the Internet for small US firms and the developing nations.

10.9 E-commerce can reduce expensive **sales and distribution** workforces, and offers new **marketing** opportunities.

Distribution

10.10 The Internet can be used to get certain products **directly into people's homes**. Anything that can be converted into **digital form** can simply be uploaded onto the seller's site and then **downloaded** onto the customer's PC at home. This is contributing to a process called **disintermediation** (see Chapter 12).

Marketing

10.11 Besides its usefulness for tapping into worldwide information resources businesses are also using it to **provide information** about their own products and services.

10.12 For **customers** the Internet offers a **speedy and impersonal** way of getting to know about the services that a company provides. For **businesses** the advantage is that it is much cheaper to provide the information in electronic form than it would be to employ staff to man the phones on an enquiry desk, and much more effective than sending out mailshots that people would either throw away or forget about when they needed the information.

10.13 For many companies this will involve a **rethink of current promotional activity**.

Marketing at Work

Peapod.com is an online supermarket and one of the more sophisticated recorders and users of customers' personal data and shopping behaviour. With over 100,000 customers in eight US cities, Peapod's website sells groceries that are then delivered to customer's homes. a list of previous purchases (including brand, pack size and quantity purchased) is kept on the site, so the customer can make minor changes from week to week, saving time and effort.

Peapod creates a database on each shopper that includes their purchase history (what they bought), their online shopping patterns (how they bought it), questionnaires about their attitudes and opinions, and demographic data (which Peapod buys from third parties). A shopper's profile is used by the company to determine which advertisement to show and which promotions/electronic coupons to offer. Demographically identical neighbours are thus treated differently based on what Peapod has learned about their preferences and behaviours over time.

Shoppers seem to like this high-tech relationship marketing, with 94% of all sales coming from repeat customers. Manufacturers like it too. the more detailed customer information enables them to target promotions at customers who have repeatedly bought another brand, thereby not giving away promotion dollars to loyal customers.

Collecting information about customers

10.14 People who visit a site for the first time are asked to **register,** which typically involves giving a name, physical address and post code, e-mail address and possibly other demographic data such as age, job title and income bracket.

10.15 From the initial registration details the user record may show, say, that the user is male, aged 20 to 30 and British. The **website can respond** to this by displaying products or services likely to appeal to this segment of the market.

Possible strategies

10.16 There are four possible strategies that a company may adopt towards e-commerce.

    (a) **Do not sell products through the internet at all,** and prohibit resellers from doing so. Provide only product information on the internet. This may be an appropriate strategy where products are **large, complex and highly customised,** such as aircraft manufacturing.

    (b) **Leave the internet business to resellers** and do not sell directly through the internet (ie do not compete with resellers). This can be appropriate, for instance, where manufacturers have already assigned exclusive territories to resellers.

    (c) The manufacturer can **restrict internet sales exclusively to itself.** The problem with this is that most large manufacturers do not have systems that are geared to dealing with sales to end users who place numerous, irregular small orders.

    (d) Open up internet sales to everybody and **let the market decide** who it prefers to buy from.

10.17 If the decision is made to enter into e-commerce a new e-business needs **support and long-term commitment from high-level management.** Ideally such a project should be 'sponsored' by the chief executive or a board-level director.

10.18 A report from Andersen Consulting points to huge differences between the US and European attitudes towards electronic commerce. It has been said that Europe is around 12 to 18 months behind the US in terms of technological and business development of the Internet. Although 82% of the 300 European executives interviewed recognise the strategic importance of e-commerce, only 39% are doing anything about it. Even within Europe, there a variations in Internet and e-commerce adoption.

10.19 Whereas US industrialists are working hard to keep government regulation out of e-commerce, European businesses want to bring governments in so that rules can be created. The contrast could hardly be more extreme.

10.20 The point being missed is that e-commerce is **not a distinct marketplace** in itself: rather, internet technology has created **new tools** that businesses can use, if they choose, to broaden their markets. E-commerce brings big changes, creating opportunities for some, threats for others; it may affect commerce in ways akin to the discovery of **new trade routes** or the invention of **faster modes of transportation** - broadening trade horizons and creating, in some fields, truly global markets, products and services.

10.21 It is unlikely that the Internet can remain totally free of political intervention and some measure of control; on the other hand, Europeans cannot expect that e-commerce will become cosily regulated.

10.22 The Internet is affecting all businesses in similar ways. Every industry is now part of a global network, with all companies in the industry equally contactable. **Information**, once valuable, is now a **commodity**. These two forces in themselves have powerful consequences: many businesses that survived merely because they were conveniently located, or because they provided information that was hard to find, must increasingly seek other sources of competitive differentiation.

10.23 On the other hand, **some organisations have benefited enormously from Internet growth**: in 1996, Forrester Research calculated that PCs, pornography and CDs and gift items such as flowers made up a little over half of all online consumer revenues. The *Economist's* survey of electronic commerce listed the following industries which are especially affected.

(a) **Financial services**

As *The Economist* points out, this is a classic example of how the Internet can open up an existing infrastructure - the financial markets' computerised information needs - to all comers, and thus transform an industry. Now that investors can get advice and market information from many (free) sources, they are less willing to pay a premium just to trade. The result is the appearance of discount online brokers; Forrester estimates that assets worth $111 billion are already managed online, and the figure is expected to rise to $474 billion. The downside is that discount broking will become a commodity service, surviving (in *The Economist's* phrase) on razor-thin margins, and depend on economies of scale - unless the companies involved can find some other way to add value, increase their margins, and differentiate themselves from their competitors.

(b) **Sex**

Forrester Research estimates that erotic material accounted for sales of $52m on the Internet in 1996, one-tenth of all retail business on the Web. Typical consumers, says *The Economist*, are 'avid, savvy and well-wired young men,' skilled in teasing out the best material at the lowest price from the thousands of sites on-line.

(c) **Travel**

Although most travellers prefer to use travel agents in order to manoeuvre themselves around opaque ticket prices, schedules and flight availability, especially since using an agent costs them no more, the emergence of the Internet has **given airlines an opportunity to cut out the middle man**. They do this in two ways. First, some airlines sell seats direct through their own web sites; second, companies like Northwest and Continental have reduced the commission they pay to online travel agencies on the grounds that much of the work is done by customers themselves. Yet online purchases still make up only about 1% of total airline ticket sales, and Forrester Research estimates that the figure will gradually creep up to no more than about 1.5%. As long as airlines are legally prevented from offering online bookers a price advantage, then most independent travellers (some of them, doubtless, driven by sheer inertia and force of habit) will continue to use agencies.

(d) **Retailing**

The most obvious advantages of **online shops** are that their **costs are lower** and they are **less constrained for space** than their physical counterparts. Yet only about a third of online retailers make money. Not only must they cope with deeply ingrained suspicions about online purchasing, but many of them appear to have entered the Internet half-heartedly. Their product ranges often consist of only a limited selection from the goods which they sell through their catalogues or shops; many items are hard to find, slow to download, and hard to see on-screen, according to *The Economist*.

(e) **Music**

In principle, because the recording industry is controlled by only a few companies, they have the power to stifle Internet competition. Most of the online CD retailers are still losing money.

(f) **Books**

Stimulated by the apparent success of Amazon.com, two of the USA's largest booksellers - Barnes & Noble and Borders - have gone online, along with some international competitors. Optimists think that online book sales will reach 8% of the market in 2000.

(g) **Cars**

In the USA, customers of Auto-by-Tel, the leading Internet car-buying service, simply tell the service what kind of car they want, and wait for nearby dealerships to make their best offer. *The Economist* says that customers report prices up to 10% lower than the best face-to-face haggling efforts could achieve, without stepping into a dealership until it is time to pay and pick up the car. It costs the dealer only about $25 to respond to an Auto-by-Tel lead, instead of hundreds of dollars to advertise and sell a car in the conventional way. In 1996, two million of the 15.1 million cars sold in America were sold through the Internet. Chrysler believes that soon it will sell around 25% of its production online.

(h) **Advertising and marketing**

The Internet, unlike any other advertising medium, is **completely customisable for each consumer**. It enables companies to target potentially interested people and communicate interactively with them. Using the Internet it is easy to know which advertising works. Just count the 'click-throughs'.

Electronic commerce: the implications and the experience

10.24 For an established company, one of the principal challenges of electronic business is **the extent to which its existing value chain is made redundant,** and whether its competitive advantage is eroded, or even fatally wounded. Successful companies usually have competitive advantages in a few parts of the value chain. Electronic commerce may mean that these advantages disappear.

10.25 Philips Evans and Thomas Wurster, of Boston Consulting Group, point out that, 'Where once a sales force, a system of branches, a printing press, a chain of stores or a delivery fleet served as **formidable barriers to entry** because they took years and heavy investment to build, in this new world they **could suddenly become expensive liabilities**. New competitors on the Internet will be able to come from nowhere to steal your customers.' Thus a bank may find its branch network threatened by the growth of online banking.

10.26 The potential threat is obvious. The conundrum for bankers is to assess the likely extent of the damage. How many customers will be lost? **Does the branch network retain important advantages in customer acquisition and retention?** Quite possibly, customers find it reassuring to know that their bank does have branches and real people whom they can visit and talk to if necessary, just as they find it pleasant to visit a bookshop.

10.27 On the other hand, **customer profiles are changing**. Those who are uncomfortable with online transactions will eventually be replaced by others who have been computer-literate more or less from birth. In addition, even if only a minority of customers were to switch from traditional banks to electronic banking, the numbers may still be sufficient to **affect product/service pricing**. In other words, the arrival of cheaper electronic transaction availability will gradually force service providers (like banks) to re-price the whole range of their activities, even for those customers who still transact their business by conventional means.

10.28 **Electronic commerce has eliminated many of the competitive advantages enjoyed by existing competitors**. Retailers can buy the ingredients they need, and rely on their brand names to help them create competitive advantage. Indeed, in an ironic twist of fortune, the major financial services companies of today may end up being little more than marginally-profitable sub-contractors to the key players (like Tesco) of tomorrow. In Martin's phrase, 'The value added will migrate to the businesses that control the customer relationships.'

10.29 On the other hand, it may be that in practice most businesses do not enjoy the relationships with their customers that they think they do. Just because a customer makes **frequent use** of a supplier - whether a retail supermarket or a bank's retail branch - does not mean that the customer is necessarily **loyal or committed**: it is equally plausible to argue that transaction frequency is a product of **necessity rather than desire**.

Marketing at Work

Hullachan is a Glasgow-based company which designs, manufactures and sells Highland and Irish dance shoes. Since opening its website, Hullachan now achieves 75 per cent of its sales through the Internet and exports to North America, Australasia and Ireland. All its overseas distributors were appointed as a result of approaches potential partners made to Hullachan after viewing its product offerings through the web; the company receives over 1000 EMails a week, which it promises to answer within 12 hours; of these, over 700 are customer enquiries which are converted to the distributors. Since January 1998 Hullachan has achieved a 60 per cent success rate with people confirming sales after looking at the site.

New problems and new products can be identified and addressed. Products are offered for testing to volunteers around the world and their feedback collected. Hullachan's owner, Craig Coussins, is currently investigating the possibility of equipping trade customers with Sony Viewcams so that product solutions can be presented visually.

BPP PUBLISHING

Global technologies and communication networks

10.30 **Global technologies** mean that it is possible to exchange data across geographical areas in a matter of seconds. Speed of transmission opens up vast possibilities for firms wanting to trade globally. The speed of data exchange also poses threats in the shape of corporate fraud which could also be perpetrated in a matter of seconds. Global communication technology has no boundaries.

Multimedia

10.31 Combining telecommunications and computers has enabled the development of a new global industry, **multimedia**.

10.32 BT expects the market for multimedia to increase to £20 billion worldwide. Of that, £13 billion will be for network operation and £7 billion for capital equipment. Multimedia is expected to **transform consumer markets,** first by using video kiosks in major shopping centres and thoroughfares and later by entering the home. Using a combination of phone, television and personal computer, people can access directly everything from groceries to holiday bookings.

Marketing at Work

Encouraged by the success of retailers such as Gap in the US, Marks and Spencer of the UK now has its own e-commerce team, which has been running a trial website for employees of BT. The venture will be the first time a major British retailer has espoused the Internet with such vigour, and the trusted M&S name will hopefully lead more people to trust the web itself.

The advantages of e-commerce for a troubled company such as M&S is the much higher profit margin. There is no rent, negligible staff costs and 24 hour opening.

---

11 GEOGRAPHY

11.1 It is easy to forget the importance of the physical environment of a country, which is relevant for the following reasons.

(a) **Climate** affects the suitability of some kinds of product, and indeed the ease of doing business (eg the extreme cold in Siberia).

(b) **Physical geography** has the most obvious impact on distribution and the economics of choosing a distribution mode, such as mountain ranges, deserts.

(c) **Environmental legislation.** The state of the physical environment is an important legal issue in many countries.

12 A KEY PITFALL: SELF REFERENCE

12.1 A key problem international marketers face is the **self-reference criterion.** This is the tendency to assume that other markets are broadly similar to the home market, so that **similar marketing approaches** can be adopted. (Remember that the home market plays an important educative role.)

12.2 This is most obviously a 'cultural' issue, but the self-reference criteria influences the following.

(a) **Determining consumer demand.** In most Western countries cigarettes are sold by the packet; in much of India they can be purchased individually.

(b) **Mistaking cultural assumptions.** Despite the common use of English, the USA is not simply a larger version of the UK. (Some examples of cultural differences are alluded to in the next chapter.)

(c) **Distribution.** The UK's sophisticated supermarket distribution system is not copied elsewhere. In the USA 'own label' has not penetrated to the extent it has in the UK: manufacturer brands are more powerful.

(d) **Approaches to management.** Management style and decision-making do vary from culture to culture.

13 COPING WITH CURRENCY FLUCTUATIONS: EXCHANGE RATES

13.1 International trading relationships in terms of either goods and services or in terms of capital flows result in demand for and supply of currencies in the market for **foreign exchange**. Most orders are quoted in **hard currency** (that is, a currency for which demand is persistently high relative to the supply, such as the US dollar).

13.2 These sophisticated foreign exchange markets co-ordinate the millions of interactions of demand and supply currency decisions that take place every day, leading to the determination of exchange rates between currencies.

The determination of exchange rates

> **Key Concept**
> An **exchange rate** is the price of a currency expressed in terms of another eg £1 = DM2.56 or 1DM = £0.39.

13.3 The **exchange rate** between two currencies is determined by **demand** and **supply** issues.

(a) The exchange rate at any given time is determined by the **demand** for a currency and the available **supply.** If, for whatever reason, people want to **buy** pounds sterling this will exert upward pressure on the price of sterling: people will be selling their own currency.

(b) People might want to buy a currency for a number of reasons.

  (i) **Trade flows.** They may need a currency to pay for goods and services. (For example, BPP books are invoiced in pounds.)

  (ii) **Physical investment.** A British firm building, say, a hotel in Sri Lanka will need to pay its workforce in rupees.

  (iii) **Capital movements.** People wanting to invest in, say, German companies listed on the Frankfurt stock exchange, will need to acquire German Deutschmarks to do so. Similarly people may be attracted because investments in certain currencies offer a **higher rate of interest,** in real terms (ie adjusting for inflation). If this increases demand, the exchange rate will rise.

(c) Obviously, trade, physical investment and capital movements are themselves influenced by a number of factors.

  (i) **Economic growth**

  (ii) Importance and **strength** of the economy

(iii) **Government policy:** the government may have certain objectives for the exchange rate. A low exchange rate increases exports because it makes exported goods cheaper for overseas customers. The interest rates affect exchange rates.

(iv) **The rate of inflation.** A country with high inflation will have a depreciating exchange rate. This is because if rising domestic prices are translated into other currencies, goods and services will become impossible to export.

Purchasing power parity (PPP) theory: exchange rates and inflation

13.4 Is sterling, at any moment in time overvalued, undervalued, or about right? In one sense, the answer is always 'just about right': sterling is worth whatever people are willing to pay for it in exchange for dollars, yen, francs, or whatever. However, according to another view, the value of sterling should, in the long run, tend to move towards the level of **purchasing power parity** (PPP), in other words the rate which equalises the domestic purchasing power of the two currencies. Thus, under PPP the exchange rate for sterling at any moment will be appropriate when it is possible to buy the same basket of goods and services in various countries for the same amount of money when that money is converted at the prevailing exchange rates, adjusting of course for distribution costs, differences in consumption patterns.

13.5 While PPP theory has been found to be inadequate in explaining movements in exchange rates in the **short** term, it is more likely to have some validity in the long run, at least in so far as it provides a rough benchmark for interpreting movements of market exchange rates.

Action Programme 5

The cheapest place to price compact discs is apparently the USA. When advised of this fact, a select committee of the House of Commons criticised UK record companies for charging more. Why might CDs be higher priced in the UK than the US?

Government policy and the exchange rate

13.6 **Exchange rate volatility** is a considerable worry in economic management, especially as the flows of foreign exchange are so large. The level of the exchange rate has social consequences.

13.7 The following aspects of government policy typically affect the exchange rate.

- **Interest rates:** most governments determine minimum lending rates
- **Credit controls:** some governments restrict the amount of borrowing directly
- **Inflation:** government policy influences inflation
- Government **borrowing**
- **Exchange controls.** Some governments regulate foreign exchange transactions

Fixed exchange rates

13.8 Some countries maintain a permanent fixed value of the exchange rate.

Advantages of a fixed rate system

13.9 The **advantages** of a fixed rate system are as follows.

(a) It **removes uncertainty** about exchange rates and therefore about the value of goods and services. It makes international trade easier because exporters/importers can agree risk free prices.

(b) Similarly, sellers can give buyers **credit** without fear of adverse movements in the exchange rate.

(c) A fixed exchange rate system also imposes a **discipline** on countries to pursue responsible economic policies. In particular, there must be broadly consistent policies about inflation and economic growth.

Disadvantages of a fixed rate system

13.10 In order to maintain their currency at a fixed rate, the authorities must have very large quantities of **foreign currency reserves**, and their own currency, to intervene in the exchange market to meet an excess supply or demand for their currency.

13.11 Consequently, a government has to take other measures **controlling economic activity** to influence the exchange rate.

(a) Cut imports (and boost exports) by **deflationary** policies to cut demand.

(b) An **inflationary** policy to correct a balance of payments surplus might also be politically unacceptable to the country concerned, because inflation has social costs. As the real value of debt falls real wealth passes from lenders to borrowers and people with fixed incomes become gradually poorer.

13.12 **Fixed exchange rates are often too rigid.** There will occasionally be structural changes in demand and supply conditions which change the **entire** balance of payments prospects for a country.

13.13 Different countries might have differing economic and political objectives, and so **international co-operation** is needed.

Floating exchange rates

13.14 Floating exchange rates are at the opposite end of the spectrum to fixed rates. At this extreme, exchange rates are left entirely to the **free play of demand and supply forces**.

Advantages of a floating exchange rate system

13.15 The **advantages** of free-floating rates are as follows.

(a) Government is not required to undertake difficult and unpopular deflationary or inflationary measures at home to support the exchange rate.

(b) Uncertainty about the future value of a currency in a floating rate system can be reduced by the use of a **forward exchange** market, in which contracts can be made to acquire or sell currency on a future date at a specified rate of exchange.

Disadvantages of a floating exchange rate system

13.16 The **disadvantages** of a free-floating system are as follows.

(a) It is by no means certain that market forces will value the exchange rate of a currency at an 'appropriate' level, because speculation might undervalue or over value the currency.

(b) In practice, governments cannot allow free floating, even if they wanted to. Even if they do not intervene in the foreign exchange markets, their policies on interest rates, control of the money supply and inflation, demand management, exchange controls, import controls and employment will all have repercussions on international trade, capital flows and the exchange rate.

(c) A free-floating exchange rate might disrupt the government's **domestic economic policies**. For example, if the exchange rate depreciates, import costs will rise and, in a high-importing country such as the UK, inflation will also increase.

Managed floating exchange rates

13.17 In practice, governments seek to combine the advantages of exchange rate stability with flexibility and to avoid the disadvantages of both rigidly fixed exchange rates and free floating. **Managed (or dirty) floating** refers to a system whereby exchange rates are allowed to float, but from time to time the authorities will intervene in the foreign exchange market.

13.18 Buying and selling in this way would be intended to influence the exchange rate of the domestic currency. Both large scale interventions (co-ordinated buying or selling by many central banks) and small scale interventions have been applied.

The costs of currency fluctuations for businesses

13.19 The cost of imports to the buyer or the value of exports to the seller might be increased or reduced by movements in foreign exchange rates. For example, if a UK importer buys goods from a US supplier for $15,000 when the exchange rate between the US dollar and £ sterling is $1.60 to £1, the importer would expect to pay £9,375 in sterling for the goods. However, if by the time the date of payment arrives, the rate of exchange is $1.50 to £1 (ie sterling has fallen in value against the US dollar) the cost to the importer would be £10,000, or £625 more than originally anticipated. The US exporter would still receive $15,000, and would not be affected by the movement.

Action Programme 6

Using the same data as in paragraph 12.19 above, what would have been the consequences for both the UK importer and the US exporter if the invoice had been in sterling (ie £9,375)?

13.20 The firm paying in a foreign currency or earning revenue in a foreign currency therefore has a potential **exchange risk** from adverse movements in foreign exchange rates. Equally, if the rate of sterling against the dollar had **improved** over the same time span, the UK importer would have benefited.

Reducing risk

13.21 There are ways of reducing or eliminating foreign exchange exposure.

(a) Banks play a central role in the foreign exchange market, because they sell foreign currency and buy foreign currency, which is of course an essential element in international trade dealings. Banks can help traders to eliminate or minimise their foreign exchange exposure, in a number of different ways. **Hedging** is a general term to describe actions to minimise financial risk.

(i) **Forward exchange contracts**. A bank will agree to sell or buy a given quantity of foreign exchange at a fixed rate of exchange for delivery at a future date, some months, or even some years, ahead. Exporters and importers can therefore eliminate their foreign exchange exposure by fixing now with their bank the rate of exchange for future foreign currency revenue or payments.

(ii) **'Pure' foreign currency options**. An alternative to foreign exchange contracts, which are provided for banks by customers who want them, are currency options. These give their holder the right but not the obligation to buy or sell in the future a given quantity of a foreign currency at a fixed rate of exchange, either on or before the expiry of the option period.

(b) **Matching receipts and payments**. When a company incurs expenditures and earns income in the same foreign currency, it can use the income to pay for the expenditures. This is the process of matching receipts and payments. Since the company will be setting off foreign currency receipts against foreign currency payments, it does not matter whether the currency strengthens or weakens against the company's 'domestic' currency because there will be no purchase or sale of the currency.

(c) **Borrowing in a foreign currency** in which payments will eventually be received, and using the payments to repay the loan.

14 EUROPEAN ECONOMIC AND MONETARY UNION

14.1 European Economic and Monetary Union (EMU) is a long-standing objective of the EU, reaffirmed in the Single European Act of 1985 and in the Maastricht agreement of 1991.

(a) **Monetary union** can be defined as a **single currency area**, which would require a monetary policy for the area as a whole.

(b) **Economic union** can be described as an unrestricted common market for trade, with some economic policy co-ordination between different regions in the union.

> **Key Concept**
> **EMU** features include a common currency and single market and monetary policy. The common currency is called the **Euro.**

Features

14.2 Although the whole package of measures included in European EMU is not paralleled anywhere else in the world, there have been many international monetary unions. For example, Belgium and Luxembourg are in a monetary union, and the UK and the Republic of Ireland were in currency union until the 1970s. There are three main aspects to the European monetary union.

(a) A **common currency**. By this, we mean that instead of using sterling in the UK, deutschmarks in Germany and francs in France, a common currency is to be used for normal everyday money transactions by everyone in the monetary union. The Euro was launched in January 1999.

(b) A **European central bank**.

- Issuing the Euro
- Conducting monetary policy on behalf of the central government authorities
- Acting as lender of last resort to all European banks

- Managing the exchange rate for the common currency

(c) A **centralised monetary policy** would apply across all the countries within the union. This would involve the surrender of control over aspects of economic policy and therefore surrender of some political sovereignty by the government of each member state to the central government body of the union.

Action Programme 7

What might be the implications of European economic and monetary union (EMU), and a single European currency, for the following UK businesses?

(1) A package holiday firm, mainly selling holidays to France and Germany.
(2) An exporter of power station generating equipment to developing countries in Asia.
(3) An importer of wine from Australia.

Do this exercise twice. (a) Assume that the UK participates in EMU, swapping sterling for the Euro. (b) Assume that it stays outside of EMU.

Advantages and disadvantages of EMU

14.3 Arguably much of the political debate about EMU has generated more heat than light. There are many ways in which European countries share or pool sovereignty (eg NATO) and no government can insulate itself from wider economic trends.

(a) Supporters of EMU claim the following advantages.

(i)   It will bed down the single European market and extend its effectiveness, securing the many benefits of EU membership.

(ii) In the long term, it will mean lower interest rates.

(iii) Exchange rate volatility makes it hard for business to plan.

(iv) It will increase the clout of Europe in world economic affairs.

(v)   The UK will attract more inward investment than if it stays out.

(b) Opponents of EMU cite the following arguments.

(i)   Political worries about sovereignty over key economic policy decisions.

(ii) Despite the EU's single market, it is not as free as the US. For example, differences in language make it hard for people to move to different areas of the EU.

(iii) EU economies are not synchronised. Interest rates appropriate for one area will not suit another.

Marketing at Work

Many retailers price goods as £1.99, £2.99, £3.99 and so forth. If the Euro is worth £0.66, £1.99 will be equivalent to EU3.02, £2.99 will be equivalent to EU4.53, and £3.99 will be equivalent to EU6.05. These prices are less easily memorable than £1.99 etc., so presumably retail mark-ups and pricing strategies will be affected. Indeed, some cynics would argue that there is a good opportunity for a windfall profit, changing prices whilst people are confused - this is reported to have happened when the UK currency was decimalised.

Chapter Roundup

- **International markets** offer firms opportunities to trade, to acquire resources and investment, but also offer threats in that other companies from overseas can do the same.

- We can analyse environmental factors using the mnemonic **SLEPT** (social, legal, economic, political, technological).

- Although trade has benefits, many countries have sought to limit its effects in order to **protect** local producers. In the long term this serves to harm economic welfare as resources are not allocated where they are most productive.

- **Regional trading blocks** promote trade between countries in groups. The environment of world trade is becoming freer, globally, with the influence of the World Trade Organisation.

- **Social factors** include overall global population growth, and the disparity between the ageing and stable (in numbers) populations of the developed world, with the young and growing populations of lesser developed countries. In individual markets, **culture** can be a determining factor of marketing success.

- **Political factors** offer extra risks to the exporter, in terms of the stability of the country, the attitude of the government to trade generally and to the company in particular.

- **Legal factors** in individual markets include product regulations and control over the marketing mix generally. Human resource usage is also determined by legal factors.

- **Economic factors** include the overall level of growth and stage of development, frequently measured by GDP. The balance of payments is an influence on government policy.

- **Technology** creates new products and industries, and enhances productivity and growth. That said, countries need an infrastructure to cope with technology.

- **E-commerce** is revolutionising the way most business is conducted.

- **Exchange rates** are determined by demand for goods and services, interest rates and inflation rates. Co-ordination in economic policy is necessary to fix or manage these rates.

- The aim of the **single European currency** is to remove the costs of volatility within the EU.

Quick Quiz

1   What are the constituents of political risk? (see para 3.2)
2   Draw up a checklist for companies to consider when dealing with the political environment. (3.8)
3   List some protectionist measures (4.1)
4   What is meant by LDC, EDC, SDC, FDC, EBC? (5.7)
5   How do you measure economic development? (5.8)
6   Describe structural adjustment programmes (5.12)
7   How do you measure market size? (5.20)
8   What are the consequences of balance of payments deficits and surpluses? (5.22, 5.23)
9   What is the Triad? (6.7) How relevant is Triad theory? (6.8)
10   Why study demography? (8.2)
11   What is the effect of growing populations? (8.3)
12   What is the significance of age structure? (8.5)
13   What is the relevance of socio-economic status to buying patterns? (8.12)
14   What is technology? (9.1, 9.2)
15   Why is technology important to international marketers examining a particular market? (9.8)
16   What is electronic commerce? (10.1)
17   What are some of the marketing issues raised by the self reference criterion? (12.1, 12.2)
18   List some factors influencing rates of exchange. (13.3)
19   How can firms limit their exposure to currency fluctuations? (13.21)
20   Define monetary union (14.1)

BPP PUBLISHING

Action Programme Review _____

1   Protectionism is about the relative benefits and drawbacks to countries of restraining trade. For commercial organisations, however, protectionism has some short run advantages.

The USA is the largest market for automobiles. US car manufacturers produce overseas for foreign markets, generally speaking, as opposed to exporting from the US itself. Free trade in motor vehicles automatically means a great deal of competition at home (particularly from Japan).

A closed market would allow them to raise prices. On the other hand, Swedish car manufacturers, such as Volvo, depend on successful exports since the home market is too small to support them. The benefits of protection would be exceeded by the disadvantages.

2   Here is one possible answer. The existence of the new wealth will encourage:

(a)   mass urbanisation
(b)   potential rural depopulation

as the new industries will encourage peasants to move in from the land in the hope of a better life. Bosanova's resources will become more and more strained. At the same time it is possible that, without parallel increases in agricultural efficiency, the ageing rural workforce, who cannot move, will become less productive.

3   There is often no right answer, but here are some ideas.

(a)   Will the foreign exchange earnings from Kwat justify the infrastructural investment at all? After all, the government will have to use the foreign exchange earnings to pay interest on loans. Option (3) might be the least risky here.

(b)   Does the country have an educational and technical infrastructure to support the technology. Road vehicles need spare parts and trained service personnel. Spare parts might be an additional drain on foreign exchange. Again option (3) might be the least risky.

4   Hints. You could write reams here, but there are a few preliminary ideas.

Western countries

(a)   Attitudes to elderly.

(b)   Distribution: over the counter? Prescribed by doctors?

(c)   Current health care of elderly.

(d)   Demographic trends: is the age structure of the country becoming more heavily weighted towards older people?

(e)   Drug testing and certification régime.

Third World country

(a)   Is Alzheimer's seen as a major problem, compared to other medical conditions (eg diseases from poor sanitation)?

(b)   Would the drug be affordable?

(c)   Attitudes to elderly.

(d)   Age structure of the country (fewer old people than in the West).

You will doubtless think of more.

5   (a)   Changes in exchange rates over time make any simplistic comparison hazardous.
    (b)   Economies of scale - the US is a far larger market than the UK.
    (c)   Differences in distribution costs and retail mark-ups.
    (d)   Different rates of consumption taxes such as VAT or sales tax.

6   If the invoice had been in sterling (ie for £9,375) the UK importer would not have had any foreign exchange risk. Instead the US exporter would have incurred a loss from the exchange rate movement from $1.60 to $1.50, receiving (£9,375 × 1.50) - only $14,062.50 instead of the $15,000 originally expected.

7   We have no wish to get involved in the ferocious political debate about this issue, nor can we offer a definitive solution, but here are some points to consider.

(a)   For companies trading primarily **within** the EU, such as the **package holiday firm**, participation in EMU will mean a reduction in exchange rate volatility - businesses will be able to compete on the essentials of cost and productivity. An analogy is the USA - although there are many 'states' there is only one currency. Most British trade is with EU countries.

Companies trading **outside** the EU (the power station supplier and wine importer) would remain subject to exchange rate risk, based on the Euro rather than sterling. It all depends on how the European Central Bank manages the currency - if the Euro becomes a 'hard' currency, like the Deutschmark, then exports will cost more to overseas customers, but imports from overseas suppliers might be cheaper. Many internationally traded goods, such as oil and aircraft, are priced in US dollars anyhow, so the impact will be indirect.

(b)   Because the UK trades with the EU, sterling will undoubtedly be affected by the Euro, much as the Netherlands guilder and Austrian schilling move in tandem with the Deutschmark. It is possible that overseas customers may prefer to be invoiced in Euros.

Now try illustrative question 2 at the end of the Study Text

BPP
PUBLISHING

3 Competing in the Global Market

Chapter Topic List	Syllabus Reference
1 Setting the scene	-
2 The competitive environment of an industry	1.2, 1.5
3 Scenario building	1.1
4 The influence of the home market: the competitive advantage of nations	1.1, 1.8

Learning Outcomes

After studying this chapter, you will have an understanding of:

- the forces facing the individual firm in the international trading environment

- approaches to global competitiveness propounded by writers like Porter, Ohmae, Hamel and Prahalad

- the theory of the competitive advantage of nations

Key Concepts Introduced

- Competitive position
- Competitive forces/five forces
- Substitute product
- Conglomerate

- Competitive advantage
- Diversification
- Cluster

Examples of Marketing at Work

- Le Shuttle
- Utility companies
- Jacobs
- Indian IT companies

- British Airways
- Medicon Valley
- Indian milk marketing
- Silicon Valley

1 SETTING THE SCENE

1.1 This chapter narrows the focus to the individual firm and industry. Despite 'globalisation', there are still major difficulties in competing internationally which do not exist in the domestic market.

1.2 Section 2 shows that global competition can have an impact on the structure of an industry and the degree of competition within it - new entrants can emerge, increasing the intensity of competition, and a firm might find itself competing in a situation where the stakes are higher than before. Comfortable local monopolies can be shattered.

1.3 In its attempt to compete in the global market, a firm's **national origin** might have an impact on its potential to succeed (section 4). Various factors in a country's endowment of raw materials, skills and government policy can offer success in some industries. However, such factors are outside the control of the individual firm, even though they can provide it with a springboard for success.

2 THE COMPETITIVE ENVIRONMENT OF AN INDUSTRY

2.1 Apart from SLEPT factors which affect all organisations, a business organisation faces **competition**. Competition comes from other organisations. Business organisations compete for customers. Competitive failure will result in the organisation collapsing, or being taken over. With increased globalisation, competition is more intense, as firms jostle for competitive position in both domestic and global markets.

> **Key Concept**
> **Competitive position** describes the market share, costs, price, quality and accumulated experience of an entity or product relative to its competition.

Competitive forces

> **Key Concept**
> **Competitive forces/five forces.** Porter's model of the competitive environment of any firm, consisting of the threats of new entrants and substitute products, the bargaining powers of customers and suppliers, and the rivalry amongst current competitors.

2.2 Michael Porter categorises **five competitive forces** in the environment of a firm as follows. Even partial 'globalisation' of the market can affect the five forces.

- The threat of **new entrants** to the industry
- The threat of **substitute** products or services
- The bargaining power of **customers**
- The bargaining power of **suppliers**
- The **rivalry** amongst current competitors in the industry

The threat of new entrants

2.3 A **new entrant** will bring extra capacity into an industry and poses a threat to established firms because they may lose market share and economies of scale.

BPP PUBLISHING

(a) The **strength** of the threat from new entrants depends on the strength of the barriers to entry and on the likely response of existing competitors. If prospective new entrants think that competitive retaliation will be strong then they might think twice before deciding to enter the market.

(b) Many overseas firms become 'new entrants' to a market if **trade liberalisation** allows them to compete.

The threat of substitute products or services

Key Concept
A **substitute product** is one that can stand in for another product eg in fast food, fish and chips might be a substitute product for hamburgers and vice versa.

2.4 The products or services that are produced in one industry are likely to have **substitutes** that are produced in another industry.

(a) Substitutes pose a threat because they limit the ability of a firm to charge high prices for its products so that demand for products becomes relatively **sensitive to price**.

(b) **Free trade** can mean that substitute products might be made available for the first time or at a lower price.

Marketing at Work
Le Shuttle and various ferry companies compete to take your car over the English Channel. Railways (Eurostar), ships and airlines offer transport to the non-motorised traveller.

The bargaining power of customers

2.5 **Customers** will look for better quality products and services at lower prices. If they have the power to get what they want, they will force down the profitability of the firms in the industry. The strength of this threat from the bargaining power of customers will depend on various factors.

- The **level of differentiation** amongst products in the industry (including 'intangible' aspects such as customer service)

- The **cost to the customer** of switching from one supplier to another

- Whether a customer's purchases from the industry represent a **large or small proportion** of the customer's total purchases

2.6 Globalisation will probably have an **indirect effect** on customers' bargaining power, depending on the industry.

(a) In some cases there are many **more potential customers,** so any one group will exert less power.

(b) At the same time, if globalisation is coupled with free investment, some industries might **consolidate** into a smaller number of companies, who will be able to exert greater pressure.

Marketing at Work

Many utilities companies are expanding overseas to escape the dominant power of the customer (represented by government regulators). National Power is operating power plants in Indonesia, to reduce its dependence on the UK market and the UK regulator. US utilities have entered the UK market to expand, because of the lighter regulatory regime in the UK.

The bargaining power of suppliers

2.7 Suppliers can influence the profitability of a firm by exerting **pressure for higher prices** or by **reducing the quality** of the goods and services which they supply.

2.8 The bargaining power of the supplier depends on a number of factors including the **number** of suppliers in the industry, the **importance** of the supplier's product to the firm and the **cost** to the firm of switching from one supplier to another.

The rivalry amongst current competitors

2.9 The **intensity of competitive rivalry** within an industry will affect the profitability of the industry as a whole. Although rivalry can be beneficial in helping the industry to expand, it might leave **demand unchanged**. In this case the individual firms will be compelled to incur costs on sales promotion campaigns, advertising battles and new product development. They will have to charge lower prices, and so make lower profits, without gaining any benefits except **maintaining market share**.

Action Programme 1

The **tea industry**, according to the Financial Times (22 March 1996), is characterised by 'chronic oversupply, with a surplus ... of about 80,000 tonnes a year'. Tea estates 'swallow capital, and the return is not as attractive as in industries such as technology or services'. Tea cannot be stockpiled, unlike coffee, keeping for two years at most. Tea is **auctioned** in London and prices are the same in absolute terms as they were 15 years ago. Tea is produced in Africa and India, Sri Lanka and China. Because of the huge capital investment involved, the most recent investments have been quasi-governmental, such as those by the Commonwealth Development Corporation in ailing estates in East Africa. There is no simple demarcation between buyers and sellers. Tea-bag manufacturers own their own estates, as well as buying in tea from outside sources.

A year later (*Financial Times*, 2 April 1997), reports were rosier. Tea prices were described in India at least as being 'exceptionally firm ... The shortage and high prices of coffee have also raised demand for tea which remains the cheapest of all beverages in spite of the recent rise in prices.' Demand from Russia, Poland, Iran and Iraq are expected to rise.'

(a) Carry out a five forces analysis.

(b) Thinking ahead, suggest a possible marketing strategy for a tea-grower with a number of estates which has traditionally sold its tea at auction.

2.10 The intensity of competition will depend on a number of factors including the **rate of growth** in the industry and whether there is a large number of balanced competitors. Obviously, globalisation increases the number of competitors.

BPP PUBLISHING

Fragmented industries

2.11 A **fragmented industry**, according to Porter is 'populated by a large number of small and medium sized companies.' Moreover, a fragmented industry is characterised by 'the **absence of market leaders** with the power to shape industry events.'

2.12 An industry is fragmented for the following reasons.

- **Barriers to entry are low:** it is easy to set up in business
- There are **few economies of scale** to be had by a large firm
- **Transport costs** are high
- Small scale businesses may be more **flexible** in coping with erratic demand
- Being too large might lead to **higher overhead costs**
- **Local image** and reputation are important
- The **market** itself might be fragmented. There may be many groups of buyers
- **Government** can forbid concentration
- If **standards** are enforced locally, this can encourage fragmentation

2.13 An industry might be fragmented for only one of those reasons: and if this can be overcome, the whole industry can be combined. For example, **new technology** can offer a cheaper way of making something, but it might require an investment of such size that only a large company can afford it.

2.14 A fragmented industry can be **consolidated** into one with fewer companies as follows.

(a) **Technological change** (as suggested above).

(b) A new standard product might be preferred to the previous 'custom-made' variety for a number of reasons. Fast food chains such as McDonald's offer a consistent standard, and customers might welcome this.

(c) Many big publishing companies have a large number of smaller **imprints,** with their own characteristics.

(d) Some industries consolidate naturally as they **age**.

2.15 Even without concentration, a firm can still grow and **specialise**.

- Offering a **standard service or product**
- Dealing with **particular customers**
- Concentrating in a **particular area**

Concentrated industries

2.16 **Concentrated industries** differ from fragmented industries in that they are dominated by a small number of large firms, which are able to exercise a significant influence over the market as a whole.

2.17 Industries become concentrated for the following reasons.

- It is cheaper to produce in bulk (ie where there are **economies of scale**)
- The **resources** needed to stay in business are significant
- **Entry barriers are high:** in other words it is hard to set up in business
- The service does not depend uniquely on the **skills** of a particular individual
- A large firm can benefit from an **integrated distribution network**
- **Customers' needs** are fairly standard in the market
- There are **economies of scale** in marketing, distribution, purchasing etc

- The company has proprietary product **technology**

2.18 The importance of industry concentration is that there is nearly always a '**market leader**' with significant influence.

- The way business is done
- Relationships with sources of supply
- Distribution

Marketing at Work

In July 1996, Klaus Jacobs, a Swiss financier, acquired Groupe Barry (France), doubling his share of the independent chocolate market to 51%. 'A duopoly in European chocolate supply is feared by many groups which do not make their own … such as Danone, Europe's largest biscuit maker which buys in almost all its chocolate.' (Other firms, such as Nestlé, continue with the messy process of making their own chocolate from beans.)

'Chocolate users could revert to making their own again. But smaller users would still be excluded.' A lot of small companies cannot afford to do their own research and manufacture.

Emerging industries

2.19 An **emerging industry** is a new, or re-formed, industry. It can be created by technological innovation, changes in costs and social and economic changes.

2.20 Examples of new, new-ish and emerging industries include the following.

- **Electronic publishing** and interactive TV
- **Waste recycling** (in some countries)
- **Internet browsing** systems
- **Road pricing** systems

2.21 The problems with emerging industries are the following.

(a) There is doubt about the **technology**. For example, there were at least three competing technologies for video cassette recorders (offered by Philips, Sony and JVC), until JVC's became adopted as standard. Currently, a battle is going on as to which firm's computer standards will end up dominating the Internet.

(b) The various participants in the industry are still **experimenting** in finding a demand for the product or building it up. Customers' needs are uncertain.

(c) New industries start with **high costs** (but these fall eventually).

(d) Consumers need to be **informed** about what the industry can offer in order to be interested in new products or services.

(e) Early **barriers to entry** include proprietary technology, access to raw materials etc.

(f) Other problems

- **Competition** for raw materials or sub-components
- Customer **confusion**
- **Obsolescence**
- **Erratic quality**
- **Scepticism** from bankers and investors

Exam Tip

The December 1997 minicase featured McDonalds' response to Jolibee, a Filipino firm which has been successful in fast food. Clearly, in the Philippines, McDonalds' brand is not such an important barrier to entry. Jolibee was able to differentiate itself by catering to the local palate.

The December 1996 case featured two US cosmetics companies trying to compete in China.

2.22 There have been various approaches in business and management literature to competing in the global market.

2.23 Kenichi Ohmae, author of *The Borderless World*, has a vision of globalisation in which businesses do not have a nationality, but are instead held together by **shared values.** This is made possible by new technology and governments opening up markets.

2.24 According to Ohmae, who has been described as 'Mr Strategy', the customer is the prime focus for a successful business, and getting to know the **overseas customer** is the primary challenge.

2.25 Competition must be analysed, both in the home market and overseas, and the company must **'globalise the mind'** by making sure its strategy recognises global trends, taking into account such factors as trade barriers.

Marketing at Work

The opportunity for Indian IT companies to exploit a $100 billion opportunity in Japan is being promoted by Kenichi Ohmae. He has concluded that 'Japanese companies are good at manufacturing, but bad at computers. They do not have a clue what to do with their computer set ups that do not talk to each other'. Indian IT experts can make these systems web-enabled and help Japanese companies to become more efficient in their computer usage. A number of US, European and South East Asian companies are also moving swiftly into this market.

Ohmae is helping to promote a software development house which will enable Indian experts to understand the work culture of Japanese companies, build relationships and understand problems before offering solutions.

2.26 In *Competing for the Future* (1994), one of the top selling business books in history, **Gary Hamel** and **C K Prahalad** argued that successful companies reshape their industry through focusing on **core competencies** rather than products. Nike, for example, has a core competency in design and merchandising rather than shoe quality. McDonald's core competency is convenience rather than gourmet dining experiences.

2.27 The **identity of a company**, according to Prahalad, must be **consistent** around the world. Sony, for example, produces both the Walkman and large sophisticated broadcasting systems. Therefore it appeals to both the mass market and high-end, innovative markets, but the skill and reputation of Sony has to be protected and the only way to do that is to maintain a consistent brand image despite product variations.

2.28 Prahalad is also concerned with whether companies are properly run so that they are able to compete in the future. **Strategy making** is often an elitist process which only involves top level managers. At the same time, he recognises that the structure and governance of a company depends entirely upon the nature and complexity of the business.

2.29 For example, a diversified conglomerate may be easily run from a small head office. A company with more closely related businesses (and therefore common competencies and opportunities) may merit more head office involvement and co-ordination to ensure that corporate objectives are met.

Key Concept

Conglomerate. An entity comprising a number of dissimilar businesses. Hanson is a prime example. Many industries diversified in the 1980s but the trend now is towards a focus on core competencies and slimming down of non-core activities.

---

3 SCENARIO BUILDING

3.1 **Scenario building** is used in strategic planning. It is the process of identifying alternative futures, ie constructing a number of distinct possible futures permitting deductions to be made about future developments of markets, products, technology and competitors.

3.2 Michael Porter (*Competitive Advantage*) tries to analyse how firms choose competitive strategy when faced with future uncertainties. Porter believes that all firms face uncertainty, but 'uncertainty is not often addressed very well in competitive strategy'.

(a) **Macro scenarios** use macro-economic or political factors, creating alternative views of the future environment (eg global economic growth, political changes, interest rates). Macro scenarios developed because oil companies (whose activities are global and were, at one time, heavily influenced by political factors) employed them.

(b) For strategy within a particular industry, macro scenarios are too **general** to be used, as they do not reflect the distinguishing dynamics of that industry.

3.3 Porter believes that the most appropriate use for scenario analysis is if it is restricted to an industry. An **industry scenario** is an internally consistent view of an industry's future structure. It is not a forecast, but a possibility.

3.4 Michael Porter believes that certain countries have advantages in certain industries. We discuss this in the next section.

Marketing at Work

A macro scenario which focuses on the world economy was employed by British Airways (BA), on the grounds that 'annual planning meetings do little to help people think what will happen a decade from now'. The easiest assumption people make is that the future will be like the present. BA, as reported in the Financial Times set up a scenario planning exercise in which two alternative futures were outlined, and managers were asked how they would react.

(a) **Wild gardens:** Conservative election victory; no single European currency; free access by European airlines to North America; Asian markets grow quickly; long US recession; unleashing of competition.

Consequences? More demanding customers; more customers who speak Asian languages than English, therefore a growing importance of language skills, and a need for BA to integrate its operations more with US Air and Qantas.

(b) **New structures:** Labour election victory; single European currency; an integrated high-speed rail network; security crisis in Asia.

Consequences? Perhaps **you** can think of some!

---

4   THE INFLUENCE OF THE HOME MARKET: THE COMPETITIVE ADVANTAGE OF NATIONS

> **Key Concept**
> **Competitive advantage** exists when a firm is able to compete successfully with other companies on a sustained basis

4.1   Michael Porter, in *The Competitive Advantage Of Nations*, suggests that **some nations succeed more than others** in terms of international competition. The UK, although prospering, has been in 'relative decline' compared to others, such as Japan.

4.2   Porter does not believe that countries or nations as such are competitive, but he asks the following questions.

(a) Why does a nation become the **home base** for successful international competitors in an industry?

(b) Why are firms based in a **particular nation** able to create and sustain competitive advantage against the world's best competitors in a particular field?

(c) Why is one nation often the home for **so many** of an industry's world leaders?

4.3   These questions are important, Porter believes, because **national origin** is a crucial factor influencing an individual firm's competitive stance. Porter's book 'seeks to isolate the national attributes that foster competitive advantage in an industry'.

4.4   Porter states that 'national' competitiveness in an industry cannot be reduced to simple factors.

- Macroeconomics
- A cheap labour supply
- Natural resources
- A government policy of promotion
- Management practices

4.5   The only meaningful measure of national competitiveness is the **productivity of its industries.**

(a) No nation can have competitive industries in every product area.

(b) International competition helps to upgrade economic prosperity and national productivity.

(c) When the exporting industries have high levels of productivity, the country enjoys high living standards and rising exports.

4.6   An explanation for **national** success is based on **comparative advantage,** which we discussed in Chapter 1. This held that relative factor costs in countries (eg the fact that some raw materials are cheaper in country A than in country B, but others are cheaper in B than A) determined the appropriateness of particular economic activities in relation to other countries. (In other words, countries should **specialise in what they are best at.**) Porter argues that industries which require **high technology** and **highly skilled employees** are less affected than low technology industries by the relative costs of their inputs of raw materials and basic labour.

(a) Technological change gives firms the power to by-pass constraints on resources (such as shortages of labour) or can nullify the advantages of other firms elsewhere (if you can do something more efficiently).

(b) Most companies have ready access to resources, through global companies and trade. Firms do not depend on their home country's endowment of a resource to become competitive. For example, BP was a successful multinational long before North Sea Oil. BP's competitive success has nothing to do with the UK's national endowment of oil.

(c) A large home market is not needed for global success (eg the success of Swiss companies in chemicals).

4.7 Given that high technology and global markets enable firms to circumvent the constraints (or advantages) of their home country's endowment of raw materials, cheap labour, access to capital and so forth, how do they become successful internationally? Or to put it another way, how do countries **develop comparative advantage**? (Going back to our example in Chapter 1, why does the UK have a comparative advantage in cars and Spain in shoes? Both countries can manufacture both.)

4.8 The **determinants of national competitive advantage,** according to Porter are outlined in the diagram overleaf. Porter refers to this as the **diamond**.

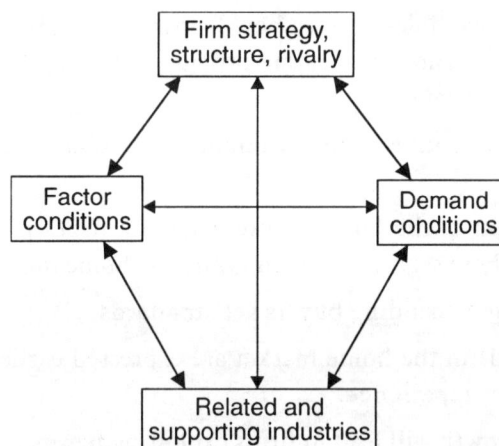

Analysing the 'diamond'

Factor conditions

4.9 **Factor conditions** is a term describing a country's endowment of inputs (eg raw materials, land, capital) to production. Different nations have different stocks of factors.

(a) **Human resources** (skills, price, motivation of labour, and industrial relations practices).

(b) **Physical resources** (land, minerals, climate, location relative to other nations).

(c) **Knowledge** (scientific and technical know-how, educational institutions).

(d) **Capital** (ie amounts available for investment, how it is deployed - eg government investment, equity shares, loans, savings rates).

(e) **Infrastructure** (transport, communications, housing).

4.10   Porter distinguishes between two types of factors.

   (a)   **Basic factors** include natural resources, climate, semiskilled and unskilled labour, and capital. Basic factors are inherited, or their creation involves little investment. Basic factors are unsustainable in the long term as a source of national competitive advantage. The wages of unskilled workers in industrial countries are undermined by even lower wages elsewhere.

   (b)   **Advanced factors** include modern digital communications, highly educated personnel (eg computer scientists), research laboratories and so forth. Advanced factors are vital for competitive success. They are necessary to achieve competitive advantages such as differentiated products and production technology.

4.11   Factors can also be **generalised** (eg a road system) or **specialised** (eg expertise in a particular technology). Specialised factors tend to be advanced. Generalised factors can be copied.

4.12   A mere abundance of factors is not enough. It is **how they are used** which matters. The former USSR had an abundance of natural resources and a well educated workforce, but collapsed economically.

Demand conditions

4.13   The **home market** demand determines how firms perceive, interpret and respond to **buyer needs**. The pressure to innovate at home provides a launchpad for global ambitions. This information role is important.

   (a)   There are fewer **cultural impediments** to communication than with 'foreign consumers'.

   (b)   The **segmentation** of the home market shapes a firm's priorities. (Companies will be successful globally in segments which typify the home market.)

   (c)   Sophisticated and demanding buyers **set standards**.

   (d)   If consumer needs in the home market are expressed earlier than in the world market this gives the firm **experience**.

   (e)   A **high rate of growth** will lead to firms exploiting new technologies at a quicker rate.

   (f)   **Early saturation** of the home market will encourage a firm to export.

Related and supporting industries

4.14   It is little use trying to be competitive when your suppliers are letting you down. The competitive success of an industry is linked to the success of the **industry's suppliers**, and other **related industries**. Porter quotes the Italian footwear industry as an example, as Italy has related success in other leather goods industries.

Firm structure, strategy and rivalry

4.15   National cultural factors do create tendencies to orientate business-people to certain industries.

   (a)   Shares of many smaller firms may only be rarely traded. This might give managers slightly **longer time horizons** in which to operate. Family businesses probably require a less exacting and predictable improvement in performance than ones with widely quoted shares. Many Italian firms are family run businesses. They are leaders in industries where economies of scale are modest. Italian firms pursue **focus strategies**.

(b) Industries have different time horizons, funding needs and so forth.

    (i) National capital markets set **different goals** for performance. In other words, the owners of Company A may require a 10% return, whereas those of company B would be happy with 5%.

    (ii) In some countries, banks are the main source of capital. Banks have a different set of priorities than equity shareholders.

    (iii) German firms, according to Porter, have a strong showing in 'industries with a high technical content.'

4.16 Firms in an industry facing difficult times can pursue one of two **strategies**.

(a) Shift resources from one industry to another, perhaps by diversification. **Unrelated diversification** 'had a strong negative correlation with national competitive advantage. Corporate parents harvested subsidiaries instead of investing to preserve competitive advantage. In other words, they milked them for profits rather than invested for the future'. Porter advises against diversification as a way of avoiding risk.

Key Concept

Diversification. Extension of a firm's activities to new products and/or new markets. It might refer to unrelated diversification, or diversification along a company's existing lines of activity.

(b) **Innovate within** the industry, to sustain competitive position. The state of **domestic rivalry** has 'a profound role to play in innovation and the ultimate prospects for international success'. Even in small countries such as Switzerland and Sweden, successful industries were composed of strong local rivals. Domestic rivalry is important for the following reasons.

- It is **visible**
- It is often **personal**
- There can be **no special pleading** about 'unfair' foreign competition
- With little domestic rivalry firms are happy to **rely on the home market**
- Tough domestic rivals teach a firm about **competitive success**
- Rivalry forces competition on grounds other than **factor endowments**
- Each rival can try a **different strategic approach**
- The **stock of knowledge** in each firm increases the knowledge of industry as a whole

---

Marketing at Work

Silicon Valley in the US is an example of strong domestic rivalry.

Influencing the 'diamond'

4.17 A country's diamond is always **vulnerable**. Chance can create discontinuities that enable shifts in competitive positions. Technological change also has an impact. Micro-electronics enabled Japanese firms to steal a march on Americans and Germans who were leaders in electro-mechanical industries.

4.18 The **role of government**, according to Porter, is to influence the determinants in the diamond.

- Changing **demand** conditions (eg as a buyer)
- **Setting policies** towards education and capital markets
- **Promoting competition** (eg through anti-trust legislation)

Interactions between the determinants

4.19 The factors in the 'diamond' are interrelated. Competitive advantage in an industry rarely rests on a single determinant. Each factor can affect the behaviour of the others.

(a) **Related industries** affect **demand conditions** for an industry. For example 'piggy-back' exporting is when an exporting company also exports some of the products of related industries.

(b) **Domestic rivalry** can encourage the creation of more specialised supplier industries.

4.20 Porter holds further that a nation's competitive industries are **clustered**. A cluster is a linking of industries through relationships which are either vertical (buyer-supplier) or horizontal (common customers, technology, skills).

> ### Key Concept
> **Cluster.** A geographically proximate collection of related businesses and industries. Clusters are supposedly a key factor in the competitive advantage of nations.

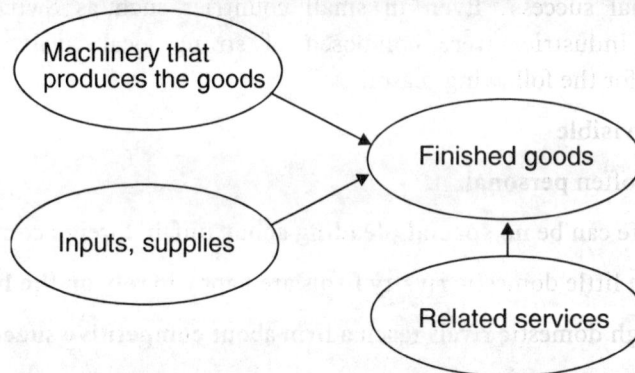

4.21 Porter cites the example of Denmark.

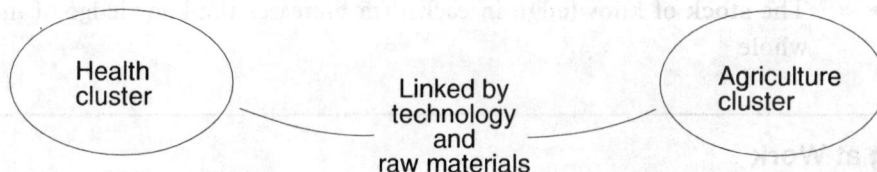

4.22 Within a country, the industry may be clustered in a particular **area**.

- The Italian ceramic tile industry is clustered in Sassuolo
- The UK merchant banking industry is largely based in London
- American information technology companies are clustered in Silicon Valley

Creating advantage

4.23 How does a country create a diamond of competitive advantage?

(a) **Factors of production** provide the seed corn. A large endowment of easily mined iron ore would suggest metal-working industries.

(b) **Related and supporting industries** can also be a foundation, if the competences within them can be configured in a new way.

(c) Extraordinary demand in the **home market** based on national peculiarities and conditions can set the **demand conditions** determinant in the diamond.

4.24 **Early mover advantages.** Being first to establish a diamond in a particular industry can raise barriers to entry for others.

Marketing at Work

The Swedish and Danish governments co-operated to form a 'Medicon Valley', comprising the areas either side of the Oresund, a waterway which forms the border between them. A Medicon Valley Academy has been set up to promote the region 'as a centre of medical and biotechnical research and production'. The area boasts two universities, three university hospitals and forty pharmaceutical and medical-technical manufacturing companies.' (*Financial Times*)

Losing competitive advantage

4.25 As industries evolve, national competitive advantage can be lost when the factors in the diamond are no longer self supporting.

(a) **Factor deterioration.** If factors such as infrastructure and human resources are not created and upgraded, competitive advantage will fade.

(i) Poor education

(ii) Inappropriate research and development

(iii) Since World War II, British firms, which had technological leadership, 'harvested market position'. In other words, they rested on their laurels and failed to invest in future technologies.

(b) **Local demand conditions** fall out of step with **global demands.**

(c) In industrial businesses, **clusters can be unwound** if industry has relocated.

(d) **Firm rivalry** is limited. Britain, Porter believes, had a small number of relatively large companies, rather than a thriving Mittestand (medium-sized businesses) as exists in Germany. Merging rather than competing was the preferred choice in many cases.

4.26 Porter's book suggested 'Britain declined because of growing disadvantages in each part of the diamond'. Yet the UK has a wider **spread** of businesses than many other economies. Porter regards this as a weakness, because in individual sectors British firms compete from a weak base, even though British firms perhaps have access to more sources of knowledge as a result of this spread. It should also be mentioned that the UK's share of the trade in world manufactures has ceased to decline, thanks to inward investment. The UK also does well in services. One of the members of the Bank of England's Monetary Policy Committee said recently: 'The future prosperity of the British economy will be largely determined by the competitive success of its service sector.'

The individual firm

4.27 The **individual** firm will be more likely to succeed internationally if there is a supporting cluster.

4.28 If a firm wishes to compete in an industry in which there is no national competitive advantage, it can take a number of steps to succeed in the long term.

(a) Aim to compete in the **most challenging market**. If a firm can compete successfully in such a market, even if this only means carving out a small niche, it holds well for its success globally.

(b) Spread **research and development activities** to countries where there is an established research base or industry cluster already.

(c) Be prepared to **invest heavily in innovation**.

(d) Invest in **human resources,** both in the firm and the industry as a whole.

(e) Look out for **new technologies** which will change the rules of the industry.

(f) **Collaborate with foreign companies.** American motor companies, particularly Ford and Chrysler, have successfully learned 'Japanese' production techniques.

(g) **Supply overseas companies.** There is some evidence that Japanese car plants in the UK have encouraged greater quality in UK components suppliers.

(h) If all else fails go for a **market niche strategy,** even if that niche is only the national market.

Stages in competitive development

4.29 Porter finally analyses economies in four different stages.

(a) **Factor driven.** Competitive advantage derives from factors (eg cheap labour, raw materials).

(b) **Investment driven.** Competitive advantage is based on investing for the future (eg buying foreign technology and improving it).

(c) **Innovation driven.** The mix of industries in which a firm competes gets broader. Firms **create** new technologies and industries.

(d) **Wealth driven.** The economy lives on its past wealth. It is concerned simply to maintain its competitive position and the social status quo. Innovation and competition narrow. Companies become less competitive except in certain special areas.

(i) Sophisticated demand (because of personal wealth) enables a country in this phase to remain competitive in areas which satisfy luxury needs.

(ii) The results of past cumulative investments provide a cushion against poverty.

(iii) Early mover advantages (eg loyalty to old and established brands) can maintain businesses.

4.30 Does Porter's analysis provide a generally applicable law, which will be relevant to all times, or is it only a 'snapshot' of a particular time?

(a) **Clustering.** The lowering of trade barriers can mean that a 'cluster' might cover several countries. If the EU is a 'single market' with free movement of goods, services and labour, clusters may be formed linking firms in a number of countries (eg between Denmark and Sweden as described in the case example earlier in this section).

(b) **Communications** are much swifter. There might be less reason for a **geographic** concentration of certain industries, especially knowledge-based ones, as communications shrink distances.

(c) **Global** (multinational) companies might become less influenced by their national origins.

(d) **Inward investment**. The UK car industry is substantial, but hardly any of it is now owned by British investors. To what extent is it a 'cluster'? Many foreign companies have invested in the UK, and there are a large number of component firms, small engineering firms and world-class engineering consultancies in the motor industry.

4.31 Research has shown that often LDC marketing with other LDCs is a more successful competitive strategy. The respective countries understand the difficulties and opportunities inherent in their markets.

Marketing at Work

India, which recently overtook the US to become the world's largest producer of milk, is helping other developing countries promote their dairy industries. (*Financial Times*, March 1999).

India is almost alone among non-European cultures in being a milk drinking nation.

The United Nations regards the Indian experience of lifting milk production through co-operatives as being relevant for most African and Asian countries. India's National Dairy Development board has taken up an assignment to help make Sri Lanka self sufficient in milk within 10 years.

The immediate objective of the venture is to meet demand for milk in Colombo and its surrounding areas. Sri Lanka currently imports large amounts of milk from New Zealand. Uganda, Kenya, Ethiopia, the Philippines, Thailand and Pakistan have also made use of India's expertise.

However, while India is at the top of the international milk production league it still remains a small player in the world market due to international food safety standards and the export subsidies of various leading dairy exporting countries. Internationally, India suffers from these subsidies, as well as discrimination against buffalo milk of which it is a big producer, and international restrictions on the use of anti-oxidants in milk - a must for tropical countries.

BPP PUBLISHING

Chapter Roundup

- International markets offer firms opportunities to trade, to acquire resources and investment, but also offer threats in that other companies from overseas can do the same.

- Porter's 5-forces model is a useful checklist for analysing the state of competition in an industry.

  - New entrants - overseas competitors.

  - Substitute products - not **necessarily** affected by international trade, unless it affects their price or availability.

  - Customer bargaining power - if customers have a greater number of suppliers they can exert pressure as they can become more choosy.

  - Suppliers - if global industries **consolidate**, firms might face fewer suppliers. In other cases, they might find more choice.

  - Competitive intensity - more competitors equals more competition.

- Industries may be fragmented, concentrated or emerging.

- Prahalad and Hamel have argued that firms should concentrate on their core competencies for competitive success.

- Some firms carry out scenario building to see what different possible futures and developments may hold for the company.

- A firm's success in overseas markets might be influenced by conditions at home: factor conditions are the resources it can use; demand conditions are the characteristics of the market; related and supporting industries; firm strategy and structure - is the firm used to competition? Many of these factors are out of the control of the **individual** firm.

Quick Quiz

1   List the five competitive forces in an industry. (see para 2.2)
2   Why do industries become concentrated? (2.17)
3   What are the main problems in emerging industries? (2.21)
4   What are macro-scenarios? (3.2)
5   What are the four constituents in a country which determine an industry's competitiveness? (4.8)
6   What is the significance of the home market for a firm's global competitive effectiveness? (4.13)
7   What is the role of government in influencing the diamond? (4.18)
8   What is a cluster? (4.20)
9   Suggest ways in which individual firms can compete in industries where there is no 'national' competitive advantage. (4.28)

Action Programme Review

1   (a)   Here are some ideas. Barriers to entry are high. There are plenty of substitute products (coffee), competitive rivalry is high because of the difficulty of stockpiling products. Customer bargaining power is high, but supplier power is low: all it needs is capital, the right sort of land and labour.

      (b)   Williamson and Magor has begun to switch from selling tea at auction to consumer marketing. The firm is aiming to build up its own brand image in the UK and Germany, by offering - by mail order - unblended, specialist teas from its Indian estates. It advertised via Barclays Premier Card magazine; replies were used to set up a customer database. When the company's Earl Grey tea was recommended on BBC2's *Food and Drink,* these existing customers could be targeted with a letter and a sample.

Now try illustrative question 3 at the end of the Study Text

4 Culture: Buyer and Organisational Behaviour

Learning Outcomes

Upon completion of this chapter you will have an understanding of the importance of cultural considerations when planning the international marketing mix.

Culture influences buyer behaviour. We consider buyer behaviour in a range of markets.

Key Concepts Introduced

- Culture
- Buyer behaviour
- Not-for-profit organisation

Examples of Marketing at Work

- Eurodisney
- French dishwashers
- Islamic banking
- USA gun laws

- Marks and Spencer and cultural issues
- Wine in the UK
- Oxfam

1 SETTING THE SCENE

1.1 Culture was introduced in Chapter 2, and is one of the most sensitive areas in international marketing. Culture refers to ways of feeling, behaving and 'seeing the world': people's basic beliefs and assumptions about who they are, what is important in life, and how they feel about themselves and their fellow humans. In marketing terms, culture has a major effect upon buyer behaviour.

1.2 Culture is particularly important for the promotion and, to a lesser extent sometimes, the product elements of the mix. It is also relevant to international marketing management in that doing business overseas requires the manager successfully to negotiate all the minefields of business behaviour that exist.

1.3 Of course many firms do negotiate these problems successfully. In some cases, this is because the product is not culturally specific, but in other cases, they ensure their managers are sensitive to cultural difference.

1.4 Culture's impact within the organisation affects buyer behaviour issues and approaches to management.

1.5 We do return to culture later in this text when we discuss promotion in Chapter 13 and the effects of a global operation on a local economy in Chapter 6.

2 WHAT IS CULTURE?

2.1 The term is used by sociologists and anthropologists to encompass the total of the learned **beliefs, values, customs, artefacts** and **rituals** of a society or group.

Key Concept

A **culture** is 'a set of beliefs or standards, shared by a group of people, which helps the individual decide what is, what can be, how to feel, what to do, and how to go about doing it' (Goodenough, cited by Usunier).

2.2 It is clear that an individual can participate in several different cultures.

(a) The 'national' culture - if such a thing exists
(b) Sub-cultures (such as 'youth culture') can be important in the early stages of product introduction. 'Computer geeks', for example, were among the first to be enthusiastic about the Internet.
(c) Corporate cultures

Marketing at Work

Consider the case of a young French employee of Eurodisney.

(a) The employee speaks the French language - part of the national culture - and has participated in the French education system etc.

(b) As a youth, the employee might, in his or her spare time, participate in various 'youth culture' activities. Music and fashion are emblematic of youth culture.

(c) As an employee of Eurodisney, the employee will have to participate in the corporate culture, which is based on American standards of service with a high priority put on friendliness to customers.

Elements of culture

2.3 'Culture' embraces the following aspects of social life.

(a) **Beliefs and values**. Beliefs are perceived states of knowing or cognition, on the basis of objective and subjective information. Values are the comparatively few **key beliefs.**

- Relatively **enduring**
- Relatively **general** - not tied to specific objects
- Fairly widely accepted as a guide to **culturally appropriate behaviour**

(b) **Customs**. Customs are modes of behaviour which represent culturally approved ways of responding to given situations. There are various types of social behavioural norms. Keith Williams (*Behavioural Aspects of Marketing*) identifies four, on a continuum ranging from lightly to rigidly enforced patterns of behaviour, corresponding to their seriousness as a threat to social survival, if violated.

- **Folkways** - appropriate patterns of behaviour, violation of which are noticeable
- **Conventions** - accustomed or 'ingrained' standards of behaviour
- **Mores** - significant social norms including moral imperatives and taboos
- **Laws** - formal recognition of the mores considered necessary in the interests of the society as a whole, with imposed sanctions for violation

(c) **Artefacts**. Culture embraces all the physical 'tools' designed by human beings for their physical and psychological well-being: works of art, technology, products, buildings etc.

(d) **Rituals**. A ritual is a type of activity which takes on symbolic meaning, consisting of a fixed sequence of behaviour repeated over time. Ritualised behaviour tends to be public, elaborate, formal and ceremonial - like religious services, marriage ceremonies, court procedures, even sporting events.

Marketing at Work

The *Guardian* carried this following report, translated from an article in the French newspaper *Le Monde* by Jean-Michel Normand.

"'Sensual couples' joy of sinks hits dishwasher makers"

The makers and marketers of dishwashers in France are in despair. For the French may object to ironing or dusting, but they don't mind doing the dishes. Washing up is seen as therapeutic by some and a sign of a happy marriage by others.

The French National Institute of Statistics and Economics has found that 80 per cent of men and 75 per cent of women don't see washing up as unpleasant, while one in 20 find it very enjoyable.

These "sensual aquariophiles", as the sociologist Jean-Claude Kaufmann calls them, constitute a lost cause for dishwasher manufacturers. For years they have found it impossible to persuade more than one in three households to buy their products.

"They regard washing up as a purification ritual", dishwasher manufacturer Gifam reports despairingly.

In daily life the washing up often represents a good way to share the household tasks. A dishwasher could endanger a rite that maintains stability between couples.

Gifam is planning a publicity campaign with the emphasis on economy. Dishwashers use three or four times less water than washing up by hand, experts say.'

The development of attitudes and beliefs

2.4 We acquire our feelings about the worth of goods and services through a process of cultural and social development. In international marketing these differences in values may be quite marked, whereas in domestic markets they may be so subtle as to be unnoticeable. For the international marketer differences in attitude and belief may affect the following.

- Attitude towards ownership of an item
- Strength and direction of attitude
- Reason for desire/antipathy
- Perception of appropriate design/style
- Meaning of colours, symbols and words

Language and symbols

2.5 Another very important element of culture, which makes the learning and sharing of culture possible, is **language**. Without a shared language and symbolism - verbal and non-verbal - there would be no shared meaning.

2.6 **Symbols** are an important aspect of language and culture. Each symbol may carry a number of different meanings and associations for different people. For example, in Western cultures, the colour white symbolises purity, but in some Eastern cultures it symbolises death. Logos, trademarks and brands all have symbolic uses.

The transfer of cultural meaning

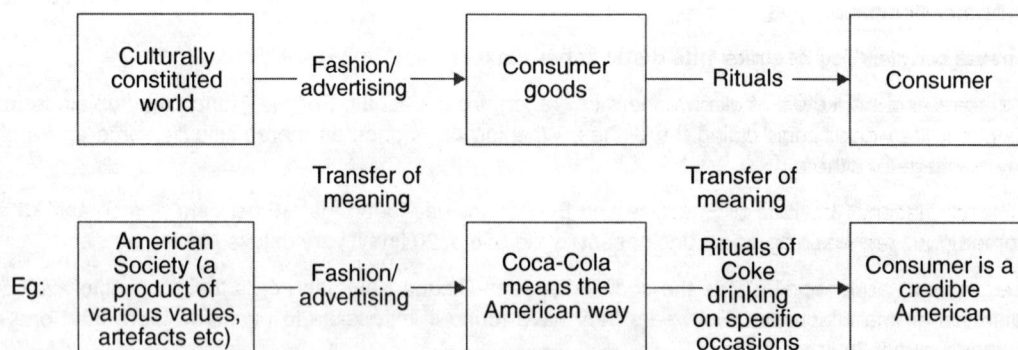

2.7 Some consumer researchers talk about the '**transfer of cultural meaning**' at different stages of the marketing process. The 'culturally constituted world' produces products which are **invested** with cultural meaning or significance by advertising and 'fashion'. Those consumer goods, symbolic of cultural values, are then sold to individual consumers, who thus absorb the cultural values. Meanwhile, by using the products in rituals of possession, exchange, grooming or whatever, the consumer adds further cultural meaning to the goods.

Cultural meaning

Culturally constituted world	Fashion/ advertising →	Consumer goods	Rituals →	Consumer

Transfer of meaning   Transfer of meaning

Eg:	American Society (a product of various values, artefacts etc)	Fashion/ advertising →	Coca-Cola means the American way	Rituals of Coke drinking on specific occasions →	Consumer is a credible American

2.8 We have already noted that each culture establishes its own norms. Often these are derived from **religious observance**. Thus alcoholic drink, beef or pork, unclad females, men doing housework and so on may all be taboo in certain cultures. A recent example was the book *The Satanic Verses* by Salman Rushdie, which caused significant offence in Muslim societies.

Cultural products

2.9 Eurodisney encapsulates some of the cultural issues in international marketing. Unlike an aircraft engine, produced on a global basis, with a high technical but a low 'cultural' content,

Eurodisney is a particular example of a service industry, tourism, which is going to be increasingly important.

2.10 In the case of Eurodisney, a number of commentators in France were horrified that it should be built there at all: one went so far as to state that Eurodisney was a 'cultural Chernobyl' which would weaken and poison indigenous French culture. Mickey Mouse, far from being a friendly cartoon character, was transformed in this view into a smiling but rapacious vampire.

2.11 Eurodisney exemplified American culture. In its early days, it was impossible to buy any alcoholic drinks on the premises, reflecting the practice of the American parent. In France, where wine consumption is embedded in the local culture, this policy was a factor hampering visitors and visitor appreciation. Similarly, at one time it was reported that European staff were less easily adapted to the company's corporate culture than American ones.

Exam Tip

Culture is a catch-all topic and can be brought into many questions on international marketing

(a) It affects the product area of the mix, as you will see later.
(b) Marketing communications are also heavily influenced by culture, for obvious reasons.
(c) Distribution might be affected – for example, the role of the shopkeeper in the local society.
(d) Even price can be influenced by culture - eg bargaining.
(e) Services are probably more affected by culture than other goods.

As well as the mix, culture can affect the success of marketing operations and even business negotiations.

Consequently, culture featured in the mini-cases in December 1995, June 1996, December 1996, June 1997 and December 1997, in such diverse contexts as food preferences, selling techniques, shopping habits and internal management.

---

3 SOURCES OF CULTURE

3.1 There are approximately 200 different countries each of which contains many different cultures, each with a myriad of beliefs, norms and taboos. It is helpful for us to have a framework showing the major categories. This is shown on page 88.

3.2 Taking the example of religion, this can affect **market entry** (religious conflict) **marketing organisation** (days of prayer) **goods** (type of clothes worn, types of food eaten) **promotion** (images shown), methods of doing **business** (eg Islamic banks) and so forth.

Marketing at Work

Islamic banking is a powerful example of the importance of culture in an economy. The Koran abjures the charging of interest, which is usury. However whilst interest is banned, profits are allowed. A problem is that there is no standard interpretation of the sharia law regarding this. Products promoted by Islamic banks include:

(a) leasing (the Islamic Bank TII arranged leases for seven Kuwait Airways aircraft)

(b) trade finance

(c) commodities trading

The earlier Islamic banks offered current accounts only, but depositors now ask for shares in the bank profits. To tap this market, Citibank, the US bank, has opened an Islamic banking subsidiary in Bahrain.

BPP
PUBLISHING

A Cultural Framework

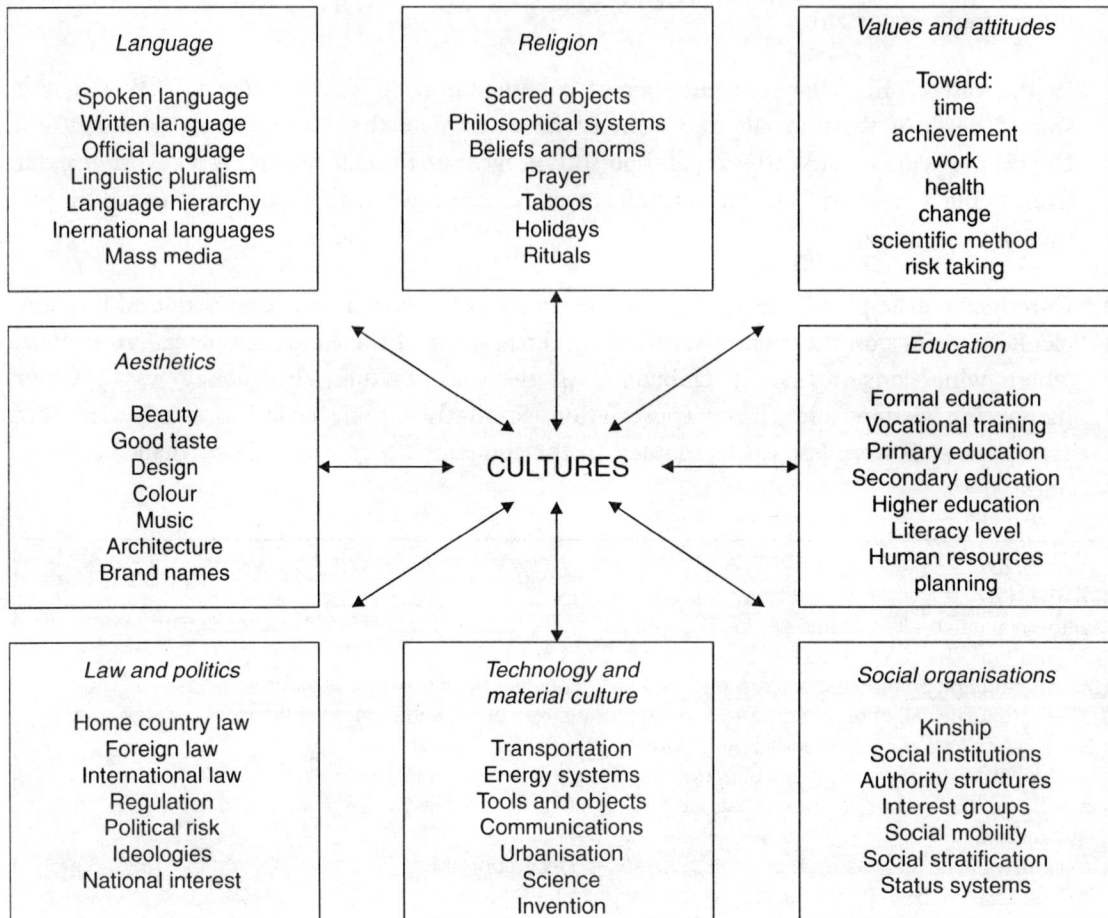

Language	Religion	Values and attitudes
Spoken language Written language Official language Linguistic pluralism Language hierarchy Inernational languages Mass media	Sacred objects Philosophical systems Beliefs and norms Prayer Taboos Holidays Rituals	Toward: time achievement work health change scientific method risk taking

CULTURES

Aesthetics	Education
Beauty Good taste Design Colour Music Architecture Brand names	Formal education Vocational training Primary education Secondary education Higher education Literacy level Human resources planning

Law and politics	Technology and material culture	Social organisations
Home country law Foreign law International law Regulation Political risk Ideologies National interest	Transportation Energy systems Tools and objects Communications Urbanisation Science Invention	Kinship Social institutions Authority structures Interest groups Social mobility Social stratification Status systems

National cultures

3.3 Many cultures can be identified with a nation, but often this does not apply.

(a) The UK is relatively small, with one language, English, predominantly spoken.

(b) A large country like India is home to many language groups, and while Hinduism is shared across many of these language groups, there is a large Moslem minority.

3.4 Some countries combine two more or less equal linguistic cultural groups. Switzerland is a nation state that is 'explicitly multi-cultural': 'precise staffing levels have been established in public bodies which prevent discrimination between linguistic communities which are not equal'.

3.5 Many of the world's **nation states**, with defined borders and central institutions, are relatively recent creations, resulting not from ethnicity or cultural homogeneity but from **colonial administration**. This is particularly true of Africa.

Marketing at Work

A huge cultural difference between the US and most other countries of similar economic development is the role of guns and firearms.

Most European states place restrictions on ownership of firearms. In the USA, the right to bear arms is embodied in the constitution and powerful lobby groups such as the National Rifle Association (NRA) seek to keep it that way.

Although hunting as a hobby is often cited as a reason, guns in the US have been given a symbolic role: the American War of Independence started with gun-shots, and the West was 'won' in this way. Even now, ownership of guns is justified as the citizen's last protection against the almighty state, and indeed against other citizens.

There is a great deal of resistance even to limited measures of gun control - quite a contrast to wide public support in the UK for banning private ownership of firearms altogether.

Oddly, the USA controls the consumption of tobacco and alcohol more strictly compared with the more tobacco- and alcohol-friendly countries of Europe.

High context and low context cultures

3.6   Edward Hall draws a distinction between high context and low context cultures. All communications have a **context,** which can influence the message.

- Where the communication takes place
- The people involved
- The content of the conversation (eg work, negotiation)

3.7   **Context** will often shape communication and can indicate how the content of a message should be interpreted.

3.8   **Low context** cultures are ones in which context is unimportant to the meaning of a message. Like railway timetables, words should mean exactly what they say. The meaning is explicit.

3.9   In **high context** cultures, messages must be interpreted from the context. In a high context culture, communication might be impossible if you do not know the person you are with.

3.10   Usunier identifies the following groups.

- Low-context and explicit messages: Swiss, Germans, Scandinavians, North Americans
- Medium-context: English, French, Italian, Spanish
- High context: Latin Americans, Arabs, Japanese

Action Programme 1

Two people, one from a low context and one from a high context culture meet for the first time to discuss a business deal. What will be the main objective of each, and where do you think each will obtain security that the deal will be ok?

---

4   CULTURE AND INTERNATIONAL MARKETING   12/99

4.1   Cultural segmentation must be considered particularly carefully, therefore, in an international (or **cross-cultural**) context: the marketer needs to understand the beliefs, values, customs and rituals of the countries in which a product is being marketed in order to alter or reformulate the product to appeal to local needs and tastes, and reformulate the **promotional message** to be intelligible and attractive to other cultures.

(a)   Nestlé, the Swiss coffee maker, sells different strengths and styles of coffee in Europe than in America. Haagen-Dazs developed green tea ice-cream for the Japanese market.

(b)   Board games such as Monopoly are sold worldwide - with nationally-relevant street/area names, money and tokens.

(c) Legal and regulatory provisions with regard to advertising vary from country to country: the showing of cigarettes in ads, for example, the use of comparative advertising, or the use of children in advertising.

(d) Products are positioned as exotic imports with the specific appeal of their country of origin (Australian lager, Italian pizza, French mineral water) - while in the domestic market they are sold on familiarity and cultural loyalty.

4.2 There are two ways of looking at cross-cultural marketing.

(a) **Localised marketing strategy** stresses the diversity and uniqueness of consumers in different national cultures.

(b) **Global marketing strategy** stresses the similarity and shared nature of consumers worldwide.

4.3 The marketer will be interested in the extent of the cultural differences between two countries with regard to the following.

Potential problems

(a)	**Language**	A promotional theme may not be intelligible - or properly translatable - whether in words or symbols.
(b)	**Needs and wants**	The benefits sought from a product in one country may be different in another.
(c)	**Consumption patterns**	One country may not use a product as much as another (affecting product viability), or may use it in very different ways (affecting product positioning).
(d)	**Market segments**	One country may have different demographic, geographical, socio-cultural and psychological groupings to another.
(e)	**Socio economic**	Consumers in one country may have different disposable income factors and/or decision-making roles from those in another.
(f)	**Marketing conditions**	Differences in retail, distribution and communication systems, promotional regulation/legislation, trade restrictions etc may affect the potential for research, promotion and distribution in other countries.

4.4 A **failure to understand cultural differences** may cause problems with each of the elements of the marketing mix.

(a) **The product**. Nestlé coffee, Camay soap and a host of similar products are marketed internationally - with different names, flavours, aromas, and other characteristics. Coffee is preferred very strong, dark and in ground form in Continental Europe - but weaker, milder and instant in the USA. Colour is another interesting element in product and packaging: it means different things to different cultures. Blue is said to represent warmth in Holland, coldness in Sweden, purity in India and death in Iran. Product benefits also vary in appeal: Pepsodent apparently tried to sell their toothpaste using the slogan 'You'll wonder where the yellow went!' in South-East Asia - where chewing betel nuts is considered an elite habit (giving status-enhancing brown teeth).

(b) **Promotion**. Customs, symbols and language do not always travel well. Apparently the Chevrolet Nova failed to sell in Latin America because in Spanish 'no va' means 'doesn't run'. 'Come alive with Pepsi' was translated as ' Pepsi brings your dead ancestors back to life' in one Far Eastern country.

(c) **Price**. Large package sizes may not be marketable in countries where average income is low, because of the cash outlay required.

(d) **Place**. Distribution tastes may vary. Supermarkets are very popular in some countries, while others prefer intimate personal stores for groceries and other foodstuffs. Newly-opening markets such as Eastern Europe exhibit poor distribution systems and very low salesperson effort and productivity - compared to Japan, say, which rates very highly.

(e) **People.** There are differing attitudes to personal service in some countries. Clearly different countries have different service cultures.

(f) **Processes.** A good example of the cultural influence on processes in some industries is the religious requirements regarding slaughtering and cooking of halal and kosher food.

(g) **Physical evidence.** In service industries such as hotels, physical evidence is of the 'essence'. Different people have different expectations as to requirements for comfort.

4.5   International business activities introduce new products, services and ways of doing business. Some cultures will resist this if no attempt is made to understand the cross-cultural dimensions of global marketing. Consideration has to be given to understanding the impact of the firm's activities. See Chapter 6 for more on this.

4.6   International marketers need to analyse the different elements of culture in order to develop an effective strategy. They need to think about the following.

- Customer needs and motivations
- Buyer behaviour
- Cultural values relevant to the product
- Decision making in the target market
- Appropriate promotion methods
- Appropriate distribution channels

Exam Tip

The December 1999 exam asked whether international marketing was merely about adjusting the marketing mix for cultural differences. There is clearly more to it than that. Culture is important in its own right.

Marketing at Work

- Marks and Spencer's Paris store is very successful and has highlighted to the French some of the best aspects of British taste, quality and value for money. By contract, the Canadian experience of M&S was not so successful, where it was assumed that tastes would be similar to those in the UK.

- The French are sensitive to companies that undermine the café culture, so hamburger and fast food restaurants are in decline.

- The Japanese culture is seen as a difficult one to export to because Japanese people often automatically regard foreign goods as inferior.

- The UK wine market has grown by an enormous amount over the past decade. UK consumers are prepared to experiment with products from different countries, and the UK supermarkets have taken a large share of the market. The French wine industry has lost UK market share to competitors from the New World (Australia, New Zealand), Bulgaria and South America.

4.7 The growth of the **service sector**, and the marketing of services, is affected by culture. Services such as travel, culture and health and fitness are becoming status symbols in many European consumer groups. Culture probably affects service products more than goods, and so the marketing of such services has to be aware of regional differences.

Cultural convergence and divergence

4.8 For certain product groups, where social exposure is important, and to the social classes where status is also important, the acquisition and adoption of an 'international' lifestyle has led to international products such as Walkman, Coke, Boss etc. Two groups seem to be most affected.

- Young people, who have an above average need for social acceptance
- International travellers, who are exposed to multicultural values

4.9 This **convergence** process has led to the idea of global products that have an appeal worldwide with little or no modification.

4.10 In an earlier chapter, we described the globalisation process. To what extent does it apply to culture?

(a) Some products and brands are of international appeal, such as the Sony Walkman, Coca-Cola, and so forth.

(b) There has been a revolution in communications with radio, television, and now the Internet. Many of these carry American shows. However, remember also that the revolution that installed the Islamic republic in Iran was facilitated by these very media. The invention of printing, analogously, did not unify the cultures of Europe: arguably it exacerbated differences between them.

(c) There is an argument that a **youth culture** has developed, susceptible to the use of particular brands. After all, many of the key experiences of 'youth' (education) are similar across many countries. However the existence of shared tastes among the affluent countries in the west should not be taken to apply globally. For example, arranged marriages are still the norm in some parts of the world. Of course, in certain markets (eg for trainers) there exists a global product.

(d) The rise in nationalism and religious fundamentalism cast doubt on a 'global' culture.

4.11 In practice, is there such a person as the 'global consumer?' Or even a Euro-consumer? This will only happen where **cultures converge**. We cite the example of wine drinking in the UK.

Marketing at Work

The emergence of Vinopolis, a 'City of Wine', is just the latest stage in the gradual transformation of British wine-drinking from a hobby pursued by cognoscenti to a mass pursuit. Back in the 1960s, Oxbridge colleges and gentlemen's clubs cultivated fine cellars, but most people stuck firmly to their beer. In the past 30 years, however, wine consumption has soared by over 450%, while it has merely doubled in America and has actually fallen by 50% in France. In 1966 British wine consumption was only about 2% of France's; now the British market is about 25% the size of the French.

As the market has expanded, so the retail trade has been transformed. Specialist off-licences, such as Victoria Wine or Thresher, each now have around 1,500 stores across the country. But in the past decade, the real story has been the rise of the supermarkets. Safeway, which stocks over 500 wines, reckons that at the moment seven out of every ten bottles of wine is sold in a supermarket compared with less than four ten years ago.

From *The Economist*

Self reference revisited

4.12 Another problem is **self reference,** in other words the tendency to interpret something according to one's own values and experience, rather than on its own terms. It is pointless getting upset about practices which are 'the norms' in the overseas market.

4.13 To avoid misinterpreting other people in the light of one's own assumptions, some firms analyse their products and promotional messages specifically for their cultural connotations, and how the product relates to them.

- **Motivation?** What needs are satisfied? (See section 5)
- What are the characteristic **patterns of behaviour?**
- What **values** are relevant to the product?
- How are **decisions** taken?
- **Promotion messages:** taboos, language etc.
- **Institution** - what types of retailing are acceptable for a product?

Exam Tip

Convergence and divergence come up in June 1996 in which candidates were asked to comment whether culture was a 'thing of the past'.
Clearly the answer must be no - even though certain cultural traits might easily cross national boundaries - as a result industrial development and communications - from culture to culture. Furthermore, some 'cultures' are actively being revived. Welsh is spoken by more people now than a few decades ago and is a language of instruction in schools.
Clearly, 'culture' will never go away - although different cultures might develop and segmentation opportunities will emerge across national boundaries.

5 MOTIVATION AND BUYER BEHAVIOUR

5.1 Whilst we have examined the effect that culture has on the marketing mix, it might be worth examining in a little more detail why this should be so, with reference to **motivation** and **buyer behaviour.**

Key Concept

Buyer behaviour is the process a buyer goes through and the weight given to various factors in arriving at a decision to purchase a product.

Motivation

5.2 We experience a need (eg for water) which motivates us to act (eg drink). Some writers, like Abraham Maslow, believe that all motivation is the result of a desire to satisfy one of several needs. He devised a **hierarchy of needs.** These are outlined below. You will have encountered these before.

- Physiological
- Safety
- Love/social
- Esteem
- Self-actualisation
- Freedom of enquiry and expression
- Knowledge and understanding needs

5.3 The 'ethnocentricity' of Maslow's hierarchy has been noted. It works, possibly, for people in the US, but does not translate well into other cultures.

5.4 However, it is a useful **model** of the sort of needs people might have. Cultural factors in a society influence a number of the needs Maslow identifies.

    (a) **Physiological needs** are likely to be powerful in societies where people are poor or where extended families and kinship networks place special demands on the working individual's role as **provider**.

    (b) **Safety needs** are powerful in particular social contexts.

        (i) For example, the practice of lifetime employment in some Japanese companies began after World War II. Safety was promised as a 'job for life' in return for dedication to work. Economic factors are now taking their toll on this concept and the 'job for life' can not now be guaranteed.

        (ii) Just as importantly, perception of 'safety' and 'risk' differ. Some societies have a variety of different attitudes to 'food' and 'health' and the risk of infection, which can have an important effect on the desirability of health products.

    (c) Satisfaction of **esteem needs**

      • The visible trappings of success
      • The respect of the group

    (d) **Self-actualisation,** the fulfilment of personal potential may not be seen as a 'need' in some societies, especially those where the success of the 'group' and conformance to its demands is the dominant value system. 'Self-actualisation' implies an individualist philosophy not always present in many cultures.

5.5 Finally, the same product will satisfy different consumer needs in different countries.

6 CONSUMER BUYER BEHAVIOUR

6.1 It is worth emphasising that buyer behaviour is influenced by a number of factors, not only motivational issues. Here are some examples.

    (a) Who takes **major purchase decisions**? The husband or wife? Or are they reached by group discussion, as might be the case in an extended family? Do people defer to the elders in their family? Is individualism or collectivism the cultural orientation?

    (b) What is the **overall buying power** of an individual in a buying situation?

    (c) What is the **retailing structure** (eg large out of town supermarkets encourage stocking up once a week)? To what extent is the population urban or suburban?

6.2 We can see that culture is an important variable in the purchase decision.

    (a) Culture can render certain products unacceptable in the first place (eg advertising pork or beef in countries where there are taboos against eating pigs or cows).

    (b) Culture can also bias a person's perception of information.

6.3 Usunier cites **institutions**, social **conventions**, **habits** and **customs** as relevant to buyer behaviour. He gives the example of **eating**. Cultures differ in the following ways.

• The number of meals consumed in a day
• The duration of meal times
• The composition of the meal (cooking style, portion size)

- The extent to which a meal is just a 'refuelling' stop or a family/social event
- Is the food prepared with basic ingredients or is it purchased part-cooked?

6.4 'The list is endless because nothing is more essential, more universal and at the same item more accurately **defined** by culture than eating habits. Eating habits should be considered as the whole process of purchasing food and beverages, cooking, tasting and even commenting. In many countries, commercials advertising ready-made foods (canned or dried soups, for instance) faced resistance in the traditional role of the housewife, who was supposed to prepare meals from natural ingredients for her family. As a result, advertisers were obliged to include a degree of preparation by the housewife in the copy strategy.'

Action Programme 2

Schiffman & Kanuk (Consumer Behaviour) give the following summary of American core values and their relevance to consumer behaviour. Consider how far they are applicable to your social culture.

Value	General features	Relevance to consumer behaviour
Achievement and success	Hard work is good; success flows from hard work	Acts as a justification for acquisition of goods ('You deserve it')
Activity	Keeping busy is healthy and natural	Stimulates interest in products that are timesavers and enhance leisure time
Efficiency and practicality	Admiration of things that that solve problems (eg save time and effort)	Stimulates purchase of products that function well and save time
Progress	People can improve themselves; tomorrow should be better than today	Stimulates desire for new products that fulfil unsatisfied needs; ready acceptance of products that claim to be 'new' or' improved'
Material comfort	'The good life'	Fosters acceptance of convenience and luxury products that make life more comfortable and enjoyable
Individualism	Being oneself (eg self-reliance, self-interest, self-esteem)	Stimulates acceptance of custom ised or unique products that enable a person to 'express his or her own personality'.
Freedom	Freedom of choice	Fosters interest in wide product lines and differentiated products
External conformity	Uniformity of observable behaviour; desire for acceptance	Stimulates interest in products that are used or owned by others in the same social group
Humanitarianism	Caring for others, particularly the underdog	Stimulates patronage of firms that compete with market leaders
Youthfulness	A state of mind that stresses being young at heart and a youthful appearance	Stimulates acceptance of products that provide the illusion of maintaining or fostering youthfulness
Fitness and Health	Caring about one's body, including the desire to be physically fit and healthy	Stimulates acceptance of food products, activities, and equipment perceived to maintain or increase physical fitness.

BPP PUBLISHING

Cultural change

6.5   Finally, it is as well to bear in mind that culture is not a static thing. Many governments recognise this, and some deplore 'Westernising' attitudes. In the west cultural values have changed.

6.6   A good example is attitudes to debt. Being in debt was regarded as a state to be avoided at all costs, and there were strong moral injunctions in some areas of UK society against indebtedness. This taboo has completely vanished. The financial services sector has been one of the UK's most prosperous industries.

7   BUSINESS AND GOVERNMENT BUYER BEHAVIOUR

Decision making units

7.1   Most models of business buyer behaviour refer to the decision-making unit, in other words the group of people responsible for making the decisions whether to buy a product. We can examine some possible problems below.

7.2   **Authority and delegation.** In some organisations, individuals have clearly defined areas of authority and decision-making power. However in some cultures, decisions have to be referred upwards to more senior figures, so the person doing the negotiating may not have the right to make the decision.

7.3   **Clarity of authority.** Henry Mintzberg writes about the ceremonial role of senior managers. In some cultures, managerial decision making is taken by consensus. The problem is to manipulate this consensus on your behalf. The way in which decisions are taken or can be overridden can be a significant problem.

7.4   **The decision process.** Does the DMU judge proposals according to the 'rational model'? In other words, are a number of alternatives evaluated in the cold light of day, or do other 'political' considerations intrude? If the firm is part of a network of other firms, it might be under pressure to buy from a group company.

'Doing business'

7.5   A factor which has an impact on organisations engaging in international industrial marketing, is the **management culture**. This is the views about managing held by managers, their shared educational experiences, and the 'way business is done'. Obviously, this reflects wider cultural differences between countries but, conversely, national cultures can sometimes be subordinated to the corporate culture of the organisation.

7.6   The way in which business practice can be affected by management culture can be indicated by an example.

(a)   The *Harvard Business Review* reported (July-August 1991) that 'the successful development of executives depends on creating a distinctive shared identity, a sense of belonging to the French managerial class'. Further quotations are illuminating.

> 'French managers see their work as an intellectual challenge, requiring the remorseless application of individual brainpower. They do not share the Anglo-Saxon view of management as an interpersonally demanding exercise, where plans have to be constantly "sold" upward and downward using personal skills. The bias is for intellect rather than for action. People who run big enterprises must above all else be clever - that is, they must be able to grasp complex issues, analyse problems, manipulate ideas and evaluate solutions. A

BPP
PUBLISHING

revealing witticism contains this rejoinder, supposedly from one senior French civil servant to another: "That's fine in practice, but it will never work in theory".

The emphasis on cleverness shows up even in executive recruiting advertisements. They hardly mention the drive or initiative looked for in Anglo-Saxon recruits, rather they call for more cerebral qualities - an analytical mind, independence, intellectual rigor, an ability to synthesise information. Communication or interpersonal skills are tacked on at the end, if they appear at all.

Recent French industrial achievements have occurred largely in fields requiring a co-ordinated, technologically and scientifically creative, and research-driven approach - rather than, say, marketing dash, financial wizardry, or manufacturing organisation.'

(b) The 'world leadership survey' conducted by the *Harvard Business Review* asked a variety of questions to managers in different countries. It could be concluded that managers in different countries do not have the same priorities when it comes to business issues. When asked what they thought of as the three most important factors in organisation success, these were listed as follows, in order of priority.

- Japan: product development, management, product quality
- Germany: workforce skills, problem solving, management
- USA: customer service, product quality, technology

7.7 The existence of these different systems of priorities and ways of doing business affects the **competitive environment, international marketing** and the **success of joint ventures** which can be damaged by communication problems.

Negotiation

7.8 Cultural differences might affect buying behaviour according to Usunier, especially in negotiation.

(a) How do you establish the salesperson's credibility? Many cultural preconceptions can underline the difficulties of assessing which person to believe. For example, frankness is to be avoided in some cultures (if it means someone else is losing face).

(b) Is the **style of negotiation** communicative or manipulative? In other words, do you want to **exchange facts** or **manipulate the other party**?

(c) To what extent are **oral agreements** the basis for business, and to what extent are contracts or written agreements preferred?

Government buyer behaviour

7.9 In many countries, government is the biggest buyer and will be responsible for buying a wide range of goods and services. The way government buys is influenced by the extent to which public accountability for expenditure is deemed to be important - so a cultural history of **public service and accountability** is critical.

7.10 The usual forms of buying procedure are the **open tender** and the **selective tender**. For a selective tender process, the firm needs to be accepted on the appropriate list. In some countries, it takes considerable persistence to get to that stage, since it may take several visits to appropriate government officials to establish a good working relationship.

7.11 In the EU, most public procurement contracts should be open to any competitor throughout the European Union - and the bidding will normally be to an open tender.

BPP PUBLISHING

Social and cultural factors

7.12 It is generally true that in dealing with governments and government departments, the significance lies, perhaps, with **who you know** rather than with **what you know**. The right political contacts are often essential.

7.13 It is also true that buying decisions may be affected as much by a lowly departmental clerk acting as a gatekeeper in a Decision Making Unit (DMU), as by a senior government official or even a politician acting as a **decision maker** or an **influencer** in the DMU. A clerk in a regional office can make life very difficult, despite support at the centre.

7.14 A clear understanding of the cultural inter-relationships in government circles, hierarchical relationships and political influence may be critical in some markets and countries.

(a) For example, a different style is necessary for dealing with officials from high context cultures than from low context cultures.

(b) Officials may formal authority but little actual power.

(c) Firms suffer if relationships between our own government and the host country government deteriorate.

(d) Different cultures have different attitudes to gifts.

(e) Some cultures prefer a high degree of legalism, others do not.

(f) There may be conflict between different government departments.

(g) Governments are susceptible to pressure from powerful interest groups at home.

8 BUYER BEHAVIOUR IN OTHER SECTORS

8.1 There are many similarities between buyer behaviour for products and services, but there are important differences.

- Attitudes
- Needs and motives
- Purchase behaviour

8.2 The personal elements involved in services can be key to a customer's decision. Customers are more likely to be dissatisfied with service purchases because services are often seen as more personal than goods. An unfriendly stewardess on an international flight will affect customer perception of the entire services.

8.3 Consumers are more likely to be influenced by friends, family and colleagues when purchasing a service. Word-of-mouth promotion is therefore frequently relied upon and should be targeted by international marketers.

Commodity, semi-processed and not-for-profit

8.4 In commodity, semi-processed products and not-for-profit sectors buyers will display a mix of motives in a range of buying situations. To use the framework outlined in paragraph 8.1 we may be able to say the following. It is not an exhaustive presentation of the issues involved. See if you can think of further examples.

	Buyer attitudes	*Needs and motives*	*Purchase behaviour*
Commodity ie raw materials; agricultural products	Goods to be bought in bulk, often from lesser developed (ie primarily agricultural) economies. Prices may vary with season and availability	For example, providing the food for population of the buyer's country. Needs could be satisfied by any one of a number of suppliers	Based upon quality considerations and availability of proper distribution facilities from the point of production. End consumers not involved
Semi-processed eg picked and frozen fruit for use in jam, yoghurts or pies	Companies may have habitual suppliers and will look to them to provide goods at reasonable price. Price may be subject to availability and seasonality.	Quality product required that complies with necessary regulations and can *add value* ie be converted to final product at a profit. Transport important	Fruit or other products examined for quality, price compared with other suppliers. Contracts may be struck on basis of previous dealings. End consumers not involved.
Not-for-profit eg charities, arts organisations, social services	Might expect some form of recognition of a charity donation; expect to enjoy output of arts/leisure organisations; vulnerable members of society need 'help' from social services. Buyers will want to know that organisation's resources are not being wasted.	'Humanitarian'; leisure time and recreation, basic needs eg for food and shelter, education or protection	Recommendation of friends and colleagues; emotional reaction to charity appeal; 'nowhere else to turn'. End consumer is usually involved.

Charity and not-for-profit marketing

8.5   Although most people would 'know one if they saw it', there is a surprising problem in clearly delimiting what counts as a **not-for-profit (NFP) organisation**. Local authority services, for example, would not be marketing in order to arrive at a profit for shareholders, but nowadays they are being increasingly required to apply the same disciplines and processes as companies which are oriented towards straightforward profit goals.

Marketing at Work

Oxfam operates more shops than any commercial organisation in Britain, and these operate at a profit. The Royal Society for the Protection of Birds operates a mail order trading company which provides a 25% return on capital, operating very profitably and effectively.

8.6   Bois suggests that we define NFP enterprises by recognising that their first objective is to be **'non-loss' operations** in order to cover their costs, that profits are only made as a means to an end (eg providing a service, or accomplishing some socially or morally worthy objective).

> **Key Concept**
>
> Bois proposes that a **not-for profit organisation** be defined as:' ... an organisation whose attainment of its prime goal is not assessed by economic measures. However, in pursuit of that goal it may undertake profit-making activities.'
>
> This may involve a number of different kinds of organisation with, for example, differing legal status - charities, statutory bodies offering public transport or the provision of services such as leisure, health or public utilities such as water or road maintenance.

8.7 **Marketing management** is now recognised as equally valuable to profit orientated or NFP organisations. The tasks of marketing auditing, setting objectives, developing strategies and marketing mixes and controls for their implementation can all help in improving the performance of charities and NFP organisations. Whilst the basic principles are appropriate for this sector, differences in how they can be applied should not be forgotten. Dibb et al (1994) suggest that four key differences exist, related to objectives, target markets (and hence buyer behaviour), marketing mixes and controlling marketing activities.

Objectives

8.8 Objectives will not be based on profit achievement but rather on achieving a **particular response** from various target markets. This has implications for reporting of results. The organisation will need to be open and honest in showing how it has managed its budget and allocated funds raised. **Efficiency and effectiveness** are particularly important in the use of donated funds.

> **Action Programme 3**
>
> List possible objectives for NFP and charitable organisations.

8.9 The concept of target marketing is different in the not-for-profit sector. There are no buyers but rather a number of different **audiences**. A target public is a group of individuals who have an interest or concern about the charity. Those benefiting from the organisation's activities are known as the **client public**. Relationships are also vital with **donors and volunteers** from the general public. In addition, there may also be a need to lobby local and national government and businesses for support.

Marketing mix issues

8.10 Charities and NFP organisations often deal more with **services and ideas** than products. In this sense the extended marketing mix of people, process and physical evidence is important.

(a) **Appearance** needs to be business-like rather than appearing extravagant.

(b) **Process** is increasingly important, for example, the use of direct debit to pay for council tax, reduces administration costs leaving more budget for community services.

(c) **People** need to offer good service and be caring in their dealings with their clients.

(d) **Distribution channels** are often shorter with fewer intermediaries than in the profit making sector. Wholesalers and distributors available to a business organisations do not exist in most non-business contexts.

(e) **Promotion is usually dominated by personal selling**. Advertising is often limited to public service announcements due to limited budgets. Direct marketing is growing due to the ease of developing databases. Sponsorship, competitions and special events are also widely used.

(f) **Pricing** is probably the most different element in this sector. Financial price is often not a relevant concept. Rather, opportunity cost, where an individual is persuaded of the value of donating time or funds, is more relevant.

8.11 Controlling activities is complicated by the difficulty of judging whether **non-quantitative objectives** have been met. For example assessing whether the charity has improved the situation of client publics is difficult to research. Statistics related to product mix, financial resources, size of budgets, number of employees, number of volunteers, number of customers serviced and number and location of facilities, are all useful for this task.

9 CULTURE AND THE ORGANISATION

9.1 We have discussed culture in a society and as a factor of a firm's environment and market for its products or services. The issue of **corporate culture** is quite important for multinational businesses. This is because many companies have their own culture.

(a) Culture embodies the common set of values: 'the way things are down around here.'

(b) Culture is embodied in rituals and behaviour.

(c) Culture is an important filter of **information** and an **interpreter** of it. For example, a firm might have a cultural predisposition against embarking on risky ventures. Finally existing behaviour patterns may make a proposed strategy incompatible with the culture and so impossible to implement.

9.2 An organisation's culture is influenced by many factors.

(a) The organisation's **founder**. A strong set of values and assumptions is set up by the organisation's founder, and even after he or she has retired, these values have their own momentum.

(b) The organisation's **history.** The effect of history can be determined by stories, rituals and symbolic behaviour. They legitimise behaviour and promote priorities. (In some organisations certain positions are regarded as intrinsically more 'heroic' than others.)

(c) **Leadership and management style**. An organisation with a strong culture recruits managers who naturally conform to it.

(d) **Structure and systems** affect culture as well as strategy.

(e) The industry (eg computer software firms in the 'silicon valley' had a reputation for being laid back on office dress).

(f) Location of head office - and its acquired culture

(g) Of most significance in this chapter, the wider **society**, discussed below.

The Hofstede model of national cultures

9.3 A model was developed in 1980 by Professor Geert Hofstede in order to explain national differences by identifying 'key dimensions' which represent the essential 'programmes' forming a common culture in the value systems of all countries. Each country is represented on a scale for each dimension so as to explain and understand values, attitudes and behaviour.

9.4 In particular, Hofstede pointed out that countries differ on the following dimensions.

(a) **Power-distance**. This dimension measures how far superiors are expected to exercise power. In a high power-distance culture, the boss decides and people do not question.

(b) **Uncertainty-avoidance**. Some cultures prefer clarity and order, whereas others are prepared to accept novelty. This affects the willingness of people to **change** rules, rather than simply obey them.

(c) **Individualism/collectivism**. In some countries individual achievement is what matters. A collectivist culture (eg people are supported - and controlled - by extended families) puts the interests of the group first.

(d) **'Masculinity'/'Femininity'**. In 'masculine' cultures, gender roles are clearly differentiated. In 'feminine' ones they are not. 'Masculine' cultures place greater emphasis on possessions, status, and display as opposed to quality of life, the environment etc.

9.5 Hofstede grouped countries into eight 'clusters'.

Group		Power-distance	Uncertainty avoidance	Individual-ism	'Masculinity'
I	'More developed Latin' (eg Belgium, France, Argentina, Brazil, Spain)	High	High	Medium to high	Medium
II	'Less developed Latin' (eg Portugal, Mexico, Peru)	High	High	Low	Whole range
III	'More developed Asian' (eg Japan)	Medium	High	Medium	High
IV	'Less developed Asian' (eg India, Taiwan, Thailand)	High	Low to medium	Low	Medium
V	Near Eastern (eg Greece, Iran, Turkey)	High	High	Low	Medium
VI	'Germanic' (eg Germany)	Low	Medium to high	Medium	Medium to high
VII	Anglo (eg UK, US, Australia)	Low to medium	Low to medium	High	High
VIII	Nordic (eg Scandinavia, the Netherlands)	Low	Low to medium	Medium to high	Low

9.6 There are dangers in using these models. In the management of individual businesses, other factors may be more important.

(a) **Type of industry**: people working in information technology from two countries might have more in common with each other than they might with people working in a different industry.

(b) **Size of company**. Some people may be accustomed to working in a bureaucracy.

Fons Trompenaars

9.7 In his book, *Riding the Waves of Culture,* Fons Trompenaars uses some case study scenarios to illustrate how people in different societies address ethical dilemmas. Here are two examples, followed by ideas advanced by managers from various countries.

(a) *Situation 1*

You are riding in a car driven by a close friend. He hits a pedestrian. You know he was going at least 35 miles per hour in an area of the city where the maximum allowed speed is 20 miles per hour. There are no witnesses. His lawyer says that if you testify under oath that he was only driving at 20 miles per hour it may save him from serious consequences.

What right has your friend to expect you to protect him?

- My friend has a definite right as a friend to expect me to testify to the lower figure
- He has some right as a friend to expect me to testify to the lower figure
- He has no right as a friend to expect me to testify to the lower figure

What do you think you would do in view of the obligations of a sworn witness and the obligation to your friend?

- Testify that he was going 20 miles per hour
- Not testify that he was going 20 miles per hour

(b) *Situation 2*

You have just come from a secret meeting of the board of directors of a company. You have a close friend who will be ruined unless she can get out of the market before the board's decision becomes known. You happen to be having dinner at the friend's house this evening.

What right does your friend have to expect you to tip her off?

- She has a definite right as a friend to expect me to tip her off
- She has some right as a friend to expect me to tip her off
- She has no right as a friend to expect me to tip her off

Would you tip her off in view of your obligations to the company and your obligations to your friend?

- Yes
- No

9.8 With situation 1, North Americans and most north Europeans emerge as almost totally **universalistic** in their approach, ie they think that the friend has no right or only some right to expect you to testify falsely. The proportion falls to under 70% for the French and Japanese, while in Venezuela two-thirds of respondents would lie to the police to protect their friend – according to the figures generated by Trompenaars.

9.9 The universalists seem to be saying that 'the law is broken and the serious condition of the pedestrian underlines the importance of upholding the law'. **Particularist cultures**, however, are more likely to support their friend as the pedestrian's injuries increase, their argument being, in effect, 'my friend needs my help more than ever now that he is in serious trouble with the law'.

9.10 For situation 2, however, Trompenaars reports some interesting differences. The Japanese in particular jump from the particularist position they showed previously to a strongly universalistic stance on corporate confidentiality. Quite possibly this occurs because the situation is broader than a particular friend: at stake here is loyalty to a group or corporation versus loyalty to an individual outside that group. Both case study scenarios show that ethical perspectives differ significantly between societies.

Corporate cultures

9.11 Dale and Kennedy (*Corporate Cultures*) consider cultures to be a function of the willingness of employees to take risks, and how quickly they get feedback on whether they got it right or wrong.

BPP PUBLISHING

High risk

BET YOUR COMPANY CULTURE ('Slow and steady wins the race') Long decision-cycles: stamina and nerve required eg oil companies, aircraft companies, architects	**HARD 'MACHO' CULTURE** ('Find a mountain and climb it') eg entertainment, management consultancy, advertising
PROCESS CULTURE ('It's not what you do, it's the way that you do it') Values centred on attention to excellence of technical detail, risk management, procedures, status symbols eg banks, financial services, government	**WORK HARD/PLAY HARD CULTURE** ('Find a need and fill it') All action - and fun: team spirit eg sales and retail, computer companies, life assurance companies

Slow feedback

Fast feedback

Low risk

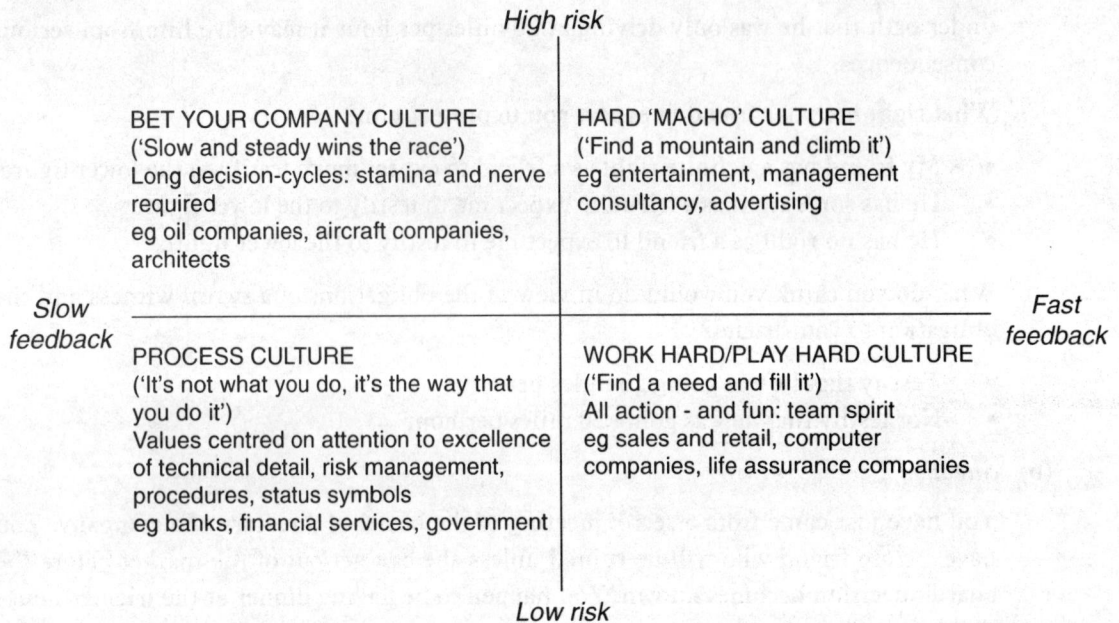

Relevance to international marketing

9.12   What is the relevance of this issue for international marketers and managers? You might like to compare Dale and Kennedy's models of culture with Hofstede's categorisation of 'national' cultures into four dimensions. In Dale and Kennedy's model, the 'hard macho culture' perhaps equates to cultures of 'high masculinity'.

9.13   This is not to say that one particular organisation culture is suited for each country; many argue that a corporate culture depends more on the **industry sector** than on the **country**.

9.14   That said, to ease communication between managers, many firms rely on corporate cultures to ensure a common value system throughout the organisation as a whole.

9.15   For example, performance related pay for individuals might be applied either in the UK or the USA, but it may have adverse consequences in cultures skewed towards collectivism such as Japan.

9.16   Some cultural problems can be solved if there is some **interchangeability of personnel**. Regular meetings, conferences, summaries, secondments etc can help instil a sense of corporate loyalty, and also give executives skills in dealing with different cultures. The senior managers of many large companies (eg ABB) need to be skilled in negotiating the many cultural minefields which exist in international businesses.

Chapter Roundup

- **Culture** is the complex body of shared beliefs, artefacts and behaviour patterns to which people are exposed in social conditioning.

- Cultures are exemplified in language, religions, customs, value systems, education, law and aesthetics.

- A variety of **frameworks** exist to analyse culture. For example, low context cultures require messages to be clear and direct. High context cultures place more emphasis on body language, and messages are not always explicit.

- Some cultures will resist new products of services if no attempt is made to understand **cross-cultural factors**.

- Culture can be an influence on **buyer behaviour**, but it should be noted that relatively simple models of motivation, such as Maslow's, do not always apply.

- Different types of buyer display different attitudes, needs and purchasing behaviour.

- Different cultures have different ways of doing business and means that people from different cultures have different expectations of a meeting, for example.

- Cultural issues need also to be considered in **organisational terms** to ensure common organisational loyalties.

Quick Quiz

1   Define culture. (see paras 2.1 - 2.3)
2   Describe four types of custom. (2.3)
3   What is the transfer of cultural meaning? (2.7)
4   Distinguish between high context and low context cultures. (3.8, 3.9)
5   What are the two ways of looking at cross-cultural marketing? (4.2)
6   To what extent has there been a 'globalisation' of culture? (4.10)
7   Why might a culture resist 'cook-chilled' foods? (6.4)
8   List three issues in business buyer behaviour. (7.1 - 7.8)
9   What influences government buying? (7.9)
10   Where are there differences in buyer behaviour for services when compared to products? (8.1)
11   What influences affect an organisation's corporate culture? (9.2)
12   What are the four dimensions of the Hofstede model? (9.4)

Action Programme Review

1   (a)   Low-context. Get down to business; security is achieved by a precisely detailed contract.

     (b)   High context. Establish if the other person is someone one can do business with; security is in the relationship.

3   Possible objectives include the following.

- Surplus maximisation (equivalent to profit maximisation)
- Revenue maximisation (as for a commercial business)
- Usage maximisation (as in leisure centre swimming pool usage)
- Usage targeting (matching the capacity available as in the NHS)
- Full/partial cost recovery (minimising subsidy)
- Budget maximisation (maximising what is offered)
- Producer satisfaction maximisation (satisfying the wants of staff and volunteers)
- Client satisfaction maximisation (the police generating the support of the public)

Now try illustrative question 4 at the end of the Study Text

5 Researching and Analysing Overseas Markets

Chapter Topic List	Syllabus Reference
1 Setting the scene	-
2 The role of international marketing research (IMR)	1.6, 1.7
3 Information sources	1.6, 1.7
4 Databases and expert systems	1.6, 1.7
5 The IMR process	1.6, 1.7
6 The uses of IMR data	1.6, 1.7
7 Some problems in IMR	1.6, 1.7
8 Managing the research effort	1.6, 1.7
9 Preparing country files	-

Learning Outcomes

Completion of this chapter will lead to a good knowledge of:

- the use of marketing research to identify international opportunities, similarities and differences

- market research agency selection for international marketing support

- the use of databases and expert systems

- the importance of Government initiatives to support exporters

- the importance of cross cultural analysis in international market appraisal

Key Concepts Introduced

- Marketing research
- Secondary data
- Primary data
- Field research

- Desk research
- Database
- Expert system
- Segmentation

Examples of Marketing at Work

- Databases (FMCG, Sears Roebuck)
- Motor car components supply industry
- CoverStory and SalesPartner
- Mountain bikes

- McDonalds and Kellogg's
- Shiseido
- Market research in Russia

1 SETTING THE SCENE

1.1 Whilst the principle of marketing research remains the same for international markets as for domestic markets, International marketing research (IMR) is often different in practice from research in the domestic market not least because of sources (section 3). Not only are countries different from each other, but there are the major problems of distance and the quality of data to contend with.

1.2 The purpose of IMR is to identify suitable countries for entry (section 6), or suitable groups of countries whose populations segment in a way that can be met by a similar marketing mix.

1.3 Much secondary data is poor (section 7), and the company is even more 'in the dark' about what is going on than they might otherwise suppose. There is greater reliance on human as opposed to documentary sources. Even primary data has to be used with care. Country borders do form barriers and outline separately identifiable markets.

1.4 The organisation of the IMR function (centralised at head office or decentralised) is analogous to most organisational problems in international marketing.

1.5 Finally, since we are concerned in this chapter about the collection of information it seemed a sensible place to put a section on preparing yourself for the examination - section 9: Preparing Country Files.

2 THE ROLE OF INTERNATIONAL MARKETING RESEARCH (IMR)

Exam Tip

Research and the underlying problems involved in researching international markets appears in the exam quite regularly in one form or another. It featured in the June 1997 mini-case. There, you had to advise an American firm on a research program to help it plan its entry into Continental Europe. You could have used the opportunity to develop an MkIS for the company. Primary research relates to buyers and their attitudes: perhaps buyer behaviour in Europe is different from buyer behaviour in the US. The 12 Cs approach (see below) would have helped you to identify information needs. Research also featured in a June 1997 short question about emerging markets.

Reasons for international marketing research

> ### Key Concept
> **Marketing research** is the objective gathering, recording and analysing of all facts about problems relating to the transfer and sales of goods and services from producer to consumer or user. It includes market research, price research etc.
>
> Marketing research involves the use of **secondary data** (eg government surveys) in **desk research**, as well as **field research** (which the firm undertakes itself) to acquire **primary data**, maybe by questionnaire.

2.1 The vast majority of UK companies export less than 10% of their total turnover. They therefore place little priority on what they see as costly market **intelligence gathering** for a minor activity. Where any intelligence is gathered it is usually through intermediaries rather than gleaned directly. However, there are a number of reasons why a company which is seriously intent on international trade should consider devoting more effort to intelligence gathering. If only a few small or medium-sized enterprises made greater commitment to exporting the impact on national finances could be significant.

2.2 The most important requirement of effective international marketing is thorough **market analysis**, both before entering the market and also once the market has been entered, in order to maintain continuous awareness of opportunities, threats and trends.

2.3 Specific objectives of international marketing research include the following.

- Identify attractive **new markets**
- Enhance profitability by pinpointing **opportunities and threats**
- Facilitate awareness of **general market trends**
- Monitor changes in **customer needs and preferences**
- Knowledge of **competitor plans and strategies**
- Identify new **product opportunities** in the marketplace
- Monitor **political, legal, economic, social** and **technological** trends
- Enhance the level and quality of **information** available for planning

2.4 It is obvious that international marketing research is more complex than domestic marketing research because of its focus on more than one country. It requires additional efforts to overcome a lack of empathy with a market and the 'foreign-factor' in general. Thus there is a need to gather information about foreign customer preferences, languages, customs, beliefs etc which in a domestic market could be assumed to be largely known and understood.

Differing IMR objectives of established and new international marketers

2.5 To a company whose horizons have so far been limited to its domestic market, all international marketing research is a new activity. Since it has no experience in foreign markets it needs information to take fundamental decisions. These may be summarised as four questions.

(a) **Should the company look to foreign markets at all?** This will involve an assessment of overseas market demand and the firm's potential share in it compared to domestic opportunities.

(b) **Which market(s) should it enter?** Potential foreign markets need to be ranked according to size, competition, investment and risk.

(c) **How should the company enter the selected markets?** Detailed analysis is required of market size, international trade barriers, transport systems and costs, local competition, government regulations and political stability.

(d) **What marketing programme is best suited to the selected market?** For each selected market a detailed knowledge of buyer behaviour, competitive practices, distribution channels, promotional methods and media will be required.

Doing research

2.6 In considering researching foreign markets, a firm has a number of options.

- Do **no research** at all
- Use **feedback** and assistance from the distribution channel
- Employ an **international research agency**
- Conduct the research '**in-house**'

2.7 There are a number of criteria that will have a bearing on the decision.

- The company's **resources**
- The company's **experience** in international trade
- The **amount of foreign trade** as a proportion of turnover
- The degree to which the foreign trade is **ongoing**

If the answer to all the above questions is 'very little' then it is probably best that the company puts little of its own resources into researching the market, since the return on investment is likely to be poor.

The small company entering a foreign market for the first time

2.8 Many small firms do not carry out any market research at all. There are a variety of reasons.

(a) Small firms generally use **indirect means** of exporting, and hence tend to rely on the channel intermediary for market intelligence.

(b) They often lack the available **resources** to devote to IMR.

(c) The **amount of foreign business** does not warrant significant expenditure on market research.

2.9 The lack of market knowledge, and reliance on the expertise of an intermediary, will limit the ability of the company to expand. For this reason most countries, including the UK, have **sources of low cost advice** and assistance targeted at the small business to encourage the company to develop and expand international trading operations.

The medium sized company wishing to extend its export business

2.10 A company in this situation will be faced with problems of finding new markets, representation, and distribution. There are several options.

- Use **existing channels of distribution** to obtain intelligence
- Use available **assistance and advice services**
- Engage an **IMR agency**

The larger company with overseas presence wishing to increase its foreign market operations

2.11 Larger companies

- Tend to be exporting on a **regular basis**
- Gain between **10% to 30% turnover** from export operations
- Have some '**in house' expertise**, usually in the form of an export department

Major multinationals introducing new products

2.12 The multinational corporation generally tries to introduce products that have a global appeal. Generally such products will be either made under contract, licensed, or made by a subsidiary. Local presence means that the multinational can call upon the expert resources of its own employees in that market. All the IMR activities are usually conducted 'in house'.

3 INFORMATION SOURCES

3.1 Before considering the IMR process in detail it is important to consider the types of data source available to the international marketer.

Human sources

3.2 **Human sources** provide the largest source of information to international marketers.

3.3 For well established international marketing companies, the principal human information source is the **managers** of subsidiaries, branches and associates abroad. Not only do they live in the foreign cultural environments but they also appreciate the company's business objectives.

- They can distinguish relevant from irrelevant information
- They can use **personal contacts** to acquire unpublished information

3.4 Managerial colleagues do not represent the sole source of human information. **Consumers, customers, distributors, suppliers** and even **competitors** are all important sources of information. These groups are particularly valuable in providing marketing assessments from their own particular standpoint. Collectively they may give a balanced view of a market, its potential and its problems.

3.5 Friends, acquaintances, consultants and professional colleagues can provide 'headquarters' marketing managers with information that is reliable and objective.

Documentary sources

3.6 **Documentary sources** are compiled without any knowledge of the reader or the precise purposes for which the information is required.

3.7 The biggest problem in using documentary sources is that there are simply so many of them, whilst none may **specifically address** the point of interest. For example, a marketing manager interested in selling shoe laces in India is unlikely to find written material on such a market, but may have access to numerous pieces on India and on the shoe trade. Without other information sources it would be dangerous to conclude that because say, ninety per cent of the population wore shoes there must be a large market for shoe laces. (The norm may be to wear sandals!)

Direct sources

3.8 Direct sources are those from which the marketing manager derives information without any intermediate analysis that could reduce its levels of accuracy and relevance. There are three general types.

(a) **Direct observation and specialist knowledge.** For example, in a tour around a plastics factory the marketing manager might be shown a new lightweight durable plastic. He knows that a persistent problem with his kitchen appliances has been that they are too heavy to be carried easily, and sees in the plastic a product that might reduce the weight of some of the motor's metal components without losing durability.

(b) **Direct observation and background information.** For example, an international marketing manager based in the UK may have heard of the French hypermarket, and received written reports about them, but only by visiting one can he properly appreciate the ambience they offer to the customer.

(c) **Personal experience supporting indirect information.** For example, a marketing manager considering the potential of the Norwegian market for the firm's product will note from a map that Norway is a geographically dispersed country with rugged terrain. But a plane trip from Oslo to Tromso will indicate just how rugged is the terrain and drive home the point that Norway extends for over 1,500 miles from north to south. Such information should encourage particular attention to distribution plans.

Sources of information and assistance to UK firms

3.9 A UK company is able to obtain considerable help and advice in its attempts to research foreign markets. Contacts may be made with a variety of organisations, including the following.

- Overseas agents and distributors
- Banks
- Trade and professional organisations
- Chambers of Commerce
- Department of Trade and Industry
- UK and foreign embassies and consulates
- Academic institutions
- Business Links

3.10 Depending on the help and advice sought there may be a charge involved but it is usually a nominal one. Financial assistance may be obtained in certain cases through the **Overseas Trade Services** under the following schemes.

- Export market research scheme
- Outward mission
- Market entry guarantee scheme
- Overseas trade fairs
- Overseas seminars
- Inward missions

Export data services

3.11 The **Overseas Trade Service** has export databases, library facilities and publications to enable businesses to conduct preliminary desk research, plus customised export intelligence.

- Export information
- The Export Market Information Centre (EMIC)
- Export publications
- Export intelligence
- Specialist market knowledge

BPP PUBLISHING

3.12 **Export information.** This gives both first time and experienced exporters access to up-to-date information concerning new opportunities. The DTI maintains a collection of overseas market information. This is complemented by numerous trade publications, directories, statistical material and published market research. This information is a great help to exporters.

- Compare different markets
- Select the best market(s)
- Analyse chosen market(s)
- Understand business methods in chosen markets
- Find out about tariff and legal requirements
- Prepare for a visit
- Identify potential agents
- Keep up with new business opportunities

3.13 **Export Market Information Centre.** EMIC is a self-help research and library facility. Information available in EMIC includes foreign statistics on trade, production, prices, employment, population and transport as well as development plans of many countries which are useful guides to the current and future state of specific economies as well as highlighting specific opportunities.

3.14 **Export publications.** The DTI publishes a wide range of country and sector reports.

3.15 **Export intelligence.** Export success frequently depends on gathering timely information about possible opportunities overseas. Exporters can arrange to be kept up to date with the export intelligence from the DTI, the EU and the World Bank. Export intelligence includes selling opportunities such as enquiries from overseas buyers and agents and market information on tariff changes, forthcoming projects, aid and loan agreements.

3.16 **Specialist market knowledge.**

- The political and economic scene
- Local conditions for doing business
- Market prospects and product suitability
- Local tariffs and other import regulations
- Business contacts
- General help doing business in that market

Specific export help

3.17 Help related to specific exporting problems is organised through a variety of services listed below.

(a) **Enterprise Initiative:** specialist consultancy advice and financial assistance in key areas.

(b) **Export Development Advisors** (EDA): identification and dissemination of good exporting practice.

(c) **Market Information Enquiry Service** (MIES): tailor-made information on the country/markets chosen.

(d) **Export Marketing Research Scheme** (EMRS): marketing research advice and financial assistance.

(e) **Export Representative Service** (ERS): advice on overseas contracts.

(f) **Overseas Status Report Service** (OSRS): information on agents and distributors.

(g) **New Products from Britain Service:** promotion of products in overseas publications.

3.18 You may have read in the newspapers about trade deals and government promotions. Overseas promotion aided by the UK government takes a number of forms.

- **Overseas trade fairs** - provide direct contact with buyers and agents
- **Outward missions** - financial and administrative support to visit overseas markets
- **Overseas seminars** - increase overseas awareness of your goods and services
- **Overseas stores promotions** - provides a shop window for the exporter's products
- **Inward missions** - influential contacts invited from overseas
- **Projects export promotion** - co-ordinate government assistance for large projects

3.19 For companies wishing to expand their business and find new markets, the **DTI Explorer Initiative** offers assistance by organising escorted trips to trade fairs, and helping with such things as interpreters and provision of up-to-date information.

3.20 Before companies seeking international marketing opportunities do anything else, they should look at the **Internet**. Sites such as 'Market Explorer' can give the first taste of a potential export market, and indicate the more accessible countries.

Action Programme 1

Why is it important for UK small businesses to consider exporting?

3.21 Other commonly consulted sources are listed below.

(a) The **Bank of England** and the major UK banks produce booklets on trade prospects for various countries.

(b) The **broadsheet newspapers,** in particular the *Financial Times* produce periodic surveys on various countries.

(c) The **Economist Intelligence Unit** produces reports on various industries, countries and long term developments.

(d) Most **major trade associations** and Chambers of Commerce hold data on trade fairs, visits and market intelligence for various countries.

(e) There are numerous **trade directories** for overseas markets including Kompass, Dunn and Bradstreet, Kluwer and Crone.

(f) The **EU** and **OECD** produce numerous reports on trade statistics and prospects for member countries.

(g) The **Department of Trade and Industry** provides many publications, statistical summaries and intelligence reports.

(h) The **CBI** produces a monthly report on foreign markets.

(i) The **Office of National Statistics** produces regular data on international trade.

- Guide to Official Statistics
- Monthly digest of statistics
- Overseas Trade statistics

(j)   Many reference libraries subscribe to **syndicated market research** and abstract services including ANBAR, Keynote, Mintel, Extel, and Euromonitor.

3.22   Various **international bodies** including the United Nations, the European Union, the Organisation for Economic Co-operation and Development and the International Monetary Fund produce statistical publications on a variety of areas.

3.23   Most of the sources surveyed here have their counterparts in other countries.

(a)   Foreign **governments and international bodies** (such as the United Nations) publish reports and statistics.

(b)   Foreign **trade associations** and industry bodies publish surveys. Many also have international links.

(c)   **International news** and information agencies (such as Reuters) publish world-wide reports.

(d)   **Resource guides** (such as *Published Data of European Markets* or the British Overseas Trade Board's *Market-Search)* provide links to recommended international sources of information.

(e)   International **newspapers and journals** are available (in print, and frequently also on the Internet).

(f)   **Internet sites** give access to foreign educational and governmental institutions and their databases, and to the websites of commercial organisations around the world. Access is not restricted to working hours (which helps when there are time differences) and information can be downloaded for later translation.

Documentation

3.24   The **red tape** of international marketing requires that a great deal of information has to be processed by a wide range of people working in different languages with different systems. **Mistakes** in the information provided by exporters and a lack of management attention often cause problems.

- **Relationships** with overseas customers are harmed by delays
- **Orders and profits** may be reduced or lost

3.25   **SITPRO** is an independent body which has the prime objective of simplifying and reducing the cost of international marketing. It has gained a worldwide reputation for the development and **standardisation** of international marketing procedures and documents as well as providing advice and guidance to UK traders on effective practices and information systems. Since non-tariff barriers have been reduced, the **complexity** of the export process has surfaced as a major barrier to trade.

Internet information

3.26   The term 'information market' reflects the growing view that information is a commodity which can be bought and sold.

3.27   **Information is a resource** that has many of the characteristics of any other resource. In particular, the growth of the **service sector** of many western economies has led to an increasing importance being attached to information.

3.28 The amount of **information** in the world is **doubling every seven years**. One half of every thing a college student learned in his or her first year is obsolete by the time they graduate. The amount of knowledge we are asking a typical A level student to learn is more information than their grandparents absorbed in a lifetime.

3.29 The communication super highway is **destroying old power structures** As knowledge flows into every home on demand, it **empowers consumers.** Consumers can scan the world's data base for the best bargains. They can instantly order products from their computers. Speciality use groups will band together to apply political pressure, share their experiences, address educational problems and strategies. The Internet allows consumers to self-educate. When consumers do these things they bypass the educational system, the medical system, the publishing system and the current political system.

3.30 Most transactions at present are done either in shops, via mail order or via the telephone. The Internet offers an alternative way of doing business, and as e-commerce increases the following social phenomena are likely to be observed.

(a) **Travel**

Rather than visiting shops and people can obtain what they want without leaving their desk. This should make shops and roads less crowded and more pleasant for those who still use the. In the long-term it may affect where people choose to live.

(b) **Consumer choice**

A computer search for an item or service can be done in seconds, whereas it could take hours, days or weeks to find exactly what was wanted by more conventional means. Consumers are also not restricted to local providers: they can do business with any company in the world that has a website. On the one hand this increases choice for consumers, but on the other it may make the purchase decision more difficult, because there are more options.

(c) **The 'size' of society**

Following on from point (b), society itself becomes global. People do business in places and with organisations that they would never have considered or even known about before.

(d) **Time management and quality of life**

Rather than being restricted to business hours people can obtain what they want 24 hours a day. This helps people to manage their time and do what they want to do at their own convenience.

(e) **Interaction**

Instead of dealing face-to-face or voice-to-voice with others, people interact with their computer. If human contact is valued, this makes the experience a poorer one. On the other hand it removes possible sources of conflict.

(f) **Work opportunities**

There will be fewer opportunities for people to work in sales roles that involve direct contact with others, but greater opportunities to work in distribution and transport. In the long-term this could be a major change since both sectors employ large numbers of people.

4 DATABASES AND EXPERT SYSTEMS 12/99

4.1 A management information system or **database** should provide managers with a useful flow of relevant information which is easy to use and easy to access.

> ### Key Concept
> In simple terms, a **database** is a large file or files of data, with the file structured in such a way that the data can be processed by different users in a larger number of different ways.

4.2 A database is, by implication, a computer file, and the collection of programs that are written to process data on the file in the many different ways is referred to as a **database management system (DBMS)**. These systems provide managers with support for their decision making. Marketing data can be analysed using statistical techniques, in models on anything from media mix to new site locations.

4.3 Our interest in databases is simply a user interest, because databases can provide valuable information to international marketing management.

(a) Computer databases make it easier to **collect and store** more data/information.

(b) Computer software allows the data to be **extracted from the file and processed** to provide whatever information management needs.

(c) Developments in **information technology** allow businesses to have access to the databases of external organisations. Reuters, for example, provides an **on-line** information system about money market interest rates and foreign exchange rates to firms involved in money market and foreign exchange dealings, and to the treasury departments of a large number of companies.

(d) The growing adoption of technology at **point of sale** provides an invaluable source of data to both retailer and manufacturer.

4.4 Many companies, ranging from direct mail houses to domestic appliance retailers, already have detailed information on their existing records.

Marketing at Work

Even organisations in the FMCG field, such as Nestlé, Pedigree Petfoods and Kraft General Foods, are consolidating data that they accumulate about their customers and in the USA, Sears Roebuck uses the computerised database information on its 40 million customers to promote special offers to specific target segments. MCI, the US phone company, has a database of 120 million subscribers.

4.5 The result is something called **mass customisation** in which a large number of customers can be reached, as in the mass markets of the industrialised economy, and simultaneously these customers can be treated individually, as in the customised markets of the pre-industrial economy.

4.6 McNamee lists nine areas of **environmental data** that ought to be included in a database for international marketing planners. These are as follows.

(a) **Competitive data**

- The threat of new entrants
- The threat from substitutes
- The power of buyers

- The power of suppliers
- The nature and intensity of competition
- The strategies or likely strategies of competitors

(b) **Economic data.** Details of past growth and predictions of future growth in GDP and disposable income, the pattern of interest rates, predictions of the rate of inflation, unemployment levels and tax rates and developments in international trade.

(c) **Political data.** The influence that the government is having on the industry

(d) **Legal data.** The likely implications of recent and future legislation.

(e) **Social data.** Changing habits, attitudes, cultures and educational standards of the population as a whole, and customers in particular

(f) **Technological data.** Technological changes that have occurred or will occur, and the implications that these will have for the organisation

(g) **Geographic data.** Data about individual regions or countries, each of them potentially segments of the market with their own unique characteristics

(h) **Energy suppliers data.** Energy sources, available and price of sources of supply generally

(i) **Data about stakeholders in the business.** Employees, management and shareholders, the influence of each group, and what each group wants from the organisation

In other words data which covers the key elements of the general and market environment should be included in a database for international marketing planners.

4.7 There is nothing magical about databases. They are just **elaborate filing systems,** and in nearly all instances the information on the database is also available in traditional hard copy format. Indeed, much of the database information may have been transferred to the database from a paper publication of some kind.

4.8 As we have said, technological developments have enabled businesses to have access to other organisations. Two premium-price on-line sources specifically tailored to the needs of marketing and advertising are Harvest and MAID (Marketing Analysis and Information Database).

4.9 There are a number of problems associated with on-line databases.

(a) Without planning and skill in carrying out on-line **database searches**, the expense can become prohibitive.

(b) Because efficient use of on-line databases requires skill, a commitment to **training** is essential.

(c) On-line databases do not yet cover all important marketing research sources. Particular omissions are parts of the trade press and some important statistical data. Total reliance on databases and an attitude of if-it-isn't-on-the-screen-it-doesn't-exist could be dangerous.

(d) On-line database searching can yield lots of **data** but not much worthwhile **information.**

4.10 Databases are becoming increasingly specialised.

Marketing at Work

One example of using external databases is found in the motor car components supply industry. Manufacturers of motor car components supply their products to the car manufacturers, and they need to be able to spot trends in the use of components by car manufacturers throughout the world. A few years ago a number of databases became available for the component suppliers.

(i)   PRS, the consultancy group, has built up a database which can provide a detailed breakdown of the constituent parts of motor vehicles produced worldwide, making it possible for component suppliers to identify trends in their market.

(ii)   Another PRS database holds data about new car registrations in Europe for at least the last ten years. This should be of interest to component suppliers who supply replacement parts to the 'aftermarket'.

(iii)   A database available from James McArdle and Associates, another consultancy firm, provides data about commercial vehicle production.

'It is possible, as just one example, to ask the database to show, over a five-year rolling period, manufacturers and their country of origin of commercial vehicles defined by the number of axles, vehicle weight, torque or power output, or cubic capacity - or a combination of these.'   *Financial Times*

Such databases could be used by component suppliers to take much of the guesswork or number-crunching out of their planning, and to assess the likely future demand both for replacement parts and for original equipment.

4.11   Databases have to be used with caution, however.

- How up-to-date are they? Some data can 'date' very quickly.
- Reliability? Is the information accurate?
- Security?
- Legality?

Expert systems

Key Concept

Expert systems are computer programs which allow users to benefit from expert knowledge, information and advice.

4.12   An expert system is therefore a program for which the master/reference file holds a large amount of **specialised data.** The user keys in certain facts and the program uses its information on file to produce a decision about something on which an expert's decision would normally be required.

4.13   Expert systems can give factual answers to specific queries, but they can also indicate to the user what a decision ought to be in a particular situation, and in this respect, expert systems can be a form of **decision support system** for managers. Applications of expert systems include the following.

(a)   In some database systems, to speed up the process of retrieving data from a database file.

(b)   In diagnostic systems, to identify causes of problems, such as in production control systems.

(c)   International tax advice.

(d)   Forecasting of economic or financial developments, or of market and customer behaviour.

(e)   Project management.

(f)   Surveillance, for example of the number of customers entering a supermarket, to decide what shelves need restocking and when more checkouts need to be opened.

Expert systems and marketing

4.14   In theory, expert systems are essential to today's goal of **precision marketing** (the mass-customisation model in which the marketing approach is matched precisely to the needs of the individual).

Marketing at Work

In the USA, Sears-Roebuck targets those of its customers who have purchased domestic appliances without any associated maintenance cover, in a drive to sell them general maintenance contracts.

4.15   Precision marketing is problematic because of the difficulty of manipulating the **vast quantities of data** involved. Until recently, even starting on such a task was near impossible; nowadays computers can easily handle the 'paperwork' involved, although they cannot so easily take decisions without being fed very elaborate sets of rules to govern every possible situation.

4.16   The expert system is the longer-term solution to this kind of dilemma. With an expert system, the computer can be taught how to make the necessary decisions using **artificial intelligence**. It may even 'learn from experience' in some circumstances.

4.17   Expert systems have been used to filter marketing data for quality problems, to develop forecasts, to set sales targets and to train sales teams. The problem to be solved must be clearly defined and narrow in scope, and the benefits of developing the ES should outweigh the costs.

Marketing at Work

Schmitz, Armstrong and Little (1990) describe a system called CoverStory which uses several expert systems to identify trends from scanned sales data then automatically writes memos that summarise important trends for marketing managers. Another system, called SalesPartner, helps sales representatives by using a retailer's historical data to develop sales presentations.

4.18   Other marketing related expert systems have been developed.

- To set marketing objectives
- To select advertising strategies
- To recommend promotions
- To filter new product ideas

5   THE IMR PROCESS

5.1   A diagram of the process of international market research is shown on the next page.

Stage 1: monitoring international markets

5.2   **Monitoring** is by far the most widespread activity in international marketing research. It involves **passive information gathering** in which the organisation has identified a particular market on which information needs to be collected but, as yet, does not warrant active measures.

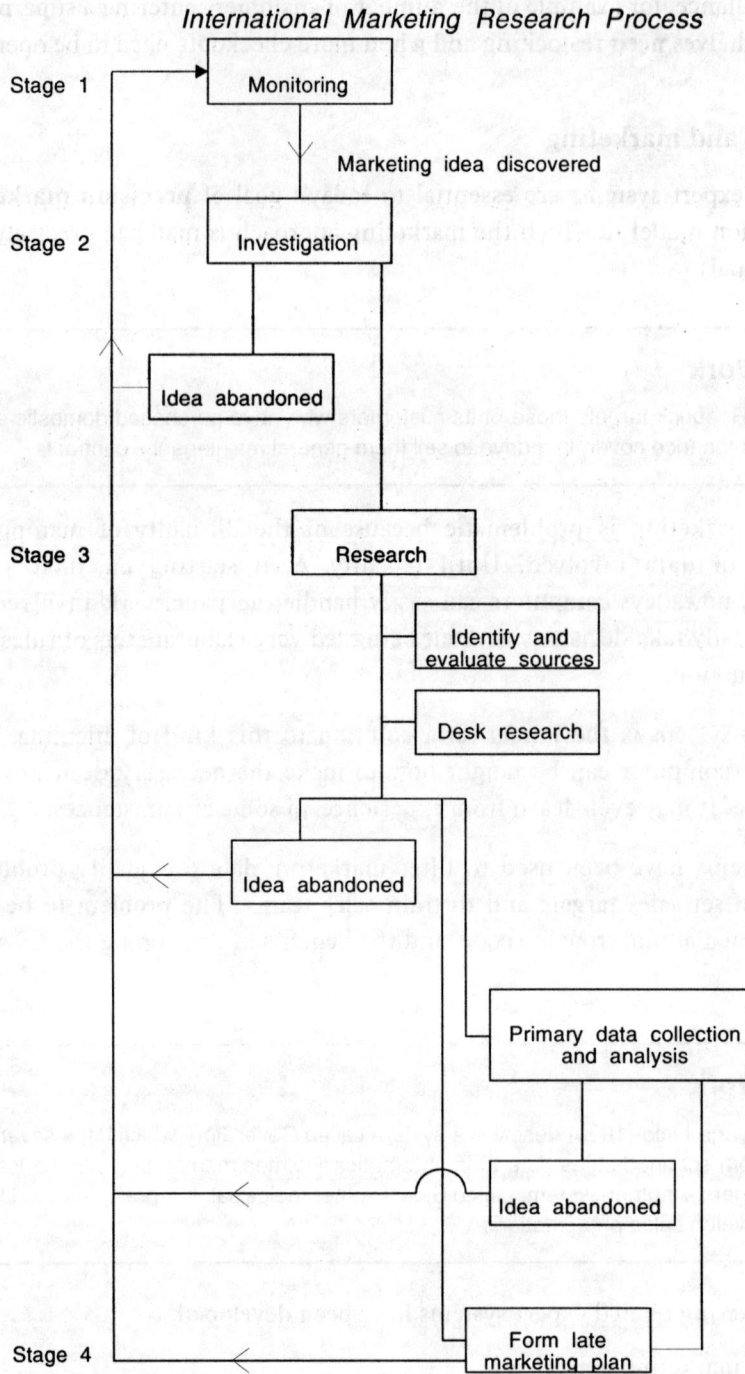

International Marketing Research Process

Stage 1 — Monitoring

↓ Marketing idea discovered

Stage 2 — Investigation

Idea abandoned

Stage 3 — Research

Identify and evaluate sources

Desk research

Idea abandoned

Primary data collection and analysis

Idea abandoned

Stage 4 — Form late marketing plan

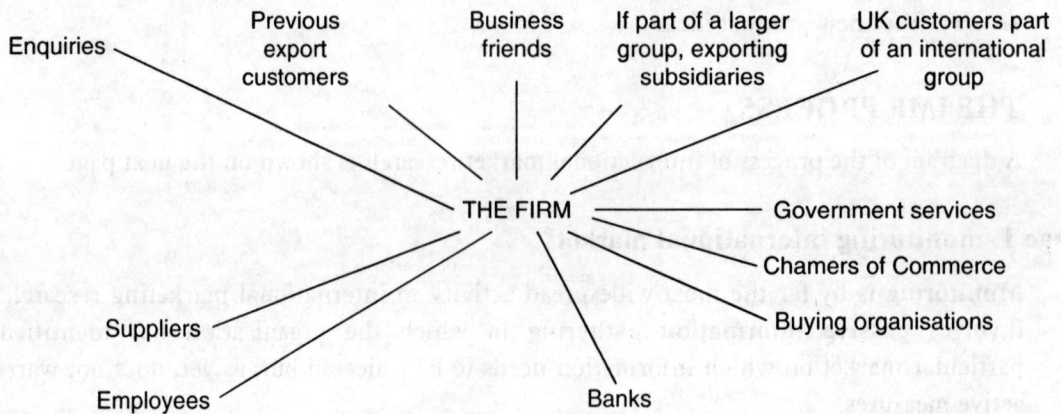

Enquiries

Previous export customers

Business friends

If part of a larger group, exporting subsidiaries

UK customers part of an international group

THE FIRM

Government services

Chamers of Commerce

Buying organisations

Banks

Employees

Suppliers

5.3   If the information that has been acquired indicates the potential for a new market, the manager will proceed to the next stage, investigation.

Stage 2: investigation

Market opportunity

5.4   The most important aspect of the investigation stage is the accurate assessment of market opportunity.

(a)   **Existing demand** concerns current purchases of the type of product. Often, it is this demand that originally attracted the company's management to the market during the 'monitoring phase'. The level of existing demand alone may be enough to justify entry to that market, to win a share.

(b)   **Latent demand** is demand which exists in the market but is currently **untapped** because of a defect in the marketing mix used by existing suppliers. Often it is simply a question of price but it may be that the distribution channels are not adequate or that the product does not offer features which that market particularly values.

Marketing at Work

The success of mountain bikes depended on new product features. Although in industrially advanced economies bicycles were regarded as a product of the leisure market rather than as a means of transport, their design gave them a rather 'tame' image, perhaps a two-wheeled version of rambling! The introduction of a more rugged design and other product features (such as styling and colour) designed to appeal to the youth market opened up a whole new segment of the bike market.

(c)   **Incipient demand** is the demand that depends on trends. It is used most often by manufacturers of goods that require wealth levels in an economy to be above a certain minimum before the volume of demand becomes sufficiently great for the market to become profitable.

5.5   It is possible to add to these categories three different types of product.

(a)   (i)   **Competitive:** the product is similar to the competition.

(ii)   **Improved:** the product is similar in nature to current products, but demonstrably better in some way.

(iii)   **Breakthrough:** the product is completely new.

(b)   These can be tracked to the assessment of demand.

(i)   An **improved** product makes it easier to enter an **existing** market.

(ii)   **Breakthrough** products are useful for entering existing markets, but where demand is latent or incipient, the marketing effort - to create the market - will be high.

Stage 3: research

5.6   By this stage of the IMR process the new marketing idea has to look sufficiently promising to be worth **committing** a significant budget to. Whereas during the investigation stage enquiries are often informal and information may be collected as part of other activities, market research proper is proactive. In the international context, this can be expensive.

BPP PUBLISHING

Planning

5.7 A vital part in any research exercise is to plan it properly. Although no entirely standard plan can be drawn up, it is likely to have the following elements.

(a) **Define the scope of the project**

Identify the geographical and political market(s) of interest, the market segments and, not least, the end objective.

(b) **Define the project's information needs**

There must always be a balance struck between the use of information and the cost and difficulty of obtaining it. Posing the following questions will help in finding the correct balance.

(i) Why is the information needed?

(ii) If it is obtained, how will it be used?

(iii) Where may information be obtained from? Is it available directly as a secondary data source, capable of production by analysis or manipulation of existing secondary data, or does it require primary data collection?

(iv) What is the information worth in financial terns?

(v) What is the cost of not obtaining it?

(c) **Evaluate the available sources for the required information**

It is no use for the international marketing manager to assume that because 'data' are available they will necessarily be valuable! Often great caution is needed and problems in interpreting data for international marketing purposes are considered later in the chapter.

(d) **Undertake the desk research and evaluate its findings**

Desk research, using documentary sources, should always be done before conducting or commissioning any primary data collection. It is almost invariably cheaper and, if its results are disappointing, the project may be abandoned without any primary data collection being undertaken at all. Even if the project does continue, and primary data is needed, careful analysis of the secondary data can focus attention on the exact primary data requirement and so reduce the costs of the research exercise.

(e) **Undertake field research**

The collection of **primary data** is sometimes known as field research. Field research is carried out 'on the spot' in a number of areas, notably customer research, advertising research, product research, packaging research and distribution research. Techniques involved in the collection and analysis of primary data are as follows.

• Experimentation	• Consumer panels
• Sampling	• Trade audits, such as retail audits
• Piloting	• Pre-tests
• Observation	• Post-tests
• Questionnaires	• Attitude scales

(f) **Knowledge of the culture** of a society is clearly of value to business. Marketers can adapt their products and appeal according to the culture of their intended export market. Multinational companies often establish new subsidiaries in a different country. Much was made of the cultural difficulties which Nissan was supposed to encounter when investing the US and UK. Nissan had to teach its new recruits about the culture of the company.

Marketing at Work

Both McDonalds and Kelloggs suffered setbacks when trying to penetrate the Indian market. McDonalds has had to come to terms with a market that considers killing cows to be sacrilege, is averse to pork, is 40% vegetarian, hostile to frozen meat and fish, and very fond of spices.

Kelloggs was unsuccessful in persuading Indians that its cereals were a healthier alternative to traditional heavy Indian breakfasts.

Desk research requirements

5.8 Phillips, Doole and Lowe (*International Marketing Strategy*) suggest a '12C' checklist for information which a marketing information system for international markets should contain. This is shown on page 120. Desk research involves work in two main areas.

(a) Collecting information

- The business environment as a whole (**general background analysis**)

- The country's economic structure of particular relevance to imports (**market access analysis**)

(b) Beyond this general level, desk research is concerned with obtaining as much information as possible on the structure of the market for the company's goods, the practices of the market and an analysis of competitor's positions. Each of these is considered below.

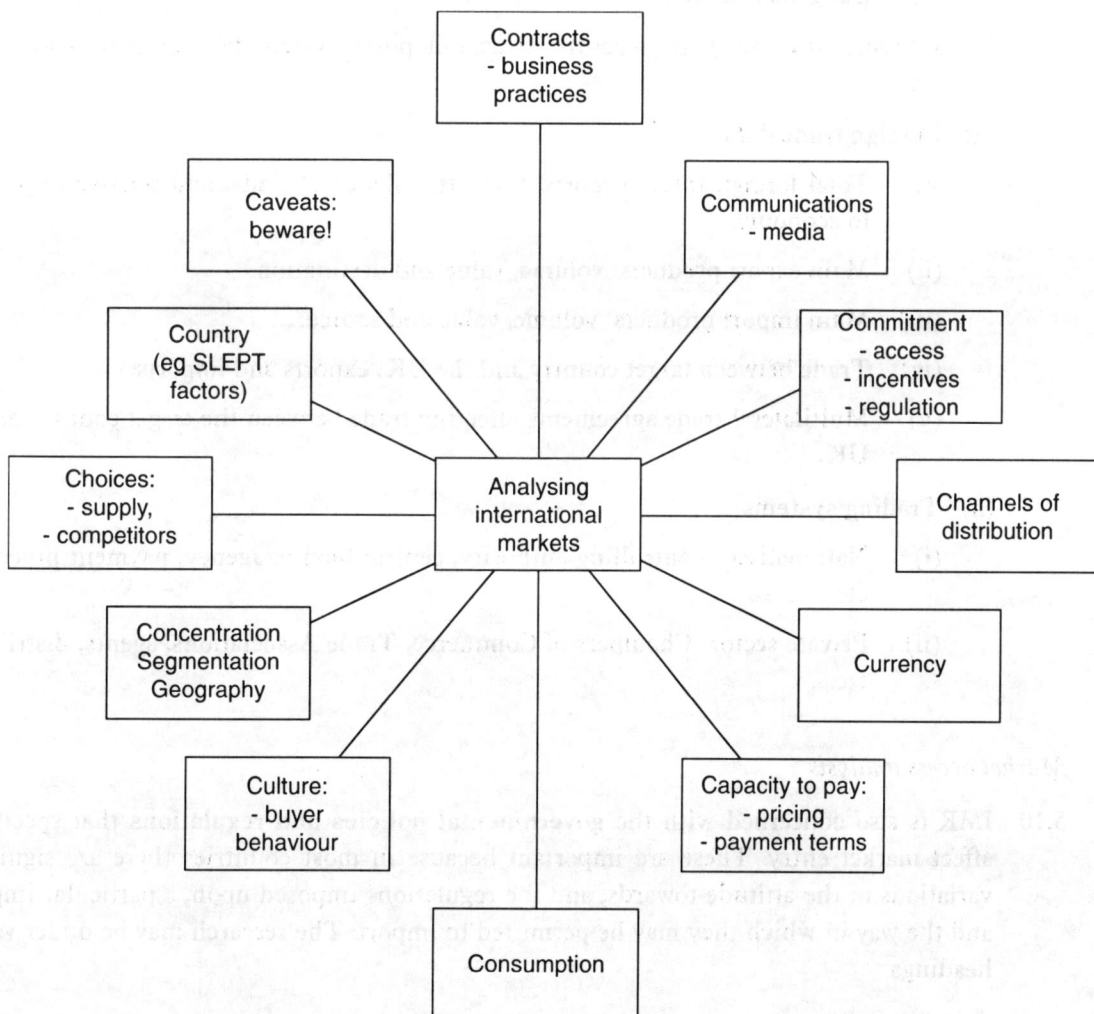

BPP PUBLISHING

General background analysis

5.9 It is important that the firm has a sound general knowledge of the country. This involves analysing various data.

(a) **Geography:** location, size, topography, climate and so on.

(b) **Population:** size, distribution by location, race, religion, income, education, age, gender etc.

(c) **Language:** official, business and other indigenous languages.

(d) **Government:** type of constitution, roles of central and local government, political climate and attitudes to foreign trade, economic and social policies.

(e) **Basic economic data**

(i) Indicators: currency exchange rates, balance of payments, foreign currency reserves, debt situation, GNP, GDP, national income, per capita income and price inflation indices.

(ii) Structure of the economy: rate and distribution of employment, output of the various industrial, service and extractive sectors.

(iii) Economic Development Plans: funds allocated, time horizon, target sectoral allocations etc.

(iv) Policy relating to foreign investment: both inward and outward.

(v) Budgetary provisions.

(f) **Infrastructure:** sea ports, airports, roads, rail, postal system, telecommunication system etc.

(g) **Foreign trade data**

(i) Total foreign trade: exports, imports, balance of trade, and relative importance to economy.

(ii) Main export products: volume, value and destination.

(iii) Main import products: volume, value and source.

(iv) Trade between target country and the UK: exports and imports.

(v) Multilateral trade agreements affecting trade between the target country and the UK.

(h) **Trading systems**

(i) Nationalised: controlling authority, central buying agency, payment procedures etc.

(ii) Private sector: Chambers of Commerce, Trade Associations, agents, distributors etc.

Market access analysis

5.10 IMR is also concerned with the **governmental policies and regulations** that specifically affect market entry. These are important because in most countries there are significant variations in the attitude towards, and the regulations imposed upon, a particular importer and the way in which they may be permitted to import. The research may be under various headings.

(a) **General import policy**

    (i)   Membership of customs union, free trade area, WTO etc.

    (ii) Special trade relationships between the trading countries involved (for example between the UK and Commonwealth countries).

(b) **Restrictive import licensing regulations:** categories, conditions for acquisition, procedures etc.

(c) **Import tariff system:** classification system, tariff rates, bases of assessment for duty etc.

(d) **Other factors:** foreign exchange controls, import deposit schemes, anti-dumping and minimum price regulations; food, health and safety regulations; selling, promotion, packaging and labelling restrictions; patents and trademark protection in that country; fair trade and anti-trust rules; taxation and shipping documents required.

(e) **Ownership of trading companies** by foreign nationals: restrictions, regulations and imposition of local ownership.

Market structure

5.11 In order to trade in a foreign market it is vital to have a detailed knowledge of the **market structure and behaviour**. Knowledge of the composition, profile and behaviour of the market is fundamental to marketing, whether domestic or internationally based. Typically in an international context, information is required on the following points.

(a) Who are the **main customers**? How, why, where, when and how much do they buy?

(b) What are the **main channels of distribution** used in such markets? Who are the main distributors, agents etc? Do reciprocal or other possibly limiting trading practices exist that could hamper market entry?

(c) What **product attributes**, specifications and developments are there in the market?

(d) Who are the **main suppliers** to the market? What are their relative positions, shares, strengths and weaknesses, strategies and performance?

(e) Are there significant **geographic variations** in customer requirements, distribution costs, product use, and promotional needs?

(f) What **facilities** are there for promoting the product into the market? What is the effectiveness of the various forms of promotion and media available?

(g) What is the **size** of the total market and potential target segments? How durable is the market? For example is it likely to disappear in adverse economic or political conditions?

Competitor analysis

5.12 World market competition is intensifying in most products and markets. If a company is interested in anything more than an insignificant niche in world trade it must have an extensive knowledge of **competitors' plans**. A firm should be aware of the following.

(a) **Major competitors:** their number, size, market shares and nationalities.

(b) Do the major competitors have **full market coverage**? Do they instead specialise in certain geographic areas or market segments? Do their product ranges contain gaps?

Market practices analysis

5.13 It is very rare that the marketing mix relevant to one country can be imported unadapted to another. Hence the international marketeer needs to assess the relevant aspects of the mix suitable for the target country. These include the following.

(a) **Transport facilities**: types, prices, reliability and risks (both within and between the relevant countries).

(b) **Distribution channels**: relative costs and benefits; possible alternatives; channel norms and trading behaviour.

(c) **Pricing strategy**: upper and lower limits, competitor prices compared to product features and appeal, discount structures etc.

(d) **Promotional factors**: methods normally used in the market, levels of expenditure and availability.

(e) **Product and services**: required features and facilities before, during and after sale. Warranties, information, credit etc as forms of product enhancement.

6 THE USES OF IMR DATA

6.1 Many firms engaged in IMR seek to spread their activities over a number of countries, and so one purpose of IMR must be to ensure that strategic positioning of products and the appropriate marketing mixes are duly identified.

6.2 IMR data can therefore be used in the following ways to identify market opportunities.

(a) To estimate product **patterns** of demand/or consumption in individual markets.

(b) To **compare** patterns of demand or consumption in different markets.

(c) To identify **clusters** of markets with similar characteristics, which can be targeted with similar mix.

(d) To identify **strategically equivalent** segments, across country boundaries.

Predicting patterns of demand

6.3 Patterns of demand change over time, for many reasons, such as changes in customer needs and expectations on the one hand, or radical product innovations on the other. Demand for computers is far higher than it used to be, because they are so much cheaper. IMR can identify trends in demand both directly, and also by inference.

Demand pattern analysis

6.4 **Demand pattern analysis** involves analysing production patterns (as a surrogate for demand) over time. It helps in identifying general marketing opportunities and, because it uses **production** statistics, it can indicate potential markets. For example, the graphs below show twentieth century trends for a variety of basic product groups with changes in GDP per capita.

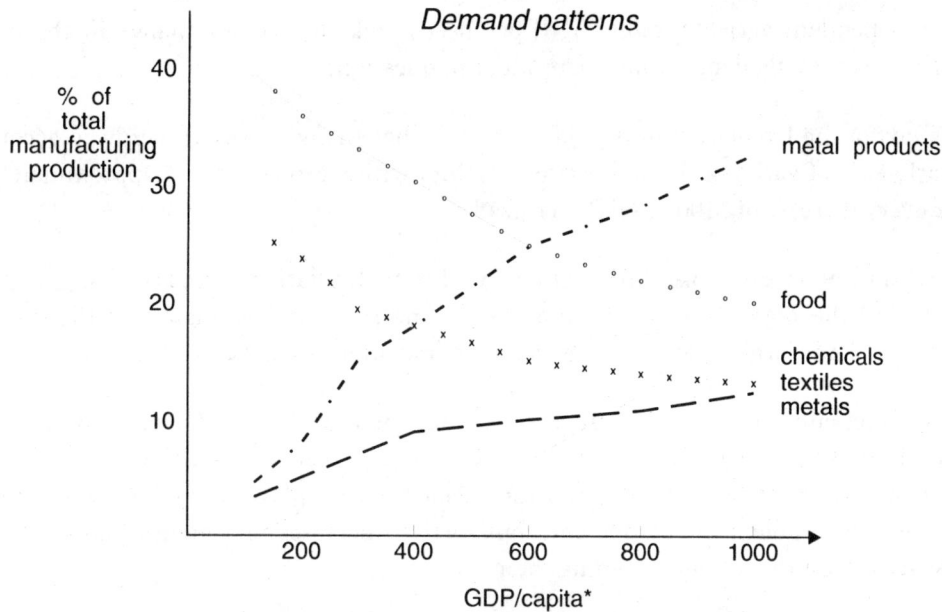

Demand patterns

* GDP translated into constant US dollars

Income elasticity

6.5 We can also estimate effective demand from how much people earn. **Income elasticity** studies are concerned with specific products. Income elasticity describes the relative changes in demand for a product with changes in income levels.

Income elasticity is expressed as:

$$\frac{\text{Change in product demand} \div \text{Product demand}}{\text{Change in income} \div \text{Income}}$$

(a) Some goods are **income inelastic**. As people get richer, demand for such goods does not increase proportionately. For example, poor people might spend over 50% of their income on basic foodstuffs. In wealthy countries such as the UK, food accounts for about 11%. British people do not eat less, but food takes up a lower proportion of their income.

(b) Goods which are **income elastic** are very sensitive to changes in people's income. These include leisure products, some consumer durables etc.

Multiple factor indices

6.6 It is commonly the case that data of the kind required for direct analysis of a market is unavailable and thus the market researcher must find alternatives. **Multiple factor analysis** attempts to surmount this problem by using surrogate variables that can be closely correlated with demand for the company's own product.

6.7 There is clearly much scope for error, but this may be reduced by using variables that are as close as possible to demand for the product. So whereas, for example, growth in total population might be found to have a good statistical correlation with demand for compact disc players, changes in population in the 15-30 age group is likely to be a better indicator. Changes in personal disposable income may be a better indicator again.

Regression analysis

6.8 **Regression analysis** takes the ideas of multiple factor indices further and adds some statistical rigour. The usual form the technique takes is **linear regression**, where change in

BPP PUBLISHING

an independent variable (often GNP per head) seeks to explain change in the dependent variable (normally demand for the product in question).

6.9 A study of the US market in the 1960s showed that changes in GNP per head accounted for nearly 80% of variation in radio set ownership, with a growth rate of approximately 25 sets for every increase of $100 in GNP per head.

6.10 Care must be taken to use this technique within its limitations. In particular, the predictive ability of the regression may be limited to a narrow band of change in the independent variable. To return to the radio sets example, one might find the situation shown overleaf.

6.11 The regression line can be extended at will but the growth rate of ownership of radios may fall above a certain income level. This is to be expected by intuition. As average wealth increases there comes a point when the majority of people who wish to own a radio have become rich enough to buy one and thus further increases in average wealth have less and less impact on the numbers owning them.

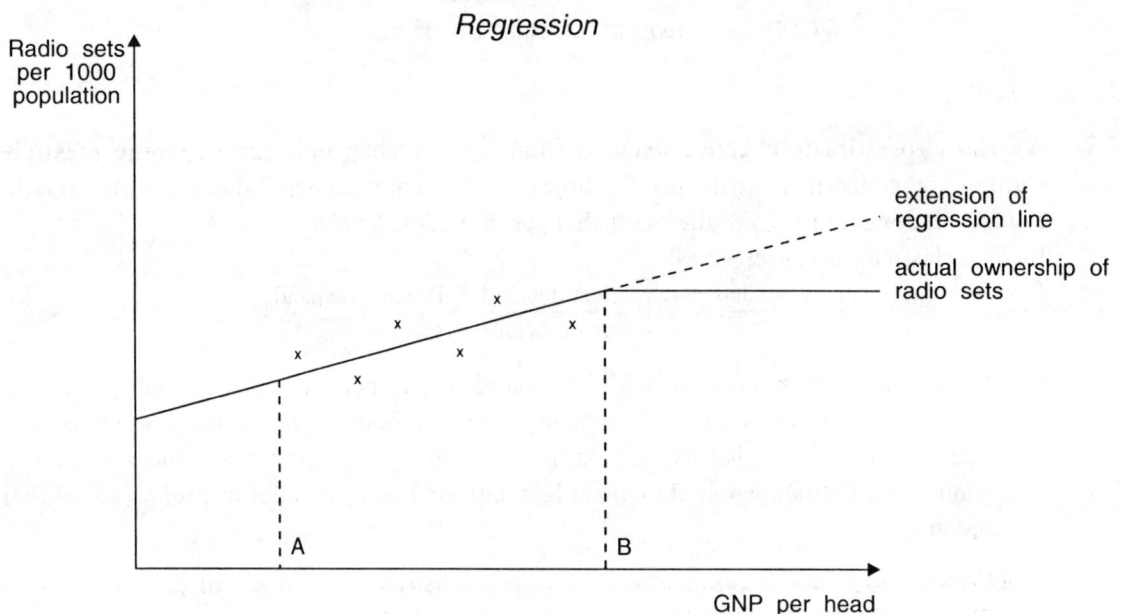

Regression

Radio sets per 1000 population

extension of regression line

actual ownership of radio sets

A   B

GNP per head

Comparing patterns of demand/consumption in different markets

Comparative analysis

6.12 **Comparative analysis** assumes that if market potential is equivalent in two markets then marketing performance should be comparable too. It usually takes the form of comparison of the same company's performance in two (or more) national markets. If the economies are broadly similar but performance is not (or vice-versa) it suggests that marketing performance is not being optimised and thus raises questions to be addressed.

Factors in a comparative analysis include many of the SLEPT factors.

- Size of population
- Age structure
- Geographic distribution
- Incomes
- Lifestyles
- Communications
- Ability to pay
- Barriers to entry

Inter-market timing differences

6.13   This technique uses the premise that certain markets have **similar demand patterns** for similar goods but that one leads and the other lags. Clearly this technique is useful only for comparing countries that can be assumed to have similar economic, social and cultural conditions. The diagram below shows the similarity in the rate of acquisition of television in the 1950s and 1960s between the UK and West Germany. At its simplest, the technique enabled the prediction of growth or decline in the then West German market by taking that of the UK market a few years earlier and adjusting for the different numbers on households in the two markets.

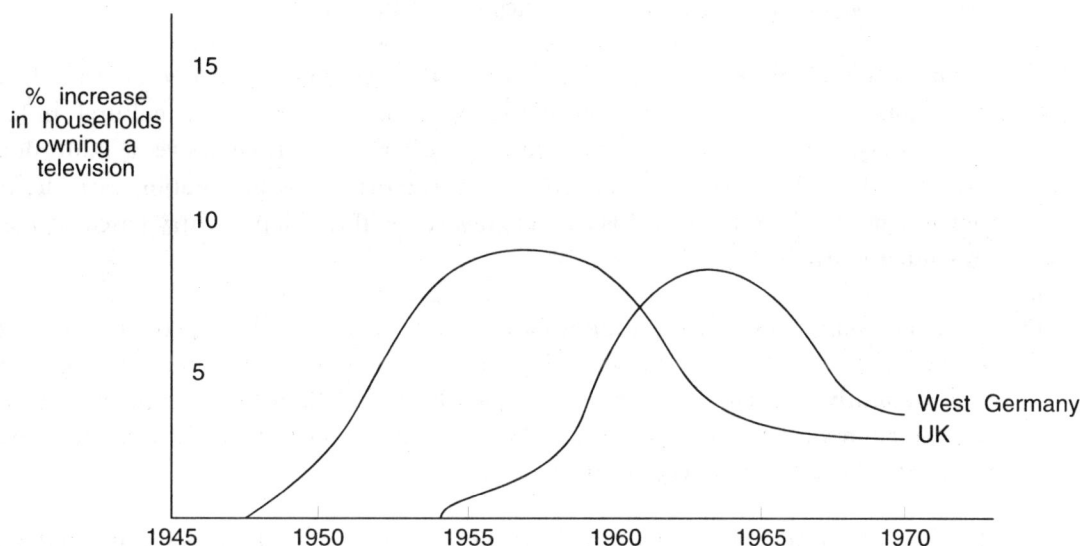

Identifying clusters of markets with similar characteristics

6.14   A logical extension of using one market to predict the behaviour of another is to identify **clusters of markets** with the same characteristics. Put another way, this is rather like segmenting groups of customers - instead the countries of the world are being segmented. (Do **not** confuse this with clustering as described by Michael Porter in *The Competitive Advantage of Nations*.) **Cluster analysis** involves mathematical techniques - too complex to describe here - to identify similar markets.

(a)   Sethi suggested four sets of variables in which each country could be compared.

   - **Production and transportation**
   - **Consumption** (income, eg number of cars)
   - **Trade data** derived from import or export figures
   - **Health and education**

   Each of these were scored, and countries were fitted into one of seven groups, with the implication that the similarity of countries within a group was strong enough to justify similar marketing approaches.

(b)   **Business International** identified indices covering market size (eg population), market growth rates and market intensity (relative concentration of wealth and purchasing power). For example the USSR, Poland and Brazil occupied one cluster, having enjoyed similar growth rates between 1986 and 1990 and having a similar 'intensity'.

Identifying strategically equivalent segments   Specimen paper

6.15   In addition to identifying clusters of countries, it is possible that a firm may wish to segment each market and pursue these segments only.

> **Key Concept**
> **Segmentation** is the subdividing of the market into increasingly homogenous subgroups of customers, where any subgroup can be selected as a target market to be met with a distinct marketing mix.

6.16 In international marketing, as in domestic marketing, firms can use more than one segmentation variable, a **primary segmentation** variable and a **secondary segmentation** variable. For example, for wet shaving equipment, the primary segmentation variable might be sex (Gillette produces different razor blade holders for men and women), and secondary segmentation variables might be age or lifestyle (or any others).

6.17 In international marketing, using **country** as the **primary** segmentation variable would seem common sense, certainly for consumer products, given the cultural influences, political risk factors and so forth identified earlier. If a firm pursues a multi-domestic strategy it will almost certainly use country as the primary segmentation variable. Even a global firm, to whom the world is a single market, will develop country-based segments in **consumer markets.**

6.18 Take the example of a firm selling walking sticks in the EU. Using country as the prime segmentation variable may cause confusion. The country markets for walking sticks are each **naturally** segmented by **age.** Consequently, rather than using country as a primary segmentation variable, it might be sensible to use **age** instead to avoid separately targeting segments whose needs are very similar.

6.19 This leads us to the notion of **strategically equivalent segments,** which transcend national boundaries. Here are some possible examples.

(a) In South East Asia, people of Chinese ethnic extraction form the business elite in many countries (eg Malaysia) despite government attempts to reduce imbalances. Therefore, for certain types of goods and services, overseas Chinese (eg in Malaysia, Singapore, Thailand etc) could be considered a strategically equivalent segment.

(b) Geodemographic segmentation can also be used. CCN **EuroMosaic** analyses ten classifications of European consumers as shown below.

• Wealthy suburbs	• Industrial communities
• Average-income areas	• Dynamic families
• Flats - luxury	• Low income families
• Low income inner city	• Farming/rural
• Municipal/social housing estates	• Holiday/retirement areas

6.20 Such worries may not exist for many **industrial markets**, where there are fewer buyers, and where purchase decisions are in theory taken according to rational criteria. The market for aircraft engines comprises the world's airlines, and it may not be possible or necessary to segment this market.

Marketing at Work

Japan's population profile is ageing more rapidly than that of most other countries. Thus, Shiseido, the cosmetics company, launched Acteaheart, a range of cosmetics specially aimed at women over 40. This might also be considered a strategically equivalent segment in other markets which Shiseido may wish to target - the US and the wealthy Asian countries.

BPP PUBLISHING

7 SOME PROBLEMS IN IMR

Researching numerous markets

7.1   In the initial stages, international marketing research may address a hundred or more markets in the broad scan for market opportunities, and certainly concentrate on a minimum of a handful of markets as enquiries become more focused. This generates a number of problems.

(a) **Cost versus profit** considerations. Researching multiple markets can give rise to economies of scale and experience but even so a marginal cost is incurred for each. Moreover many markets are small, heterogeneous and with limited profit prospects. This then justifies only moderate market research expenditure and has forced IMR practitioners to develop methods and techniques geared to limited budgets. It also requires the researcher to exercise judgement as to which countries would be worth investigating. Hence the importance of informal methods of research at the initial stages.

(b) **Differences between countries** gives rise to several problems.

(i)   **Definition:** defining the problem with respect to various countries. Bicycles are treated as recreational items in the UK, largely sporting in nature in parts of continental Europe, and as a means of transport in much of the Third World. Thus the definition of research to be carried out and the categories provided in surveys should be sufficiently broad to encompass the variety of uses, reasons and responses that might be evoked.

(ii) **Classification:** meaning and classification problems in surveys and their analysis due to different behavioural and living patterns.

(iii) **Frame:** sources of sampling frames from which to draw samples may not be reliable, especially in under-developed countries.

(iv) **Non-response:** the desire to co-operate with a survey will largely depend on the norms of that culture. It should not be assumed that questions freely answered in one country will be accepted in another.

(v)   **Comparability** is weakened by many factors, particularly differing cultural values, consumption patterns, political influences and reliability of data sources.

Secondary data problems

7.2   There are normally three critical deficiencies regarding secondary data that are important to the international market researcher.

(a) **Lack of data.** Without doubt, the USA has the best documented commercial information. Key economic indicators, compilations of trade statistics and the work of trade associations, state and local government, and management groups, are readily available to the market researcher. But few countries come close to matching the sheer volume and diversity of data collected in the USA. Until the United Nations began assimilating world economic data, there was often little available other than very rough estimates for many lesser developed countries.

(b) **Comparability** and **timeliness.**

(i)   This problem is at its most acute in less economically developed countries which, despite recent attempts to remedy the situation, often choose to devote a rather lower proportion of their resources to data collection than advanced economies. As a consequence data is often many years out of date and collected on an infrequent and unpredictable schedule.

(ii)   More specific problems involve different definitions used in data collection, the fact that different base years have been used for comparative purposes and that gaps may exist. As an example a television is classified as household furniture in the USA but not in Germany (where it is treated as a recreational purchase) leading to problems of comparability of data collected in different countries.

(c)   **Lack of reliability** of some of the secondary data that are collected. Much of it has to be analysed with great care.

(i)   In many economically underdeveloped countries, national pride takes precedence over statistical accuracy.

(ii)   Moreover, companies have been known to reduce their production statistics so that they reconcile to sales reported to the tax authorities!

7.3   As a practical matter, before basing a marketing strategy on the analysis of secondary data, it is worthwhile asking the following questions.

(a)   **Who** collected the data? Would there be any reason for deliberately misrepresenting the facts?

(b)   For what **purpose** was data collected?

(c)   **How** was the data collected (ie what was the survey methodology used?)

(d)   Is the data **consistent with one another** and are they logical (in the light of known data sources or market factors)?

Marketing at Work

One of the problems of doing market research in Russia is identifying groups of consumers. Official statistics leave a lot to be desired, given the enormous social changes over the past few years.

Researchers have begun, however, to identify new segments, from wealthy entrepreneurs to poorer people dependent on state pensions. Rather than outlining a simple rich/poor divide, a number of groups have been identified.

Problems in collecting primary data

7.4   Where the informal and secondary sources are inadequate, as a last resort the market researcher must turn to collecting **primary data**. This is both expensive and difficult and the task is often handed over to specialist agencies to carry out. The problems involved in primary data collection include the methods of data collection, non-response, survey control, illiteracy and language.

Data collection

7.5   Except in the most unusual circumstances it is too time-consuming and too expensive for the market researcher to survey the whole of the target population for the product under consideration (even if it can be defined adequately in the first place). Consequently a **sample** needs to be taken.

Questionnaires

7.6 Survey research, to obtain primary data, normally requires a questionnaire. There are three main characteristics of a good questionnaire.

- The questions are easy for interviewees to answer and for the interviewer to record
- It acquires the necessary information but keeps the interview to the point
- It is straightforward

7.7 In order to make sure that the questionnaire achieves these characteristics, a number of **design principles** need to be adhered to. The main ones are as follows.

- Questions should **address** one point only
- Questions that suggest their **own** answer should be avoided
- Ensure that questions **mean** one thing only
- Make the language in which the questions are framed easy to understand
- If at all possible, the questionnaire should list the possible replies to questions
- Avoid asking questions of a personal and potentially embarrassing kind

---

Action Programme 2

Design a short questionnaire about a product of your choice. Try it out on a colleague and ask your colleague to give you marks as to whether you have satisfied all the criteria above.

Problems in response

7.8 People's unwillingness to provide information is a feature of many countries. Several reasons can be suggested for this.

(a) **Tax evasion and avoidance of responsibility**. Anyone asking questions may be suspected of being a government employee.

(b) **Wish to preserve secrecy**. Many business managers regard data relating to their company or markets as potential help to competitors and accordingly response rates are low when they concern anything that might be regarded as an aid to a competitor.

(c) **Cultural taboos and norms**

(i) Topics that are freely discussed in some countries (for example birth control methods) are taboo for discussion in others except in the most intimate situations.

(ii) Similarly the authority to respond may not be the same in all cultures. Thus whilst in one country a female head of household may feel authorised to discuss a topic with a researcher, in other countries there may be a marked reluctance to give information.

7.9 In carrying out surveys, firms in the UK take many things for granted that may not exist in other countries, particularly less developed ones.

(a) There may be no suitable lists (**sampling frames**) from which a representative sample can be selected.

(b) In many countries there is a dearth of economic, demographic and social **statistics** on which to base sampling methods.

(c) Inadequate **communication infrastructure** can be a severe practical handicap.

(d) Low levels of **literacy**.

(e) Problems of **language and comprehension** are widespread in IMR. Differences in idiom and problems of precise translation lead to great misunderstandings. In large countries such as India the researcher has to be prepared to deal with some fourteen languages and 200 dialects when planning a survey.

7.10 This discussion should make it clear that there is a greater necessity for **care, understanding and skill** in IMR data analysis.

(a) Thus the analyst requires an extensive understanding of the cultural environment of the countries being researched and a talent for interpolating data that contains gaps or has other deficiencies.

(b) A final requirement would be a **healthy scepticism** towards both primary and secondary data since they are very likely to be imperfect, resulting in a desire to cross check and substantiate data wherever possible.

8 MANAGING THE RESEARCH EFFORT

8.1 International marketing intelligence is crucial for a firm's strategic decisions and for the on-going implementation and review of marketing plans. The collection of strategic intelligence has to be co-ordinated.

- At the appropriate level in the organisation
- At the appropriate time

8.2 Not only does data have to be collected, it has to be **communicated** to the right area of the organisation.

8.3 For decisions made by local **subsidiaries**, the information will be gathered and stored locally. The international **headquarters**, however, can operate as a clearing house for research studies, actively passing on information to those who might benefit from it.

8.4 **International head office** may conduct research on its own, perhaps on issues relevant to all markets or in areas where there would be duplication if the subsidiaries did all the work themselves.

8.5 Some firms have **regional** HQs as well, covering a number of countries. The advantages of one MR department are economies of scale, and the ability to concentrate efforts.

8.6 Co-ordinating the **timeliness** of information is important. After all, if a product launch is critically dependent on marketing intelligence, any delay can be costly.

8.7 An important management decision is the extent to which firms use **agencies** to conduct their IMR.

Using external agencies

8.8 IMR managers face considerable problems in obtaining useful information at a reasonable cost. The manager may consider hiring an external agency to carry out IMR. Before hiring such an agency however the firm must make three crucial decisions:

Whether to hire an agency or not

8.9 There are a number of factors favouring the hire of an agency.

(a) The firm may have little or no **marketing research resources**.

(b) The firm does have marketing research resources but these are subject to **peak demands**. Thus it may be more economical to hire agencies to meet peak loads than to increase the firm's permanent resources.

(c) The firm may have little or no **experience of the foreign market** to be analysed. Here an agency with that specific market experience may be of great value.

(d) The research is of a **highly specialised** kind involving skills not present in the firm (for example behavioural studies).

(e) The research is a 'one-off' exercise and thus it would be uneconomic to develop 'in-house' expertise.

(f) The firm anticipates **language or cultural problems** in carrying out the research that their own expertise cannot cope with.

(g) Management requires an **objective view**, which is often difficult when its own employees are aware of the pressures within the firm for a particular answer.

8.10 On the other hand, there are also several factors that would favour 'in-house' research.

(a) **Lack of suitable marketing research agencies** in the foreign markets to be investigated.

(b) The firm is **well experienced** in IMR and has a good understanding of the cultural and other conditions that might affect the research.

(c) The relevant **resources and skills** already exist in the firm.

(d) The firm needs to develop a **thorough knowledge** of the market. Agencies do provide information, but they may leave the firm without the extensive knowledge which is required to get a 'feel' for the market.

(e) The firm would find it difficult to **brief** the agency adequately on its research objectives and the technical parameters and applications of the product.

(f) The research project is a **small** one, requiring few interviews and relatively little time.

(g) It may be **cheaper** for the firm to execute its own marketing research. It is quite likely that economies of scale and experience can be achieved when studies are duplicated in multiple countries.

Which type of agency to select

8.11 In general terms the firm may engage any one of three types of agency to execute its IMR.

(a) **Foreign agency domiciled in the target country.** This offers the major benefit of having a comprehensive understanding of the local market, language, culture and business environment. However, it requires costly and time consuming visits by the firm's personnel to select and brief the agency, and then to supervise the project.

(b) **Domestic agency sending competent staff to the target country.** This is beneficial insofar as it permits easy and cheap selection, briefing and supervision of an agency. It should also offer a high standard of marketing research skills and may be less costly than hiring a foreign agency. A serious disadvantage would arise, however, if the

BPP
PUBLISHING

agency or its personnel were not in fact thoroughly familiar with the foreign market, its culture or its environment.

(c) **Domestic agency with foreign agency subsidiaries, associates or subcontracting arrangement.** This is the synthesis of the above two alternatives. Here the domestic agency works in conjunction with its overseas associates.

(i) The benefit for the firm is that it only has to select, brief and supervise the domestic agency which in turn acts on behalf of the firm with the foreign agency. Further it is assumed that the foreign agency will have a thorough understanding of the target market, its culture and its environment.

(ii) The major disadvantage of such an arrangement is that the firm has little or no control over the selection and supervision of the foreign agency. Additionally there may be some communication problems between the two agencies, and the cost of utilising two agencies may be greater than with direct hiring.

(d) **Global agency** with a worldwide presence.

Selecting a particular agency

8.12 Whatever type of agency the firm finally decides to hire, it must select an appropriate agency to carry out the research. This involves obtaining information about the various agencies to evaluate their suitability and acquiring a research proposal from each for assessment. Agencies might be invited to tender.

8.13 **Briefing.** Each agency approached will require certain **guidelines** from the firm to ensure that the proposal which it prepares is appropriately formulated.

- A clear written statement of the **research problem**

- An indication of the **way in which the research findings will be used**

- An indication of the approximate **budget**

- An opportunity for the agency to **discuss** the proposed programme

8.14 **Shortlisting.** In making a shortlist, the firm should take the following factors into account.

(a) Evidence of suitable **background and experience** of the agency staff in IMR and the target markets.

(b) Details of any **specialist staff** (statisticians, analysts, psychologists and so on) used by the agency.

(c) **Agency experience** in relevant IMR areas, foreign markets, products and research techniques.

(d) **Quality and reliability** of field operations including the selection and training of staff, levels of supervision, and control and monitoring procedures.

(e) Where large amounts of data are to be collected, the agency's **facilities for data processing**, analysis and report preparation.

(f) The financial **status** and reputation of the agency.

A **recommendation** from other satisfied users of an agency can be a significant aid in shortlisting a suitable agency. The informal network outlined earlier in this chapter can be utilised here.

8.15 **Final choice.** The agency selected from among the shortlisted and submitted proposals will be the one which puts forward the most appealing blend of the following.

(a) A demonstration of a sound grasp of the research problem and its objectives.

(b) A detailed description of the research including a statement of the scope and nature of preliminary desk research, pilot studies and qualitative research. Where quantitative research is involved, a statement of the data collection method, the population to be sampled, the sample size and the sampling technique.

(c) A statement of the staff involved and their duties.

(d) A statement of the total cost with a detailed breakdown of the component costs, and a reasonably detailed timetable for the research programme, including a final reporting date.

9 PREPARING COUNTRY FILES

9.1 In *Marketing Success*, the examiner noted the following.

'Questions often require candidates to compare and contrast international marketing planning from countries in different stages of economic development. Create a series of country files, for underdeveloped, emerging and industrialised countries. The quality press do country profiles. This saves you having to "think on your feet" during the examination'.

Selecting countries

9.2 The examiner suggests creating files for underdeveloped, emerging and industrialised countries, as well as one for Europe.

(a) Do not rely on outdated perceptions of which countries are undeveloped and which are not. Try to be up-to-date.

(b) Some industrialised countries, such as the US, are huge markets in their own right, and you would almost certainly drown in data. The US is the world's most advanced economy, but it is more regionally diverse than might appear.

(c) Do not insist on using your holiday destinations as examples, unless you can back them up with other data. In some countries, the tourist industry is distinct from the rest of the economy.

(d) Look at a map of the world - only there will you get some idea of the choice available to you. Do not rely on memory alone. Although the Pacific Rim is developing fast, Latin America and the Middle East can be considered, and what about the new states in ex-Soviet Central Asia?

(e) Choose your countries from different regions of the world. For example, you might choose an emerging country from the Americas, an industrial country from Asia and an underdeveloped country from the Middle East. This will give you some geographical scope.

(f) You might also like to include in your assessment an element of political risk (ie low, medium and high), as well as other developments.

Arranging your file

9.3 When you have chosen your target countries, you need to set up a file as follows.

Basic data

9.4 First of all you need **basic data,** hopefully recent, about the country. This you can glean from the most recent *Hutchinson Encyclopaedia,* or similar publication. Data might be as follows.

- Area
- Capital city
- Other major towns
- Environment (eg mountainous, desert, wet, dry)
- Physical infrastructure
- Communications infrastructure
- Political system (eg liberal democracy, military republic) and political parties
- Main exports
- Currency
- Population: this gives the potential size of the consumer market
- Life expectancy
- Gross national product, and gross domestic product
- Religion
- Level of literacy
- Media (independent? state controlled? Number of newspapers, TV stations)
- Recent political developments

9.5 **Gross national product** gives some idea of the overall **size of the economy. Gross domestic product** identifies the economic output of the country. Dividing gross domestic product by the population gives an approximation to gross domestic product per head, an indication of the wealth of the country.

9.6 **Life expectancy** gives some assessment of **wealth** and **health.**

Examples

9.7 Once you have got hold of this information you should collect articles from marketing journals, quality newspapers, and so forth. The *Financial Times* and the *Economist* regularly profile overseas countries. The UK government publishes *Overseas Trade* about overseas markets and successful UK exporters. Look for articles which offer one or more of the following.

(a) **Significant relevant background data about the country.** For example, a slow rise in the Japanese yen will mean higher-priced, hence less competitive, Japanese exports and cheaper imports.

(b) **Items relating to international marketing. Do not** stick **only** to fast moving consumer goods. Many developing and expanding countries are investing heavily in large **infrastructure** projects, which provide major opportunities for overseas producers.

(c) Describe the activities of **individual companies** in the region.

- Strategic issues
- Mode of entry issues
- Tactical implementation issues
- Problems and opportunities
- Organisation structure

(d) Look also for exporters **from** your chosen country.

Exam Tip

The examination paper has been 'internationalised', so you could get a question about a Japanese firm investing in Thailand, say, or even in the UK.

Chapter Roundup

- **International marketing research** is more complex than domestic marketing research, as there are additional factors to consider. Some foreign markets may be attractive commercially, but there may be legal barriers to entry. Detailed **analysis** of international trade regulations could be appropriate, as would be a general background analysis of the country, its market structure, competitors, market practices and access.

- IMR information can be used to predict patterns of demand, to compare different markets, to cluster countries and to identify strategically equivalent segments.

- **Databases and expert systems** can provide useful information. Expert systems in particular represent a leap in information effectiveness because of their ability to make 'decisions' and promote precision marketing.

- Some **government agencies** offer specific export assistance, often in terms of advice and promotional help.

- International market research is made difficult by the existence of different **cultural assumptions** in the foreign market, which may distort the results of research designed for use in the home country. Moreover, secondary data may be non-existent and unreliable.

- **Cross cultural differences** must be recognised when undertaking IMR.

- The commissioning of a **research agency** experienced in the overseas market might be advisable, although the market knowledge provided may not be less thorough than it would be if the firm did the research itself.

Quick Quiz

1   What are the objectives of IMR? (see para 2.3)
2   What four IMR options exist? (2.6)
3   What is the main source of marketing information? (3.2)
4   What are the sources of assistance available to UK companies considering conducting IMR? (3.9)
5   What export data services are provided by the Overseas Trade Service? (3.11 - 3.16)
6   What is SITPRO? (3.25)
7   What is a database? (4.2)
8   What environmental data should be included on the database of the international marketer? (4.6)
9   What is an expert system? (4.12)
10 Outline the process of IMR. (5.1)
11 Why might latent demand exist? (5.4)
12 Outline a plan for an IMR project. (5.7)
13 When a company has selected a potential target country for possible market entry, what general background information would be required to develop effective marketing plans? (5.9)
14 What are the uses of IMR data? (6.2)
15 What is a comparative analysis? (6.12)
16 List problems in IMR. (7.1)
17 What are the characteristics of a good questionnaire? (7.7)
18 What are the problems to be considered in deciding whether or not to use an agency to carry out IMR? (8.9-8.10)

Action Programme Review

1   Aside from the possibility of increasing sales, exporting provides exposure to more rigorous market disciplines than might be available in the home market. Moreover, it might provide information about competitors' products. The foreign market may also be a source of new ideas.

Now try illustrative question 5 at the end of the Study Text

Part B
International strategic planning

6 Going International: Planning for International Marketing

Chapter Topic List	Syllabus Reference
1 Setting the scene	-
2 The features of international marketing	2.1, 2.2
3 The reasons for starting to market internationally	2.1, 2.2
4 Choice of market and extent of involvement	2.1, 2.6
5 The marketing programme and type of marketing organisation	2.2
6 Good practice in IM planning	2.2
7 Some issues and problems in IM planning	2.2
8 The international marketing planning process	2.8, 2.9
9 Competitive and product-market strategy decisions	2.2
10 Lesser developed economies	2,1, 2.8

Learning Outcomes

After completing this chapter you will have an understanding of:

- differences in marketing planning between developed and lesser developed countries

- organisational and management issues pertinent to international marketing planning

- non-linear approaches to planning such as emergent strategies

- the effect of global operations on a host country

- sources of global finance (an introduction)

Key Concepts Introduced

- Economies of scale
- Risk
- Undifferentiated, differentiated and concentrated marketing
- Planning
- Mission
- Position audit

- Ethnocentrism
- Polycentrism
- Geocentrism
- Emergent strategy
- Cost leadership, differentiation and focus
- Emerging market

BPP PUBLISHING

Examples of Marketing at Work

- Standardisation and cultural influences
- Contrasting cultural values in the US and Japan
- National Power
- Thorntons
- Heineken
- Skoda
- Jollibee/McDonalds
- Bajaj/Honda
- Ford Union
- Mars
- Unilever, Snickers and Heinz

- Johnson and Johnson
- Volvo
- Pepsi
- British Airways
- Tandy
- Honda
- Hoffman-La Roche
- Pharmaceuticals
- Eurofighter
- Vehicle manufacturers
- Tata group of companies

1 SETTING THE SCENE

1.1 Having in Part A outlined the pressures and obstacles in the international trading environment, in this chapter we narrow the focus to the decisions taken by the individual company in its international marketing (IM) activities.

1.2 This chapter refreshes what you have learnt so far, and forms an opening to the rest of the Study Text. Of course, general marketing principles apply, but particular international planning issues are also covered in this chapter.

1.3 We describe the contents of a typical international marketing plan, and the different levels for which international considerations are necessary.

1.4 Mode of entry and organisational issues are covered in Chapters 7 and 8. Part C deals with the detailed implementation of the marketing mix, and control.

2 THE FEATURES OF INTERNATIONAL MARKETING

2.1 At one extreme IM may consist of **exporting** from one nation to another while at the opposite extreme it refers to a company which both **produces and markets** in many countries without its goods crossing national frontiers. Ford, for example, exports cars from the UK and imports cars into the UK.

2.2 It is possible to identify the following.

- The **marketing mix** (product, place, price, promotion, and people, processes and physical evidence), in other words the **controllable factors**

- **Uncontrollable factors** arising from SLEPT or PEST factors and competition

2.3 A key factor in IM is the concept of **'foreignness'**. This arises due to environmental differences among countries and it is a principal difference between domestic marketing and IM.

Marketing at Work

Some major companies such as IBM disregard the notion of 'foreignness', treating different countries as distinguishable businesses to be managed using orthodox SWOT analysis.

Industries such as aircraft engines, memory chips, and telecommunications face enormous fixed costs for product development, capital equipment, marketing and distribution. Consumers are satisfied with standardised products in such areas because cultural influences on product design and promotion are relatively low.

2.4 A final issue is the relative **complexity** of international marketing which (according to Doole, Lowe and Phillips, *International Marketing Strategy*) might involve the following.

   (a) **Export marketing** (eg the export from the UK of goods to another country).

   (b) **Multinational marketing:** an organisation operates in more than one country.

   (c) **Global marketing** treats the world as a single market, or at least as one which can be addressed on a worldwide basis.

Some differences between domestic and international marketing

2.5 Sound marketing principles are generally applicable universally. However, there are major environmental differences between home and overseas markets and therefore marketing principles need to be adapted accordingly.

Action Programme 1

Draw up a list identifying the main differences between domestic and international marketing.

Differences among international markets

2.6 An obvious, but important, point is that there are often very large differences among **environmental conditions** in different overseas markets.

Marketing at Work

The table below contrasts cultural values in two of Britain's export markets - namely the USA and Japan.

Contrasts in culture, tradition and behaviour

United States	*Japan*
1 Individualistic	1 Collective
2 Independent	2 Dependent
3 Authoritative decision making	3 Participative decision making
4 Competitive	4 Co-operative
5 Style: confrontation	5 Style: compromise
6 Quick decision making but slow implementation	6 Slow (due to consensus) decision making but quick implementation
7 Direct	7 Indirect
8 Short-term view	8 Long-term view
9 Communications are one way and secretive	9 Communications are interactive and open
10 Efficiency orientated	10 Effectiveness orientated
11 Management is control orientated	11 Management is customer orientated
12 High job mobility and low loyalty	12 High loyalty
13 Incompetence is fatal	13 Shame is fatal

BPP PUBLISHING

United States	Japan
14 Heterogeneous society: dynamic melting pot	14 Homogeneous society: gradual screening process
15 Relaxed and casual in attitude	15 Tense and formal in attitude
16 Enjoyable	16 Serious
17 Specialist is valued	17 Generalist is valued
18 Freedom and equality	18 Reliance upon order and hierarchy

Source: Keegan

2.7 To what extent are international and domestic marketing radically different?

(a) Can the **same approach** to marketing be applied to each market?

(b) Should each country be treated as a **separate market**?

(c) **Is globalisation** eroding the differences between markets?

(d) **A global niche marketer** would view national and international markets as essentially the same.

Some key decisions for international marketing

2.8 Firms must deal with six major issues in IM.

- Whether to market abroad at all
- Which markets to enter
- The mode(s) of entry
- Marketing programmes
- Marketing organisation
- Marketing mix

3 THE REASONS FOR STARTING TO MARKET INTERNATIONALLY

3.1 Firms may be **pushed** into IM by domestic adversity or **pulled** into IM by attractive opportunities abroad. More specifically, some of the reasons firms enter into IM are the following. They can be classified as either **internal** or **external** factors.

(a) **Chance.** Firms may enter a particular country or countries by chance. A company executive may recognise an opportunity while on a foreign trip or the firm may receive chance orders or requests for information from potential foreign customers.

(b) **Life cycle.** Home sales may be in the mature or decline stages of the product life cycle and IM may provide for sales growth since products are often in different stages of the product life cycle in different countries.

(c) **Competition.** Intense competition in the domestic market sometimes induces firms to seek markets overseas where rivalry is less keen. This was a major reason in Gillette's decision to begin marketing razor blades outside its US home markets.

(d) **Reduce dependence.** Many companies enter into IM to diversify away from an over-dependence on a single domestic market. For example, many UK firms entered into or increased their IM involvement to escape the worst effects of the economic recession which began in the 1970s.

(e) **Economies of scale.** Technological factors may be such that a large volume is needed either to cover the high costs of plant, equipment, R&D and personnel or to exploit a large potential for economies of scale and/or experience. For these reasons firms in the aviation, ethical drugs, computer and automobile industries are often obliged to enter multiple countries.

> ### Key Concept
> **Economies of scale** come about as reductions in the average cost of producing a commodity, as the output of that commodity increases. To take a retailing example, Wal-Mart's size means that an American DIY enthusiast can pick up a hammer in one of its stores for the same price a British retailer would buy it from the manufacturer. Wal-Mart's buying power can command a far lower price.

(f) **Variable quality.** IM can facilitate the disposal of discontinued products and seconds since these can be sold abroad without spoiling the home market. Many Third World customers, for example, are willing to accept imperfect goods sold at low prices. Conversely, many companies, such as most UK pottery manufacturers, reserve their first quality outputs for sale in lucrative high income countries like the USA, selling only seconds in the home country.

(g) **Finance.** Many firms are attracted into IM by favourable opportunities such as the development of lucrative Middle Eastern markets, marked depreciation in their domestic currency values, corporate tax benefits offered by particular countries and the lowering of import barriers abroad.

(h) **Familial.** Many countries and companies trade because of family or cultural connections overseas. For example, the Kenyan horticultural industry exports to the UK.

(i) **Aid agencies.** Countries that benefit from bilateral or unilateral aid often purchase goods which normally they would not have the money for. Toyota vehicles have been bought for aid projects in Africa via UNDP funds.

3.2 In terms of formal marketing objectives, the **traditional** view is that in domestic markets firms are concerned mainly with profits, whereas overseas they are primarily motivated by volume objectives. Empirical evidence from the 1980s, however, contradicts this. In Piercy's sample of UK firms and Shipley's samples of both UK and US companies, **volume objectives** were subordinate to **profit objectives** in both domestic and overseas markets. Against this, however, is the well known example of Japanese manufacturing companies whose principal objective in the early stages of internationalisation has been, traditionally, **market share**.

Marketing at Work

The decision to market internationally can be driven by a number of factors, as shown by the example of National Power, the UK power generating company. Power generation in the UK has been liberalised, and National Power inevitably has lost market share as the market was opened. The company was reported as investing £1bn overseas by the year 2000, including sites in Bangladesh, Portugal and Spain, with more planned. The firm now has 5% of its generating capacity outside the UK market.

3.3 Walsh gives a number of reasons for and against involvement in IM.

(a) **Reasons supporting involvement in IM**

(i) **Profit margins** may be higher abroad.

(ii) Increase in **sales volume** from foreign sales may allow large reductions in unit costs.

(iii) The **product life cycle** may be extended if the product is at an earlier stage in the life cycle in other countries.

(iv)   **Seasonal fluctuations** may be levelled out (peak periods in some countries coinciding with troughs in others).

(v)   It offers an opportunity of **disposing of excess production** in times of low domestic demand.

(vi)   International activities **spread the risk** which exists in any single market (eg political and economic changes).

(vii)   **Obsolescent products** can be sold off overseas without damage to the domestic market.

(viii)   The firm's prestige may be enhanced by portraying a **global image**.

(b)   **Reasons for avoiding involvement in IM**

(i)   Profits may be unduly affected by factors outside the firm's **control** (eg due to fluctuation of exchange rates and foreign government actions).

(ii)   The **adaptations** to the product (or other marketing mix elements) needed for success overseas will diminish the effects of economies of scale.

(iii)   Extending the product life cycle is not always **cost effective**. It may be better to develop new products for the domestic market.

(iv)   The **opportunity costs** of investing abroad may be better utilised at home

(v)   In the case of marginal cost pricing, **anti-dumping duties** are more quickly imposed now than in the past.

Marketing at Work

Thorntons, the UK chocolate company, has had two forays into the International market place, neither with great success. The first market entry was to the United States but although US customers loved the product, the location of stores was too widespread for efficient administration and losses were incurred. Withdrawing from the US in 1987, the company nevertheless decided that the proposed single European Market presented an opportunity not to be missed and entered the French market in 1988, first by buying a few shops here and there in good locations - but later taking over a small chain from Nestle.

Problems were encountered integrating the French operation to Thorntons management style. Eventually a new Managing Director, coming in from another company background, decided in 1997 to concentrate on the company's core business in a still expanding home market and closed their French operation. The opportunity cost of operating in France could be devoted to making more profits in the domestic market by freeing up investment money for refurbishment and the development of new UK shops.

3.4   However, before getting involved in IM, the company must consider both strategic and tactical issues.

(a)   **Strategic issues**

(i)   Does the strategic decision to get involved in IM fit with the company's overall mission and objectives? Or will 'going international' cause a mis-match between objectives on the one hand and strategic and tactical decisions on the other?

(ii)   Does the organisation have (or can it raise) the resources necessary to exploit effectively the opportunities overseas?

(b)   **Tactical issues**

(i)   How can the company get to understand customers' needs and preferences in foreign markets?

(ii)   Does the company know how to conduct business abroad, and deal effectively with foreign nationals?

(iii)   Are there foreign regulations and associated hidden costs?

(iv)   Does the company have the necessary management skills and experience?

4   CHOICE OF MARKET AND EXTENT OF INVOLVEMENT

4.1   In making a decision as to which market(s) to enter the firm must start by establishing its objectives. Here are some examples.

(a)   What proportion of total sales will be overseas?

(b)   What are the longer term objectives?

(c)   Will it enter one, a few, or many markets? In most cases it is better to start by selling in countries with which there is some familiarity and then expand into other countries gradually as experience is gained. Reasons to enter fewer countries at first include the following.

- Market entry and market control costs are high
- Product and market communications modification costs are high
- There is a large market and potential growth in the initial countries chosen
- Dominant competitors can establish high barriers to entry

(d)   What types of country should it enter (in terms of environmental factors, economic development, language used, cultural similarities and so on)? Three major criteria should be as follows.

- Market attractiveness
- Competitive advantage
- Risk

4.2   The matrix below can be used to bring together these three major criteria and assist managers in their decisions.

Evaluating which markets to enter

Source: Kotler

(a)   **Market attractiveness.** This concerns such indicators as GNP/head and forecast demand, and market accessibility.

(b)   **Competitive advantage**. This is principally dependent on prior experience in similar markets, language and cultural understanding.

(c) **Risk**. This involves an analysis of political stability, the possibility of government intervention and similar external influences.

4.3 The best markets to enter are those located at the top left of the diagram. The worst are those in the bottom right corner. As described in Chapter 5, obtaining the information needed to reach this decision requires detailed and often costly international marketing research and analysis. Making these decisions is not easy, and a fairly elaborate **screening process** will be instituted, described in Section 7 below, in the context of international marketing planning.

Risk

Key Concept

In economic terms, **risk** is the potential volatility of returns on an investment, which is compensated for by a higher return. In other words, a rational investor will accept a higher risk in the hope of reaching a higher return.

4.4 In international marketing there are several categories of risk.

(a) **Political risk** relates to factors as diverse as wars, nationalisation, arguments between governments etc.

Marketing at Work

Heineken withdrew from Burma as a result of public hostility regarding the political situation.

(b) **Business risk**. This arises from the possibility that the business idea itself might be flawed. As with political risk, it is not unique to international marketing, but firms might be exposed to more sources of risk arising from failures to understand the market.

(c) **Currency risk**. This arises out of the volatility of foreign exchange rates. Given that there is a possibility for speculation and that capital flows are free, such risks are increasing.

(d) **Profit repatriation risk**. Government actions may make it hard to repatriate profits.

4.5 Assessing risk is not a straightforward exercise. A useful model is the *Business Environment Risk Index (BERI)*. A variety of environmental factors are scored between 0 and 4 (where 0 is unacceptable and 4 superior). These are then weighted, according to their significance. The total is added up and each country receives a score. A score of less than 40 would denote high risk.

Involvement in international markets

4.6 Firms develop through various stages of learning as commitment to IM grows and there are choices to be made along the way as to the extent to which a company commits itself to the International market. These stages are identified below.

(a) **Domestic marketing**. The firm is preoccupied with home marketing.

(b) **Pre-export stage**. A search is conducted and export opportunities are assessed.

(c) **Experimental involvement**. There is some limited involvement in exporting: unsolicited and easy-to-get orders are accepted.

(d) **Active involvement**. This indicates systematic analysis of export opportunities and expansion into foreign markets.

(e) **Committed involvement**. The firm allocates its resources according to opportunities in different countries.

4.7   Different levels of involvement in IM are shown below

LEVELS OF COMMITMENT TO INTERNATIONAL MARKETING

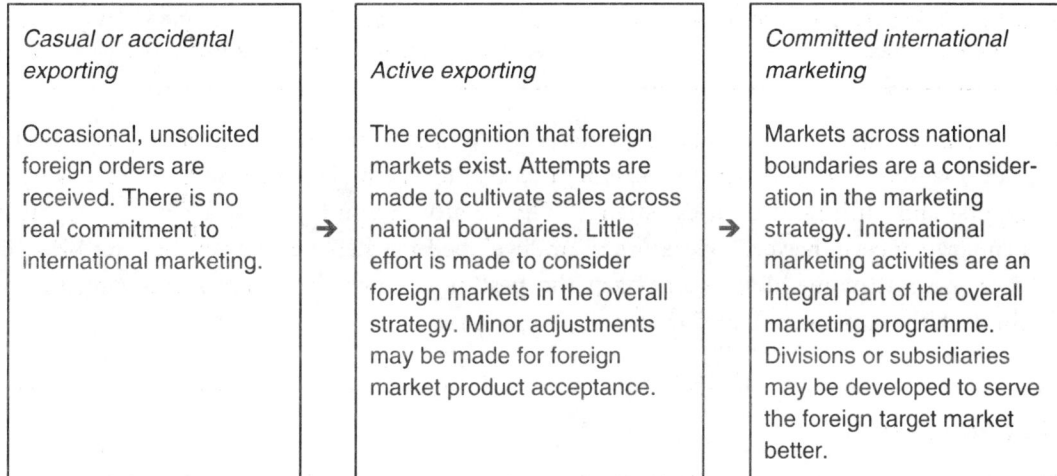

Casual or accidental exporting Occasional, unsolicited foreign orders are received. There is no real commitment to international marketing.	→	*Active exporting* The recognition that foreign markets exist. Attempts are made to cultivate sales across national boundaries. Little effort is made to consider foreign markets in the overall strategy. Minor adjustments may be made for foreign market product acceptance.	→	*Committed international marketing* Markets across national boundaries are a consideration in the marketing strategy. International marketing activities are an integral part of the overall marketing programme. Divisions or subsidiaries may be developed to serve the foreign target market better.

Source: Adapted from Pride and Farrell

4.8   Another model (by Richard Daft) identifies **four** stages.

(a) **Domestic stage**. Firms are happy to concentrate on the home market. Exports are made, but without direction: overseas buyers may order products. Where domestic demand is weak, exporting is a 'second-best' means of getting rid of surplus stock. There is no particular relationship with organisation size. Many small, specialist organisations export. Many large companies do not (many of the UK's large utilities only began overseas activities after privatisation).

(b) **International stage**. The firm's exporting activities are taken more seriously, and an export department might be set up to develop export markets. At this stage a **multi-domestic** strategy is pursued, in which each country is regarded as a separate market. Arguably, this is sensible market segmentation. However, this relies mainly on exports; only a few activities are conducted overseas.

(c) At the **multinational** stage the company has a large number of activities in different countries, including both marketing and production facilities. However, the firm still has a recognisable 'home'.

(d) A **global company** is one which transcends any country.

The local effects of an international global operator

4.9   The presence (actual or potential) of a global operator can either encourage or send fears into a community. The arrival of a multinational company can be a boon to local consumers, who benefit from wider choices becoming available. For local companies, however, the arrival of a large competitor may be disastrous. If their business is only valuable in the home country, then the best course may be to sell out entirely.

BPP PUBLISHING

Marketing at Work

The Czech car maker Skoda sold out to Volkswagen after the collapse of the Soviet Union. Only choice-starved consumers in the former Eastern bloc could appreciate the cars, and even they recognised that Skoda models were outdated, of poor quality and limited in appeal. These shortcomings became even more apparent when the markets opened up and multinational carmakers arrived. Volkswagen has invested heavily in repositioning Skoda cars as the value brand in its global line of vehicles.

Some local companies are successful at fending off foreign competition. Jollibee Foods fought off McDonalds in the Philippines to capture 75% market share. Bajaj Scooters in India held its market position against an invasion from Honda, who eventually withdrew. Both Jollibee and Bajaj had significant home advantage in terms of local tastes and distribution networks that proved considerable barriers to entry. Multinationals are often seeking to exploit global scale economies while local businesses fragment the market and serve the needs of distinct niches.   Adapted from an article in the *Harvard Business Review*

4.10   If the newcomer is welcomed, particularly by countries in dire need of foreign investment, they may be rewarded with government assistance with resources such as cash and land grants, and pulling of political strings. The loyalty of employees at a new plant will be a primary concern, because operators in undeveloped markets will always be afraid that later investors will come along and poach the best staff, once the pioneer company has gone through the expense of training them.

Marketing at Work

Ford Union, a shared venture between Ford, the Belarusian government and Lada, opened an assembly plant at Obchuck, near Minsk, and made efforts to win loyalty by laying on free transport to the plant and paying for English lessons for those who were interested.

4.11   The effects of inward investment by a foreign company can be extremely positive, both for the local economy and the investor. At the end of August 1998, Nissan's plant in Sunderland was declared the most efficient in Europe, producing three times as many cars as the Rover plant in the same town. A recent survey by the London School of Economics suggested that British workers in a Japanese company make far fewer mistakes than UK-employed counterparts.

4.12   Cross-cultural influences will also have a part to play. Companies who invade an underdeveloped or otherwise struggling economy with overt messages and advertising may find the policy backfiring after initial success, with consumers in the new market becoming alienated. It is easy for successful companies to overestimate the value of their reputation in underdeveloped markets.

Marketing at Work

The US chocolate bar giant, Mars, stormed the Russian market early and to great effect (*The Economist Intelligence Unit 1998*). For several years it was the leading foreign advertiser, launching the Mars and Snickers brands with the message that 'this is what good-looking, going-places young people in the West eat for fun; you should too.' For a time, Mars bars were the only thing apart from cheap vodka that could be found throughout the Soviet Union, but Russians soon became tired of the carefree American image being rammed down their throats at a time when economic reality was painfully difficult. 'By putting Snickers everywhere at a time when few Russian families could afford tomatoes, the company gave many Russians the impression that it was conspiring to undermine national nutrition'.

4.13   Local laws need to be understood. For example, in India an employer with more than 10 workers cannot fire them without permission from a government labour commissioner, which is usually impossible to obtain. In countries where there is widespread poverty, government officials will speak only about protecting jobs.

5 THE MARKETING PROGRAMME AND TYPE OF MARKETING ORGANISATION

5.1 Once a firm has decided on which markets it is going to operate in and the level of involvement in each market, it has to determine its marketing mix.

Programme

5.2 A business has three broad possibilities for its international marketing mix.

Key Concepts

Undifferentiated marketing. The company offers to the whole market a standard product with a standard price and promotional activities. It aims to minimise both production and marketing costs.

Differentiated marketing. Here the company segments its market. It sells in a large number of markets, but adjusts its product and marketing programmes to the needs and environmental variables of each.

Concentrated marketing. With this approach a company devotes all its marketing effort to one or a very few markets. It will choose a market where its standardised product and marketing programme will be best suited. It is the best approach for a company with limited resources.

Action Programme 2

Identify one product. Enquire how it is sold in the UK, and in another country of your choice, and assess whether undifferentiated or differentiated marketing is being applied.

5.3 Most firms would prefer to sell the same product at the same price through similar distribution channels, using the same means of communication in all its markets. As we will see later, this is rarely possible because of very dissimilar marketing environments.

5.4 The diagram on page 154 shows examples of barriers to standardisation caused by environmental differences.

Barriers to standardisation

Environmental variable	Product	Price	Distribution	Promotion
Economy	Usage	Varied income level	Different retail structures	Media availability
Culture	Consumer tastes and habits	Price negotiating habits	Buying habits	Language and attitude differences
Competition	Nature of existing products	Competitors' objectives, costs and prices	Competitors' monopoly and use of channels	Competitors' budgets appeals
Law	Product regulation	Price controls	Restriction on distribution	Advertising and media restrictions

Organisation

5.5 The type of organisation structure adopted is influenced heavily by the level of involvement in IM.

5.6 For a firm whose involvement in IM is simply exporting, an **export department** will meet its needs. However, as a firm becomes more involved and chooses other entry methods - licensing, contract manufacturing, joint venture and so on, then it will have to create an **international division** to meet its needs. In the truly multinational company, where marketers have stopped thinking of themselves as national marketers who have ventured abroad, a **global organisation** might need to be adopted.

6   GOOD PRACTICE IN IM PLANNING   Specimen paper

> **Key Concept**
> **Planning** is the establishment of objectives, and the formulation, evaluation and selection of the policies, strategies, tactics and action required to achieve them. Planning comprises long-term/strategic planning, and short-term operation planning.

6.1 An **international marketing plan** should feature the following.

(a) **Mission.** The international marketing plan should be consonant with the overall mission of the organisation, and so this might be stated. Mission answers the question: 'What business are we in?'. It also is crucial in spreading the right corporate culture.

> **Key Concept**
> The **mission** is an organisation's rationale for existing at all and/or its long term strategic direction and/or its values.

(b) The **mission statement** might be supported by the various goals, which aim to satisfy the stakeholders in the organisation (ie will those who have a legitimate interest in what it does). For businesses, profit as return is an important goal. Some companies pursue other goals such as corporate social responsibility **worldwide,** especially with regard to the environment.

(c) **Position/situation audit.** This will be based on past performance in each major market. The significance of each market is then evaluated.

Key Concept

The **position audit** is part of the planning process which examines the current state of the entity in respect of: resources of tangible and intangible assets and finance; products, brands and markets; operating systems such as production and distribution; internal organisation; current results; returns to stockholders.

(d) A statement of basic assumptions about key **environmental factors** both in the long term and short term, ie social, technological, economic and political developments in its existing and potential markets.

(e) (i) SWOT analysis of external **opportunities** and **threats** for its various products and markets.

(ii) An analysis of the company's **strengths** and **weaknesses** relative to its competitors, ie strengths and weaknesses concerning products, facilities, financial situation, reputation, market share and distribution. The BCG or GEC matrix may be used here (see below).

(f) A statement of long-term **objectives** and the strategy options for achieving them (for example, marketing, financial and growth).

(g) A statement of objectives and strategies for the **short-term** (one year) that is broken down by product, country and market segment.

(h) **Detailed programmes** to co-ordinate the sequence of marketing activities, with budgeted costs.

(i) Less detailed statements of **objectives for subsequent years**.

6.2 There are three levels of planning which apply equally to International as well as domestic marketing.

(a) **Operational plans** (short range 1-3 years). At this level planning is the responsibility of each overseas operating unit. The format of the plan may be supplied by a headquarters planning department. Plans should include sales forecasting, profit and cash flow projections for each product or product line, market share and capital expenditure requirements. These individual unit operational plans may be integrated at regional level or at headquarters, depending on organisational orientation and structure.

(b) **Strategic plans.** National operating units plan ahead on a longer timescale. Strategic planning addresses the product/market portfolio and acquisitions/divestments. Headquarters reviews the plan but provides only general guidelines. The plans are usually confined to the operating unit's country of operation.

(c) **Corporate plans.** These are global plans developed at international headquarters and are consistent with (but subordinate to) overall corporate objectives and strategies. It is long range in nature, monitoring worldwide changes in environments while looking for opportunities for growth.

6.3 Good planning achieves the following general objectives.

(a) It obliges management to **examine all the factors** that affect the potential effectiveness of each given strategy.

(b) It **involves and informs** all the people concerned with implementing a strategy, thereby motivating and possibly developing and improving them.

(c) It forces management to form **realistic objectives** and to adopt a satisfactory philosophy for IM (**ethnocentrism, polycentrism, geocentrism**).

> ### Exam Tip
> The specimen paper contained a question on the operational issues (human resources, production, financial) which need consideration when implementing a market entry plan.

6.4 Specifically, planning enables a company to achieve the following.

- To minimise the problems associated with environmental **threats** and organisational **weaknesses**

- To match available company **resources** with the global opportunities

- To facilitate the **co-ordination of data** concerning multiple countries

- To co-ordinate and integrate the activities of a **decentralised organisation**

Product-market matrices

6.5 The product-market matrix is a simple technique used to classify a product or even a business according to the features of the market and the features of the product. It is often used at the level of **corporate strategy** to determine the relative positions of businesses and select strategies for **resource allocation** between them. Thus, for example, a bank might apply the technique to evaluate the relative position and profitability of its corporate division and its personal division, its international division, its merchant banking division and so on. The same techniques are equally valuable when considering products and the management of the product portfolio. The two most widely used approaches are the **Boston Consulting Group (BCG) growth-share matrix** and the **General Electric (GE) Business Screen**.

The BCG matrix

6.6 **The BCG matrix, illustrated below, classifies products (or businesses) on the basis of their market share relative to that of their competitors and according to the rate of growth in the market as a whole.**

(a) The split on the horizontal axis is based on a market share identical to that of the firm's nearest competitor, while the precise location of the split on the vertical axis will depend on the rate of growth in the market.

(b) Products are positioned in the matrix as circles with a diameter proportional to their sales revenue. The underlying assumption in the growth-share matrix is that a larger market share will enable the business to benefit from economies of scale, lower per unit costs and thus higher margins.

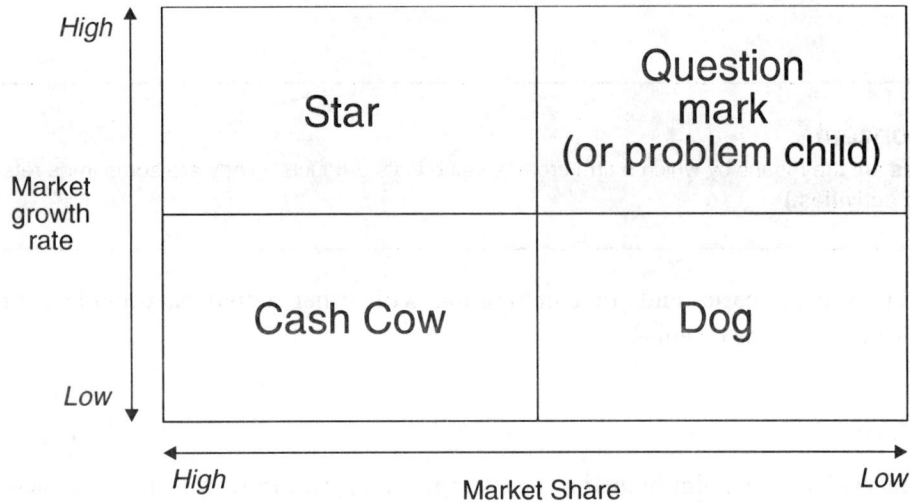

6.7 The framework provided by the matrix can offer guidance in terms of developing appropriate strategies for products and in maintaining a **balanced product portfolio**, ensuring that there are enough cash-generating products to match the cash-using products.

The General Electric Business Screen (GEBS)

6.8 The approach of the GE Business Screen is similar to that of the BCG matrix. The GEBS includes a broader range of company and market factors. A typical example of the GE matrix is provided below. This matrix **classifies products (or businesses)** according to **industry attractiveness** and **company strengths**. The approach aims to consider a variety of factors which contribute to both these variables.

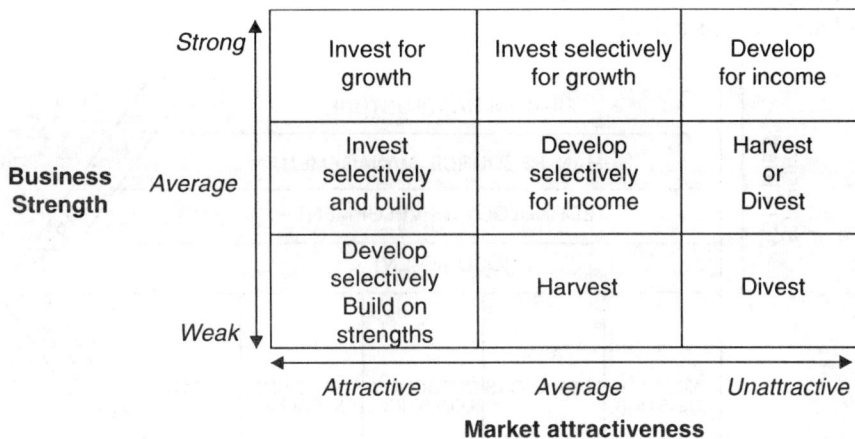

6.9 The broader approach of the GE matrix emphasises the attempt to match competences within the company to conditions within the market place. Difficulties associated with measurement and classification mean that again the results of such an exercise must be interpreted with care.

Converting resources: the value chain

6.10 The **value chain** model of corporate activities, developed by Michael Porter, offers a bird's eye view of the firm and what it does. Competitive advantage, says Porter, arises out of the way in which firms organise and perform **activities**.

Activities

> **Key Concept**
>
> **Activities** are the means by which a firm creates value in its products. (They are sometimes referred to as **value activities.)**

6.11 Activities incur costs, and, in combination with other activities, provide a product or service which earns revenue.

6.12 EXAMPLE

Let us explain this point by using the example of a **restaurant**. A restaurant's activities can be divided into buying food, cooking it, and serving it (to customers). There is no reason, in theory, why the customers should not do all these things themselves, at home. The customer however, is not only prepared to **pay for someone else** to do all this but also **pays more than the cost of** the resources (food, wages etc). The ultimate value a firm creates is measured by the amount customers are willing to pay for its products or services above the cost of carrying out value activities. A firm is profitable if the realised value to customers exceeds the collective cost of performing the activities.

(a) Customers **'purchase' value**, which they measure by comparing a firm's products and services with similar offerings by competitors.

(b) The business **'creates' value** by carrying out its activities either more efficiently than other businesses, or combine them in such a way as to provide a unique product or service.

6.13 Porter (in *Competitive Advantage*) grouped the various activities of an organisation into a **value chain**. Here is a diagram.

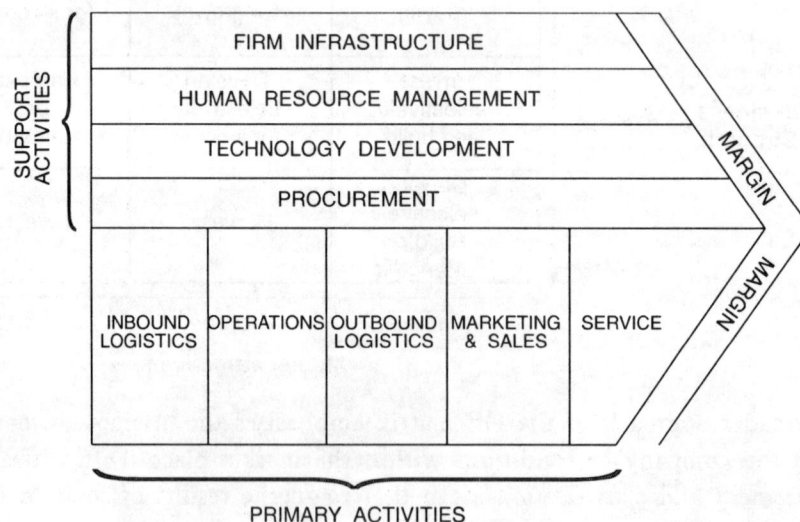

The **margin** is the excess the customer is prepared to **pay** over the **cost** to the firm of obtaining resource inputs and providing value activities. The needs of the customer are affected by all the activities in the value chain, because he does not only encounter sales staff. The service he receives is also dependent on accounts and warehouse staff for example. Pressure therefore exists throughout the value chain to service the customer profitably.

> **Key Concept**
>
> The **value chain** is the sequence of business activities by which, in the perspective of the end user, value is added to the products or services produced by an organisation.

Activity

6.14 **Primary activities** are directly related to production, sales, marketing, delivery and service.

	Comment
Inbound logistics	Receiving, handling and storing inputs to the production system (ie warehousing, transport, stock control etc).
Operations	Convert resource inputs into a final product. Resource inputs are not only materials. 'People' are a 'resource' especially in service industries.
Outbound logistics	Storing the product and its distribution to customers: packaging, warehousing, testing etc.
Marketing and sales	Informing customers about the product, persuading them to buy it, and enabling them to do so: advertising, promotion etc.
After sales service	Installing products, repairing them, upgrading them, providing spare parts and so forth.

6.15 **Support activities** provide purchased inputs, human resources, technology and infrastructural functions to support the primary activities.

Activity	Comment
Procurement	Acquire the resource inputs to the primary activities (eg purchase of materials, subcomponents equipment).
Technology development	Product design, improving processes and/or resource utilisation.
Human resource management	Recruiting, training, developing and rewarding people.
Management planning	Planning, finance, quality control: Porter believes they are crucially important to an organisation's strategic capability in all primary activities.

6.16 **Linkages** connect the activities of the value chain.

(a) **Activities in the value chain affect one another.** For example, more costly product design or better quality production might reduce the need for after-sales service.

(b) **Linkages require co-ordination.** For example, Just In Time requires smooth functioning of operations, outbound logistics and service activities such as installation.

Value system

6.17 Activities that add value do not stop at the organisation's **boundaries**. For example, when a restaurant serves a meal, the quality of the ingredients - although they are chosen by the cook - is determined by the grower. The grower has added value, and the grower's success in growing produce of good quality is as important to the customer's ultimate satisfaction as the skills of the chef. A firm's value chain is connected to what Porter calls a **value system**.

159

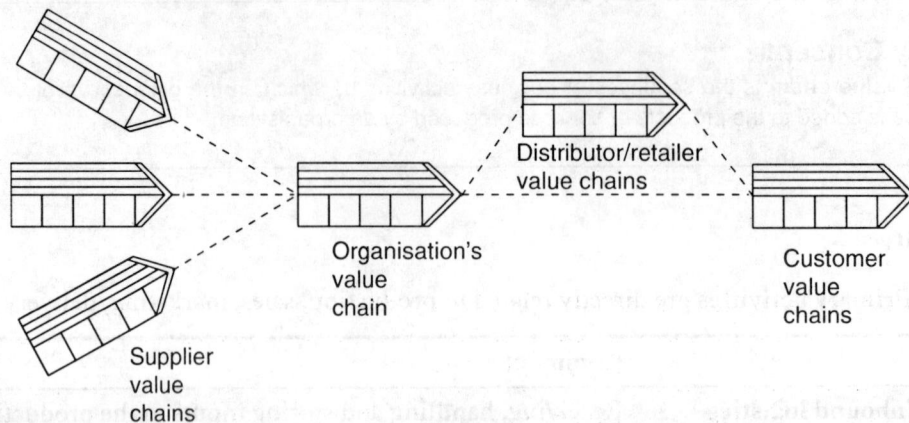

Distributor/retailer value chains

Organisation's value chain

Customer value chains

Supplier value chains

6.18 **Using the value chain**, a firm can secure **competitive advantage**.

- Inventing new or better ways to do activities
- Combining activities in new or better ways
- Managing the linkages in its own value chain
- Managing the linkages in the value system

6.19 The value chain is an important analytical tool.

- To see the **business as a whole**
- To identify potential **sources of competitive advantage**
- To suggest **strategies**
- To analyse **competitors**

7 SOME ISSUES AND PROBLEMS IN IM PLANNING

7.1 Compared with domestic marketing planning, international marketing planning is a much more complex and involved process.

Top down vs bottom up

7.2 **Top down planning** originates at a company's headquarters and is implemented by local managers. It is appropriate when managers of operating units around the world are not familiar with the process and practice of planning or where conditions do not vary greatly from region to region.

7.3 **Bottom up planning** is initiated locally, although it should be reviewed centrally to ensure that conflicts between operating units do not arise. It is appropriate where local environmental differences exist, necessitating local plans. Local managers need to have planning experience and skills. A problem with bottom up planning is that if you add together all the 'bottom up' plans there may be too few resources to meet them, and selection will be a 'political' rather than a rational process.

Marketing at Work

Uniform branding is not always possible at IM level. Unilever allows local managers to take branding decisions, and even decisions as to packaging changes.

However some firms insist on uniform branding. Snickers bars used to be known as Marathon in the UK. Heinz has ambitious plans to globalise its brands. Its tomato ketchup is the only brand which carries the same name and similar packaging all over the world. Its seafood category carries at least six different brand names in different markets. 'It is a fundamental problem for Heinz, that unlike Proctor and Gamble, Mars and Colgate Palmolive, it does not have a worldwide brand.' (*Marketing Week*)

The process of planning

7.4   There are also difficulties to be encountered in the planning **process,** in particular the strategic planning process. As far as the **management structure and culture** are concerned, the following issues may pose problems.

(a) **Domestic headquarters**

(i)   Managers may be ignorant of overseas markets, and their decisions might be taken with little regard to local attitudes or feelings.

Marketing at Work

In the early 1990s, managers of Johnson and Johnson in the Philippines discovered that young Filipino women were using Johnson and Johnson baby talcum powder to freshen their makeup during the day, carrying a small amount in a knotted handkerchief.

Johnson and Johnson Philippines developed a compact holder for the talcum powder, and an advertising campaign was devised.

A few days before the product launch, corporate HQ in the US asked that it be cancelled, because 'we are not in the cosmetics business'. It was only after the chief marketer in the Philippines flew to headquarters and pleaded for the product's life that it was allowed to go ahead.   Adapted from *Harvard Business Review*

(ii)   Furthermore, if the organisation is centralised, all the 'political' battles within its leadership will be focused around the **domestic** agenda.

(b) **Local level problems**

- Resentment at being bossed around.
- Unclear goals.
- Different ways of doing business.
- Inadequate control.
- A lack of a strategic outlook and marketing expertise.
- A completely different attitude to the product and marketing task.

(c)   International marketing planning also involves **human resources considerations.** The local subsidiary will have its own human resource needs, and these will be met by and large by local personnel. A problem is to ensure that the corporate culture is strong enough to withstand any potential clashes caused by cultural differences between Head Office and subsidiaries.

Marketing at Work

The following case is drawn from *Corporate Culture: From Vicious to Virtuous Circles,* by Charles Hampden-Turner.

The attitude of the staff of Volvo in France to the product they were selling was this.

'The Swedish people who make Volvo don't understand the French. We are hot-blooded Latins, with dash, romance and style. We like cars that perform and are in fashion. Volvos are too sober, too safe, too pedestrian, too cerebral and too practical, consisting of largely old models, which have not changed noticeably in years. Scandinavians have a temperament that dwells on accidents and upon keeping warm. The French have more joie de vivre. Despite heroic efforts to move these melancholy motors, we have not been very successful.'

A crucial aspect of changing a culture is to retell, reinterpret or transform a story which otherwise spells defeat. Goran Carstedt did that in Volvo France. By taking the dealers and their wives to Sweden and giving them the grand tour, the story of moody Scandinavians and dull cars was totally recast to read as follows.

'Volvos are made in Sweden by small, dedicated groups of craftsmen who make and sign each entire car and who manage themselves. Volvo symbolises for the world an individualism married to social concern, to which

161

the virtues of safety and reliability are the key. There are enough French people of discernment and good sense to think of their families and future responsibilities. With the new support we are getting, the Volvo message is one we can deliver with pride and success.'

7.5 As far as **management processes and decision making** are concerned, typical problems include these.

(a) **Poor information systems and communications.** However, the rapidly falling costs of telecommunications in real terms, the development of e-mail and video-conferencing facilities make this less excusable than before.

(b) **Interpretation of information.** Culture filters information. It can also determine the priorities of the planners. By **failing to allow for diversity**, planners can make marketing on the ground more difficult.

   (i) Managing a local market in a large country with a low population density and whose main source of earnings is natural resources would be different from marketing to a small country with a high population density.

   (ii) High tech products may not be suitable to a country with a poorly developed educational and technological infrastructure as there might be no-one to service the equipment. So a high tech strategy at home would not work abroad.

   (iii) Consumers in countries with very high rates of inflation will have different priorities to those who live in countries with low inflation. Managers' priorities will be to minimise any holdings of local currency, by converting it into a harder currency or into tangible assets. However, this makes financial reporting difficult.

Distance and implementation problems

7.6 The distance, as it were, between the corporate plan and its implementation 'on the ground' is greater than it is for a company which only deals with one market.

(a) **Physical**

   (i) The degree of variation in environmental conditions is so much greater. Managers, in trying to get a global picture, may **aggregate data** from very dissimilar markets.

   (ii) In order to compete effectively, local management must be able to respond to differing environmental conditions.

(b) **Psychological.** Corporate planners may not share the same assumptions as local managers.

7.7 As a consequence of the greater variety of factors involved in IM planning, any attempt at central control is likely to be much less certain.

(a) **Lack of experience.** The expertise and experience of head office planners might be limited by their careers in the 'head office' or by a gradual loss of a feel for their local roots.

(b) **Time horizons.** Corporate planners will be seeking to satisfy the firm's **investors,** whose desire for a return might be dominated by their local considerations. This is typically a problem when a long term investment is required in an overseas market. Japan is a notoriously difficult and expensive market to get into - it is not impossible, but a great deal of time must be taken to build up contacts, arrange distribution etc.

The slowness of the return may result in corporate planners dictating marketing strategies, for reasons of cost, not necessarily appropriate to the overseas market.

8 THE INTERNATIONAL MARKETING PLANNING PROCESS 12/99

8.1 **Strategic planning** is a systematic means of effectively managing a company's resources, its strengths and weaknesses in line with the opportunities and threats which arise in the continuously evolving marketing environment.

Objectives

8.2 The starting point for all successful strategic marketing planning must be the formulation of **objectives**. Defining objectives clarifies the international orientation of the firm (see below). Failure to define objectives clearly may lead to a firm attempting to penetrate otherwise attractive markets that involve activities which conflict with or detract from the firm's principal objectives. If there is a mismatch (as there often is) between corporate objectives and foreign market opportunities then either plans must be modified (or even abandoned) or objectives need to be reconsidered.

Orientation

8.3 A firm's basic IM orientation can be one of the following.

Ethnocentrism

> **Key Concept**
> **Ethnocentrism** is a **domestic country orientation** in which IM is secondary to home marketing. Firms adopting this orientation will tend to adopt objectives which involve marketing the same products with the same marketing programmes in overseas countries as at home.

8.4 The approach simply ignores any inter-country differences which exist. Market opportunities may not be fully exploited with this orientation, or foreign customers may be alienated by the approach.

Marketing at Work

Pepsi experienced customer alienation when it attempted to mechanically import its global 'younger challenger to Coke' image into Russia. It lost ground to an obscure Swiss rival, Herschi, which used Russian sports stars and celebrities in its campaign.

Polycentrism (multidomestic)

> **Key Concept**
> With **polycentrism**, objectives are formulated on the assumption that it is necessary to adapt almost totally the product and the marketing programme to each local environment. Thus the various country subsidiaries of a multinational corporation are free to formulate their own objectives and plans (bottom up planning).

BPP PUBLISHING

8.5 Sometimes the outcome of this orientation is too much differentiation.

Geocentrism (or regiocentrism)

> **Key Concept**
>
> **Geocentrism** is the synthesis of the two previous orientations. It is based on the assumption that there are similarities and differences among countries which can be incorporated into regional or world objectives and strategies. This approach favours neither the home approach nor total adaptation.

8.6 Geocentrism considers the issues of standardisation and adaptation on their merits so as to formulate objectives and strategies that exploit markets fully while minimising company costs.

8.7 Clearly geocentrism is preferable since it does not involve preconceived assumptions. It is usually firms with this orientation that use formal international strategic planning.

8.8 Companies which have successfully 'gone global' must plan to maintain their competitive position. Just as the company has to work to maintain a presence in the domestic market, the international market does not stand still. For example, **emerging markets** such as India, China and Brazil are providing challenges for existing multinational corporations. These markets will be key arenas for competition in the future, with a new consumer base of hundreds of millions of people. Multinationals have tended to bring their existing products and marketing strategies to such markets without fully understanding the consumer market. When Revlon introduced its Western beauty products to China in 1976 and India in 1994, only the very top tier of the population could afford. it. To compete more effectively with local producers, multinationals have to constantly re-think their strategies.

Marketing at Work

British Airways is one of the world's most respected companies. It is been transformed from a state-owned airline into a profitable company against the background of the rapidly changing world of aviation. It faces numerous international competitive pressures.

- New alliances being formed, creating larger networks
- Emergence of budget carriers such as Easy-Jet
- Competition from other forms of transport eg high speed railways
- High fleet maintenance costs
- Government regulations

Such pressures add up to a series of challenges which the company can only face by rigorous planning. Strategic decisions to cut the workforce have had to be made.

Modelling the strategic planning process

8.9 Whether a firm is new to international marketing or is already operating in many overseas countries it is essential to adopt a **systematic approach**. A company new to international marketing has to select which countries to enter with which products, marketing programmes and levels of resources. The diagram on the following page illustrates a model of the strategic planning process for IM.

Phase 1: preliminary analysis and screening: matching company and country needs

8.10 Whether it is new to or heavily involved in IM, the company's first step is an **evaluation of available markets**. The purpose here is to identify which countries, on the basis of very rough screening criteria, are obviously not suitable for investment. For example, a company marketing downhill skiing holidays would automatically rule out Holland and Egypt as locations for its activities.

Screening criteria

8.11 The next step in Phase 1 is the development of further screening criteria against which to evaluate the prospects of the remaining alternatives. Such criteria vary from company to company, being determined by their own objectives, strengths and weaknesses. Central to the evaluation are the company's reasons for entering a foreign market and the returns expected from it. Examples of typical **screening criteria** are as follows.

- Specified minimum acceptable levels of profits
- Market share and volume
- Acceptable levels of competition
- Acceptable legal conditions
- Political risks

8.12 When screening criteria have been outlined, the next step of Phase 1 is a thorough analysis of the **environmental conditions** prevailing in each prospective country (ie economic, demographic, political and social factors). At this stage, the company must consider any links between its domestic environment and its ambitions for overseas markets. For example, domestic laws may forbid exporting to a particular country or company language capabilities may favour a particular market. The results of Phase 1 yield the following information.

- Identify obviously inappropriate countries
- Assess the potential of each overseas market
- Identify where further environmental research and analysis is needed
- Select the most appropriate overseas markets
- Determine whether and how the marketing mix needs to be adapted to meet local needs
- Formulate and implement a marketing action plan

8.13 It seems likely that one of the consequences of globalisation might be a blurring of national boundaries when it come to segmentation decisions, although we should not underestimate the dangers of assuming that national borders do not exist.

Choosing countries

8.14 That said, it is unlikely that a firm would export to its chosen segment in **every country**. After all there are practical and logistical problems in exporting everywhere, and, as should be apparent, the political and currency risk profiles of the various countries may differ, and the competitive environments may vary.

8.15 So, just as it is common to have a screening process for new products, it is worth having a screening process for new **country markets**, if of course such a screening process is carried out rationally.

8.16 In practice, the segmentation and screening process will be based on economic factors, and might follow a number of stages. Jeannet and Hennessy suggest a four-stage approach to screening.

BPP
PUBLISHING

Part B: International strategic planning

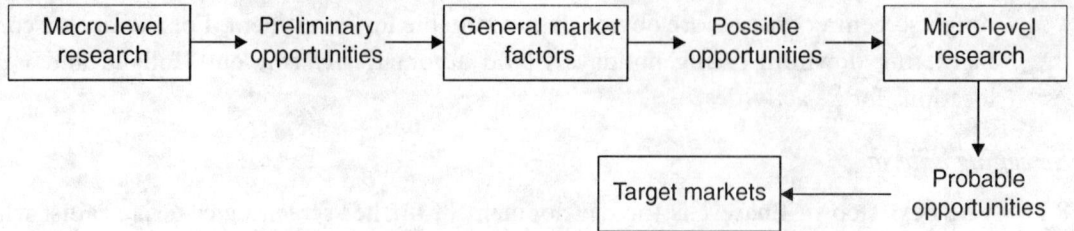

```
┌──────────────┐     ┌──────────────┐     ┌──────────────┐     ┌──────────────┐     ┌──────────────┐
│  Macro-level │ →   │  Preliminary │ →   │General market│ →   │   Possible   │ →   │  Micro-level │
│   research   │     │ opportunities│     │   factors    │     │opportunities │     │   research   │
└──────────────┘     └──────────────┘     └──────────────┘     └──────────────┘     └──────────────┘
                                                                                             │
                                                                                             ↓
                     ┌──────────────┐                                            ┌──────────────┐
                     │Target markets│ ←──────────────────────────────────────────│   Probable   │
                     └──────────────┘                                            │opportunities │
                                                                                 └──────────────┘
```

Information derived from each phase, market research and evaluation of performance

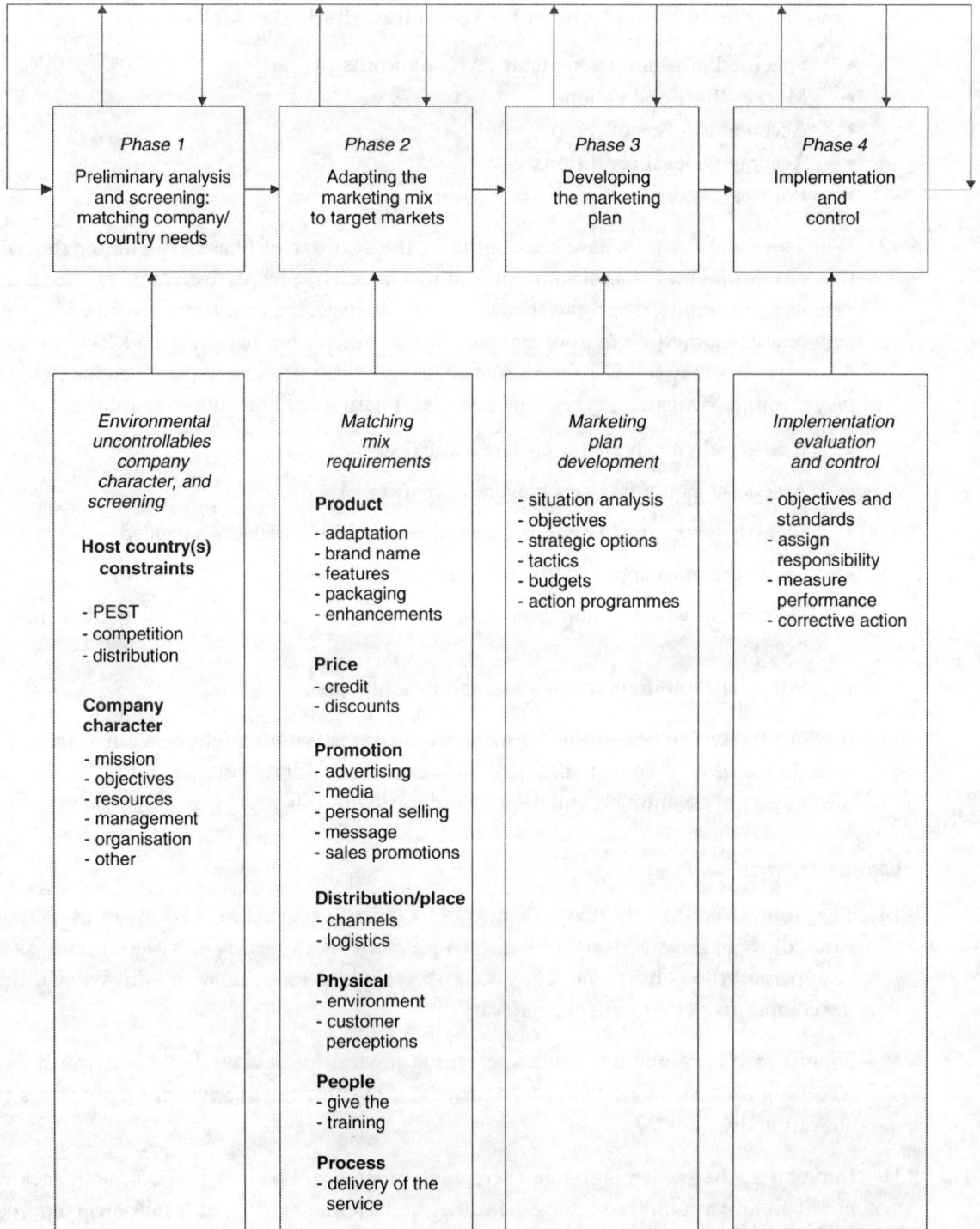

Phase 1	Phase 2	Phase 3	Phase 4
Preliminary analysis and screening: matching company/ country needs	Adapting the marketing mix to target markets	Developing the marketing plan	Implementation and control

Environmental uncontrollables company character, and screening	*Matching mix requirements*	*Marketing plan development*	*Implementation evaluation and control*
Host country(s) constraints - PEST - competition - distribution **Company character** - mission - objectives - resources - management - organisation - other	**Product** - adaptation - brand name - features - packaging - enhancements **Price** - credit - discounts **Promotion** - advertising - media - personal selling - message - sales promotions **Distribution/place** - channels - logistics **Physical** - environment - customer perceptions **People** - give the - training **Process** - delivery of the service	- situation analysis - objectives - strategic options - tactics - budgets - action programmes	- objectives and standards - assign responsibility - measure performance - corrective action

(a) **Macrolevel research.** Such information relates to the overall SLEPT factors in the overseas market. If the country is too poor, for example, or in the throes of a civil war, then such countries might be ignored altogether, as being too risky. Indicators of the total size of the market might include area, climate, demographic factors or gross domestic product (in other words much of the background data you should have established for your country file).

(b) The next level is the **general market** relating to the product.

    (i) Market size can be estimated by proxy statistics. The number of households with dishwashers can suggest the market size for dishwasher powder. If telephone ownership is widespread, there is likely to be a bigger market for answering machines than if telephones are a rarity.

    (ii) Are there specific regulations controlling the market? For example, trade in financial services has yet to be completely liberalised.

    (iii) Are the products culturally acceptable?

(c) **Microlevel research** identifies specific factors relating to the product.

    (i) Competition, existing and potential. For example, some markets might be very open and host to a large number of competitors. Others may be closed, arising to regulation, or foreigners may have restricted access. Air travel is heavily regulated.

    (ii) The market might be similar in certain key respects. Measures of similarity include production and transportation, personal consumption, trade, health and education. We can also add similarity of legal systems, and enforceability of contracts. For example, Jeannet and Hennessy note that 'a US firm will enter Canada, Australia, and the United Kingdom before entering less similar markets such as Spain, South Korea or India... Entering a market that has the same language, a similar distribution system, and similar customers is, less difficult than entering a market in which all these variables are different'.

    (iii) Finally this leads to **target markets** or segments which are screened for their suitability.

8.17 There are a number of problems with this approach.

(a) It assumes that markets segment naturally into countries. After all, in using this approach, you might end up exporting to Germany and not to Austria, on the grounds that, despite other similarities, the Austrian market is too small.

(b) A criticism of strategic planning generally is that it fails to capture all the necessary information about the demand for the product.

(c) Furthermore, developments in world trade lead to leakages across national boundaries.

Financial issues

> **Exam Tip**
> The examiner is very keen for students to assess the financial implications of international marketing decisions.

8.18 Whilst getting carried away with how attractive or unattractive a country is, keep in mind that the ultimate objective of the whole exercise is to make money. **Financial issues** are always of vital importance.

(a) Will the company make profits? Which mode of entry will be profitable?

(b) Will the profit be acceptable given the risk? Normally, the higher the risk, the higher the return.

(c) What is the size of the investment required, and how much will it cost to finance the investment? Is money being taken away from other, potentially more profitable, investments?

(d) **Global operations finance.** This is essential. When an exporter sells to a foreign buyer, that buyer will often be allowed a period of credit. This may create a cash shortage for the exporter, who can approach a financial institution. short term solutions may be provided by an overdraft facility, while loans may solve longer term problems. The method of payment will depend on individual agreements but is likely to be one of the following.

- Payment in advance
- Irrevocable letter of credit
- Payment on the shipment of goods
- Documentary collection
- Open account
- Bill of exchange

More detail on these can be found in Chapter 11.

(e) **Cash-flow.** Will the firm be able to repatriate dividends and cash from the country? Cash flow is the life-blood of a business. If there are restrictions on export of cash, this makes the investment less attractive.

(f) **Exchange risk.** Will this affect the financial results? Transactions risk is the risk that particular transactions will be affected by exchange rate volatility. Translation risk occurs when the value of a firm's assets when shown in the accounts are affected by exchange rates. A factory in an overseas market might be valued in local currency, but if the exchange rate changes, its reported value in sterling in the accounts will change too.

Without an extensive search and appraisal programme, firms entering IM are liable to make major and costly mistakes.

Marketing at Work

The Tandy Corporation, a US firm, did without such an exercise and consequently made many errors when attempting to enter the Western European Market. For example, in Holland, Tandy staged its first Christmas promotion for December 25 unaware that the Dutch exchange Christmas presents on December 6 (St Nicholas). Tandy also launched citizen band radios as a product only to find that in many European countries it was illegal to use them.

8.19 The scanning process should give information on markets.

- **Existing markets,** where customer needs are already serviced

- **Incipient markets** where potential customers are currently recognised but are not being serviced

- **Latent markets** where there is a foreseeable, but not a present, market for products. The Gilligan and Hird model taken from Doole, Lowe and Phillips is shown below - and this model shows the relationships between the costs and risks associated with such marketing opportunities

Gilligan and Hird model

Type of product		Existing	Latent	Incipient	
	Competitive			Existing brands are positioned to take advantage of possible developing needs; no direct competition, but consumers need to be found and then persuaded of the product's value to them. Risk and cost of failure may be high	*Low*
	Improved	Superior product offers competitive advantage and eases market entry	Increasingly advanced profile offers greater benefits to the market; no direct competition		*Cost and risk of launching the product*
	Breakthrough	Breakthrough product offers self-evident superiority and the competitive advantage is high	Breakthrough product offers significant advantages but markets need to be identified and developed. Little likelihood of competitors in the short term and medium term, but customer resistance may be high		*High*

Low   *Cost and risk of*   *High*
opening up the
market

Phase 2: adapting the marketing mix to target markets

8.20   When target markets have been chosen it is necessary to examine the blend of mix elements in greater detail. Specifically the company should be seeking answers to two major questions.

(a)   What cultural or other environmental **adaptations** are needed to ensure customer satisfaction with the mix offered?

(b)   Will adaptation **costs** prevent profitable market entry?

8.21   Often the answers to either of these questions indicate that the marketing mix requires such major **adaptation** that a decision is taken to eliminate the country from any further consideration. For example, the high cost of many textbooks published in the USA means that prices set for them in the UK would be too high to generate adequate volume. Alternatively, products sometimes have to be adapted to meet differences in measurement systems (eg metric and British Standard) and this may be prohibitively expensive.

8.22   Conversely, further research in this phase may suggest ways in which the marketing programme can be **standardised** for two or more countries.

Phase 3: developing the marketing plan   12/99

8.23   At this point a marketing plan is formulated for a specific country or target market. It begins with a situation analysis and includes all of the 'usual' elements of a typical marketing plan. As in the earlier phases, the firm may decide to drop a particular country if it becomes evident that it cannot design a marketing plan that will result in the achievement of marketing objectives for the country.

Phase 4: implementation and control

8.24 Finally, specific marketing actions are implemented, co-ordinated and **controlled**. The last of these is very important, being much neglected despite the fact that effective monitoring and control enhances performance substantially. Control requires continuing monitoring of performance against targets to identify when remedial action is needed, in what form and by whom. We look at control issues in Chapter 14.

Phases 1 to 4: information flows

8.25 There are both flows of information into each of the four phases and outflows of data. Information is also obtained from marketing research. Hence firms are able to store data in their **marketing information systems** for use in later strategic planning cycles.

Problems with formal planning

8.26 A formal IM planning process at corporate level is likely to be compromised by the following factors.

(a) The distance which market sensitive information has to travel from the local market to corporate head office.

(b) The preoccupation of the corporate planners with domestic marketing considerations may prevent them from asking the 'right' questions about overseas markets.

(c) Unequal allocation of resources, as domestic projects might be given priority.

(d) The loss of local responsiveness in search for economies of scale (eg inventing a 'global product' where there is no real demand for it).

8.27 Recently, the very notion that strategy-making can be reduced only to planning processes has come under a sustained attack from Henry Mintzberg, in his book *The Rise and Fall of Strategic Planning*. He makes the following assertions.

(a) Strategic planning models fail to account for how strategies are made **in practice**.

(b) Empirical studies have **not** shown that planning activities **necessarily** contribute to improved performance. The jury is out.

(c) Strategic planning occurs often in an **annual cycle**. But a firm 'cannot allow itself to wait every year for the month of February to address its problems.'

(d) Formal planning can **discourage strategic thinking**. Once a plan is locked in place, people are unwilling to question it.

(e) Planning can result in an **obsession with control**, which results in a reluctance to consider truly creative ideas and a fear of risk.

8.28 Mintzberg went further and identified what he regarded as fundamental fallacies in strategic planning.

(a) **Formalisation.** The assumption is that strategy formation is a job which, like other jobs such as bricklaying, can be analysed into its component parts. But how can an intuitive judgement be analysed into a logical sequence of steps?

(b) The **assumption of detachment.** Senior managers at the top of the pyramid 'think great thoughts' while others scurry beneath them. This assumes that managers do not really need any day to day knowledge of the product or customer.

(c) **Defining** strengths and weaknesses in isolation is actually very difficult. Discovering strengths and weakness is a **learning process.**

(d) **Predetermination.** Planning assumes that the environment can be forecast, and that its future behaviours can be controlled, by a strategy planned in advance and delivered on schedule. This is only true in **stable** environments.

No strategic planning: 'freewheeling opportunism'

8.29 The **freewheeling opportunism approach** suggests firms should not bother with plans and should exploit opportunities as they arise, judged on their individual merits and not within the rigid structure of an overall corporate strategy.

(a) **Advantages**

(i) **Opportunities** can be seized when they arise, whereas a rigid planning framework might impose restrictions so that the opportunities are lost.

(ii) A formal corporate plan might take a long time to prepare and is fully documented. Any sudden, unexpected change (eg a very steep rise in the price of a key commodity) might cause serious disruption. A freewheeling opportunistic approach would **adapt to the change** more quickly.

(iii) It might encourage a more **flexible, creative attitude** among lower-level managers.

(b) **Disadvantages**

(i) **No co-ordinating framework** for the organisation as a whole
(ii) It cannot guarantee that all opportunities are **identified and appraised**
(iii) The firm ends up **reacting** all the time rather than acting purposively

No strategic planning: incrementalism

8.30 Herbert Simon suggested that managers do not **optimise** (ie get the **best** possible solution), but instead they **satisfice.** In other words they muddle through with a solution which is reasonable, if not ideal. Managers are limited by **time,** by the **information** they have and by their own **skills,** habits and reflexes. This is called **bounded rationality.**

8.31 This has the following implications.

(a) Managers including international marketing managers, do not in practice evaluate **all** the possible options open to them in a given situation, but choose between relatively **few alternatives.**

(b) Strategy making tends to involve **small scale extensions of past policy - incrementalism** - rather than radical shifts following a comprehensive rational 'search' and evaluation of the alternatives.

(c) Strategy making often does not proceed according to any coherent plan but rather proceeds **disjointedly.**

8.32 The **dangers** of incrementalism are these.

(a) This approach can lead too easily to **strategic wear-out.**

(b) In marketing terms, **small scale adjustments** of current marketing programmes may not be enough.

- To 'move' with existing customers' and their needs
- To identify new markets or sets of customers

No strategic planning: crafting emergent strategies

8.33 Some strategies do not always arise out of **conscious** strategic planning. Instead they emerge 'from below'.

> ### Key Concept
>
> An **emergent strategy** is one developed out of a pattern of behaviour not consciously imposed by senior management.

(a) They can result from a number of **ad hoc choices,** perhaps made lower down the hierarchy, which may not be recognised at the time as being of strategic importance.

(b) They develop out of **patterns of behaviour,** in contrast to planned strategies which are imposed from above. An exercise will make the point clearer.

Action Programme 3

Aldebaran Ltd is a public relations agency founded by an entrepreneur, Estella Grande, who has employed various talented individuals from other agencies to set up in business. Estella Grande wants Aldebaran Ltd to become the largest public relations agency in North London. Management consultants, in a planning document, have suggested 'growth by acquisition'. In other words, Aldebaran should buy up the other public relations agencies in the area. These would be retained as semi-independent business units, as the Aldebaran Ltd group could benefit from the goodwill of the newly acquired agencies. When Estella presents these ideas to the Board there is general consensus with one significant exception. Livia Strange, the marketing director, is horrified. 'How am I going to sell this to my staff? Ever since we've been in business, we've won business by undercutting and slagging off the competition. My team have a whole culture based on it. I give them champagne if they pinch a high value client. Why acquire these new businesses - why not stick to pinching their clients instead?'

What is the source of the conflict?

Crafting strategy

8.34 Mintzberg uses the metaphor of **crafting strategy** to help understand the idea. Mintzberg uses the image of a potter's wheel. The clay is thrown, and through shaping the clay on the wheel, the potter gives shape to the clay lump through a gradual process.

Marketing at Work

Honda

Honda is now one of the leading manufacturers of motorbikes. The company is credited with identifying and targeting an untapped market for small 50cc bikes in the US, which enabled it to expand, trounce European competition and severely damage indigenous US bike manufacturers. By 1965, Honda had 63% of the US market. But this occurred by accident.

On entering the US market, Honda had wanted to compete with the larger European and US bikes of 250ccs and over. These bikes had a defined market, and were sold through dedicated motorbike dealerships. Disaster struck when Honda's larger machines developed faults - they had not been designed for the hard wear and tear imposed by US motorcyclists. Honda had to recall the larger machines.

Honda had made little effort to sell its small 50 cc motorbikes - its staff rode them on errands around Los Angeles. Sports goods shops, ordinary bicycle and department stores had expressed an interest, but Honda did not want to confuse its image in its 'target' market of men who bought the larger bikes.

The faults in Honda's larger machines meant that reluctantly, Honda had to sell the small 50cc bikes just to raise money. They proved very popular with people who would never have bought motorbikes before. Eventually the company adopted this new market with enthusiasm with the slogan: 'You meet the nicest people on a Honda'. The strategy had emerged, against managers' conscious intentions, but they eventually responded to the new situation.

How to craft strategy

8.35 Mintzberg mentions the following essential activities in strategic management.

(a) **Manage stability.**

    (i) Most of the time, managers should be effectively implementing the strategies, not planning them.

    (ii) Obsessions with change are dysfunctional. Knowing **when** to change is more important.

    (iii) Formal planning is the detailed working out of the agreed strategy.

(b) **Detect discontinuity.** Environments do not change regularly, nor are they always turbulent. Strategists should realise that some small environmental changes (eg technological changes) are much more significant than others

Marketing at Work

Technological developments are hard to assess. Hoffmann-LaRoche, a Swiss based pharmaceutical company, began as a small firm making dyes. It acquired the patents to vitamins when no one else wanted them, and invested and borrowed all it could for producing and selling them. It is now an industry leader.

(c) **Know the business.** Strategic management involves an intimate feel for the business. This has to include an awareness and understanding of **operations**.

(d) **Manage patterns**. 'A key to managing strategy is the ability to detect emerging patterns and to help them take shape'.

8.36 So, some IM planning might be less organised and rational because of the **environmental volatility** the firm is subjected to, the lack of many true global products or brands, and the longer lines of communication. The emergent strategy approach should therefore be taken into account.

Evolutionary strategies

8.37 Such opportunities emphasise the importance of the market place, where **change** is to be expected. Rational planning approaches cannot possibly keep up, and ultimately long term survival cannot be planned at all. Managers can only ensure that the **organisation is prepared** for whatever hand the competition deals it.

8.38 In a study of major multinational businesses Quinn concluded that the management process could be described as **logical incrementalism,** with managers moving towards where they want to go in an evolutionary way. This is done largely in stages.

- Develop a strong yet flexible **core business**
- Build on that experience to decide on **future development**
- **Experiment** with 'side' issues and ventures
- **Test changes** in strategy via small-scale steps

8.39 They must be sensitive all the time to **environmental signals** and cannot possibly know everything about the environment itself. Logical incrementalism is the deliberate development of strategy by '**learning through doing**'.

8.40 Johnson and Scholes (*Exploring Corporate Strategy*) quote the following benefits of such an approach.

- Improved quality of information because of continual testing
- Better sequencing of decisions
- Commitment to change is fostered throughout the organisation
- Managers learn from each other
- Smaller changes face less resistance
- The organisation keeps itself in line with environmental changes

9 COMPETITIVE AND PRODUCT-MARKET STRATEGY DECISIONS

Competitive strategy

9.1 **Competitive strategies** are the strategies an organisation will pursue for competitive advantage (a condition which is proof against 'erosion by competitor behaviour or industry evolution'). They determine **how you compete**. Competitive advantage is anything which gives one organisation an edge over its rivals in the products it sells or the services it offers.

9.2 Porter believes there are three **generic strategies** for competitive advantage.

> ### Key Concept
> **Cost leadership** means being the lowest cost producer in the industry as a whole.
> **Differentiation** is the offer of a product or service which is unique or in some way different from other products
> **Focus** involves a restriction of activities to a segment through:
> (i) providing goods and or services at lower cost to that segment (a cost-focus);
> (ii) providing a differentiated product or service for that segment (differentiation-focus).

Cost leadership and **differentiation** are industry-wide strategies. **Focus** involves market segmentation, but involves pursuing, **within the segment only,** a strategy of cost leadership or differentiation.

9.3 Although there is a risk with any of the generic strategies, Porter argues that a firm must pursue one of them. A **stuck-in-the-middle** strategy is almost certain to make only low profits, he says. Recent research has indicated that this is too simplistic. Being the lowest cost producer does not mean you have to compete on price.

9.4 It is, of course, fairly easy to see how such competitive strategy decisions can be taken in a large domestic market, such as the US, where many economies of scale are readily available. But IM involves recognising differences between country markets, the barriers to entry caused by national and cultural borders, and the global market.

9.5 Is it hard to achieve overall **cost leadership.** In terms of international and global marketing it perhaps only applies to a few companies, and even they might face restrictions on market entry.

(a) Only a few companies are available to take advantage of global sourcing and the economies this offers.

(b) Cost leadership is a dangerous strategy, as companies from developing countries might, for a short time, benefit from those countries' comparative advantages in lower labour costs. (Generally speaking higher productivity in advanced economies neutralises many of the gains from cheap labour. Thus, the NAFTA agreement has not led to a collapse in US employment. US workers are far more productive than Mexican ones and there is some evidence that as workers become more productive, their wages increase.)

(c) Domestic producers might have substantial cost advantages owing to their proximity to the local markets.

(d) A firm's ability to compete as the lowest cost producer in certain markets will be hampered.

- **Tariffs** raise the price of your goods in relation to competitors (eg producers of Scotch whisky trying to export to Japan)

- **Exchange fluctuations** can render your efficiently-made products more expensive than a those of local producers

(e) Many of the costs of goods can be increased by factors outside management control, such as intricacies of the distribution system.

9.6 Clearly, then, a strategy of **differentiation** or **focus** can be more realistic.

(a) Products can be **differentiated** for the international market, whilst keeping the same brand name (eg coffee).

(b) The fact that, despite trade liberalisation, there are real differences between markets might suggest that focus is appropriate. Use national boundaries as a means of segmentation, or, as has been suggested, concentrate on those consumers in the international market who share characteristics **across** national segments.

Marketing at Work

An example of having the right 'product' for emerging markets is provided by the Bangladeshi firm, Beximco Pharmaceuticals, which pursues a differentiation-focus strategy.

Western firms, such as Glaxo, invest heavily in research and development, producing sophisticated but expensive products. Beximco, which sells to poorer markets, makes simple products cheaply. In developing countries, such as Vietnam and Iran, and even in Russia, a good supply of basic drugs is what is required. It is felt that there will be less emphasis on vertical expansion, which involves growing sales of sophisticated products to a small section of the population at ever-increasing prices.

Beximco has low wages and low research. Although tighter patent rules may make things worse, western drugs may go out of patent and can be copied.

Product-market strategies

9.7 Models such as the Ansoff matrix can also be applied, although its application might be more complex than in the single domestic market. To remind you, here follows a diagram.

Product

	Present	*New*
Present	Market penetration; (for growth) or consolidation (to maintain position) or withdrawal	Product development
New	Market development	Diversification

Market

9.8 How can this be applied to international marketing strategy? Unfortunately the categories tend to shift.

(a) It is obviously easy to suggest what the **new market** might be: another country.

(b) What, however, do we mean by '**new product**'? Is the product new to the company? Has it only been developed? Is the company still on a learning curve in its domestic market? In this case there might be a choice.

(i) Introduce the new product **simultaneously** in domestic and overseas markets.

(ii) Have a continuing rolling programme.

Year 1: the domestic market is dealt with first
Year 2: existing overseas markets are serviced
Year 3: genuinely new overseas markets are addressed

By year 3, the decision to introduce new products into new markets has effectively become one of market development, on the grounds that product has already been on sale at home and in existing overseas markets.

(c) It would appear **unlikely** that a company would set up abroad in a completely unfamiliar market with a completely new product, when there are easy opportunities to minimise the risk.

9.9 Of course, there are other models available such as the BCG or GEBS (covered in section 6).

Strategies for established global operators

9.10 The Ansoff matrix above can be applied equally to a company looking for new international development or to an established global player. Many strategic developments are concerned with building on where the organisation currently sits in global market, via current products and competences and stretching them to improve competitive position. There are a number of options for expanding or contracting operations.

Diversification

9.11 **Diversification** occurs when a company decides to make **new products for new markets**. It should have a clear idea about what it expects to gain from diversification.

(a) **Growth.** New products and new markets should be selected which offer prospects for growth which the existing product-market mix does not.

(b) **Investing surplus** funds not required for other expansion needs. (The funds could be returned to shareholders.)

Related diversification

> **Key Concept**
> **Related diversification** is 'development beyond the present *product market,* but still within the broad confines of the industry ... [it] ... therefore builds on the assets or activities which the firm has developed' (Johnson and Scholes). It takes the form of vertical or horizontal integration.

9.12 **Horizontal integration** refers to development into activities which are competitive with or directly **complementary** to a company's present activities.

9.13 **Vertical integration** occurs when a company becomes its own supplier.

(a) **Supplier** of raw materials, components or services (**backward vertical integration**). For example, backward integration would occur where a milk producer acquires its own dairy farms rather than buying raw milk from independent farmers.

(b) **Distributor** or sales agent (**forward vertical integration**), for example: where a manufacturer of synthetic yarn begins to produce shirts from the yarn instead of selling it to other shirt manufacturers.

9.14 **Advantages of vertical integration**

- A secure supply of materials, thus lower supplier bargaining power
- Stronger relationships with the 'final consumer' of the product
- Win a share of the higher profits at all stages of the value chain
- Pursue a differentiation strategy more effectively
- Raise **barriers to entry**

9.15 **Disadvantages of vertical integration**

(a) **Overconcentration.** A company places 'more eggs in the same end-market basket' (Ansoff). Such a policy is fairly inflexible, more sensitive to instabilities and increases the firm's dependence on a particular aspect of economic demand.

(b) The firm **fails to benefit from any economies of scale or technical advances** in the industry into which it has diversified. This is why, in the publishing industry, most printing is subcontracted to specialist printing firms, who can work machinery to capacity by doing work for many firms.

Unrelated diversification

> **Key Concept**
> **Unrelated or conglomerate diversification** 'is development beyond the present industry into products/ markets which, at face value, may bear no close relation to the present product/market.'

9.16 Conglomerate diversification is now very unfashionable. However, it has been a key strategy for companies in Asia, particularly South Korea.

9.17 **Advantages of conglomerate diversification**

- **Risk-spreading**
- **High profit opportunities**
- **Escape** from the present business

- **Better access to capital** markets
- **No other way to grow**
- **Use surplus cash**
- **Exploit under-utilised resources**
- **Obtain cash,** or other financial advantages (such as accumulated tax losses)
- **Use a company's image and reputation** in one market to develop into another

9.18 **Disadvantages of conglomerate diversification**

- The **dilution of shareholders' earnings**
- **Lack of a common identity and purpose** in a conglomerate organisation
- **Failure in one of the businesses will drag down the rest**
- **Lack of management experience**

Withdrawal

9.19 It might be the right decision to cease producing a product and/or to pull out of a market completely. This is a hard decision for managers to take if they have invested time and money or if the decision involves redundancies.

9.20 **Exit barriers** make this difficult.

- **Cost barriers** include redundancy costs and the difficulty of selling assets
- **Managers** might fail to see that it is no use throwing good money after bad
- **Political barriers** include government attitudes
- **Marketing considerations** (eg loss leaders) may delay withdrawal
- **Psychology** (managers hate to admit failure)
- People might wrongly assume that carrying on is a **low risk** strategy

9.21 **Reasons for exit**

(a) The **company's business** may be in buying firms, selling their assets and improving their performance, and then selling them at a profit.

(b) **Resource limitations** mean that less profitable businesses have to be abandoned. A business might be sold to a competitor, or occasionally to management (as a buy-out).

(c) A company may be forced to quit, because of **insolvency.**

(d) **Change of competitive strategy**. In the microprocessor industry, many American firms have left high-volume DRAM chips to Asian firms so as to concentrate on high value added niche products.

(e) **Decline in attractiveness of the market.**

(f) **Funds can earn more elsewhere.**

Guidelines for a product-market strategy

9.22 Johnson and Scholes suggested the following principles and guidelines for product-market planning.

(a) **The potential for improvement and growth.** It is one thing to eliminate unprofitable products but will there be sufficient growth potential among the products that remain in the product range?

(b) **Cash generation.** New products require some initial capital expenditure. Retained profits are by far the most significant source of new funds for companies. A company investing in the medium to long term which does not have enough current income from existing products, will go into liquidation, in spite of its future prospects.

(c) **The timing decision for killing off existing products**. There are some situations where existing products should be kept going for a while longer, to provide or maintain a necessary platform for launching new models.

(d) **The long-term rationale of a product or market development**.

(e) **Diversification by acquisition**. It might pay to buy product ranges or brands in a takeover deal. If the product-market strategy includes a policy of diversification, then the products or services which the expanding company should seek to acquire should provide definite benefits. We discuss acquisitions in the next chapter.

Country alliances

9.23 Countries can get together to pool resources and enter global markets which would otherwise be unavailable.

Marketing at Work

Eurofighter is a 1996 collaboration between Germany, the UK, Italy and Spain. It Is overseen by the NATO Eurofighter and Tornado Management Agency. The consortium foresees an available global market of 800 combat aircraft between 2005 and 2025, worth over $70 billion. Each of the partner companies is taking the lead for the consortium in different markets. British Aerospace is responsible for marketing to Canada, Australia, Malaysia, Singapore, Bahrain, Saudi Arabia and the United Arab Emirates.

The advantages of four leading European nations collaborating on such a project include:

- each contributes the expertise of their aerospace industry
- high technology jobs assured
- cost savings for the partner nations
- global competitiveness of Europe's aerospace industry

Adapted from the Eurofighter Website

---

10 LESSER DEVELOPED ECONOMIES   12/99

10.1 In industrially advanced countries companies can normally adopt the marketing strategy they choose; they have little or no restriction in using the marketing mix in the way most appropriate for each market. Marketing planning for **lesser developed countries** (LDCs) is notoriously difficult. A lesser developed country relies heavily on primary industry, with low GDP per capita and poorly developed infrastructure.

10.2 It is well known that **cultural differences** between markets pose one of the greatest challenges in international marketing. A means of countering this in marketing planning is to involve nationals from each market (an example of **bottom up** planning). In industrially advanced countries, with developed marketing professions, this is a practical method of trying to overcome the differences produced by culture. In LDCs, however, it can rarely be done and planning normally involves **top down** planning from the company's headquarters or input from expatriate managers who are unlikely to have the same cultural appreciation as local nationals.

10.3 At a lower level than the marketing planning system itself, each element of the marketing mix requires examination to ascertain the likely changes that need to be made to cater for LDCs.

10.4 The most obvious need for changes in a company's marketing plans is in **product adaptation**. In general terms products must be of more robust design and construction, and technologically simpler. For example, electrical equipment such as refrigerators often have to be constructed to function on a range of different voltages, and even from portable generators. The instruction booklet that accompanies the product may also have to be redesigned to cater for the lower average literacy levels. The robust and simple design and construction element of product adaptation meets a number of local needs.

(a) The **physical environment** may be harsher.

(b) Lack of available **repair facilities** may necessitate a low maintenance design.

(c) **Lower average income levels** may make customers more **price sensitive** and unable or unwilling to pay for the more sophisticated features used for product differentiation in industrialised markets.

Marketing at Work

Vehicle manufacturers are well aware of the need for these kinds of product adaptation. For example diesel models, which are more robust and easier to maintain, make up a greater proportion of the product range of all the major manufacturers in LDC markets.

10.5 **Price planning** also differs in LDCs when compared to industrially advanced markets. The most prevalent interference with free trade is **government restrictions** and controls on price. These may come in a number of forms, the most obvious being legal controls on either the maximum price that may be charged for the product, or the minimum, or both. Governments may also influence pricing less overtly by using **import duties**. The foreign exporter may be able to create some flexibility in pricing by adapting the product design (for example to include a minimum local content) to maximise the advantage from the tariff structures.

10.6 **Distribution** in LDCs also frequently requires a different approach. There are often three kinds of adaptation required.

(a) Governments, especially in countries that are centrally planned to a greater or lesser extent, may **dictate what distribution channels are used**, and indeed own them. For example, many African countries adopt such a system.

(b) Even if the distribution channels are free from government interference, the **range of channels** found in advanced economies may not exist, requiring the foreign exporter to adapt its plans or, if feasible, create an entirely new distribution system.

(c) As LDCs are often found in geographically 'difficult' places, the **speed and availability** of transportation may be restricted. This applies particularly in tropical countries with marked wet seasons, during which road transport is often impossible and rail or air the only alternatives. For products such as food, and particularly perishable food, this basic problem can be a severe disadvantage.

10.7 **Promoting** the product in LDCs requires similar adaptation of marketing planning to that for distribution. Restrictions may be placed on the type of advertising because of **cultural taboos** (for example women's clothing in many Muslim countries). Alternatively **communications media** may be government controlled and not accept commercial advertising. The communications infrastructure itself is often underdeveloped. Vast stretches of India and China, for example, do not have telephones.

10.8 Even when no controls are placed on the foreign company, the range of potential **promotional techniques** are likely to be fewer than for advanced economies. Direct mail, for example, may not be possible. Not only may the **source data** to compile suitable mailing lists be unavailable, but the target audience may also be unable to read it.

10.9 Each of the differences in planning the marketing mix between industrially advanced economies and LDCs may be tackled and an alternative put in place. What is often difficult or impossible to plan for adequately, however, is **political risk**. Changes in the political climate can occur overnight and bring with them wholesale changes in the business environment.

10.10 In marketing planning terms, all that is normally possible is to **minimise financial exposure** in LDCs with significant political instability. For example. the foreign company should avoid locating manufacturing plants in the country (which might be expropriated). Whilst it is normally good marketing practice to concentrate resources on a few markets, so that a significant impact is made in each, this policy should not be pursued in a group of LDCs that show high levels of political instability.

Emerging markets

Key Concept

An **emerging (or developing) market** is a variant of the lesser developed country, but is one which is opening up to the global economy. Other factors such as size and growth rate are important in the definition, as is how well the economy brings buyers and sellers together. An emerging economy can be seen as placed between an advanced economy and one which is stagnant or in decline.

10.11 Companies in emerging markets cannot generally adopt the same strategy as those in advanced economies. For example, an article in the *Harvard Business Review* (July-August 1997) suggested that while large diversified corporations have had their day in economies such as the USA or the UK, in developing countries such as Korea or the Latin American countries they are still a useful form of business organisation because they can **imitate the functions** of institutions found only in advanced economies (such as access to financial markets, education and training of managers, communications). Companies in emerging markets must take responsibility for a wide range of functions in order to do business well.

10.12 Because of problems with communications and other factors, companies in emerging markets find it much more difficult to establish **reputable brands**. When they are successful, they can extend that reputation across multiple products, eg Samsung. Promoting group identity is often pursued rather than promotion of individual product lines.

Marketing at Work

The Tata group of companies in India has interests in information technology, process control, advanced materials, oilfield services, and computer manufacturing. Its reputation has led to ventures with Daimler-Benz and AT&T. The philosophy of the company is reflected in the words of one of its executives: 'If we don't start these businesses, no one else will either, and society will be worse off.'

Chapter Roundup

- Firms can be **pushed** into **international marketing** by domestic adversity or **pulled** into it by attractive opportunities abroad. The level of commitment may be casual, active or committed.

- There are many reasons why international marketing is a more complicated exercise than domestic marketing.

- The **key decisions** are:
    - whether to market abroad at all
    - where to market
    - the mode of entry
    - marketing programmes
    - marketing organisation
    - marketing mix.

- The presence of a **global operator** can be a boon or a source of fear for the local community. Local businesses may feel particularly threatened.

- **International marketing planning** is sometimes the 'poor relation' of domestic marketing planning, if the firm has not really committed its resources to IM.

- Plans should state **assumptions, objectives and strategies**. The difficulties of IM planning reflect the difficulties of international marketing generally (ie fragmented markets, cultural problems).

- Planning orientation can be **ethnocentric**, **geocentric** or **polycentric**.

- **Information** is needed for each phase of the planning process.
    - Analysis and screening, matching company and country needs
    - Adapting the marketing mix to target markets
    - Developing the plan
    - Implementation and control

- The **problems** of planning and implementation include distance, characteristics of each market and domestic priorities. Sometimes 'bottom-up' or emergent planning or management is more effective than rigid 'top down' planning.

- In **competitive strategy**, cost leadership is compromised by the costs imposed by international trade and trade barriers, so focus or differentiation is perhaps a better choice. Using the Ansoff matrix, market development would naturally suggest overseas markets.

- **Lesser developed economies** present their own marketing problems and challenges.

Quick Quiz

1   What activities are covered by international marketing? (see para 2.1)
2   List six key decisions for IM. (2.8)
3   Why do firms become involved in IM? (3.1)
4   Why might a firm decide against getting involved in international markets? (3.3 (b))
5   How might a firm assess country attractiveness? (4.2)
6   List some types of risk. (4.4)
7   What three levels of involvement might a firm have in IM? (4.7)
8   List three possibilities for a firm's international marketing mix. (5.2)
9   Identify some barriers to standardisation. (5.4)
10 What would you expect to find in an international marketing plan? (6.1)
11 What general and specific objectives does good marketing planning achieve? (6.3)
12 What is the starting point in strategic marketing planning? (8.2)
13 Identify screening criteria. (8.11)
14 Describe a screening process. (8.16)
15 What financial issues might be relevant to screening? (8.18)
16 What is an emergent strategy? (8.33)
17 What are the problems of pursuing cost leadership, as a generic strategy, in global markets? (9.5)
18 What adaptations to distribution may be required when marketing in an LDC? (10.6)

Action Programme Review

1   See table on page 7

3   Livia Strange's department has generated its own pattern of competitive behaviour. It is an emergent strategy. It conflicts directly with the planned strategy proposed by the consultants. This little case history also makes the additional point that strategies are not only about numbers, targets and grand plans, but about the organisational cultures influencing a people's behaviour.

Now try illustrative question 6 at the end of the Study Text

7 Market Entry Methods

Chapter Topic List		Syllabus Reference
1	Setting the scene	-
2	Three methods of entry to overseas markets	2.9
3	The criteria for selecting a method of entry	2.9
4	Exporting: introduction	2.9
5	Indirect exports	2.9
6	Direct exports	2.9
7	The rationale for overseas production	2.9
8	Methods of overseas production	2, 3, 2.9

Learning Outcomes

After completing this chapter you will have an appreciation of the issues facing a company planning its international marketing strategy as it determines its market entry choices.

You will understand what factors influence the selection of market entry methods and the implications for strategy.

Different methods imply a different levels of involvement in each market.

Key Concepts Introduced

- Indirect exports
- Direct exports
- Overseas manufacture
- Complementary exporting

- Licensing agreement
- Franchise
- Joint venture
- Organic growth

Examples of Marketing at Work

- The Shanghai Forever Bicycle Company
- Distribution in Japan
- Castlemain XXXX, Pilkington and Philips
- Marks and Spencer

- Joint ventures
- Tesco and Samsung
- Bass

1 SETTING THE SCENE

1.1 Once a market has been selected, a **method of market entry** must be chosen. The method of entry to the overseas market has a number of wide reaching implications for the marketing mix, and is a critical indicator of a firm's depth of involvement in, and vulnerability to, the overseas market. Why might this be so?

1.2 A product might be manufactured at home or abroad. If the product is manufactured at home and exported (Sections 4 and 5), the firm is vulnerable to exchange rate fluctuations. On the other hand, a substantial investment might be needed for overseas operations (Section 7).

1.3 Mode of entry also has implications for the **distribution channel.** Although, in domestic markets, firms often give some control over distribution to intermediaries, this problem is magnified in international terms. In some cases, a firm has no choice but to enter into a joint venture. For many firms, overseas operations means they are forced into the aims of intermediaries even though this may not be the ideal means of the satisfying the needs of the end consumer (Section 8). In fact, as we shall learn in Chapter 8, the method of entry has significant implications for the structure of the organisation.

1.4 The method of market entry is of strategic importance. A market may not appear so attractive as in the initial assessment if the mode of entry requires unusual effort. So although method of entry decides 'how' a firm goes about international marketing it has strategic implications as it affects the **risk** a firm encounters. It is therefore important that you recognise that market entry **strategies** and market entry **methods** must be consistent and complementary. The latter is the way to achieve the goals of the former.

2 THREE METHODS OF ENTRY TO OVERSEAS MARKETS

2.1 If an organisation has decided to enter an overseas market, the way it does so is of crucial strategic importance. The mode of entry affects a firm's entire marketing mix and its control over the mix elements.

2.2 Broadly, three ways of entering foreign markets can be identified: direct exports, indirect exports and overseas manufacturing.

Key Concepts

Indirect exports. These are sales to intermediary organisations at home which then resell the product to customers overseas. It is the outsourcing of the exporting function to a third party.

Direct exports. These are sales to customers overseas without the use of export houses etc. These customers may be intermediary organisations based abroad or end-users.

Overseas manufacture. A firm may set up its own production operation overseas or enter into a joint venture with an enterprise in the overseas market. As an example, a number of Japanese companies have established factories in the UK to manufacture for the UK and European markets.

2.3 Each of these methods is discussed in more detail below, but here is a diagram in outline.

```
                              Decision to
                             enter overseas
                             markets: but
                            which mode of entry?
```

A flowchart with two main branches: **Exporting** and **Overseas production**.

Under **Exporting**:
- **Indirect**
  - Home-based export managers
  - Buying offices
  - Piggy-backing
- **Direct**
  - Overseas export agent
  - to final user
  - via company branch offices
  - E-commerce and Internet

Under **Overseas production**:
- Licensing
- Contract manufacture
- Joint venture
- Wholly owned overseas production
  - Acquisition
  - Organic growth

Key issues?	Exchange rates Protectionism Lack of knowledge	⟶	Political risk Partnership Managing overseas facilities
Involvement	Usually less involved, but an exporter might *depend* on the overseas market	⟶	Usually more involved, but overseas subsidiaries might act independently: varying levels of control

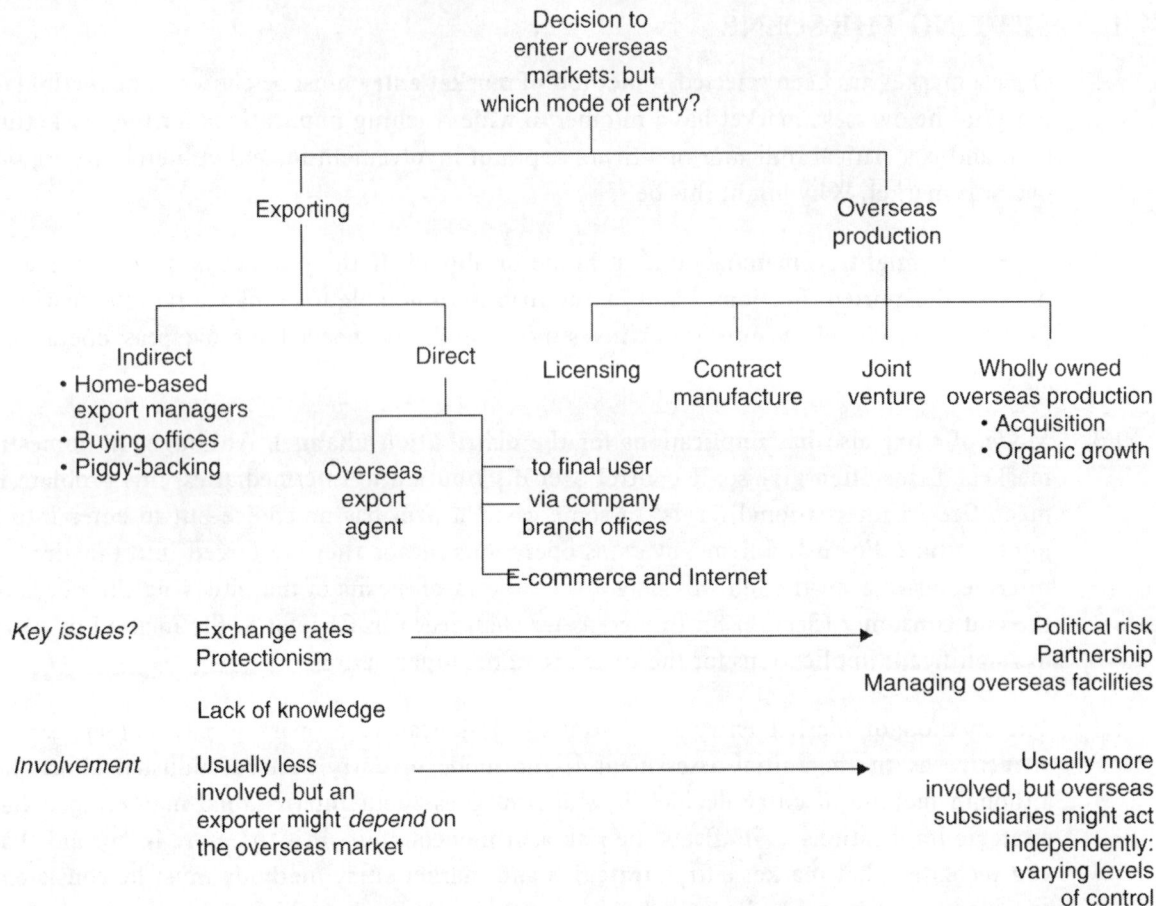

3 THE CRITERIA FOR SELECTING A METHOD OF ENTRY Specimen paper

3.1 The most suitable method of entry varies.

(a) Among firms in the same industry (eg a new exporter as opposed to a long-established exporter)

(b) According to the market (eg some countries limit imports to protect domestic manufacturers whereas others promote free trade)

(c) Over time (eg as some countries become more, or less, hostile to direct inward investment by foreign companies)

3.2 To choose a method of entry to a particular market, a firm should consider the following issues.

(a) **Firm's marketing objectives,** in relation to volume, timescale and coverage of market segments. Thus setting up an overseas production facility would be inappropriate if sales are expected to be low in volume, or if the product is only to be on sale for a limited period.

(b) **Firm's size**. A small firm is less likely than a large one to possess sufficient resources to set up and run a production facility overseas. Not only would the firm have to provide investment capital and organisational ability, but it would also have to support the costs of continuing operations.

(c) **Mode availability.** A firm might have to use different methods of entry to enter different markets. Some countries only allow a restricted level of imports, but will welcome a firm if it builds manufacturing facilities which provide jobs and limit the outflow of foreign exchange. In this case, overseas manufacture is a better option than direct export.

(d) **Method quality**. In some cases, all modes may be possible in theory, but some are of questionable quality or practicality. The lack of suitably qualified distributors or agents would preclude the export, direct or indirect, of high technology goods needing installation, maintenance and servicing by personnel with specialist technical skills.

(e) **Human resources requirements**. These vary according to which method of entry is used. When a firm is unable to recruit suitable staff either at home or overseas, indirect exporting or the use of agents based overseas may be the only realistic option.

(f) **Market information feedback**. In some cases a firm can receive feedback information about the market and its marketing effort from its sales staff or distribution channels. In these circumstances direct export or joint ventures may be preferred to indirect export.

Marketing at Work

One small UK company manufacturing and selling a range of leather goods decided to set up a direct export model using a sales subsidiary in France. Having done so they discovered from closer contact with the customers that the reason that one of their best selling lines in the UK was a flop in France was that French customers thought the regal red lining to their wallets was 'too vulgar'. A modest product change using a muted brown lining made the product very acceptable to French customers and sales rocketed.

(g) **Learning curve requirements**. Firms which intend a heavy future involvement might need to learn from the experience that close involvement in an overseas market can bring. This argues against the use of indirect exporting as the method of entry.

(h) **Risks**. Some risks, such as political risk or the risk of the expropriation of overseas assets by foreign governments, might discourage firms from using overseas production as the method of entry to overseas markets. Instead, firms might prefer the indirect export mode as it is safer. On the other hand, the risk of losing touch with customers and their requirements would encourage either direct export or overseas production.

(i) **Control needs**. Control over the marketing mix and the distribution channel varies greatly by method of entry. Production overseas by a wholly owned subsidiary gives a firm absolute control while indirect exporting offers virtually no control to the exporter.

Exam Tip

The December 1997 exam featured a question on choice of entry criteria. You could have used the list above as a starting point to your answer.

---

4 EXPORTING: INTRODUCTION

4.1 **Exporting** is the easiest, cheapest and most commonly used route into a new foreign market. Many firms become exporters in an unplanned, haphazard and reactive way, simply by accepting orders from potential customers who happen to be based overseas. However, it is also common for a firm to take a proactive approach to exporting, by systematic planning and the identification and selection of target markets for its exports. This gives rise to several advantages over those entry methods which require greater involvement in the overseas market.

(a) The principal benefit is that exporters are able to concentrate production in a **single location**, giving economies of scale and consistency of product quality.

(b) Firms lacking the **know-how and experience** can try international marketing on a small scale.

(c) Exporting enables firms to **develop and test** their plans and strategies.

(d) Exporting enables firms to minimise their **operating costs,** administrative overheads and personnel requirements.

Marketing at Work

The Shanghai Forever Bicycle Company, which has built 100m bicycles since 1949, is making low profits as China's bicycle market is oversupplied. To use the capacity, the firm is investing in new types of bike and, as importantly, has been exporting heavily to Africa and South America. Excess domestic capacity makes establishing overseas plants a waste of money. (*Financial Times*)

4.2 Although exporting requires a **low involvement** in the overseas market, this does not necessarily imply that only low investment is needed. Exporting requires investment in **market research, strategy** formulation and careful **implementation of the marketing mix**. The initial success of Japanese car firms in the USA and Europe was based on research and strategic planning that was both extensive and costly.

5 INDIRECT EXPORTS

5.1 **Indirect exporting** is where a firm's goods are sold abroad by other organisations. There are four ways of indirect export.

- Export houses
- Specialist export managers
- UK buying offices of foreign stores and governments
- Complementary exporting

Export houses

5.2 **Export houses** are firms which facilitate exporting on behalf of the producer. There are three main types of export house.

(a) **Export merchants** act as export principals. They buy goods from a producer and sell them abroad.

(b) **Confirming houses** also act as principals. Their main function is to provide credit to customers when the producer is unwilling to do so.

(c) **Manufacturers' export agents** are based at home, but sell abroad for the producer. An agent will usually cover a particular sector or industry, (eg pottery). Remuneration is by commission.

5.3 **Advantages of export houses**

(a) The producer gains the benefits of the export house's market knowledge and contacts.

(b) Except in the case of export agents the producer is relieved of the need to do the following.

- **Finance** the export transaction
- Suffer the **credit risk**
- Prepare **export documentation**

(c)   The producer does not bear the **overhead costs** of export marketing.

(d)   In some cases export merchants receive preferential treatment from foreign institutional and organisational customers.

(e)   Where export agents are used, the producer retains considerable **control** over the market.

5.4   **Disadvantages of export houses**

(a)   Ultimately, it is not the producer's but the merchant's decision to market a product, and so a producer is at the merchant's mercy.

(b)   Any goodwill created in the market usually benefits the merchant and not the producer.

(c)   As with all intermediaries, an export house or merchant might service a variety of producing organisations. An individual producer cannot rely on the merchant's exclusive loyalty.

(d)   Export houses are not normally willing to enter into long term arrangements with a producer.

Specialist export managers

5.5   Specialist **export management firms** (SEMs) offer a full export management service. In effect, they perform the same functions as an in-house export department but are normally remunerated by way of commission.

(a)   Advantages of using a specialist export manager are the same as those for export houses. In addition, the manufacturer (or service provider) immediately gains its own export department without incurring overheads, retains full market control and can normally expect a long term relationship with the export manager.

(b)   Disadvantages do exist however.

(i)   As the export manager is an independent organisation, it can leave the producer's service and the producer will have gained **no in-house exporting expertise.**

(ii)   As the producer does not learn from the experience of exporting, this may adversely affect future options by restricting those available.

(iii)   The SEM may not have sufficient knowledge of all the producer's markets.

UK buying offices of foreign stores and governments

5.6   Many foreign governments and foreign companies (eg department stores) have buying offices set up permanently in the UK. In addition, other foreign companies send representatives on buying expeditions to the UK.

Complementary exporting

> ### Key Concept
>
> **Complementary exporting** ('**piggy back exporting**') occurs when one producing organisation (the **carrier**) uses its own established IM channels to market the products of another producer (the **rider**) as well as its own. The carrier may act as:
>
> (a)   a simple transporter, using spare capacity in its distribution network;
>
> (b)   an agent, selling the rider's goods for commission;
>
> (c)   a merchant, buying and selling the rider's goods.

5.7   **Advantages of complementary exporting**

(a)   The carrier earns increased profit from a better use of distribution capacity and can sell a more attractive product range.

(b)   The rider obtains entry to a market at low cost and low risk.

5.8   **Turnkey contracts** may also provide opportunities for complementary exporting. A single firm engaged on a particular project overseas (eg construction and civil engineering projects in the Middle East) will often acquire products and services from other firms in the home country for the project.

6   DIRECT EXPORTS

6.1   **Direct exporting** occurs where the producing organisation itself performs the export tasks rather than using an intermediary. Sales are made directly to customers overseas who may be the wholesalers, retailers or final users. Sales may increasingly be made via e-commerce on the Internet.

Sales to final user

6.2   In this case there are clearly no intermediaries. Typical customers include industrial users, governments or mail order customers. Marketing in this environment is similar to marketing in the domestic market, although there are the added problems of distance, product regulations, language and culture.

Overseas agencies

6.3   Strictly speaking an **overseas export agent** is an overseas firm hired to effect a sales contract between the principal (ie the exporter) and a customer. Agents do not take title to goods; they earn a commission. In practice, however, the phrase is often understood to include distributors (who do take title). Some agents merely arrange sales; others hold stocks and/or carry out servicing on the principal's behalf.

6.4   **Advantages of overseas agents**

(a)   They have extensive knowledge and experience of the overseas market and the customers.

(b)   Their existing product range is usually complementary to the exporter's. This may help the exporter penetrate the overseas market.

(c)   The exporter does not have to make a large investment outlay.

(d)   The political risk is low.

6.5 **Disadvantages**

(a) An intermediary's commitment and motivation may be weaker than the producer's.

(b) Agents usually want steady turnover. Using an agent may not be the most appropriate way of selling low volume, high value goods with unsteady patterns of demand, or where sales are infrequent.

(c) Many agents are too small to exploit a major market to its full extent. Many serve only limited geographical segments.

(d) As a market grows large it becomes less efficient to use an agent. A branch office or subsidiary company will achieve economies of scale.

As with all intermediaries, the use of an agent requires careful planning, selection, motivation and control.

Regulation of agency agreements

6.6 From January 1994, as part of Single European Market harmonisation, UK companies have had to apply European Union-wide legislation to agency agreements. The difference is that what were in the past freely negotiated agreements, are now based on a structure of law.

6.7 EU regulations apply to all agency agreements **within** the EU (including the domestic market), through not agents outside the EU. The law draws on German law. Both sides, the principal and agent, have precise rights and duties.

(a) Agents have the right to commission on sales within a reasonable time after the agreement has ended. The length of the period is not specified, so it has to be negotiated at the outset.

(b) Principals cannot delay paying their agents simply because the principals themselves have not received payment from customers.

(c) To terminate a contract, written notice is required (one month in the first year, two months in the second, and three months subsequently).

(d) Provided the agent has not breached contract terms, the agent is liable for compensation for termination of the agreement.

6.8 Small businesses, especially, will have to pay attention to agency contracts.

Distributors/stockists

6.9 **Distributors** are customers with preferential rights to buy and sell a range of a firm's goods in a specific geographical area. Distributors earn profit, not commission. They differ from wholesalers only in that their selling and marketing activities on behalf of a producer are restricted geographically.

6.10 **Stockists** are distributors who receive more favourable financial rewards than distributors as they normally undertake to carry at least a certain minimum level of stock. The advantages and disadvantages of distributors and stockists are similar to those associated with overseas agents.

BPP PUBLISHING

Marketing at Work

In some markets, such as Japan which has a complicated distribution system of retailers, a knowledgeable local distributor is essential. Tie-ups with Japanese partners and expensive marketing are necessary before discussions can start.

Company branch offices abroad

6.11 A firm can establish its own office in a foreign market for the purpose of marketing and distribution.

6.12 **Advantages**

(a) When sales have reached a certain level, branch offices become more effective than agencies.

(b) Sales performance will improve, as the commitment and motivation of a producer's own staff should be more effective than those of an agent.

(c) The producer retains complete marketing control.

(d) The producer should be able to acquire more accurate and timely market information.

(e) Customer service should improve. Intermediaries are notorious for poor performance in this respect.

6.13 **Disadvantages**

(a) Higher investment, overhead and running costs are entailed.

(b) There can be a political risk, particularly expropriation of assets.

(c) The firm will be subject to local employee legislation (eg minimum number of local staff, dismissal, trade union membership) which it may not welcome.

E-commerce

6.14 This is a newer method of direct market entry for the international marketer. Although it is still in its infancy, it is set for expansion according to most forecasts. It was explored in more detail in Chapter 2, where some examples were given.

7 THE RATIONALE FOR OVERSEAS PRODUCTION

7.1 Firms that are fully committed to international marketing are often drawn into overseas manufacture. This gives rise to several major benefits.

(a) Location abroad can offer a better understanding of the problems and needs of customers in the overseas market.

(b) Some markets (eg the USA) are so large that economies of scale can still be gained from overseas production.

(c) Production costs are lower in some countries overseas than at home.

(d) For firms producing weighty or bulky products (eg brewers), overseas production can reduce storage and transportation costs.

(e) Overseas production can overcome the effects of tariff and non-tariff barriers to imports.

(f)   Where an overseas government is a customer, manufacture in the overseas market may be a factor in winning orders.

7.2   For firms which are late entrants to a market, taking over a firm in the overseas market can be a more effective way of establishing a production facility overseas than building one from scratch. Alternatively the firm might enter into co-operative agreements with firms in the overseas market.

7.3   The figure below (adapted from Doole, Lowe and Phillips) shows the balance between **control** and **risk** of the key market entry methods. We have already covered risks.

Political
Exchange risk
Business risk

Clearly the greater the level of involvement, the greater the risk.

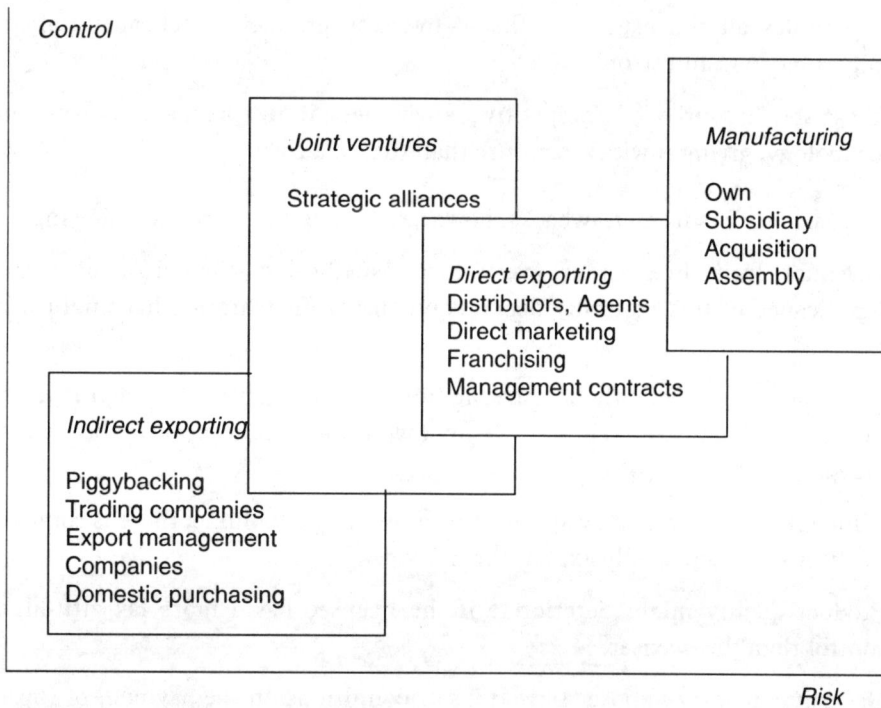

Control

Joint ventures

Strategic alliances

Manufacturing

Own
Subsidiary
Acquisition
Assembly

Direct exporting
Distributors, Agents
Direct marketing
Franchising
Management contracts

Indirect exporting

Piggybacking
Trading companies
Export management
Companies
Domestic purchasing

Risk

8   METHODS OF OVERSEAS PRODUCTION

8.1   A firm's strategic choice of overseas production method depends on its objectives, resources and level of commitment to international marketing.

Licensing

> **Key Concept**
>
> A **licensing agreement** is a commercial contract whereby the licenser gives something of value to the licensee in exchange for certain performances and payments.

8.2   The licenser may provide any of the following.

- Rights to produce a patented product or use a patented production process
- Manufacturing know-how (unpatented)
- Technical advice and assistance

- Marketing advice and assistance
- Rights to use a trademark, brand etc

8.3 Licensing is growing in extent and importance throughout the world. It is used by small, medium and large firms, as it has many advantages. These are listed below.

(a) It requires no investment save the continuing costs of monitoring the agreement.

(b) It enables entry into markets that would otherwise be closed (eg by tariffs, government attitude and policies).

(c) As a method of entry, it is relatively simple and quick.

(d) The licenser gains access to knowledge of local conditions.

(e) New products can be introduced to many countries quickly because of low investment requirements.

(f) It provides all the usual benefits of overseas production (cheaper transport, lower import barriers and so on).

(g) It can be a source of competitive advantage, if it spreads the firm's proprietary technology, giving it wider exposure than that of a rival.

8.4 Licensing also suffers from drawbacks, however. Among these are the following.

(a) Revenues from licenses are very low, usually less than 10% of turnover. The significance of this naturally depends on the profit margins that might otherwise be expected.

(b) A licensee may eventually become the licenser's competitor. During the license period, the licensee may gain enough know-how from the licensor to be able to operate independently.

(c) Although the contract may specify a minimum sales volume, there is some danger that the licensee will not fully exploit the market.

(d) Product quality might deteriorate if the licensee has a more lax attitude to quality control than the licenser.

(e) Governments may impose restrictions or conditions on the payment of royalties to the licenser or on the supply of components.

(f) It is often difficult to control the licensee effectively. The licensee's objectives often conflict with those of the licenser and disagreements are common.

(g) With some new contracts the firm may not be able to manage.

8.5 Astute management of the license agreement is essential. Therefore licensers should:

(a) be careful in the choice of licensees (eg identify criteria that must be satisfied);

(b) design contracts that protect both parties;

(c) control the licensee, by, say, having an equity interest in the licensee's business or by retaining control over key input components;

(d) take action to motivate the licensee.

Marketing at Work

(a) *Consumer marketing.* Many beers are brewed under licence. For example, Castlemaine XXXX, an Australian beer, is brewed in the UK under licence.

(b) *Industrial marketing.* Pilkington's developed the float glass process. It licensed the use of this process to other firms world-wide, and still collects revenue.

(c) *Consumer and industrial applications.* The technology behind CDs was devised by Philips, but has been licensed world-wide.

Franchising

8.6 Franchising is a type of licensing.

> ### Key Concept
> The **franchise** agreement specifies, in more detail than a license agreement, exactly what is expected of the franchisee. In a franchise arrangement, the franchiser supplies a standard package of goods, components or ingredients along with management and marketing services or advice. The franchisee supplies capital, personal involvement and local market knowledge. Avis, Holiday Inn, Pepsi Cola, Kentucky Fried Chicken, the Body Shop, and McDonald's have franchise arrangements in many countries.

Marketing at Work

Marks and Spencer, when announcing in late 1997 a major move to become a global retailer, indicated that one rapid way to become established, particularly in the far eastern markets, was to franchise its highly regarded name to partner organisations who had money to invest in prime retail locations. It would be much quicker than having to negotiate for each of the necessary sites themselves.

8.7 The advantages and disadvantages of franchising are largely the same as those of licensing.

(a) An extra benefit, however, is that it provides some leverage for controlling the franchisee's activities as the franchiser supplies ingredients or components.

(b) A particular disadvantage of franchising is that the search for competent candidates is both costly and time consuming where the franchiser requires many outlets (eg McDonalds in the UK). This has led to decisions by Burger King and Kentucky Fried Chicken to reduce the number of franchised outlets in the UK.

Contract manufacture

8.8 In the case of contract manufacture a firm (the contractor) makes a contract with another firm (the contractee) abroad whereby the contractee manufactures or assembles a product on behalf of the contractor. The contractor retains full control over marketing and distribution whilst the manufacture is done by a local firm. Firms such as Del Monte, Colgate, and Procter and Gamble, use this method of entry to overseas markets.

Advantages of contract manufacture include the following.

(a) There is no need to invest in plant overseas.

(b) Risk associated with currency fluctuations is largely avoided.

(c) The risk of asset expropriation is minimised.

(d) A product manufactured in the overseas market may be easier to sell, especially to government customers.

(e) Lower transport costs and, sometimes, lower production costs can be obtained.

8.9 Contract manufacture

- Countries where the **small size of the market** discourages investment in plant
- Firms whose main strengths are in **marketing** rather than production

8.10 Contract manufacture does involve some disadvantages, which include the following.

(a) Overseas contractee producers who are **reliable and capable** cannot always be easily identified.

(b) Sometimes the contractee producer's personnel must receive intensive and substantial **technical training**.

(c) The contractee producer may eventually become a **competitor**.

(d) **Quality control** problems in manufacturing may arise.

Joint ventures

Key Concept

A **joint venture** is an arrangement where two or more (often competing) firms join forces for **manufacturing, financial and marketing purposes** and each has a share in both the equity and the management of the business, sharing profits, risks and assets.

8.11 Forming a joint venture with a technologically advanced foreign company can lead to new product development, maybe at a lower cost.

8.12 Licensing, franchising and contract manufacture are loose forms of joint venture. However joint ventures are bound by much stronger formal ties. They essentially focus on a single national market. When based abroad, they usually involve partners of unequal strength, for example when a developed country multinational, contributing capital and technology joins forces with a local firm in a developing country, offering local market knowledge and contacts.

Marketing at Work

Ford and Mobil Oil in the US announced a strategic alliance to work on new fuel systems for the automotive industry. Faced with threatened and actual new exhaust emission standards in California and, probably, the rest of the world, together with resource shortages in oil stocks possible in the foreseeable future, these two companies have chosen to pool R & D expertise to find a solution which can benefit both corporations.

US car manufacturers have acquired parts of Japanese firms to participate in small car development eg Ford and Mazda.

Coca Cola and Cadbury Schweppes bottle and distribute Coca Cola in Great Britain.

8.13 A joint venture is usually an alternative to seeking to buy or build a wholly owned manufacturing operation abroad and can offer substantial advantages.

(a) As the **capital outlay is shared,** joint ventures are attractive to smaller or risk-averse firms, or where very expensive new technologies are being researched and developed (such as the civil aerospace industry).

(b) When funds are limited, joint ventures permit **coverage of a larger number of countries** since each one requires less investment by each participator.

(c) A joint venture can reduce the risk of **government intervention** as a local firm is involved (eg Club Mediterranee pays much attention to this factor). The strong role of government in China means that nearly all foreign ventures in China are alliances with Chinese partners.

(d) Licensing and franchising often give a company **income based on turnover,** and any profits from cost reductions accrue to the licensee. In a joint venture, the participating enterprises benefit from **all sources of profit.**

(e) Joint ventures can provide **close control** over marketing and other operations.

(f) A joint venture with an indigenous firm provides **local knowledge.** This is a big advantage for firms seeking to do business in difficult markets, such as Russia. Political know-how, site selection expertise and business connections are important.

(g) In **oligopolistic** markets, where a few firms are dominant, a foreign firm may find the cost of market entry too high, and seek an alliance with an established competitor.

Marketing at Work

Tesco is to invest £130 million in developing a chain of hypermarkets in South Korea in partnership with Samsung (*The Times*). Tesco is to invest £80 million in cash, with Samsung contributing two hypermarkets and three development sites worth a similar amount.

Tesco said the move was part of a coherent long term strategy of expanding into underdeveloped markets. It has acquired 13 hypermarkets in Thailand. Outside the UK, Tesco now operates in countries with a total population of 170 million people.

8.14 Partners in a joint venture do not necessarily hold equal shares, and the contribution from each partner may vary. Funding, technology, equipment and marketing organisation may be contributed. There are several forms of joint venture.

- **Spider's web,** which consists of many firms in a network
- **Go-together then split** after a period of time, either due to success or failure
- **Successive integration**

8.15 Killing categories joint ventures into **dominant** and **shared** partnerships, depending upon which party's particular know-how or competencies are more critical.

8.16 The major disadvantage of joint ventures is that there can be major **conflicts of interest** between the different parties.

- **Profit** shares
- Amounts **invested**
- The **management** of the joint venture
- The **marketing strategy**

For these reasons firms such as IBM have, in the past, been reluctant to engage in joint ventures, although this policy has changed with the announcement of co-operative agreements with Apple (for work stations) Siemens and Dell.

8.17 Some protectionist **governments** discourage or even prohibit foreign firms setting up independent operations. Instead, they encourage joint ventures with indigenous firms.

    (a) Some governments regard uncontrolled investments from overseas as a type of colonial exploitation.

    (b) They are averse to sending foreign exchange outside the country.

    (c) Joint ventures generally involve a transfer of **know-how and technology** that benefits the local economy. Joint venturing between outside and local firms is encouraged, for example, in India, Nigeria and the former USSR.

8.18 There is always a potential for conflict. There are ways to minimise it.

- Careful selection of partners
- Formulation of jointly beneficial contracts
- Pre-arranging for arbitration to resolve any clashes that occur

---

Marketing at Work

From the *Financial Times*, March 2000:

Bass, the UK's second largest brewer, is set to pull out of a brewing joint venture that came to symbolise the intemperate expectations of some foreign companies in China's vast potential market.

The cultural chasm that divided the two partners was apparent at the 1996 launch. The Chinese tried to eat haggis and neeps and tatties with chopsticks, while the strains of bagpipes followed a Beijing opera performance.

Soon after the joint venture began production, growth in the local beer market, which had averaged over 20 per cent a year for more than a decade, began to decline.

As the market became over-supplied, local protectionism grew and road blocks went up across China to prevent deliveries to areas with one of the country's 850 breweries.

The Bass venture was in too isolated a location to command a large local market.

The cost of advertising in China's big cities was steep and largely failed to convince consumers to pay the extra price premium over local brands.

The market for premium beer remains limited in China, where fashionable bars are rarities beyond the large cities.'

The consortium

8.19 Under this approach, member firms create a **working relationship,** but not a new entity. The aircraft industry offers several examples, such as the European airbus, because the risks and costs associated with producing several hundred aircraft are so high.

8.20 The major jet engine companies have also been involved in this type of arrangement. Rolls Royce aero engines indulge in project specific ventures.

8.21 The consortium approach has the obvious advantage that the involvement of several high profile firms from several countries should ensure a certain level of sales.

Strategic alliances

8.22 These have become a popular model for global expansion. Some writers such as Kenichi Ohmae have argued that they are vital for survival in a world of fierce competition and shorter product life cycles.

8.23 The participants tend to be **competing firms from different countries,** seeking to enhance their competencies by **combining resources**, but without sacrificing autonomy. The strategic alliance is usually concerned with gaining market entry, remaining globally competitive and attaining economies of scale. According to Jeannet and Hennessey, they can be categorised as follows.

- **Production** based alliances - improving manufacturing and production efficiency
- **Distribution** based alliances - sharing distribution networks
- **Technology** based alliances pooling R & D costs

8.24 Alliances may be **horizontal** (between two firms in the same industry) or **vertical**, involving collaboration between a supplier and a buyer. Sometimes, they involve firms with no such connection, such as when Toys R Us and McDonalds formed a venture in 1990 to build Toys R US stores in Japan which had a McDonalds restaurant attached.

8.25 Strategic alliances have mainly concentrated in manufacturing and high tech industries, and increasingly in services (notably airlines, such as the 'One World' alliance involving British Airways, Qantas and several other international collaborators).

8.26 Strategic alliances have the following features.

(a) They are collaborations between two or more competing companies of similar strength, generally from industrialised countries.

(b) The relative contributions by the companies are balanced.

(c) The motivation for the alliance is generally broadly strategic or competitive, rather than purely for market access or economies of scale.

(d) The relationships are reciprocal and provide the opportunity for learning.

(e) They have a strategic and global focus, and seek to enhance global competitiveness via gaining access to a whole series of resources and skills.

Wholly owned overseas production

8.27 Establishing and running a **production facility** in an overseas market demonstrates the fullest commitment to that market. Production capacity can be built from scratch, or an existing firm acquired.

8.28 **Advantages of wholly owned overseas manufacture**

(a) The firm does not have to **share its profits** with partners of any kind.

(b) The firm does not have to **share or delegate decision making** and so there are no losses in efficiency arising from inter-firm conflict.

(c) There are none of the **communication problems** that arise in joint ventures, license agreements etc.

(d) The firm is able to operate a completely **integrated** and synergistic international system.

(e) The firm gains more **experience** from overseas production.

8.29 There are also major disadvantages.

(a) The **substantial investment** funding required prevents some firms from establishing operations overseas.

(b) **Suitable managers,** whether recruited in the overseas market or posted abroad from home, may be difficult to obtain.

(c) Some **overseas governments** discourage 100% ownership of an enterprise by a foreign company.

(d) This method of entry forgoes the benefits of an **overseas partner's market knowledge, distribution system** and other **local expertise.**

Action Programme 1

You are marketing chocolate for a large UK confectionery firm. The UK style of chocolate is not widely appreciated in Europe although a recent EU ruling has paved the way for British chocolate to be stocked on the continent. If you wished to expand into European markets, what method of entry would you use?

Acquisition vs organic growth

8.30 **Acquisition,** as a method of entry, is rapid and offers the benefits of an existing management team, market knowledge and all the other trappings of a 'going concern'. General Motors, for example, enjoyed these gains on entry to the UK market by the acquisition of Vauxhall Motors. At the same time, acquisitions which go wrong (eg the Midland Bank's purchase of the California based Crocker Bank) can have serious and long term penalties.

8.31 **Acquiring** a company can also be a way of ensuring a market presence in an overseas market or segment.

8.32 Acquiring an overseas subsidiary has the following justifications, in **marketing** terms.

- Shared **distribution networks** (ie getting more share out of your existing network)
- Access to **new markets,** in which the acquired company already has a presence
- Access to **new brands,** so that a variety of brands can be promoted

Product range

8.33 Another reason for acquiring a company is to expand the product range.

8.34 The difficulties of **acquisitions** in international markets are expanded versions of their problems in the domestic markets, in other words problems with corporate culture, operational disruption and so forth.

Organic growth

Key Concept
Organic growth is the expansion of a firm's size, profits and activities, achieved without taking over other firms.

8.35 Organic growth offers fewer of the 'quick' advantages of acquisitions: it involves building up a presence from scratch.

(a) The disadvantages are the time and effort it takes to build a new market presence, especially in **mature** markets, where growth in market share involves a war of attrition, and where a firm has little **knowledge** of the market.

(b) However, it offers control over the process of growth, and there need be fewer clashes of corporate culture. For **new** products it might be better than acquisitions.

8.36 **Franchising**, discussed earlier might be a useful way of promoting 'organic growth', both with control and with a sharing of resources and local knowledge. After all, local franchisees can be bought out at a later stage.

8.37 Entry to an overseas market by creating new capacity can be beneficial if there are no likely candidates for takeover, or if acquisition is prohibited by the government.

(a) This entry method enables the use of the newest production technology.

(b) The investing company may also be able to start afresh with new forms of managing industrial relations.

8.38 These were major benefits for Nissan Motors when the company created new capacity in Sunderland and Tennessee. However, another reason for direct inward investment by Japanese companies in Europe is the threat of being excluded from the single European market. The UK has been a prime site because of government support and relatively low labour costs, for example when compared with Germany.

Chapter Roundup

- It is possible to identify **three methods of entry** to foreign markets.

  - indirect exports
  - direct exports
  - overseas manufacture

- The **choice** of method of entry is affected by:

  - the firm and its products and history
  - the foreign market
  - the degree of involvement the firm wants in the foreign market

- **Indirect exporting** occurs when a firm uses an intermediary. **Direct exporting** is when the firm exports directly to the overseas markets or overseas agency.

- Some firms set up **overseas branch offices** to facilitate direct exports, but others enter the overseas market for good, as it were, by setting up **production facilities** overseas.

- Firms can choose **acquisition** or **joint venture** arrangements or can choose to go it alone. Joint ventures and acquisitions might be preferred as they offer greater expertise.

Quick Quiz

1   What are the main ways of entering foreign markets? (see para 2.2)
2   What factors might affect the method of entry decision for a prospective international marketing company? (3.2)
3   What are the advantages of exporting over methods of market entry requiring greater involvement? (4.1)
4   What are the ways of exporting indirectly? (5.1)
5   What are the advantages and disadvantages of using overseas agents? (6.4 - 6.8)
6   Why should a company consider overseas manufacturing? (7.1)
7   What are joint ventures and why are they so popular? (8.11 - 8.13)
8   What is a consortium? Give an example. (8.19 - 8.20)
9   What are the advantages and disadvantages of wholly owned overseas manufacture? (8.28-8.29)
10 Why do some companies choose to enter overseas markets by acquisition? (8.30)
11 When might firms pursue organic growth? (8.35 - 8.38)

Action Programme Review

1   You would probably manufacture overseas, perhaps by buying an overseas company with the expertise and available brands.

Now try illustrative question 7 at the end of the Study Text

8 Organising for International Marketing

Learning Outcomes

After studying this chapter you will have an understanding of:

- various types of organisational structure

- how they are relevant to international marketing planning

- human resource issues behind the choice of expatriate or local staff

Key Concepts Introduced

- Matrix organisation
- Human resources management

Examples of Marketing at Work

- Working in the Middle East
- British Airways

1 SETTING THE SCENE

1.1 In Chapter 7, we discussed international market entry methods, and identified that different methods require a different level of involvement for each market. This different level of involvement is mirrored in how a firm organises and manages its own operations. (Some principles of organisation are discussed in sections 2, 3 and 4.)

1.2 An exporter, the lowest level of involvement, might have a separate export department - this is a step further on from subcontracting all export activities to outside agents. However once a firm establishes overseas operations, the international dimension adds a layer of complexity to organisational choices (section 5): firms are likely to consider geographic departmentation even though the market may not segment naturally by country.

1.3 Whatever form of organisation is chosen, there is still a question as to where decisions are actually taken. In head office? In each local subsidiary? Different firms have different approaches to solving this problem.

1.4 In Part A of this text we discussed the global market: but we ask in section 7 if there are truly global companies to go with it. Perhaps there will be in future, but most companies still have a 'home': no firm is genuinely stateless.

1.5 Finally, in section 8 we show that a higher level of involvement in overseas operations brings special management problems.

2 GUIDELINES TO ORGANISATION

2.1 In organising for international marketing, management is concerned with the way a firm structures **relationships and communication**.

- Who does what in an organisation (division of labour)
- The allocation of responsibilities
- Delegation, power, authority
- Centralised/decentralised decision making

2.2 There are some general principles that may be applied in establishing an organisation structure.

(a) There should be a clear **chain of command** in the organisation.

(b) Everyone should **know to whom they report** and who reports to them.

(c) **Responsibility** should be matched by **authority** but remember that responsibility cannot be delegated.

(d) Authority should be **delegated** as far down the line as possible.

(e) The number of **levels of authority** should be kept to a minimum.

(f) The **span of control,** that is the number of subordinates reporting to a manager, should not be too great.

(g) The structure should be **flexible**. One of the main tasks of the marketer is to ensure that the organisation can adapt to meet customer needs.

2.3 There are special problems in multinational organisations arising from **communication difficulties**.

2.4 The task of an international company's organisation is to integrate these separate foreign operations into a co-ordinated effort, and overcome **communication gaps.**

3 THE FACTORS AFFECTING INTERNATIONAL MARKETING ORGANISATION

12/99

3.1 The actual form of organisation chosen depends on many factors.

(a) The **size of the firm and its business,** total volume and overseas volume. Clearly, the smaller the overseas volume, the less complex will be the organisational needs.

(b) The **number of foreign countries** in which it operates.

(c) The **level of involvement** and mode of operation in its overseas markets. Exporters will have different organisational structures from firms involved in joint ventures or direct overseas manufacturing.

(d) The **firm's overseas objectives for its foreign business.** A company with the aim of selling surplus abroad will not require the same structure as one which wishes to become truly international.

(e) The **firm's experience in international business.** A firm with no experience will require a structure which relies heavily, at least initially, on intermediaries or joint ventures.

(f) The **value and variety of its products.** Firms with products that are technically complex, requiring installation, maintenance and servicing will have to adopt organisational structures which cater for this.

(g) The **nature of its marketing task.** For example if the marketing task requires close contact with customers or intermediaries then this will need to be reflected in the organisational structure.

> **Exam Tip**
> The December 1999 paper asked about the internal factors to be considered by a company deciding to go global for the first time.

4 LOW INVOLVEMENT ORGANISATION STRUCTURES

4.1 For firms **initially** engaged in international marketing there is a basic choice for organising.

- To set up an **export department**
- To establish an international division
- To integrate international business with domestic business

The export department

4.2 If the firm is an occasional exporter, responding to orders from abroad without actively seeking them, then there is no need to adapt. The existing domestic sales section can deal with such orders.

4.3 However, if foreign sales increase, it must establish an export department, in recognition of the special nature of export marketing. Initially, all that is required is an export sales manager with administrative and clerical support. As export sales increase so the export department will need to expand and adapt in one of the ways discussed below (ie by area, product or function).

BPP
PUBLISHING

4.4 Such an export department can no longer depend wholly on the services of domestic marketing staff. It will possibly need some **functional specialists**, even if it adopts an area or product based organisation, eg market research, publicity and so on. One possible organisational structure for a company with significant export volume is shown below.

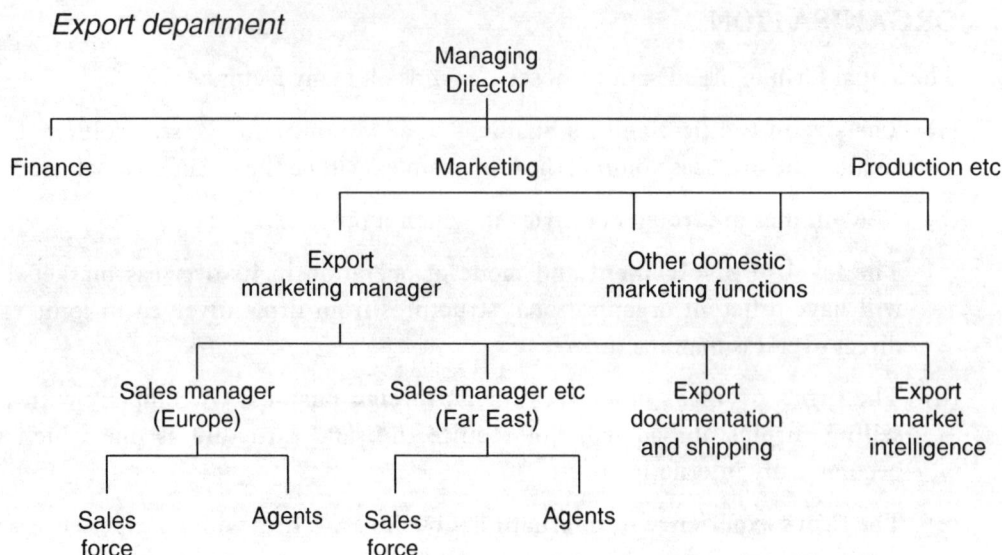

Export department

```
                        Managing
                        Director
        ┌──────────────────┼──────────────────────┐
     Finance            Marketing            Production etc
              ┌────────────┼──────────┬──────────┐
           Export      Other domestic
        marketing manager  marketing functions
      ┌──────────┬──────────────┬──────────────┐
  Sales manager  Sales manager etc   Export        Export
   (Europe)       (Far East)    documentation     market
                                and shipping    intelligence
   ┌─────┬─────┐  ┌─────┬─────┐
  Sales  Agents Sales  Agents
  force         force
```

The international division: integration or separation?

4.5 As exporting firms become more heavily involved in international marketing, through licensing, joint ventures, manufacturing subsidiaries and so on, the export department is no longer able to manage the complexities of international business. Most export departments are primarily sales and marketing departments. International divisions on the other hand must be concerned with all the business functions, production, finance, human resource management etc. These centralised specialist staff provide services to the various operating units around the world.

4.6 The international division may be organised on any of the three bases discussed overleaf (**area, product, function**) or a combination of them. By far the most common however is the area organisation.

4.7 There are two key **advantages** in treating international business separately.

(a) Centralising specialist skills and expertise in one place makes for **efficiency**.

(b) **Opportunities** in international business are less likely to be lost or overlooked since the division's principal focus is to develop international business.

4.8 There are also **disadvantages**

(a) In many firms the international division is subordinate to domestic marketing staff, and thus does not have enough control over resources to exploit opportunities.

(b) As international business grows, other divisions may wish to control their own international operations and **conflicting objectives** may develop.

*Functional organisation
with international division*

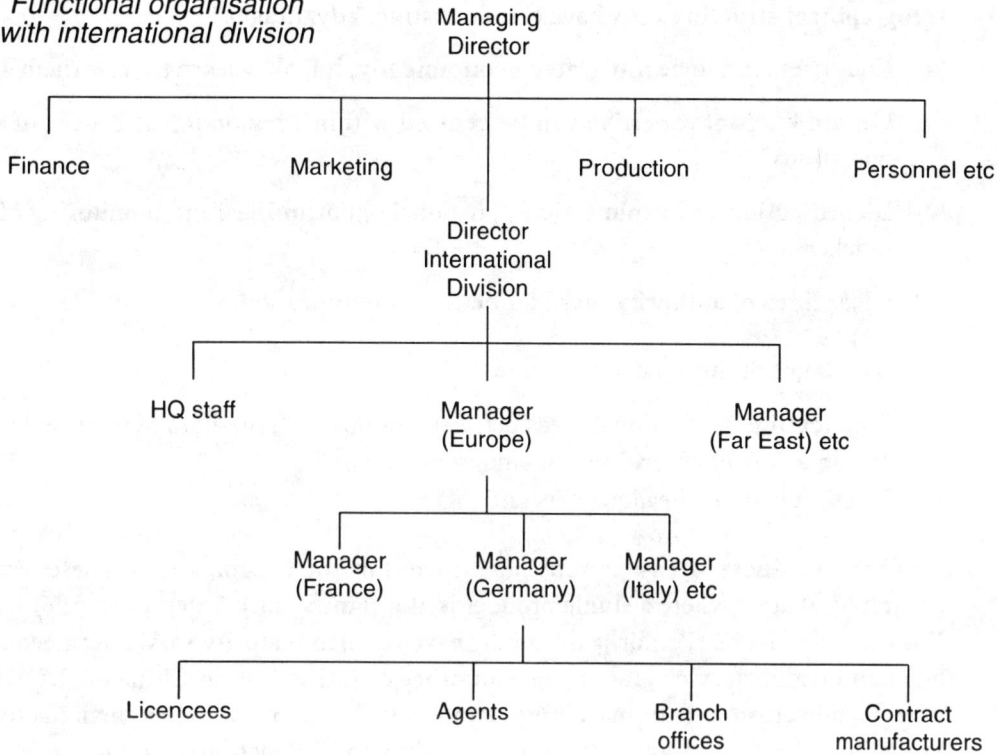

```
                        Managing
                        Director
   ┌──────────┬────────────┼────────────┬──────────┐
Finance    Marketing                 Production   Personnel etc
                        Director
                      International
                        Division
        ┌───────────────────┼───────────────────┐
     HQ staff            Manager              Manager
                         (Europe)           (Far East) etc
                 ┌──────────┼──────────┐
              Manager    Manager    Manager
              (France)  (Germany)   (Italy) etc
        ┌──────────────┼──────────────┬──────────────┐
     Licencees       Agents        Branch        Contract
                                    offices     manufacturers
```

5   MORE ELABORATE ORGANISATION STRUCTURES

5.1   Unless a multinational opts for a matrix structure (see 5.12 below), it must organise staff along **regional, product, functional** or **project** lines. This section outlines the advantages and disadvantages associated with each.

Organisation by geography (eg region)

5.2   This form of structure is attractive to a marketing orientated company with relatively stable product technology, such as consumer non-durables, pharmaceuticals or cars.

*Area organisation,
with product groups*

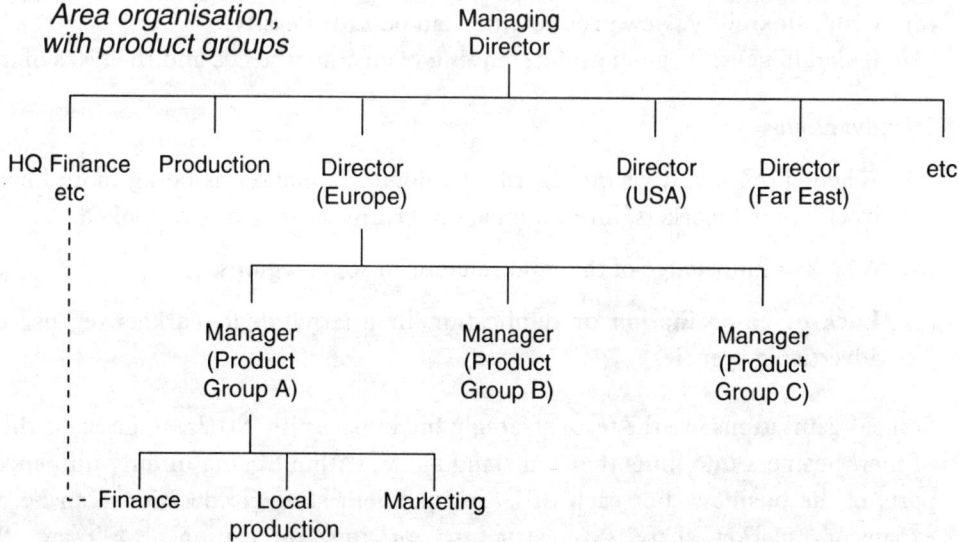

```
                              Managing
                              Director
   ┌──────────┬──────────┬───────┼──────────┬──────────┬────────┐
HQ Finance  Production  Director          Director   Director   etc
   etc                  (Europe)           (USA)     (Far East)
             ┌────────────┼────────────┐
          Manager      Manager      Manager
          (Product     (Product     (Product
          Group A)     Group B)     Group C)
        ┌─────┼─────────┐
     Finance  Local   Marketing
             production
```

Line relationship ──────────
Functional relationship ─ ─ ─ ─ ─ ─

BPP PUBLISHING

5.3 **Geographical structure** does have certain distinct **advantages**.

   (a) Countries tend to be **integrated economically**, it makes sense to treat them as a unit.

   (b) Certain kinds of **expertise can be centred** within a region to the benefit of all country operations.

   (c) **Identification and exploitation** of regional opportunities, and monitoring of threats, is quicker.

   (d) **Clear lines of authority** make for better communication.

5.4 **Disadvantages** of this type of structure.

   - **Duplication** in functional areas between regions (eg a plethora of finance departments)
   - Possible **lack of co-ordination** among the regions
   - **Friction** between headquarters and regions

5.5 **Strategic business areas** can be identified for some companies. These are different geographical areas where a single product is at a significantly different stage of its life cycle. For example, the market for jeans might have reached maturity in Western economies, but be at an introductory or growth stage in other countries, say in China or the Middle East. The manufacturing and marketing strategies for a major jeans manufacturer would probably differ according to the product's situation in each geographical market, and an organisation structure for the company might be based accordingly on separate strategic business areas.

Organisation by product or brand

5.6 Organising along product lines requires **product or brand groups** to undertake **global responsibility** for marketing. It is common for companies with several unrelated product lines, especially if the marketing task varies more by **product** than by **region**, eg Lucas Industries (aerospace products, automotive products).

5.7 **Advantages**

   (a) It aids **flexibility**. New product lines can be added easily.
   (b) It should generate **good understanding** of customer needs and the tasks of marketing.

5.8 **Disadvantages**

   (a) Where a product division regards the domestic market as being more important than international markets, international opportunities may be overlooked.

   (b) A **lack of knowledge** of the requirements of some regions.

   (c) **Lack of co-ordination** or duplication in international markets (eg use of different advertising agencies).

5.9 Some organisations use the term **strategic business units** (SBUs) to describe the separation of their business into units that can stand alone, without being unduly influenced by other parts of the business. For each SBU, independent strategic decisions can be made about expansion, market share, cost structure, pricing, innovation, R&D etc. Within the organisation structure, each SBU should stand as a major investment centre.

Product divisionalisation, with areas

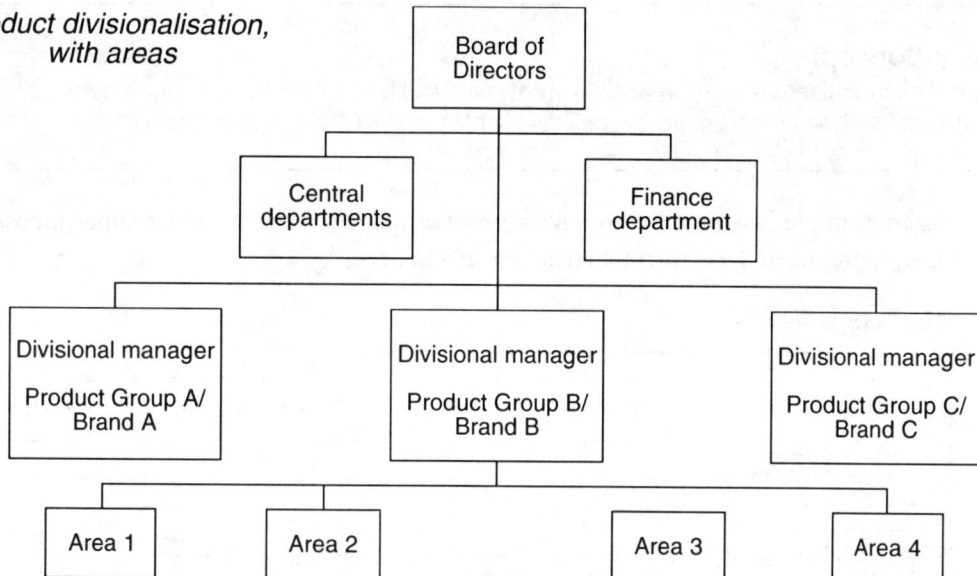

```
                          ┌──────────────┐
                          │  Board of    │
                          │  Directors   │
                          └──────────────┘
             ┌──────────────┐        ┌──────────────┐
             │  Central     │        │  Finance     │
             │  departments │        │  department  │
             └──────────────┘        └──────────────┘

┌──────────────────┐  ┌──────────────────┐  ┌──────────────────┐
│ Divisional manager│  │ Divisional manager│  │ Divisional manager│
│                  │  │                  │  │                  │
│ Product Group A/ │  │ Product Group B/ │  │ Product Group C/ │
│ Brand A          │  │ Brand B          │  │ Brand C          │
└──────────────────┘  └──────────────────┘  └──────────────────┘

  ┌────────┐  ┌────────┐      ┌────────┐  ┌────────┐
  │ Area 1 │  │ Area 2 │      │ Area 3 │  │ Area 4 │
  └────────┘  └────────┘      └────────┘  └────────┘
```

Organisation by function

5.10 In **functional organisation,** top managers in the various management functions (marketing, finance, production and so on) each have global responsibilities for their function. It is a form of organisation suitable for firms with narrow product lines or where product expertise is not an important factor. It also requires there to be few regional variations in operations. For these reasons it is not very common in multinational firms and most examples are small and medium sized European firms whose domestic markets are fairly small.

Action Programme 1

The Erewhon Bank plc has branches in the UK, Eire, France, Germany and Denmark. It grew from the merger of a number of small local banks in these countries. These local banks were not large enough to compete single-handedly in their home markets. The Erewhon Bank hopes to attract both retail and corporate customers, through its use of home banking services and its heavily advertised Direct Bank service, which is a branchless bank to which customers telephone, fax or post their instructions. The bank also specialises in providing foreign currency accounts.

What sort of organisation structure do you think would be appropriate?

Organisation by project

5.11 Where a multinational company is involved in large scale production or assembly operations (such as large civil engineering concerns), then it may be organised into a series of **project groups** which temporarily bring together staff drawn from wherever needed in the organisation. The groups change frequently to reflect changes in the company's operations.

Matrix organisation

5.12 **Matrix organisation** is a structure which provides for the formalisation of management control between different functions, whilst at the same time maintaining functional departmentation.

BPP PUBLISHING

> **Key Concept**
>
> A **matrix organisation** is one in which unity of command is sacrificed to co-ordination across business functions, such as projects or people reporting to both product managers and area bosses.

5.13 As an example it is possible to have a product management structure superimposed on top of a geographical departmental structure in a matrix.

Matrix organisation

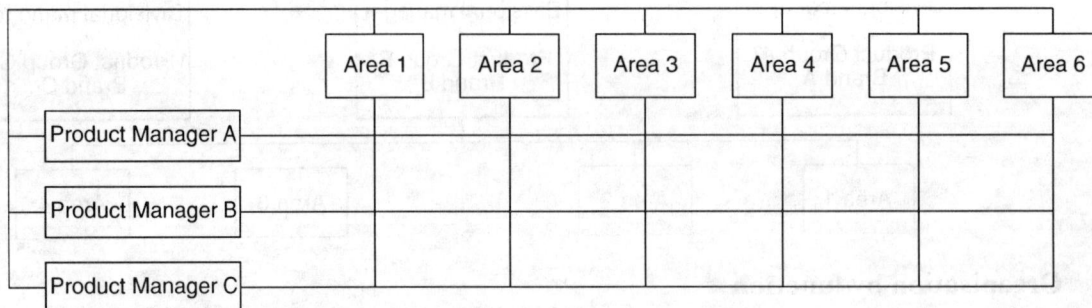

	Area 1	Area 2	Area 3	Area 4	Area 5	Area 6
Product Manager A						
Product Manager B						
Product Manager C						

* The product managers may each have their own marketing team; in which case the marketing department itself would be small or non-existent.

5.14 Matrix organisation means that subordinates have two (or more) 'bosses', in the sense that they must report to both a functional boss and a project boss.

5.15 The matrix structure recognises that there are a number of **basic competences** in international business.

(a) **Regional** and environmental knowledge (which suggests a need for national subsidiaries).

(b) **Product** knowledge and know-how (suggesting that product managers with global responsibilities are required).

(c) **Functional** competence in marketing, finance, production, (which means that both line and function (dotted line) relationships are desirable).

(d) Knowledge of **customer** needs. Again, line and function relationships have to be established.

5.16 The matrix structure is intended to focus these competences on the firm's worldwide business objectives. Within such a structure, the task of management is to:

(a) Achieve an organisational balance that brings together the necessary perspectives and skills (regional, product, functional, customer) to accomplish the organisational objectives.

(b) Ensure that both national organisations and product divisions are responsible for profitability, ie both are viewed as profit centres.

(c) Initiate the substantial changes in organisational culture and management behaviour which will be necessary.

6   CENTRALISATION AND DECENTRALISATION

6.1   A major concern of management when considering organisational structure is **division of labour** or **specialisation,** in other words who does what, where does responsibility lie, what authority/control over resources do individuals have.

6.2   The concept of division of labour has two aspects.

(a)   The **span of control** (or horizontal division of labour). In international marketing the decision concerning region, product, function, matrix or project structure covers horizontal division of labour.

(b)   The **chain or levels of command** (ie vertical division of labour). This is the centralisation/decentralisation decision. Here management is concerned with questions of delegation of power and authority and the level at which different types of decisions will be made.

6.3   For the global company, senior management must consider the division of labour between corporate headquarters and its foreign market operations.

Factors affecting the extent of decentralisation

6.4   **Organisation type chosen.** The five organisation types previously discussed (regional, product, function, project and matrix), vary in the extent to which they lend themselves to a decentralised structure.

6.5   **The nature of the management function.** Marketing tends to be a **decentralised** function, compared with finance for example, because of the importance of understanding local customer needs, responding to environmental differences and changes, developing relationships with customers and so on.

6.6   **The size of subsidiaries.** The larger a subsidiary is the more autonomy it will tend to have in its decision making, ie more decentralised.

Headquarters/local subsidiary roles

6.7   Whether a company adopts a centralised or a decentralised philosophy there is a role for both corporate headquarters and local subsidiaries in international marketing. Headquarters normally does the following.

(a)   Sets **overall marketing objectives**

(b)   Controls the three key areas

(i)   Basic **policy** decisions, eg changes in marketing policy, product elimination, expansion of production capacity

(ii)   Major **capital expenditure**

(iii)   **Appointment** of top executives

(c)   Provides **ideas, techniques and resources** for effective local marketing

(d)   **Co-ordinates the marketing efforts** of its various subsidiaries

Local/national subsidiary

6.8   Local business unit responsibility

- **Formulating and carrying out marketing mix plans**
- Undertaking **market research** and analysis
- Recruiting, motivating and managing the **sales force**

Advantages and disadvantages of centralisation

6.9 Advantages of centralisation

- Better planning (providing that 'top-down' planning is indeed the most effective)
- Better co-ordination in achieving overall corporate objectives
- Optimum use of resources (operational, financial and human)

6.10 Disadvantages of centralisation

- Motivation of senior staff at subsidiary level may be adversely affected if they do not have control over decisions or resources which affect their targets

- Centralisation may lead to misunderstandings and delays in management communications

---

Action Programme 2

You work for a small company which sells youth fashion goods products to three different countries of the EU: the UK, the Netherlands, and Germany. There are separate marketing departments and finance departments in each country. A new finance director arrives. The finance director regards the whole arrangement as inefficient, and wishes to return to a centralised structure.

What would you consider would be the advantages and disadvantages of such a change in policy?

Which arrangement?

6.11 The choice of planning organisation will depend partly on the preferences of the company's top management, and the style they like to adopt, but there are other influences as follows.

(a) In terms of the marketing mix, the element most likely to be centrally determined is **product**. Distribution channel decisions may be shared between head office and local management.

(b) **Advertising and promotion decisions** may need to be made at a local level for linguistic and cultural reasons.

(c) When big **capital investments** are planned, head office should be involved in the decision.

(d) When **cash flow** is tight, other strategies must be sacrificed to the paramount concern for short term survival and attention to cash flow.

(e) **Widely diversified** organisations, and organisations in industries which are facing rapid change, would be better managed by a greater decentralisation of authority.

(f) Organisations in a single industry which is fairly **stable** would perhaps be more efficiently managed by a hierarchical, centralised management system.

Exam Tip

You may be asked how an organisation could maintain a global perspective while acting with local flexibility. Key issues are adaptation, duplication and control.

7 DO GLOBAL FIRMS REALLY EXIST?

7.1 Some writers believe that there is an increasing number of 'stateless corporations', whose activities transcend national boundaries, and whose personnel come from any country. Global firms are 'stateless entities'. Many of their activities are subcontracted to outsiders, or foreign component-making firms. Firms are places where 'enterprise webs' are spun, which tie together capital, resources, skills and technology from all over the world. For Reich, (*The Work of Nations*), it does not matter if a company is American or Japanese, providing it is doing high-value work in your country. Perhaps we can summarise the differences between so-called 'global' companies and most firms operating internationally by taking a visual approach.

(a) **Non-'global' firms**

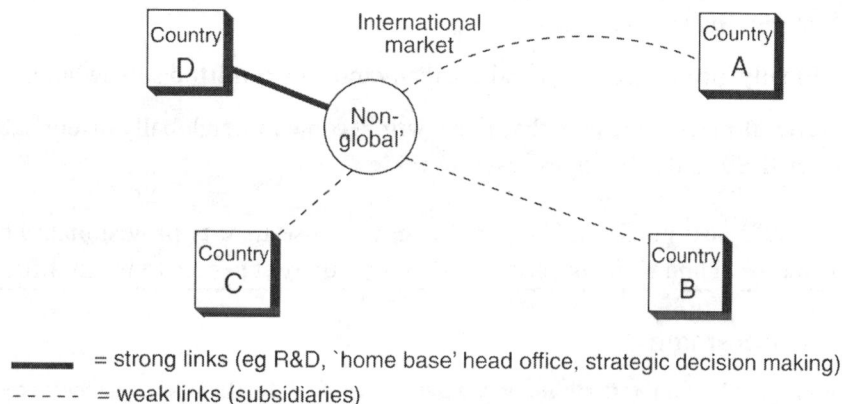

```
————  = strong links (eg R&D, `home base' head office, strategic decision making)
- - - - -  = weak links (subsidiaries)
```

In the case above the links between the company and countries C, B and A are likely to be severed before those with D, which is the home country.

(b) **'Global'/'stateless'**

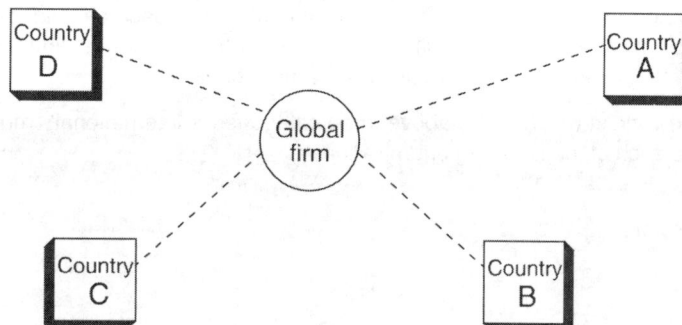

The global corporation can shift between countries.

7.2 This theory looks attractive on the surface, particularly in a relatively open economy like that of the UK, which is host to a number of multinational corporations and has attracted a fair degree of inward investment.

7.3 Do these global or stateless corporations really exist? Against Reich's view the following objections have been raised (by Yao-Su Hue and John Cantwell of Reading University).

(a) Most multinationals, other than those based in small nations, have **less than half of their employees abroad**.

(b) **Ownership and control** of multinationals remain **restricted**. This is partly because of the way in which capital markets are structured. Few so-called global companies are quoted on more than two stock markets.

(c) **Top management** is rarely as multinational as the firm's activities. This is particularly true of Japanese companies. A foreigner is rarely seen on the Tokyo-based board of a Japanese multinational. The *Financial Times* reported that the membership of the Board of Directors of UK firms is the most cosmopolitan.

(d) **National residence and status** is important for tax reasons. Boundary-less corporations are not recognised as such by lawyers or tax officials.

(e) The bulk of a multinational's **research and development** is generally done in the home country. Indeed Porter says that the home market is important for product development in the information it gives about consumers.

(f) Where capital is limited, 'global' companies stick to the home market rather than developing overseas ones.

(g) Finally, **profits** from a global company must be **remitted** somewhere.

7.4 However, it may be the case that firms will become more globally orientated if they are able to specialise and if it becomes easier to trade.

7.5 You should also note that the terminology we use here is provisional. The words **global, multinational** and **transnational** are used by different people to mean different things.

Action Programme 3

Some organisations are **international** in the sense that they distribute and sell their products/ services in more than one country, but operate centrally form a single location, or from several locations, in one country - usually the country of the organisation's origin. Other organisations are **multinational,** ie they will operate independent businesses in different parts of the world, though control is still exercised chiefly through a systems of expatriate managers and business strategies which are centrally imposed. Finally, a few organisations are genuinely **global**: they function worldwide, through a network of managers and executives who are appointed to positions as they become vacant, without any regard for national connections; such 'global' organisations will have research and development units and manufacturing plants (where appropriate) scattered across their territories, and may grant considerable autonomy (in strategic terms) to the various parts of the organisation.

Given this framework, in which of the above three categories – 'international', 'multinational' or 'global' - would you place each of the following organisations?

(a) Philips
(b) General Motors
(c) Sony
(d) Coca-Cola
(e) McDonalds
(f) Hutchinson Telecom
(g) News International
(h) IBM

What do you think are the reasons for the fact that so few organisations are 'global' in the genuine sense of the term?

Exam Tip

The examiner regards the above question as reflecting a very important issue. When reviewing this text he commented: 'I see too much sloppy thinking on this issue. I would be glad if you would reinforce the importance of clarity on these issues.' Consider yourself forewarned!

8   HUMAN RESOURCES ISSUES   Specimen paper

Expatriates or locals?

8.1   For an international company, which has to 'think globally' as well as act 'locally', there are a number of problems.

- Do you employ mainly **expatriate staff** to control local operations?
- Do you employ **local managers**, with the possible loss of central control?
- Is there such a thing as the **global manager**, equally at home in different cultures?

8.2   Expatriate staff are sometimes favoured over local staff.

(a)   Poor **educational opportunities** in the market may require the 'import' of skilled technicians and managers. For example, expatriates have been needed in many western firms' operations in Russia and Eastern Europe, simply because they understand the meaning of 'profit'.

(b)   Some senior managers believe that a business run by expatriates is easier to **control** than one run by local staff.

(c)   If the firm is a macropyramid, expatriates might be better able than locals to **communicate** with the corporate centre.

(d)   The expatriate may **know more about the firm** overall, which is especially important if he or she is fronting a sales office.

8.3   The use of expatriates in overseas markets has certain disadvantages.

(a)   They **cost** more (eg subsidised housing, school fees).

(b)   **Culture shock**. The expatriate may fail to adjust to the culture (eg by associating only with other expatriates). This is likely to lead to poor management effectiveness, especially if the business requires personal contact.

(c)   A substantial training programme might be needed.

(i)   **Basic facts** about the country will be given with basic language training, and some briefings about cultural differences.

(ii)   **Immersion training** involves detailed language training, simulation of field experiences etc. This is necessary to obtain an intellectual understanding and practical awareness of the culture.

8.4   Employing local managers raises the following issues.

(a)   A '**glass ceiling**' might exist in some companies. Talented local managers may not make it to board levels if, as in many Japanese firms, most members of the board are drawn from one country.

(b)   In some cases, it may be hard for locals to assimilate into the corporate culture, and this might led to communication problems.

(c)   They will have greater local knowledge - but the difficulty of course is to get them to understand the wider corporate picture, but this is true of management at operational level generally.

8.5   Those firms which export sporadically might employ a home-based sales force. Their travel expenses will of course be high, and it might not always be easy to recruit people willing to cope with the pace.

Marketing at Work

In *A Western manager in the Eastern world,* (Administrator, October 1995) Adrian Burnett describes how his experiences of being a senior administrator and manager in the Middle East have shaped his thinking. Despite organisations' structural resemblance to European ones, there were significant differences in values and processes.

- 'Fluency counted for nothing ... the right message, haltingly expressed, was infinitely preferable to being stylishly wrong. Drive and activity were not valued as such, and experience was as useful only as the owner's ability to adapt it.'

- 'Raw intelligence and originality were held in high esteem ... Personal standards were extremely important in deciding who to do business with.'

- 'Managers who succeeded had a constantly running mental programme which asked "Why should he do what I want/ask/suggest?" The fact that one was entitled, by virtue of position, terms of reference and so on, to expect to be obeyed meant absolutely nothing, since the worker at the bottom of the 'food chain' was often related to someone senior, and would use nepotism to ensure that he got his way. A manager's mental attitude therefore had to be that of always making sure that his workers and colleagues actually wanted, and were able, to act in a particular way. Without this it was like being in a nightmare where one can see and feel, but cannot move or change anything.'

- 'Also the identification of personalities with issues was largely avoided. There was wheeling and dealing, but conducted in a manner that avoided loss of face; a result of this was that when the organisation wanted to act it could do so with surprising speed and purpose. Sometimes though there was only token action, or simply none at all. However this never had anything to do with technical reasons, and was always because the party supposed to act did not like and trust the other party.'

Management effectiveness

8.6 A problem is that there are often severe cultural differences as to what constitutes 'management' in the first place. Are **management** principles universally applicable? The marketing function needs awareness of effective management approaches in different cultures.

8.7 Two American writers, Gonzalez and McMillan, suggested after a two-year study of management in Brazil that no general conclusions on management principles can be arrived at, and that different principles will apply in different cultures. It even opens up the possibility that general management principles may not be applicable throughout a large country such as the United States because of the variety of sub-cultures that may exist.

8.8 Koontz, O'Donnell and Weihrich (KOW) on the other hand have argued that apparent differences between management **principles** in different countries are actually differences of **application,** and that this distinction has been blurred by careless use of terminology. Their idea is that certain universal **fundamentals** of management exist, which may be applied in different ways depending on the local culture.

8.9 R N Farmer and B M Richman emphasise the importance of the external environment in which an organisation operates. They developed a model to illustrate the distinction between the management process and the environment of managing.

The Farmer-Richman model

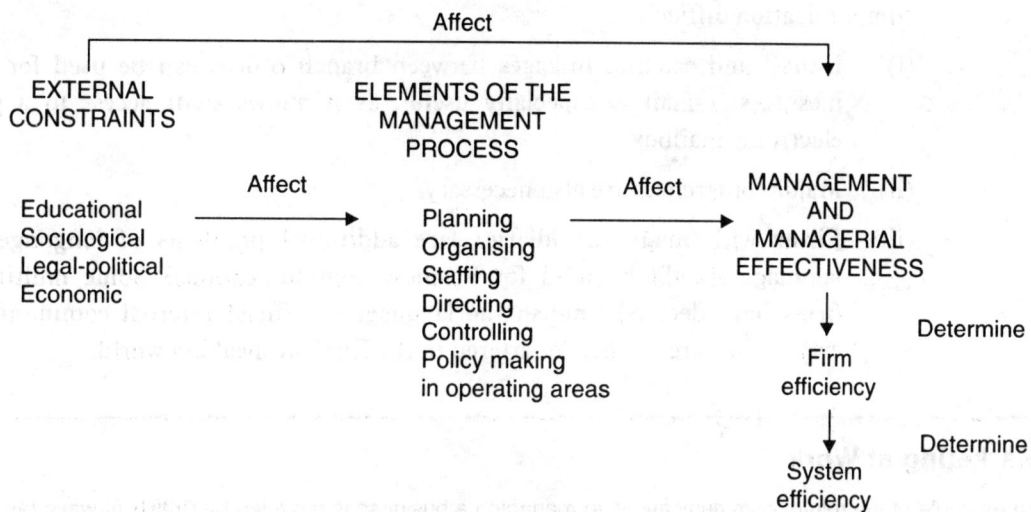

```
                            Affect
        ┌──────────────────────────────────────────────────┐
        │                                                   ▼
EXTERNAL              ELEMENTS OF THE           MANAGEMENT
CONSTRAINTS           MANAGEMENT                AND
                      PROCESS                   MANAGERIAL
         Affect                     Affect      EFFECTIVENESS
Educational    ───────►  Planning   ──────►
Sociological             Organising                        Determine
Legal-political          Staffing
Economic                 Directing                  Firm
                         Controlling               efficiency
                         Policy making
                         in operating areas                Determine

                                                  System
                                                 efficiency
```

8.10   Farmer and Richman elaborate on the four categories of external constraints identified in the model.

(a)   **Educational** constraints include the level of literacy in the environment (country) and the availability of secondary education, vocational training and higher education. Poor educational facilities will inevitably result in poor management.

(b)   **Sociological** constraints are the most numerous category. For example, one country may have a tradition of antagonism between trade unions and management whereas another might have a history of mutual trust and co-operation.

(c)   **Legal and political constraints.** In the UK, managers can hire and fire at will. In other countries, there are laws governing this.

(d)   **Economic constraints.** Some countries suffer from high rates of inflation and other symptoms of economic instability. The availability of capital is another important factor which varies from one environment to another.

Human resources management

> **Key Concept**
>
> **Human resources management** involves recruitment and selection, training, appraisal systems and such like, in other words the organisation's relationship with its employees. From management's point of view, HRM is designed to get the best possible performance from employees.

8.11   Relevant issues to keep in mind are these.

(a)   **Recruitment and training.** In countries with low levels of literacy, more effort might need to be spent on basic training.

(b)   **Career management.** Can overseas staff realistically expect promotion to the firm's highest levels if they do well?

(c)   **Appraisal schemes.** These can be a minefield at the best of times, and the possibilities for communications failure are endless. For example, in some cultures, an appraisal is a two way discussion whereas in others arguing back might be considered a sign of insubordination.

(d) **Communications**. HRM tries to mobilise employees' commitment to the goals of the organisation. In far-flung global firms, the normal panoply of staff newsletters and team briefings may be hard to institute but are vital. Time differences also make communication difficult.

    (i) **E-mail** and satellite linkages between branch offices can be used for routine messages: e-mail is especially useful, as it allows swift access to a person's electronic mailbox.

    (ii) Major conferences are also necessary.

    (iii) Firms with many subsidiaries face additional problems of **language**. What language should be used for business communications? Some multinational firms have decreed English the language of official internal communications, even if they are not headquartered in the English speaking world.

Marketing at Work

An example of the role of communications in managing a business is provided by British Airways (as reported in the *Guardian*).

After privatisation, BA cut its staff by almost 20,000 to 35,000 although since that staff levels have increased as airline traffic has expanded.

BA attaches great important to internal corporate communications, as it wishes to make staff feel involved.

At a series of business seminars, costing £750,000, senior board members made detailed presentations to 4,500 junior and senior managers, and, as importantly, invited - and received - feedback and criticism. BA's senior managers 'say they benefit enormously from hearing how staff feel that BA can continue to improve its performance.'

Chapter Roundup

- Firms can choose between:
    - treating the international marketing function separately from the domestic marketing function;
    - integrating international marketing with domestic marketing.

- Some companies design their marketing organisation on an **area** basis, others by **product**.

- In a **'global'** company, no country is considered as the home country market. In practice global companies are hard to find.

- **Matrix organisation** is where organisation by product is combined with organisation by area.

- **Human resource management** must get the best performance possible from a personnel resource which may be taken from many different cultures. The international company must decide whether to use expatriate or local staff.

Quick Quiz

1 What general principles may be used in establishing an organisation's structure? (see para 2.2)
2 What factors affect the organisational structure of a firm involved in international marketing? (3.1)
3 Why do some firms establish a separate division for handling overseas business? What are the drawbacks of doing so? (4.5, 4.8)
4 What are the advantages of organisation by region? (5.3)
5 What is a matrix structure? (5.12)
6 What are the advantages and disadvantages of centralisation? (6.9, 6.10)
7 Why might you question the view that 'stateless' corporations actually exist? (7.3)
8 Describe the advantages and disadvantages of using expatriate managers. (8.2, 8.3)

Action Programme Review

1 Although some of the technical details of the products described might have appeared daunting, you should have realised that the bank basically serves two markets, the personal sector and the corporate sector. However, you would perhaps be ill advised to organise the bank **solely** on that basis. Why?

(a) The banking needs of customers in the personal sector are likely to be quite distinct. This market is naturally segmented geographically. Users of the telephone banking service, for example, will want to speak in their own language. Also, despite the Single European Market, the competitive environment of financial services is likely to be different in each country (eg credit cards are widely used in France, but hardly used at all in Germany).

For the personal sector, a geographic organisation would be appropriate, although with the centralisation of common administrative and account processing functions and technological expertise, so that the bank gains from scale economies and avoids wasteful duplication.

(b) For the corporate sector, different considerations apply. If the bank is providing sophisticated foreign currency accounts, these will be of most benefit to multi-nationals or companies which regularly export from, or import to, their home markets. A geographical organisation structure may not be appropriate, and arguably the bank's organisation should be centralised on a Europe wide basis, with the country offices, of course, at a lower level.

2 The finance director might have a point when it comes to the possible duplication and inefficiencies arising out of a centralised finance department. The marketing implications are quite different. Having a localised management structure gives the firm the advantage of a flexible response to local market conditions. In the youth fashion market, keeping an 'ear to the ground' is probably more advantageous than centralisation.

3 In our view, the classification for the organisations listed is as follows.

'International': None
'Multinational': General Motors, Sony, Coca-Cola, McDonald's, Hutchinson Telecom
'Global': Philips, News International, IBM

Few organisations are genuinely global because they fear loss of control if too much discretion is devolved from the centre; they may also be sceptical about the abilities of locally-recruited managers, and cannot easily manage the culture clashes when groups of managers, from differing countries, have to operate as a team.

Now try illustrative question 8 at the end of the Study Text

Part C
International strategy implementation and control

9 International Product Management: Standardisation and Differentiation

Chapter Topic List	Syllabus Reference
1 Setting the scene	-
2 What is a product?	3.1
3 Standardisation vs. adaptation	2.8
4 Product and communications	3.1
5 Other aspects of product decisions	3.1
6 New product development for overseas markets	3.1, 3.9
7 Product life cycles and international marketing mix decisions	3.1
8 International branding decisions	3.1
9 Services and other product forms	1.1, 3.1, 3.6, 3.7

Learning Outcomes

Upon completion of this chapter you will have knowledge of the issues behind international product management. Specifically, this will include:

- the standardisation v adaptation issue

- packaging and labelling

- new product development and product launch

- the product life cycle and international trade life cycle

- branding

- other types of product such as services and commodities

Key Concepts Introduced

- Product
- Market positioning
- The international trade life cycle
- Brand
- Commodity

BPP PUBLISHING

Examples of Marketing at Work

- Packaging and product features
- Clockwork radio
- Motor vehicles
- Chocolates and soft drinks
- Rolex and Unilever
- Nestlé
- Gillette
- Nissan

- Toshiba and Intel
- Volkswagen Beetle
- Brewing industry
- General Motors and Mars
- Budweiser
- BAA
- Business travellers
- American Facility Guarantee Programme

1   SETTING THE SCENE

1.1   Product/market decisions are perhaps the most critical area in corporate planning on an international scale and the issue that sets international marketing apart from domestic marketing probably more than any other. We start this chapter off by reviewing the question of what a product is. This should be very familiar ground from other elements of the CIM courses.

1.2   The focus of this chapter is the issue surrounding the choice of whether to standardise or differentiate the product offering by adapting it to the various markets in which the company seeks to operate. On the one hand, if you are expecting to achieve economies of scale, the last thing you want to do is customise each product. On the other hand, many products have to be adapted for overseas markets.

1.3   This adaptation does not only relates to legal and technical requirements, but also to the different cultures in each market. This applies also to augmentations of the product such as packaging, labelling and servicing. The development and introduction of new products also is influenced by international marketing considerations, in particular the fact that product life cycles can differ in each country.

2   WHAT IS A PRODUCT?

> **Key Concept**
> A **product** is anything that can be offered to a market for attention, acquisition, use or consumption that might satisfy a want or need. It includes physical objects, services, places, organisations, ideas, and people.

2.1   In marketing terms a product is the total **utility** or **satisfaction** that a buyer receives as a result of a purchase. It exists at three levels - **core, formal and augmented.**

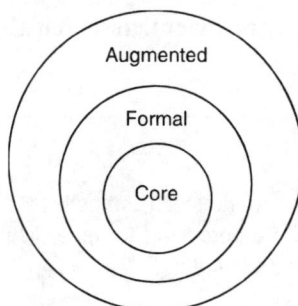

Core product

2.2 The **core product** refers to the need which is being satisfied or the problem which is being solved by the product. This is a vital concept in international marketing, eg the 'core' product varies between Third World countries and industrially developed countries. In the case of a bicycle we can say the following.

- In the Third world - used as a means of transport
- In the developed world - used for recreation, sport

Marketeers must always view a product in terms of its ability to satisfy needs or solve problems, ie perceived benefits which may vary between countries.

Formal product

2.3 The **formal product** is what the market recognises as the tangible offer. It comprises the features, styling, quality, packaging and brand name. Again this may have important implications for international marketing. Variations in quality, size, colour etc may have to be used from country to country.

Marketing at Work

(a) For computer programs and software, features might include special adaptation for the local language or, indeed, different keyboard layouts.

(b) Ethical pharmaceuticals in some Scandinavian countries are expected to be sold in packaging which is primarily white. So branded products emanating from other markets are likely to be adapted to take account of this

Augmented product

2.4 The **augmented product** includes core and formal product and the additional services and benefits which 'surround' a product. They may offer the following.

- Reputation
- Delivery
- Before and after sales services
- Installation and maintenance
- Guarantee
- Finance
- Credit

According to many marketers (for example Levitt) it is at this level of the product that the 'new' competition is taking place. Customers may value reliable delivery, credit or after sales service more than quality or price. So it is vital for the international marketeer to be aware of **needs and expectations** and the extent to which they vary between different countries when making product decisions.

Key Concept

Market positioning is 'the attempt by marketers (domestic and international) to give the product a distinct identity or image so that it will be perceived to have distinctive features or benefits relative to competing products'. (*Economist Pocket Marketing*)

Marketing at Work

Clockwork radios

Most radios are powered by batteries, or by mains electricity supply. Batteries are expensive, and many rural areas in poorer countries do not have mains electricity. Whereas in the west, broadcasting is a source of entertainment, in poorer countries it can be a vital source of education and modernisation.

Invention of the clockwork radio was the subject of a BBC TV documentary. The inventor, Trevor Bayliss, shown shaking hands with Nelson Mandela, was credited with having brought broadcasting within reach of many poorer people.

The clockwork ratio converts kinetic energy into electricity - the spring powers a tiny generator, which powers the radio. It is hard to think of a product better adapted to poorer markets.

In July 1996, Trevor Bayliss won the BBC design award. An example of the radio's use is in health education in Eritrea (reconstructing itself after a war of independence from Ethiopia which has lasted several decades). Villagers can learn about simple ways of reducing children's exposure to infection.

---

3 STANDARDISATION VS ADAPTATION 12/99

Factors encouraging product standardisation

3.1 Factors encouraging standardisation are as follows.

(a) **Economies of scale**

- Production
- Marketing/communications
- Research and development
- Stock holding

(b) Easier management and **control**.

(c) **Homogeneity** of markets, in other words world markets available without adaptation (eg denim jeans).

(d) **Cultural insensitivity,** eg industrial components and agricultural products.

(e) **Consumer mobility** means that standardisation is expected in certain products.

- Camera film
- Hotel chains

(f) Where '**made in**' image is important to a product's perceived value (eg France for perfume, Sheffield for stainless steel).

(g) For a firm selling a **small proportion** of its output overseas, the incremental adaptation costs may exceed the incremental sales value.

(h) Products that are positioned at the **high end of the spectrum** in terms of price, prestige and scarcity are more likely to have a standardised mix.

Factors encouraging adaptation/modification

3.2 **Mandatory modification.** Mandatory product modification normally involves either adaptation to comply with government requirements or unavoidable technical changes. Using car manufacture as an example it may concern:

(a) **Legal requirements**

- Health and safety law
- Economic law

(b) **Technical requirements** such as:

- Modification of heating/cooling systems for different climates
- Engine modification to use locally available fuels

3.3 **Discretionary modification**

(a) Discretionary modification is called for only to make the product more appealing in different markets. It results from differing customer needs, preferences and tastes. These differences become apparent from market research and analysis, intermediary and customer feedback etc.

(b) Levels of customer **purchasing power**. Low incomes may make a cheap version of the product more attractive in some less developed economies.

(c) **Levels of education** and technical sophistication. Ease of use may be a crucial factor in decision-making.

(d) Standards of **maintenance/repair** facilities. Simpler, more robust versions may be needed.

(e) **'Culture-bound' products** such as clothing, food and home decoration are more likely to have an adapted marketing mix.

3.4 These strategies can be exercised at global and national level, depending on the type of product.

Marketing at Work

A current example of standardisation and adaptation issues relates to world markets for motor vehicles. In particular, the US government has taken up arms on behalf of the US car industry to increase US manufacturers' market share in Japan, claiming that there are structural barriers and non-tariff barriers.

In fact, Japan is one of the few countries (the others being the UK, the Republic of Ireland, Australia, New Zealand, South Africa and Sri Lanka) with right hand drive.

The real problem, according to the *Economist* is that Detroit (ie the US car industry), 'has never catered for those strange foreign markets, such as Japan and Britain, where cars are driven on the left and steered on the right ... GM (General Motors) doesn't sell a single car in Japan with the steering wheel where the drivers want it ... Meanwhile how about bashing those villainous Saudi Arabians for not buying American ski-equipment?'

3.5 Not all products are suitable for standardisation.

Marketing at Work

Take the example of Cadbury-Schweppes which deals with chocolate and soft drinks.

(a) The UK consumer's taste in chocolate is not shared by most European consumers, who prefer a higher proportion of cocoa-butter in the final product. Marketing Cadbury's UK brands of chocolate on a Europe-wide basis would not seem to be appropriate: instead the acquisition of a European company would be the best way to expand into this market. The UK is thus a segment of a global market with its unique needs.

(b) The market for soft drinks on the other hand is different, with Schweppes tonic water well established as a brand across Europe.

3.6 To conclude, there are four possible decisions for products.

- Sell products unmodified/standardised
- Modify or adapt products where necessary
- Develop new products for a specific market or group of markets
- Eliminate old/weak products

Global product

3.7 Coca-Cola could be a good example of a global product, in that it is widely available over most of the world, although it is not globally priced and does not contain the same ingredients the world over. It first established its worldwide presence during the Second World War when the drink accompanied US troops. However, you ought to think of others.

Marketing at Work

- The Rolex watch is the same all over the world. Its positioning as the watch for the high achiever is the same across the globe. It is an upmarket product and will be found in upmarket outlets.

- Unilever's Lifebuoy soap is positioned identically in India and East Africa, despite having different ingredients. It is promoted as an inexpensive soap that protects health.

3.8 Ideally, a firm would prefer to offer the same product, with the same pricing policy using the same promotional methods and through the same distribution channels in all its markets, for ease of management, if nothing else. But in practice, this is never possible.

3.9 Complete **global standardisation** would greatly increase the profitability of a company's products and simplify the task of the international marketing manager. The extent to which standardisation is possible is controversial in marketing. Levitt wrote:

> 'The global corporation operates with resolute constancy, at low relative cost, as if the entire world (or major regions of it) were a single entity; it sells the same things in the same way everywhere.'

3.10 At the other end of the spectrum, it has been argued that adaptability is the key ingredient for global success. Much of the decision making in an international marketing manager's role is concerned with taking a view on the necessity, or lack of it, of adapting the product, price and communications to individual markets.

3.11 A firm's approach to this decision depends to a large extent on its attitude towards internationalisation and its level of involvement in international marketing. There are broadly three types of approach in this context, as we have discussed earlier.

(a) **Ethnocentrism.** Overseas operations are viewed as being secondary to domestic operations and are often simply a means of disposing of surpluses. Any plans for overseas markets are developed at home with very little systematic market research overseas. There is little or no modification of any aspects of the mix with no real attention to customer needs. This is the first step into international marketing and involves a centralised strategy.

(b) **Polycentrism.** Subsidiaries are established, each operating independently with its own plans, objectives and marketing policies on a country by country basis. Adaptation will be at its most extreme with this approach. Polycentrism can be viewed as an evolutionary step and involves a decentralised strategy. It is easy to fall into a **multidomestic** pattern of operations that does not take advantage of co-ordinating actions across differential markets.

(c) **Geocentrism.** The organisation views the entire world as a market with standardisation where possible and adaptation where necessary. It is the final evolutionary stage for the multinational organisation and involves an integrated marketing strategy.

3.12 In general terms, the extent to which the mix has to be adapted depends on the type of product. Some products are extremely sensitive to the environmental differences, which bring about the need for adaptation; others are not at all sensitive to these differences, in which case standardisation is possible.

3.13 A useful way of analysing products internationally is to place them on a continuum of **environmental sensitivity**. (We are referring to the social, legal, economic, political and cultural environments here.) The greater the environmental sensitivity of a product, the greater the necessity for the company to adapt the marketing mix.

Environmentally sensitive   Environmentally insensitive

|———|

Adaptation necessary   Standardisation possible

- Fashion clothes
- Convenience foods

- Industrial and agricultural products
- World market product, eg denim jeans

3.14 A more sophisticated approach is a two-dimensional matrix. The vertical dimension measures the advantages of standardised marketing and the horizontal dimension takes the need for localised marketing into account. This is illustrated below.

3.15 There are strong forces in the business environment drawing companies towards global marketing strategies, the most important of which are as follows.

(a) **Demographic, cultural** and **economic convergence** among consumer markets and increasing homogeneity in the needs of industrial customers worldwide.

(b) Increased need for **investment and research** to ensure long term competitiveness, longer lead times involved in bringing products to market and the growing return needed for this process.

(c) The growing importance of **economies of scale** (purchasing, manufacturing, distribution).

(d) Changes in **regional economic cooperation** resulting in freer movement of goods and capital.

(e) The impact of technology on manufacturing, transportation and distribution.

(f) The **deregulation** of national markets, in areas such as air transport, financial services, telecommunications and power generation.

	Sector 1 GLOBAL • Aircraft manufacturing • Computers • Industrial machinery Automobiles	Sector 3 BLOCKED GLOBAL • Telecommunications • Generators Pharmaceuticals	High
	Sector 2 MULTINATIONAL/ MULTIMARKET • Medical equipment • Synthetic fibres • Cash dispensers • Electrical equipment	Sector 4 NATIONAL/ LOCAL • Breweries • Cement • Retail trade Processed food	Low
	Low	High	

*Advantages of
standardised
marketing*

Need for localised marketing

3.16 However, despite these strong worldwide forces, there are still many situations where the advantages of or need for local adaptation is high.

(a) **Sector 1** contains true global marketing companies with a geocentric orientation. Local adaptation is inappropriate and globalising forces can be exploited to great advantage to the company. Examples include aircraft, computers and industrial machinery.

(b) **Sector 2.** Multinational or multimarket companies with a polycentric orientation adopt this approach. Products require only a low degree of local adaptation. The world market for such multinational organisations is divided into regions or countries with different characteristics, such as W Europe, S America or the Far East. Products in this sector include electrical equipment.

(c) **Sector 3.** Blocked global businesses are those in which both the need for local adaptation and the globalising factors discussed above are strong. This sector includes businesses that are dominated by economies of scale and would be global but for the influence of legal or political constraints (eg government purchasing policies) creating the need to adapt their products. Regional telephone networks offer a typical example.

(d) **Sector 4** contains true local businesses. Strong local adaptation is necessary for success and there are no strong arguments in favour of globalisation (eg brewing and retail trade).

3.17 Kenichi Ohmae writes (in *The Borderless World*) that 'the lure of a universal product is a false allure', simply because local tastes are so different (eg American cars are generally too large and bulky for Europe's narrow streets). It is a similar story with brands. Some brands are global while many others are present in only one country.

Marketing at Work

Out of 560 brands that Nestlé had in 1995, 250 were present in only one country. Only 19 were found in more than 50 per cent of the countries where Nestlé operates.

3.18 Some products suit globalisation

- Watches and cameras
- Fashion-oriented, premium price branded goods including luxury items

---

Action Programme 1

What are the arguments in favour of product adaptation?

---

4 PRODUCT AND COMMUNICATIONS

Standardisation vs adaptation

4.1 The question of whether or not to adapt the product is often considered in conjunction with the **promotion/communication** issue. This gives us four possible product and communication strategies. We will be returning to communications issues generally in Chapter 11.

	Product standardised	Product adapted
Communications standardised	Standardisation worldwide of both product and communications	Adaptation of product only
Communications adapted	Adaptation of communications only	Both product and communications adapted

Source: Keegan

Standardised product and communications

4.2 This is the obvious strategy for the occasional exporter but also some major international companies seeking economies of scale.

4.3 PepsiCo has been successful with this strategy. Many perfumes and cosmetics are marketed in this way. (For example, the actress Elizabeth Hurley has been adopted to be the 'face of Estée Lauder' worldwide.) Polaroid, however, failed in France with their instant picture camera because of failure to modify their product and communications activities from the successful USA version. This failure was due to the fact that the product was at a different stage in its product life cycle in France and the United States.

Standardised product/adapted communication

4.4 This strategy is used where a product meets different needs in different countries. Take bicycles for example. The product is the same, but communications can suggest different uses.

- France/Belgium - sport-recreation
- UK - recreation
- Third World - means of transport

Adapted product/standardised communication

4.5 This strategy is relevant where the product satisfies the same need (or solves the same problem) in many markets but conditions of use vary.

(a) Petrol companies adapt their fuel to climactic conditions but standardise their advertising and other promotional activities.

(b) Car manufacturers need different tyres and temperature control systems in Saudi Arabia than they do in the UK.

Adaptation of both product and communications

4.6 This strategy is the most costly one but may be necessary to exploit a market fully. For example, take these two stereotypes.

(a) US product - can be made or packaged in plastic and be disposable.

(b) German product - must be made or packaged in metal and must be durable and repairable because of German concern for environmental issues. Promotional activities must reflect these product attributes.

5 OTHER ASPECTS OF PRODUCT DECISIONS

5.1 Other aspects of the product decision principally concern packaging, labelling and after sales service.

Packaging

5.2 Again, standardisation vs adaptation is the major question. A problem might be the different sizes required in different countries. There are three aspects of packaging.

(a) **Protection**. Packaging may have to be adapted/modified if climate, handling facilities, time spent in distribution chain or usage rate vary.

(b) **Promotion**. Packaging will be adapted if package size, cost of packaging, colour preference, legal constraints, literacy, reputation/recognition varies from market to market.

(c) **Recyclability**. The issue of recyclability is becoming increasingly important. Germany, in particular, has a complex scheme for collecting and recycling household packaging materials. An EU directive has recently come into force in all European countries requiring a reduction in packaging use, greater re-use and recycling. This has had a significant impact on pack design and distribution channel management for some companies (**"reverse logistics"** for the return of packaging is now becoming standard in some industries)

5.3 Consumer needs and wants are not identical across markets.

Marketing at Work

The market research agency, Research Business International, was commissioned to carry out some overseas work for its client, Gillette. Gillette wanted to know more about the market for its razor products in Africa. The agency discovered that in Nigeria, razors were used mainly for skinning animals, not for shaving. Gillette responded by developing a special holder which facilitated this product use.

Labelling

5.4 Labelling is an example of mandatory modification required by government regulations.

(a) This usually concerns listing contents or use of appropriate language or languages.

(b) Some countries have strict laws regarding describing the contents of each package.

(c) Eco-labelling is now becoming important in some markets (primarily European markets at the moment) informing consumers of the environmental aspects of the product - for example the energy usage over the lifetime of refrigerators.

Servicing

5.5 This is an increasingly important part of the augmented product (particularly in the developed economies) and is of great importance in international marketing. If the availability or quality of servicing is doubtful, consumers may choose to buy domestic products.

5.6 The service problem is a complex one for the exporter. It involves decisions about facilities, personnel and training. Should they use distributors which would involve training foreign staff and sending out HQ personnel to monitor or should they operate a direct servicing policy in which case they would fly out maintenance staff when required? The appropriate decision varies with the technical sophistication and value of the product.

6 NEW PRODUCT DEVELOPMENT FOR OVERSEAS MARKETS

6.1 Sometimes international marketing managers may need to develop new products for a specific overseas market or group of markets. If a product has been developed for one geographical market, taking it to other countries sometimes requires little extra developmental effort, eg pharmaceuticals.

- Idea generation
- Idea screening
- Concept tasting
- Business analysis
- Product development and testing
- Test marketing
- Commercialisation

6.2 New product development that co-ordinates efforts across national markets does tend to lead to better products. **Unilever** has four global research laboratories that develop products for different national markets while also investigating components for global products. The **internet** has widened the potential for scouring the world for information for product design.

Success of new products

6.3 The success of new products in an international environment depends on a number of factors.

(a) It is important to have an appropriate **organisational structure**. An international division, responsive to international rather than purely domestic marketing concerns, is far more likely to introduce new products overseas successfully.

(b) There should be a commitment to **market research**. As we have seen, international market research is more complex than domestic market research.

(c) Sources of **idea generation** should be as wide as possible: customers, intermediaries, competitors, research and development, sales staff etc.

(d) The new product development process should be implemented for **each country**, ie screening, business analysis, test marketing etc.

Marketing at Work

Designing a new version of one product for each market is prohibitively expensive, but a company may want more than one product covering all markets. Nissan has been a pioneer in finding the right balance. It reduced the number of different chassis designs from 40 to 8, for cars destined for 75 markets.

The development of new products for specific markets is especially relevant to developing nations, although if the market potential is not high a modification to an existing product may be more commercially viable.

6.4 Furthermore, there is increasing evidence of **time-based competition**. In other words many firms are reducing the time spent to get new products researched, designed and launched.

- It wrongfoots competitors (eg early mover advantages)
- It enables the firm to get the maximum return from patents
- It might enable the firm to set industry standards for new products
- It enables a premium or skimming pricing strategy

6.5 Speed in NPD can be facilitated by co-ordination between marketing and R&D throughout the design process. There are many good reasons why R&D should be more closely co-ordinated with marketing.

(a) If the firm operates the marketing concept, then the 'identification of customer needs' should be a vital input to new product developments.

(b) The R & D department might identify possible changes to product specifications so that a variety of marketing mixes can be tried out and screened.

6.6 Other measures to speed NPD

(a) **Parallel engineering** (ie different aspects of the design are carried out simultaneously, rather than being shuffled to and fro in a sequence)

(b) **Design for manufacture** (ie product design specification should, as far as possible minimise new equipment or machine modification, which can be time consuming)

(c) Setting up relationships with **distributors** early on to encourage rapid takeup

6.7 When it comes to launching a product, companies decide on different **launch strategies** for different product types. Arvind Sahay (Financial Times *Mastering Marketing* series) suggests that the following criteria apply when deciding upon the launch strategy (simultaneous launch, or one country at a time?) to be adopted.

(a) Is the product purchased **separately** by the consumer, or as a component for another product or service?

(b) How much **promotion** is required?

(c) What is the **price** of the product? It has been suggested that a product which is satisfactory for its purpose and costs less than $300 is likely to be a mass market item. (This of course would not necessarily apply in developing economies.)

6.8 These points are illustrated by the following example.

Marketing at Work

- Toshiba launched the Digital Video Disk (DVD) at varying stages, sequentially, starting with Japan in 1996 and going to Europe a year later. Intel, however, launched its component PC chips simultaneously to all markets, because it is a standard component.

- Higher priced products are going to be bought by 'innovators' or 'early adopters' who do not mind price skimming strategies. A launch of such a product is unlikely to be simultaneous in all markets, eg car navigation systems are standard in Japan but unknown in developing countries.

Exam Tip

NPD has been examined. The issues have included:

(a) the speed of NPD

(b) comparing an exporter's ability to obtain useful inputs to the NPD process from overseas with that of a firm with plants throughout the world.

---

7 PRODUCT LIFE CYCLES AND INTERNATIONAL MARKETING MIX DECISIONS

7.1 Many marketing mistakes have been made because firms have failed to take into account the fact that in different countries a product may be at different stages in its **product life cycle**. By now, you should be thoroughly familiar with this concept.

7.2 Marketing principles tell us that products, prices, marketing communications and channels of distribution need to be adapted as a product 'ages' during its life cycle. The marketing mix programme for a new product should be fundamentally different from the mix programme for a mature product.

7.3 The product life cycle is relevant to international marketing management. Traditionally many firms have tended only to operate at home as long as performance there was satisfactory. Then, when domestic performance declined, they tried to close the gap by exporting. But this is possible only if there are **different product life cycle patterns** in different countries. In the diagram on the following page, the product is in the decline stage in the home market, in the growth stage in country X, and in the introduction stage in country Y.

7.4 This approach was very convenient. Firms were simply able to classify markets according to their economic development and launch declining products in rapid succession into countries with progressively less market development. Nowadays, however, this type of strategy is less feasible, although not entirely impossible. The revolution in communications among countries during recent years has narrowed the time gap between when saturation occurs in the home market and the last overseas market entered. Hence, the **total** duration of the profit life cycle, aggregated across all the firm's markets, has shortened. For some products the profit life cycle pattern is exactly the same for home sales as for some/most/all overseas markets.

BPP PUBLISHING

Product life cycles in different countries

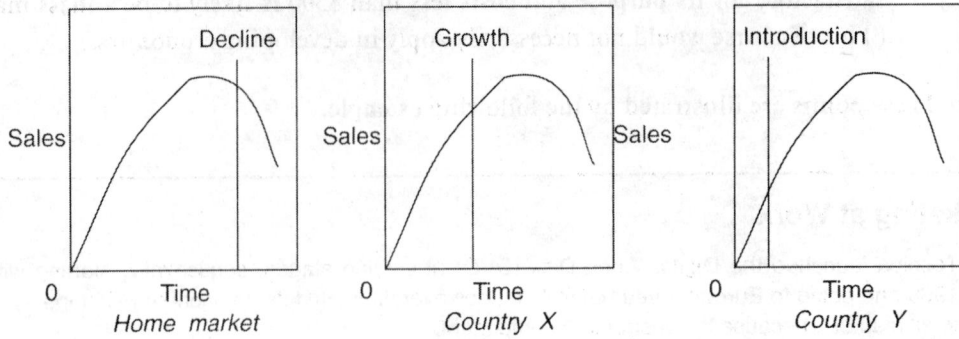

Home market — Country X — Country Y

7.5 As a result of these developments, international marketing must consider many markets simultaneously, with a view to implementing a global introduction.

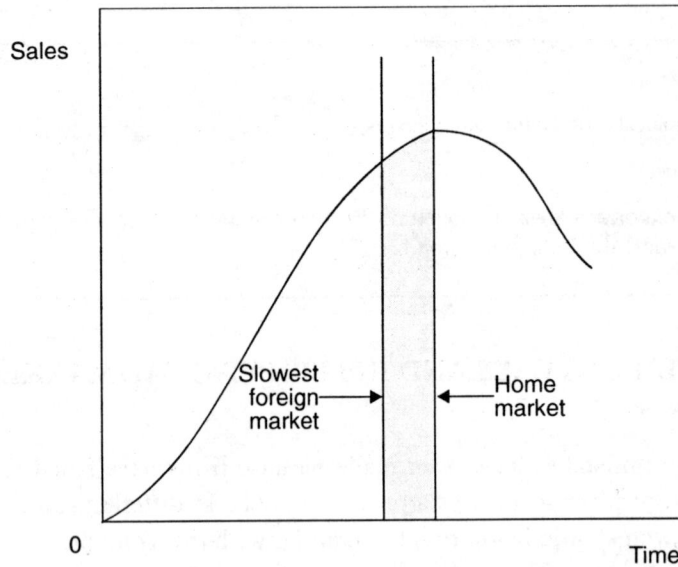

7.6 This is necessary to ensure that the product is launched in all potential markets before rivals have time to pre-empt the firm and to ensure that introduction everywhere coincides with the most appropriate demand conditions.

Marketing at Work

The old Volkswagen 'Beetle' car is manufactured and sold in Mexico and Brazil, long after it ceased production in Germany, as a 'cheap and cheerful' means of transport.

Product life cycle and the market/country

Key Concept
The **international trade life cycle** (ITLC) is the adaptation of the product life model to international conditions.

7.7 The **International Trade Life Cycle** (ITLC) is used in developing long-term product strategy. It postulates that many products pass through a cycle during which high income, mass-consumption countries are initially exporters but subsequently lose their export markets and ultimately become importers of the product.

7.8 From the perspective of the initiator high income country the pattern of development is as follows.

(a) **Phase 1. The product is developed in the high income country** (eg the USA). There are two main reason for this.

   (i) High income countries provide the greatest demand potential.

   (ii) It is expedient to locate production close to the market during the early period so that the firm can react quickly in modifying the product according to customer preferences.

(b) **Phase 2. Foreign production starts.** Firms in the innovator's export markets (such as the UK) start to produce the product domestically. Thus, for example, the UK market is then shared by the innovative US firm and the UK firms.

(c) **Phase 3. Overseas producers compete in export markets.** The costs of the UK producers begin to fall as they gain economies of scale and experience. They may also enjoy lower costs of labour, materials etc than the US firms. The UK firms now start to compete with the US producers in third-party export markets such as, say, Greece or Brazil.

(d) **Phase 4. Overseas producers compete in the firm's domestic market.** The UK firms become so competitive, due to their lower production costs that they start to compete with the US firms in the US domestic market. The cycle is now complete.

   The cycle may well, however continue as firms in less developed countries enter and ultimately take over the market. The extent and speed of the process depends largely on the product's technical sophistication.

7.9 The major significance of the ITLC concept is in long-term strategic planning.

(a) A firm developing a new product in a high income country should try to penetrate foreign markets as quickly as possible so as to maximise early returns before lower-cost firms located elsewhere enter the market.

(b) Moreover, the innovator would do well to consider the benefits of establishing production capacity overseas as early as is technically feasible.

Product elimination

7.10 Elimination (**divestment**) should be part of a procedure for product portfolio analysis, where for each country a periodic review of product range is undertaken. Factors to be taken into consideration during this review would include the following.

   • Current profitability
   • Effects of elimination on the sale of other (complementary) products
   • After sales service implications
   • Alternative product opportunities in each country
   • The effect on sales/profits of product life extension/rejuvenation

7.11 All these factors become much more complex for the multinational company with overseas operations. The multinational company may be producing the product under consideration in a number of countries, under a number of different market conditions.

7.12 However, the multinational company's range of alternatives to product elimination for a marginal product is greater than for an exporter. A multinational company can export or license or arrange for contract manufacturing as an alternative to direct manufacturing abroad.

8 INTERNATIONAL BRANDING DECISIONS

> ### Key Concept
> A **brand** is a name, term, sign, symbol or design intended to identify the product or service of a seller and to differentiate it from those of competitors. It is a particular make of a product form.

8.1 Not long ago, and this is still the case in many less developed countries, most products were sold unbranded from barrels and bins etc. Today in developed and even developing countries hardly anything goes unbranded. Salt, oranges, nuts and screws are often branded. There has however been a limited return recently in some developed countries to 'generics'. These are cheap, unbranded products, packaged plainly and not heavily advertised.

Marketing at Work

Brewing is an industry with significant economies of scale. Apart from Heineken and Guinness, it is only recently that big brewers have become 'international'. There are a variety of aspects of this development.

(a) Beers are branded across markets. Stella Artois is available in the UK as a premium product, whereas in Belgium it is 'a decent modestly price lager'.

(b) Other firms are expanding by acquisition. Interbrew, the brewer of Stella Artois has purchased Labatt of Canada, to gain access to markets in North and South America.

(c) Big brewing companies see many European and American markets are stagnant: they are trying to revive them with imported or foreign brands.

(d) Firms co-operate in some markets but compete in others. (Guinness distributes Bass in the US, whilst competing with Bass in the UK.)

(e) The greatest potential seems to be east Asia, where beer consumption is rising by 10% pa and South America, where growth is 4% pa.

Ultimately, even if the beer market eventually becomes truly global, it will remain fragmented for a long time to come.

To brand or not to brand?

8.2 The advantages of branding include the following.

(a) Branding facilitates **memory recall,** thus contributing to self-selection and improving customer loyalty.

(b) In many cultures branding is preferred, particularly in the **distribution channel**.

(c) Branding is a way of obtaining **legal protection** for product features.

(d) It helps with **market segmentation**.

(e) It helps build a strong and positive **corporate image**, especially if the brand name used is the company name (eg Kelloggs, Heinz). It is not so important if the company name is not used (eg Procter and Gamble).

(f) Branding makes it easier to link **advertising** to other marketing communications programmes.

(g) **Display space** is more easily obtained and point-of-sale promotions are more practicable.

(h) If branding is successful, other **associated products** can be introduced.

(i) The need for expensive **personal selling** may be reduced.

8.3 Branding is not relevant to all products

- Only those that can achieve **mass sales** because of the cost of branding and advertising

- Those whose attributes can be **evaluated** by consumers

Thus chocolate bars can be branded, but not concrete slabs. Whisky can be branded but not coal.

8.4 The most successful examples of worldwide branding occur where the brand has become **synonymous with the generic product** (eg Sellotape, Aspirin).

Types of brand

8.5 There are four choices of brand.

(a) **Individual brand name.** This is the option chosen by Procter and Gamble for example, who even have different brand names within the same product line, eg Bold, Tide. The main advantage of individual product branding is that an unsuccessful brand does not adversely affect the firm's other products, nor the firm's reputation generally.

(b) **Blanket family brand name** for all products, eg Hoover. This has the advantage of enabling the global organisation to introduce new products quickly and successfully. Also the cost of introducing the new product in terms of name research and awareness advertising will be reduced (eg Honda lawn mowers).

(c) **Separate family names** for different product divisions. Alcoholic drinks fall into this category. Most brands of spirits for example are owned by one of a small group of firms.

(d) **The company trade name combined with an individual product name,** eg Kelloggs - Corn Flakes, Rice Krispies etc. This option both legitimises (because of the company name) and individualises (the individual product name).

Success criteria for branding

8.6 Qualities of a brand name

(a) Suggests **benefits,** eg Ultrabrite toothpaste, Slimline tonic

(b) Suggests qualities such as **action** or **colour,** (eg Shake 'n Vac)

(c) Be **easy to pronounce,** recognise and remember

(d) Be **acceptable in all markets** both linguistically and culturally. For international companies name research can avoid possible faux pas because of cultural and language differences, eg 'Body Mist' when translated into German means 'manure'!

(e) Be distinctive

(f) Be meaningful. When Procter and Gamble wished to launch 'Crest Tartar Control' into South American countries, research found that there was no recognised Spanish translation for dental tartar. The brand name had to be changed

Global or local brand?

8.7 The key differences between a standardised global brand approach and an approach based upon identifying and exploiting global marketing opportunities are as described below.

(a) **Standardised global brand approach**

(i) A standardised product offering to market segments which have exactly similar needs across cultures

(ii) A common approach to the marketing mix and one that is as nearly standardised as may be, given language differences

(b) **Global marketing opportunities**

(i) A recognition that the resources of the company may be adapted to fulfil marketing opportunities in different ways, taking into account local needs and preferences but on a global basis

(ii) A willingness to sub-optimise the benefits of having a single global brand (eg advertising synergy) in order to optimise the benefits of meeting specific needs more closely

---

Marketing at Work

(a) It is possible to move from the latter approach to a global brand approach as demonstrated by the Mars Corporation with their Snickers brand. In the UK market, the biggest 'candy market' in Europe, Mars had decided to use the brand name Marathon for the chocolate bar known as Snickers in the US and elsewhere around the world. Reportedly, this was done to avoid confusion with the word knickers. There was a very distinctive brand identity in the UK to the extent that the company would sponsor the London Marathon and other sporting events to tie in with the brand name. Competition from Nestlé in Europe persuaded the company that they needed to take up the potential benefits of a standardised global brand approach rather than merely relying on a global marketing approach. They, therefore, changed the name to Snickers in the UK market at very considerable cost of advertising support.

(b) General Motors who operate as Opel in Germany and elsewhere in Europe, and Vauxhall in the UK, chose to use the brand name Vectra for the 1996 update of the Vauxhall Cavalier in the UK market. This was done in order to standardise the name across the European market - since the 'Cavalier' model had been known as the Opel Vectra in most markets anyway. General Motors still use the Vauxhall company name in the UK market since it has strong brand equity in its own right.

8.8 For the international company marketing products which can be branded there are two further policy decisions to be made.

- The problem of deciding if and how to protect the company's brands
- Whether there should be one global brand or different national brands for a product

8.9 The major argument in favour of a single global brand is the economies of scale that it produces, both in production and promotion. But whether a global brand is the best policy or even possible depends on a number of factors, which address the two basic policy decisions above.

Legal considerations for branding

8.10 (a) Legal constraints may limit the possibilities for a global brand, for instance where the brand name has already been registered in a foreign country.

(b) Protection of the brand name will often be needed, but internationally is hard to achieve.

- In some countries registration is difficult
- Brand imitation and piracy are rife in certain parts of the world

There are many examples of imitation in international branding, with products such as cigarettes, and denim jeans.

(c)   Worse still is the problem of piracy where a well known brand name is counterfeited. It is illegal in most parts of the world but in many countries there is little if any enforcement of the law. (Levis is one of the most pirated brand names.) Piracy is also a problem for intellectual property.

Action Programme 2

Even with trademark protection the impact of a market leader's branding may be weakened by consumers who perceive the brand name as a generic term. Can you think of some examples?

Marketing at Work

Budweiser is a US beer - but a beer with an identical name - through a very different taste - is made in the Czech Republic and is sold throughout Europe. Anheuser-Busch, the American owner, has been unable to buy the Czech beer's trademark.

Cultural aspects of branding

8.11   Even if a firm has no legal difficulties with branding globally, there may be cultural problems, eg unpronounceable names or names with other meanings. There are many examples of problems in global branding, for example Maxwell House is Maxwell Kaffee in Germany, Legal in France and Monky in Spain. But sometimes a minor spelling change is all that is needed, such as Wrigley Speermint in Germany.

Other marketing considerations

8.12   Many other influences affect the global branding decision, including:

(a)   Differences between the firm's major brand and its secondary brands. The major brand is more likely to be branded globally than secondary brands.

(b)   The importance of brand to the product sale. Where price, for example, is a more important factor, then it may not be worth the heavy expenditure needed to establish and maintain a global brand in each country; a series of national brands may be more effective.

(c)   The problem of how to brand a product arising from acquisition or joint venture. Should the multinational company keep the name it has acquired?

Exam Tip

Questions in this area often will specifically ask for examples so you should keep your eyes peeled on the business press.

---

9 SERVICES AND OTHER PRODUCT FORMS

9.1 Services have the following characteristics.

- **Intangibility**: although it is more accurate to speak of a continuum
- **Inseparability**: many services are created when consumed
- **Variability**: services depend on who delivers the service and when it takes place
- **Perishability**: services cannot be stored
- **Ownership**: services do not result in a transfer of property

9.2 Services are harder to trade than goods, for obvious reasons: you cannot 'export' haircuts or physiotherapy, for example. However, many services are produced and marketed on a global scale.

- Financial and banking services
- Transportation (eg airlines)
- Tourism
- Legal, accounting and consultancy services
- Telecommunications and media services
- Retailing
- Utilities, such as power generation
- Fast food

9.3 The marketing mix for services also includes people, processes and physical evidence but there are issues of overall service decision, quality and delivery and management.

(a) **Overall service design.** Some service ideas transport easily from one country to another. The classic example is the American hamburger bar, such as **McDonald's** or **Burger King** (owned by a British firm).

(b) **Service quality and delivery.** Service improvements in one country can be introduced by a firm to another country, providing the market is open. The UK has a very competitive market in credit cards. Many American banks, including MBNA, Beneficial Bank and Advanta have entered the UK, offering tailored mixes of service and price to targeted segments in the UK market. This offers improvements and enhancement on existing offerings.

(c) **Service management.** Service companies in one country can expand by buying up service facilities elsewhere, to provide resources of finance and expertise.

These have a number of implications for the marketing mix.

9.4 **People** are a key element in service delivery. Firms providing international services with high customer-contact, such as airlines, have been well aware for many years of the need to motivate service staff to give of their best.

(a) Airline cabin crew can be trained to speak the languages relevant to the routes they fly.

(b) If service quality depends on **consistency**, training is very important.

(c) **Spatial zones** can communicate messages. In Western societies, we give work colleagues or acquaintances a large zone of personal space. Only family and close friends will enter an individual's near zone. If a colleague comes too close, our reaction is to back off, as our personal space is being invaded. This is not so in some Far Eastern countries, where space is at a premium and people have far less privacy. There, it is acceptable to stand far closer to others.

Marketing at Work

BAA (formerly British Airports Authority) aims to be acknowledged 'as the best run airports company in the world'. It has ambitions to run airports in Italy, Australia and South Africa.

It has developed its own MBA (Master of Business Administration) course, with the University of Surrey, with special emphasis on the needs of running an airport. (Diploma of Management Studies courses are also available.) BAA says 'it wants to see employees from terminal duty managers to firefighters and security staff doing the courses'.

9.5 **Processes** describe the way the service is delivered. Of course, this is infinitely bound up with people, but well designed processes are essential to service design and delivery.

Marketing at Work

Most business travellers like flexibility in a hotel. Important 'processes' in catering for business travellers might be:

- delivery of fax messages
- datapoints to enable laptop computers to work
- provision of town maps
- fast and responsive laundry service
- security at the check-in desk

Processes must also be **adapted** to the legal environment of each country, for example with legal or financial services. Failure to follow 'due process' might lead to a weak legal position in litigation.

9.6 **Physical evidence** in international marketing terms can include factors such as these.

(a) Coherent **branding** across service outlets in the world. This will be reflected in packaging (of materials supplied with the service), staff uniforms and so on.

(b) Attention to the design, layout and lighting of any physical environment, such as aircraft cabins, hotel rooms, restaurant.

(c) People communicate both by using language and non verbal signs. A shake of the head to us means no and a nod yes. This convention is reversed in some cultures.

9.7 We discuss services marketing further in Chapter 13.

Exam Tip
Questions have asked to identify key characteristics of services which make them difficult to market internationally.

Commodities

Key Concept
A **commodity** is something that is bought and sold, especially raw materials, industrial products or agricultural products. We first referred to them in Chapter 4 when we looked at buyer behaviour.

9.8 A key example of raw material commodities is provided by **agricultural produce**. Many countries do not have the population to consume all that they produce, so the export market is extremely important. Conversely, some countries do not have enough raw materials for their needs. Access to adequate **transport facilities** is key.

Marketing at Work

In America, the Facility Guarantee Programme (FGP) has been set up to enhance facilities in emerging markets (such as Jamaica, Trinidad and Tobago, Cost Rica, El Salvador, Panama and Peru) that process, handle, store or transport agricultural products imported from the US. Improved and expanded grain handling and storage at a discharge port will ultimately increase efficiency and lower the costs.

9.9 The state of Oregon in the USA exports about 40% of its total agricultural production to overseas markets, chiefly to Pacific Rim countries which have been badly affected by the Asian economic crisis, so it can be important to **diversify markets** for commodities, as with other products.

9.10 Commodity marketing has been transformed by **communications technology** in much the same way as other product types. Print media has been overtaken by the internet. Overseas marketing has been helped by the development of refrigerated containers and shipment tracking systems.

9.11 Commodity exporting often accounts for a significant proportion of a **developing country** economy. To take the example of Ethiopia, the export of hides, skins, meat, animals and leather products accounted for about 15% of 1997/98 exports. Coffee accounts for 62% and the remainder is taken up by textiles, fruit and vegetables and pulses and seeds.

9.12 The price of commodities can be set on the **commodity exchanges** of international stock exchanges or in **futures contracts,** eg cocoa futures.

Semi processed products

9.13 These are the products that are neither in their basic nor their final form, but which have been processed by the producer to some extent (eg fruit harvested and frozen prior to further processing). Examples might also include the leather and animal skins exported by Ethiopia, perhaps to be made into handbags or clothing by factories in a more developed country, or industrial components that have been partly finished before transfer to another company for further processing and installation in industrial machinery.

9.14 Semi-processed products are sold to buyers who know they can **add value** to them by further processing. This further processing may not be possible in the country of origin due to lack of skilled labour or other resources.

Chapter Roundup

- A **product** is the satisfaction purchased by the buyer. The same physical object, however, can have different uses and meanings.

- In international marketing, the choice is between **standardising** the product in all markets to reap the advantages of scale economies in manufacture and, on the other hand, **adaptation** which gives the advantages of flexible response to local market conditions. Adaptation may be unavoidable in some circumstances (eg if different countries have different legal standards for safety).

- Packaging, labelling - and even branding - must sometimes be sensitive to the **local conditions**.

- A product's stage on the **product life cycle** may vary from country to country, and different marketing strategies will be appropriate in each case.

- **Time based competition** is becoming increasingly important in **new product development**. Product development may be co-ordinated across several international markets.

- Different product types may require different **launch strategies**.

- Companies may have a single global brand, because of the economies of scale that may be realised, but **global branding** may not be the best strategy.

- **Commodities** and **semi-processed products** provide variations on the standard product form.

- **Services** can be said to have their own marketing mix.

Quick Quiz

1   What are the three levels of attribute associated with a product? (see para 2.1)
2   What is discretionary modification? (3.3)
3   List three approaches to standardisation. (3.11)
4   What forces encourage global marketing strategies? (3.15)
5   Identify four strategies for product and communications. (4.1 - 4.6)
6   What are the aspects of packaging? (5.2)
7   What factors govern success of new products in an international environment? (6.3)
8   What is the consequence of reduced gaps between product life cycles in different markets? (7.5,7.6)
9   What are the stages of the international trade life cycle? (7.8)
10 What factors should be taken into account when deciding whether or not to develop a global brand for a product? (8.2)
11 What are the advantages of a blanket family brand name? (8.5)
12 What characteristics do services have? (9.1)
13 What is a commodity? (9.8)

Action Programme Review

1   Arguments in favour of product adaptation include the following.

   (a) **Greater sales potential**, where this also means greater profitability, which it may not!

   (b) **Varied conditions of product use** which may force a company to modify its product.

   - Climatic variations (corrosion in cars produced for dry climates)

   - Literacy or skill levels of users (languages which can be used on a computer)

   - Cultural, social or religious factors (religious or cultural requirement for food products - Halal slaughtering of New Zealand lamb for Middle Eastern Markets, for instance, or dolphin-friendly tuna catching methods of Europe and the USA)

   (c) **Variation in market factors.** Consumer needs are in their nature idiosyncratic, and there are likely to be distinctive requirements for each group not met by a standard product.

    (d)   **Governmental or political influence**. Political factors may force a company to produce a local product.

- Taxation
- Legislation
- Pressure of public opinion

    (e)   Local competition

2   (a)   How can people 'Hoover' with an Electrolux machine?

       (b)   Have you ever 'xeroxed' on a photocopier not made by Rank?

       (c)   Hence the messages 'It's the real thing' or 'Always Coca Cola' from Coca Cola.

Now try illustrative question 9 at the end of the Study Text

10 International Pricing Decisions

Chapter Topic List	Syllabus Reference
1　Setting the scene	-
2　The role of pricing	3.2
3　Approaches to pricing	3.2
4　The factors influencing international marketing pricing decisions	3.2, 3.9
5　Export pricing	3.2
6　Transfer pricing	3.2
7　Export quotations	3.2
8　Methods of payment	3.2
9　Countertrade and barter	3.2

Learning Outcomes

On completion of this chapter you will have a greater appreciation of pricing issues in international marketing. Specifically, you will:

- understand various pricing strategies for international markets, including skimming and penetration pricing;

- understand the concepts of price escalation, the futures market, hedging/forward buying, tendering and bartering;

- understand export quotations, pricing and transfer pricing

- understand the meanings and specifics of Incoterms and specific payment methods

Key Concepts Introduced

- Ethnocentric, polycentric and geocentric pricing
- Cost based pricing
- Market penetration pricing
- Marketing skimming
- Price escalation

- Dumping
- Transfer price
- Foreign currency pricing and hedging strategies
- Documentary credits
- Countertrade

BPP
PUBLISHING

Examples of Marketing at Work

- Motor vehicles in the EU
- Cable television
- Telefonica
- Telecommunications and music industries

1 SETTING THE SCENE

1.1 At the best of times, pricing is a difficult decision for marketers, as it is what the consumer is actually giving in response for the satisfactions offered by the marketing mix. This crucial decision is one in which the firm is most vulnerable to wider developments in the economic environment, through changes in exchange rates. Changes in the exchange rate increase the risk profile of overseas operations.

1.2 However, you should not allow this to blind you to other considerations in the price element of the international marketing mix. Price is, after all, influenced by cost, competitive strategy, whether the product is new and so on (sections 3 and 4).

1.3 Some pricing issues are especially pertinent to international activities. Transfer pricing - the price at which goods and services are transferred between business units in different countries - is something governments have a keen interest in (section 6). The firm can use price as a competitive weapon, by offering to take all the foreign exchange risk or to augment the product/service offered by paying for distribution (section 7). Getting paid (section 8) is obviously the ultimate objective, and the complexities and risks of exporting have enabled banks to offer a variety of services to ease the process. One unusual form of payment is counter-trade or barter (section 9).

2 THE ROLE OF PRICING

2.1 Pricing is the only mix decision that produces revenue. The other elements involve costs. It is often the major mix decision yet its importance can be overstated. For many products, other mix aspects are more important, eg product quality or augmented product features.

2.2 Many companies do not handle pricing well. **Common mistakes** include the following.

- Pricing is too **cost-orientated** (see below)
- Pricing is not **revised** often enough to reflect changing market conditions
- Pricing is **decided in isolation** rather than as part of an integrated marketing plan
- Pricing is **not flexible** enough to meet the needs of different segments or countries

2.3 **Flexible pricing** is necessary to cover the following situations.

(a) When a **new product** is launched.

(b) When the company wants to **initiate a price change**.

- Cost increases
- A decision to sell as a loss leader
- A sales promotion
- A change in the product life cycle stage
- A change in discount policy
- A decision to reposition the product

(c) As a response to price change by **competitors**.

(d) When the company wants to decide on a price policy for an **entire product line**.

2.4   Successful international marketing involves an analysis of the extent to which prices should be **adapted** to meet the different **environmental and competitive situations** in the company's markets.

Standardisation and adaptation in prices of exported goods

2.5   Firms can adopt three approaches to pricing goods exported from the home market. These are explained below.

Key Concepts

(a)   **Standardised, ethnocentric pricing.** A single price is charged to recover costs and earn the return. As this is translated at local exchange rates, this can lead to price volatility in local terms and a lower volume of sales than would be possible. The demand curve in the overseas market may differ, and using a fixed standard price may not result in a maximised marginal revenue in the overseas market.

(b)   **Adaptation or polycentric pricing.** Each local subsidiary sets its own prices. There is no co-ordination. Headquarters has no control, and 'grey markets' develop.

(c)   **Geocentric pricing** aims to have a global pricing strategy, but in the short term at least (eg introducing a new product) local subsidiaries have some autonomy.

Marketing at Work

There have been many reports in the press about the relative price differentials on motor vehicles in the various countries of the EU. Buyers in the UK can face prices 50% more than those found on the continent. The manufacturers claim that these are supported by differences in specification, distribution costs etc. These different prices are reinforced by restrictions which make it hard for dealers in, say, the Netherlands to sell a car to a UK citizen for export to the UK. Consumer groups think that competition is inhibited. The car market in the UK is already being affected, with consumers delaying the purchase of new cars in the expectation of Government action soon to force cheaper UK car prices. In some cases, prices are already coming down.

Standardisation and adaptation in prices of goods both produced and sold in the overseas market

2.6   Here we are concerned with pricing strategies for products that are both produced and marketed in an overseas country. The extent of pricing control exercised from outside that country will depend on the organisation's structure.

(a)   **Ethnocentric approach:** group headquarters dictates its subsidiary's pricing decisions totally.

(b)   **Polycentric approach:** the subsidiaries are autonomous. This is fine if it manufactures its products locally, as costs and revenues will be in the same currency.

(c)   **Geocentric approach:** control varies depending on the situation, perhaps the best of both worlds.

2.7   **Foreign governments** influence pricing decisions. An international company must be aware of the legislation in each of the countries in which it operates. There are broadly two types of government influences in pricing decisions.

- **Price controls**
- **Restrictive practices** control

Price controls

2.8 These tend to become more widespread when inflation takes hold. Governments either forbid or lay down certain conditions for price increases. Price controls still feature in some countries for basic commodities (eg bread in Egypt). Governments may also take the view that setting minimum prices is in the public interest by maintaining competition.

Restrictive practices controls

2.9 A **restrictive practice** is one practice which prevents, restricts or distorts competition. The government control of such practices will have effects on foreign market pricing. Many countries have a government agency whose main task is to protect the public interest by controlling such practices (in the UK, the Office of Fair Trading).

3 APPROACHES TO PRICING

3.1 In the international context the need for flexibility in pricing arises because different conditions may exist in different markets and firms may adopt different marketing objectives (see section 4 below).

> ### Key Concept
> With **cost based pricing**, price is based purely on the cost of making goods, with little thought about market conditions.

Cost based pricing

3.2 **Total cost** is often the basis for pricing. This is a sensible policy in markets where price is the only or most important factor in the purchase decision and where there is little differentiation among product offerings, both at a formal and augmented level, (eg industrial nuts, bolts and screws).

3.3 However, research tends to suggest that too many firms adopt cost based pricing for all their products and in all their markets when other approaches would be more effective in achieving their objectives. For example, even in industrial product markets demand intensities can vary between countries, which gives opportunities for **price differentiation**.

Demand based pricing

3.4 **Demand based pricing** enables marketers to set prices according to the customer's ability and willingness to pay. These demand levels may vary from one country to another, within the same country among different segments, or even within the same segment over time.

3.5 This is the true **marketing based approach** and puts customers' needs and preferences at the heart of the pricing decision. Demand based prices are most prevalent in branded consumer goods but are increasingly possible in many industrial goods markets.

Competition and pricing

3.6 There are two aspects of **competition based pricing** relevant to the international context.

(a) Where there is almost perfect competition individual suppliers of a product have no control over the price they charge. This is the case with **commodity prices** such as those for tea and coffee. Here current world market prices are known to customers and any change is established as a result of interaction among a large number of buyers and sellers.

(b) Where a firm can base its price levels in relation to its competitors in order to achieve certain objectives the price charged must be consistent with those objectives. The **price/quality diagram** below illustrates the competitive price strategies open to an international firm.

Relative price

		High	Medium	Low
	High	1 Premium pricing strategy	2 Penetration pricing strategy	3 Super bargain strategy
Relative product quality	**Medium**	4 Overpricing strategy	5 Average pricing strategy	6 Bargain pricing strategy
	Low	7 Hit & run pricing strategy	8 Shoddy goods pricing strategy	9 Cheap goods strategy

A full analysis of this model can be found in many textbooks concerned with marketing principles.

3.7 Some examples of the model's application in the international context would be as follows.

(a) A firm might adopt Strategy 3 (at least in the short term) in one country in order to penetrate a difficult competitive market while adopting Strategy 1 in another where it already has a good reputation and fewer real competitors.

(b) A firm might adopt Strategy 9 (cheap goods strategy) in a less developed country because of low disposable income levels while producing a better quality product at a higher price in a market where disposable incomes are higher (Strategies 5 or 1).

(c) Any of strategies 4, 7 or 8 (over pricing, hit and run pricing or shoddy goods pricing) might be adopted in markets where customers are unaware that they could obtain the same quality at a lower price or a higher quality at the same price. In another, more knowledgeable market, a cheap goods strategy (9) might be used.

Kotler states that strategies 4, 7 and 8 should be avoided by professional marketers. Selling shoddy goods devalues the brand name, and will discourage repeat purchases.

New product pricing

3.8 J Dean (in *Fundamentals of Marketing* ed by Taylor, Robb and New) has suggested that there are three elements in the pricing decision for a new product. These are as follows.

- Getting the product **accepted**
- **Maintaining a market share** in the face of competition
- **Making a profit** from the product

3.9 When a firm launches a new product on to the market, it must decide on a pricing policy which lies between the two extremes of **market penetration** and **market skimming**.

Penetration

> ### Key Concept
> **Market penetration** pricing is a policy of low prices when the product is first launched in order to gain sufficient penetration into the market. It is therefore a policy of sacrificing short-run profits in the interests of long-term profits.

3.10 The circumstances which favour a penetration policy are as follows.

(a) The firm wishes to **discourage rivals** from entering the market.

(b) The firm wishes to **shorten the initial period** of the product's life cycle, in order to enter the growth and maturity stages as quickly as possible.

(c) There are significant **economies of scale** to be achieved from a large output. A firm might therefore deliberately build excess production capacity and set its prices very low; as demand builds up, the spare capacity will be used up gradually, and unit costs will fall; the firm might even reduce prices further as unit costs fall. In this way, early year losses will enable the firm to dominate the market and have the lowest costs.

Skimming

> ### Key Concept
> **Market skimming** pricing involves the following. Some firms set a high initial price to achieve high unit profits, knowing that a certain number of customers will buy at the high price. This is possible where rival firms are not expected to undercut these high prices, where the fixed costs of output are fairly low, so that economies of scale are relatively insignificant and where the customer believes that high prices signify a quality product.

3.11 Market skimming involves the following.

(a) Charging high prices when a product is **first launched.**

(b) **Spending heavily on advertising** and sales promotion to win customers.

(c) As the product moves into the later stages of its life cycle **progressively lower prices** will be charged. The profitable 'cream' is thus 'skimmed' off in progressive stages until sales can only be sustained at lower prices.

3.12 The aim of market skimming is to gain **high unit profits very early** on in the product's life. Conditions which are suitable for such a policy are as follows.

(a) Where the product is **new and different,** so that customers are prepared to pay high prices so as to be 'one up' on other people who do not own one. Many new technology items come into this category.

(b) Where **demand elasticity is unknown.** It is better to start by charging high prices and then reducing them if the demand for the product turns out to be price elastic than to start by charging low prices and then attempting to raise them substantially when demand turns out to be price inelastic.

(c) High initial prices might not be profit-maximising in the long run, but they generate **high initial cash flows.**

(d) Skimming may also enable the firm to identify **different market segments** for the product, each prepared to pay progressively lower prices. If product **differentiation** can be introduced, it may be possible to continue to sell at higher prices to some market segments.

Marketing at Work

Cable TV

For many German, Japanese and US firms (and others) the UK is an overseas market with its own peculiar cultural, legal and marketing characteristics. The British government in the 1980s encouraged a number of US cable TV companies to set up business, dig up pavements and sell their services in Britain.

The American companies have invested several billion pounds in the UK: how are they to recoup this money?

In the event, demand for television services has been less than anticipated: in the US, cable TV offered far better reception but in most parts of the UK, 'ordinary' TV reception is good. Furthermore, in addition to terrestrial channels, satellite channels such as BSkyB offer other programs. So was the huge investment justified?

The cable companies have made more of the fact that they offer an alternative telecommunications network to BT. The aim is to win market share from BT and so with phone services start to make a profit.

The cable firms have used penetration pricing as a key aspect of their market entry strategy. Skimming is not an option where British citizens have easy access to TV and phone services.

3.13 If you relate these ideas to the International Trade Life Cycle, you can end up with different pricing strategies in different markets. Some of the possible consequences of this are discussed in the next section.

4 THE FACTORS INFLUENCING INTERNATIONAL MARKETING PRICING DECISIONS

4.1 Pricing is affected both by a company's own objectives and a variety of external factors.

(a) The **company's marketing pricing objectives**. These are as follows.

(i)	**Financial**	- cash generation, profit, return on investment
(ii)	**Marketing**	- maintain/improve market share
		- skim/penetrate depending on stage in product life cycle
(iii)	**Competitive**	- prevent new entry
		- follow competition
		- market stabilisation (tacit agreements)
(iv)	**Product differentiation**	- high price aids perception of product differences

A company may have **different objectives in different markets** and may thus need to adopt different pricing policies. For example, in one market early cash recovery may be the objective leading to premium pricing. In another, larger market the objective might be longer term market share, suggesting a more penetrative pricing strategy.

(b) **Level of demand**. This is influenced by the market's state of economic development, stage in the product life cycle and cultural attitudes. Relatively low prices would be suitable in the following circumstances.

- In markets of low economic development
- In the maturity/saturation stages of the product life cycle
- Where the product is perceived as a basic one

253

(c) The **intensity of competition,** both domestic and international.

(d) **Cost**.

(e) **Government restrictions** and controls. Many governments have both maximum and minimum permitted prices for certain products.

(f) The number and type of **intermediaries** in the distribution channel.

(g) **Pricing in foreign currency.** A sales value in a company's home currency is uncertain due to exchange rate fluctuations.

Marketing at Work

Telefonica, which has invested in cable TV in Peru, requires its subscribers to pay in US dollars.

Buyer behaviour, culture and pricing

4.2 The price of a good is something definite, but this should not blind us to some of the **cultural** implications which can affect its use in the marketing mix in different countries. This does not mean that the economic factors in pricing are unimportant - quite the opposite - but culture does enable a firm to 'tinker at the margins'.

4.3 We are used to **fixed** prices in the West for many goods largely because the relationship between the customer and supplier is often impersonal.

(a) **Bargaining** still exists for certain purchases.

(i) On the one hand, the end **consumer** does not bargain over the price of a Mars bar, a packet of aspirin tablets or a newspaper.

(ii) On the other hand, buying or selling a used car, say through a newspaper advert often involves bargaining to arrive at a mutually acceptable figure.

(b) Bargaining still exists in industrial marketing, under the name of volume discounts etc. After all, Michael Porter refers to the **bargaining** powers of customers and suppliers.

4.4 In **developing countries,** bargaining is often still the rule. Time is not a scarce resource, but money is. There are many rituals involved in bargaining. The key lesson for international marketers is that in a society where bargaining is the norm, price may end up being determined by local short-term considerations.

Quality and price

4.5 Although price is the only element of the marketing mix that generates revenue, it has, in addition to its economic function, a **symbolic function.** A price conveys information about something. (There is a theory which says that the price of a share being traded in the Stock Exchange reflects **all** the information available about it.)

4.6 Price is used as a **surrogate for quality.** In other words some people assume that something of a high price must be of a high quality.

4.7 Furthermore, it can be argued that the price of something does not necessarily reflect the **actual cost** to the user of 'consuming' the product.

(a) DIY equipment is popular as people prefer to spend the time on home improvements rather than, for example, working overtime to earn the money to hire somebody to do the job professionally. In the user's eyes, the price of DIY equipment is very favourable compared with getting a building firm to do the job.

(b) Is there a national preference for disposable items? For example, in a country where people move home every five years, there are disadvantages in getting a high price high quality cooker, say, with a long life span, as it is inconvenient to transport it to a new house where it might not fit in.

4.8 High prices often have a 'snob' value (the **Veblen effect**: snobbish consumers prefer high prices).

4.9 To counter this, customers have recently begun demanding high quality and high levels of service at **low prices**. This is a relatively new phenomenon and is demonstrated clearly with new cars and mobile phones. In the mobile phone market high levels of competition between many dealers have allowed the customer to become more demanding of features such as free calls and the abolition of peak/off peak tariff systems.

5 EXPORT PRICING

5.1 **Export pricing** involves all the complexities of the domestic pricing decision plus some major additional complications.

- Greater difficulties of acquiring **reliable market information**
- Problems in reacting to **frequent changes in demand** in multiple markets
- Greater complexities in accurately **allocating costs**
- Problems of responding to **exchange rate fluctuations**
- Additional difficulties in deciding on **payment terms**
- **Barter trading** which may sometimes be an unfamiliar practice
- Other complications, such as **legal and cultural factors**

Price escalation

> **Key Concept**
> **Price escalation** occurs when a product moves through the value chain and has additional costs associated with it. It is especially obvious with exported goods as the domestic costs of production will be augmented by shipping, storage, insurance etc costs as the products are sent abroad.

5.2 As we have seen, the cost structure of any firm is a major factor in determining price. This is true of exporters, but they must also take other costs into account which will impact the final price at which the product can be sold for a profit.

- Additional **transport** costs
- **Insurance and storage**
- **Taxes**
- Additional overseas **advertising**
- **Product enhancements** if these are needed
- Costs associated with **agents or distributors**

5.3 All these additional costs mean that the **international** price of the product is very much higher than the domestic price, and will cause it **escalate**. Here is a numerical example.

	Domestic sale £	Export sale (via agent) £
Net price of a child's bicycle	50.00	50.00
Shipping overseas		6.00
		56.00
Duty payable when landed (say 15%)		8.40
Cost to foreign agent		64.40
Foreign agent's expected margin (10%)		6.44
Cost to wholesaler	50.00	70.84
Wholesaler's margin (15%)	7.50	10.63
Cost to retailer	57.50	81.47
Retailer's margin (20%)	11.50	16.29
Selling price	69.00	97.76

5.4 In this example the 'international' price of the bicycle is 42% higher than the domestic price.

5.5 The exporting firm can limit price escalation by amending the channel of distribution. In our example, the firm could decide to do away with foreign agents or set up its own manufacturing plant abroad. This could entail a significant investment in resources which would need to be thoroughly evaluated.

5.6 It may press the wholesalers and retailers to accept a lower margin. The success or failure of this strategy would depend upon the relative strengths of these intermediaries. If they are dependent on this firm for bicycles, they may be more willing to accept a lower margin.

Export pricing procedure

5.7 As in any other pricing exercise, export pricing should be based on an integrative approach. While the guidelines prescribed constitute a sound basis for price decision-making, they are incomplete in the particular context of export pricing. For sales overseas price determination must incorporate additional considerations in relation to individual markets. A comprehensive set of export criteria are set out below.

(a) **Pricing discretion**

(i) What, if any, **product** factors give us pricing discretion? (For example, product differentiation, patents, cross elasticity, specialisation?)

(ii) What, if any, **market** factors give us pricing discretion? (For example, market share, number and size of rivals, number and size of customers, market segmentation?)

(iii) What, if any, **customer** factors give us pricing discretion? (For example, loyalty, degree of knowledge?)

(iv) What, if any, **company** factors give us pricing discretion? (For example, dependence on exports, attitudes concerning exporting, objectives?)

(v) Overall, in this particular market, are we a **'price taker'** or a **'price maker'**?

(b) **Costs and export pricing**

(i) Which costs are most suitable for export pricing? Are these full costs or marginal costs? For example, does exporting form a major part of our business or is it subsidiary or even marginal? Are we adopting a long term or short term view?

(ii)   What are the true incremental costs of exporting? For example, what extra packaging, transportation, insurance, tariffs etc are involved?

(iii)   What contribution to overheads and profits do we require from export sales?

(c) **Buyer behaviour and export pricing**

(i)   What level of buyer awareness prevails in the particular market? Do customers know how competing prices compare? Do they try to compare prices? Should we try to strengthen or reduce buyer awareness?

(ii)   What degree of price awareness (elasticity) prevails? Are buyers more responsive to price or other variables? Are there segmental differences? Are there any important psychological influences on price-induced behaviour? How does our price compare to the 'going rate'? Should we try to strengthen price elasticity or to dilute it?

(iii)   What evidence is there concerning price interpretation? Are prices used to judge quality? Is price compatible with our brand image? Is there a market stereotype influence on price perceptions?

(d) **Marketing factors and export pricing**

(i)   Is our marketing mix designed to emphasise price or non-price elements? Is our price consistent with other mix factors like quality, advertising and channels? Are the various components of price consistent (eg list price, discounts, credit).

(ii)   If price is used as a promotional tool, is this effective and are there any significant side-effects?

(iii)   At what stage is the product in its life cycle? Does this vary across markets and segments? Is price compatible with the life cycle stage?

(iv)   Is there scope for viable differential pricing? Should prices be equal to, above or below domestic prices? How should prices vary across export markets?

(e) **Export price management**

(i)   What are the specific company objectives to be sought through export pricing? What are the constraints? What control and remedial procedures are there?

(ii)   Can we construct a price plan for each market based on the elements of this checklist?

(f) **Currencies for export pricing**

(i)   Do we have a general policy concerning currencies for export pricing?

(ii)   What currencies do we quote and price in for export sales? Could we improve exporting performance by changing.

(iii)   Is our export currency policy consistent with the role of price in our marketing/ competitive strategy?

(iv)   How do we monitor and respond to currency fluctuations? How should we do this?

A set of guidelines is provided below.

Avoiding parallel imports

5.8   Parallel imports occur when a product is sold more cheaply in one market than another, giving third parties an incentive to import goods from the cheaper to the more expensive market, thereby wrecking the manufacturer's carefully crafted segmentation strategy.

Integrated pricing guidelines

1 Set consistent objectives

(a) Make sure that objectives are clearly stated, operational and mutually consistent.

(b) When there are several objectives, develop priorities, or otherwise clarify the relationships between the objectives.

(c) Make sure that everyone concerned with a pricing decision, at any level in the firm, understands the relevant objectives.

2 Identify alternatives

(a) Identify enough alternatives to permit a sensible choice between courses of action.
(b) Avoid traditional thinking, encourage creativity.

3 Acquire relevant information

(a) Be sure that information about buyers and competitors is current and reflects their current and future situations.

(b) Make sure information is for the future, not just a report of the past.

(c) Involve market research people in the pricing problem.

(d) Make sure cost information identifies which costs will be affected by a particular pricing alternative.

(e) Communicate with and involve accounting people with the cost aspects of a pricing decision.

(f) Analyse the effect a particular alternative will have on scarce resources, inventories, production, cash flows, market share, volume and profits.

4 Making the pricing decision

(a) Make full use of the information available.

(b) Correctly relate all the relevant variables in the problem.

(c) Use sensitivity analysis to determine which elements in the decision are not important.

(d) Consider all human and organisational problems which could occur with a given pricing decision.

(e) Consider the long-run effects of the pricing decision.

(f) Base the pricing decision on the life cycle of each product.

(g) Consider the effect of experience in reducing costs as the cumulative production volume increases.

5 Maintain feedback and control

(a) Develop procedures to ensure that pricing decisions fit into the firm's overall marketing strategy.

(b) Provide for a feedback mechanism to ensure that all who should know the results of individual price decisions are fully informed.

To summarise, pricing decisions should be logically made and should involve rigorous thinking, with minimum difficulty from human and organisational factors. Further, it should be recognised that judgement and prediction are needed about the future, not the past. Finally, pricing decisions should be made within a dynamic, long-run marketing strategy. Source: Monroe

Marketing at Work

(a) The world telecommunications industry is facing competition from 'call-back' companies, because of differential prices: it is cheaper to make phone calls from the US to Germany than vice versa. A call-back service enables a person in Germany who wants to phone a number in the US to phone a call-back company in the US which phones him back enabling him to call from Germany much more cheaply.

(b) In the case of CDs, there have, in the past, been restrictions to the extent that they could be re-exported. In the case of CDs, retailers have been prohibited from importing a CD from the US independently of the publisher's chosen European distributors as this would undermine the publisher's pricing strategy in the European market. (Usunier uses the music industry as an example: an album is released in the UK before it is released officially in Italy; an Italian fan buys many copies in London, sells them as rarity items in Italy and pockets an inflated profit; the record company's sales may be adversely affected in Italy, and it might end up short of stock in the UK.)

5.9 Many manufacturers go to considerable lengths to control the ultimate destination of their products. However, exclusive distribution agreements and bans on parallel imports are hard to enforce.

5.10 Solutions to this problem might be as follows.

(a) Alter the pricing strategies in home or overseas market to **erode the differential** - but this might have serious implications for marketing strategy generally.

(b) **Change or re-specify the product**. Car manufacturers justified price differentials in EU countries on the grounds that in the UK, for example, as many of the cars were purchased as part of a company fleet, they were more likely to have costly extras, such as alloy wheels etc.

(c) **End dealership arrangements** if the dealer indulges in parallel importing.

(d) **Buy back** the goods.

Marginal cost pricing: 'dumping'

Key Concept

Dumping is the sale of goods in an overseas market at a price lower than would be charged in the home market. Alleged dumping has been an excuse for protectionist measures particularly by the US and EU against companies from Japan and the Third World, to protect national/regional firms. Examples abound in consumer electronics industries.

5.11 When a company reaches a level of output which generates enough revenue to cover all the costs of producing that output (fixed and variable) then it is said to be at **break even point**. Any output above break even point yields a profit, provided the price charged exceeds the variable cost, since fixed costs (eg the factory rent) have already been covered.

5.12 Clearly any company has to sell well above marginal cost price (the price at which only variable costs are covered) in most of its markets. If, however, an isolated market can be found where conditions for **marginal cost pricing** apply (see below) without jeopardising price levels in established markets, total profit will be increased by selling below market price but above variable cost.

Conditions for marginal cost pricing

5.13 In order to penetrate a difficult competitive market, it is worth considering marginal cost pricing in the following four situations.

(a) Where there is **little possibility of speedy intervention** by the foreign government. If the government of the importing country or authorities in the economic block wishes to protect firms in a domestic industry it may try to impose 'dumping' duties. **Dumping** takes place if the price of the product exported from one country to another is less than the comparable price, in the ordinary course of trade, for the like product when destined for consumption in the exporting country. It is a lengthy, complex procedure to investigate a claim of dumping. Hence, anti-dumping legislation is not a serious threat to the occasional or short term marginal cost price.

(b)   Where the output being sold at marginal cost price forms only a small proportion of total output.

(c)   Where the resources used to produce the marginal output cannot be used more profitably elsewhere in the company.

(d)   Where it will not jeopardise prices in the principal markets.

If a company has **surplus stock** it is justified in selling it even below marginal cost. Provided that the costs of distribution and sale are covered it is worth selling the stock rather than scrapping it.

6   TRANSFER PRICING

> ### Key Concept
> The **transfer price** is the price at which goods or services are transferred from one process or department to another or from one member of a group to another. The extent to which costs and profit are covered by the price is a matter of policy. A transfer price may, for example, be based upon marginal cost, full cost, market price or negotiation. Transfer pricing is important in global businesses which source components from many countries from their various operating divisions.

6.1   When a multinational firm adopts a decentralised organisational structure, each of its manufacturing units becomes a **profit centre**. Components, semi-finished or finished products may have to be transferred between these manufacturing or assembly units. It is in this context that the question of **transfer pricing arises**. If these components or products are sold on the open market they will be sold at arms length price (market price). Multinational firms must decide whether the transfer price between units of the same organisation should be equal to, higher than or lower than the open market arm's length price. Once again, problems associated with transfer pricing in a domestic marketing situation become more complex in an international context.

Setting the transfer price

6.2   (a)   **Transfer price less than open market price.** A multinational organisation will find it beneficial to set its transfer price below the open market price in the following situations.

   (i)   If the importing country has a lower rate of profits than the exporting country. In this situation, for the ethnocentric organisation, dividend repatriation is easy. The problem here is that operating revenues and profits are distorted and problems of managerial motivation and appraisal arise.

   (ii)   If the importing country has high tariff barriers, the impact of those barriers may be lessened by charging a price below open market price and thus improve overall corporate profits.

   (iii) As a competitive pricing strategy, it may be possible to penetrate a new, competitive market more quickly by adopting a low initial transfer price (provided the market has high price elasticity).

   (iv)   If inflation is high in the exporting country it may be possible to transfer funds by high transfer pricing to an economically 'safe' country.

   (b)   **Transfer price greater then open market price.** In the following circumstances it may be beneficial to the organisation to set the transfer price above open market price.

(i)   If the importing country taxes profits at a higher rate of tax than the exporting country.

(ii)   If dividend repatriation is restricted.

(iii)   If tariffs are at a relatively low level in the importing country.

(iv)   If there is a fear of expropriation of assets the organisation will wish to hold its cash assets in the most politically 'stable' country.

Problems of transfer pricing

6.3   The problem of managerial motivation and evaluation may override a transfer price that has the best economic justification.

6.4   **Tax avoidance strategies** are increasingly attracting the attention of governments and their tax authorities. In the UK the Inland Revenue (for profit tax effects) the Department of Customs and Excise (for tariff effects) and the Monopolies and Mergers Commission (for the effects on fair competition and trading) are all concerned with transfer pricing practices of multinational organisations. Because of this 'public surveillance' international companies increasingly feel the need to be seen to be playing fair to both domestic and host countries and to unions and other groups.

6.5   Finally, transfer pricing might, indirectly, be the subject of **anti-dumping actions**.

7   EXPORT QUOTATIONS

7.1   Here we are concerned with the make up of the export price. There are two important aspects of quoting export prices.

- The currency of the quotation
- The terms

Foreign currency pricing

Key Concept
Foreign currency pricing involves pricing your goods in foreign currency, thereby suffering the exchange risk. This risk can be controlled by **hedging** strategies.

7.2   About 70% of UK imports are paid for in foreign currency. However about 90% of UK exports are invoiced in sterling. When sterling was in decline in the early 1990's there were advantages to UK exporters in a change towards invoicing in selected foreign currencies (or indeed notional units of account, such as ECUs). In recent years, partly because there were doubts about the UK adopting the Euro with the first batch of EU countries, interest rates in this country have been higher and the value of the pound has increased again. Many companies are complaining in 1998 that markets have become much more difficult for them to compete in because their prices have become much less competitive.

Foreign exchange risk

7.3 In international trade, the exporter must invoice the buyer in a foreign currency (eg the currency of the buyer's country) or the buyer must pay in foreign currency (eg the currency of the exporter's country).

7.4 It is also possible that the currency of payment will be the currency of a third country; for example, a UK firm might sell goods to a buyer in Brazil and ask for payment in US dollars. One problem for importers is therefore the need to obtain foreign currency to make a payment, and for exporters there can be the problem of exchanging foreign currency received for currency of their own country. Banks provide the service to importers and exporters of buying and selling foreign currency.

7.5 What is the risk? The **cost of imports** to the buyer or the **value of exports** to the seller might be increased or reduced by movements in foreign exchange rates. Although there is a chance of making a profit out of favourable movements in exchange rates, movements in foreign exchange rates - introduce a serious element of risk ('gambling' or a 'lottery' on the way exchange rates move) which might deter firms from entering international sales or purchase agreements.

Reducing risk

7.6 **Match receipts and payments.** The foreign exchange risk does not arise for a business that makes payments and earns receipts in the **same foreign currency**, because payments in the currency can be made out of cash income in the same currency. For example, if a UK company buys goods from supplier X costing US $10,000, and at the same time the UK company sells goods abroad to customer Y for US $10,000 (in dollars), the company can use the US $10,000 it receives from customer Y to pay the US $10,000 dollars to supplier X. If 'matching' receipts and payments is carried out in this way, the exchange rate between the foreign currency and the company's domestic currency would be irrelevant and exchange risk would be avoided. (Matching receipts and payments is made easier by the ability of organisations or individuals in the UK to hold a **foreign currency** bank account.)

7.7 Matching currency receipts and payments (or currency receipts and the repayment of currency loans) is only feasible if the international trader has receipts and payments in the same currency to match. Many traders are not so lucky.

- They must make a (net) payment in a foreign currency
- They must earn (net) receipts in a foreign currency

The futures market

7.8 **A futures contract** is a contract for the delivery of a standard package of a standard commodity at a specific point in the future. The 'commodity' may be currency or a commodity in the traditional sense, ranging from aluminium and cattle to wheat, wool and zinc.

7.9 To take an example, let's say that the price today for a ton of cocoa is £500. An international marketer of cocoa knows he will have one ton of cocoa available for sale in a month's time. He does not know what the price will be, so he may decide to reduce the risk by selling at the current price a contract for a ton of cocoa to be delivered in one month. He has removed uncertainty. Whatever happens to the price of cocoa over the next month, he knows how much money he will get.

7.10 The futures market can therefore help a company by allowing it to plan ahead on the basis of known prices.

Forward markets and hedging

7.11 It is up to the international company to protect itself against the swings of currency value. There are various ways that this risk can be controlled by **hedging**.

7.12 There is a **forward market** in currencies as well as a **spot market**. In the forward market, currencies are bought and sold for delivery in the future. Spot prices are quoted for immediate delivery. Suppose a UK company knows it is due to receive Danish krone (and will therefore have Danish krone to sell) in two months' time. It will be worried that the value of the krone will fall, meaning it will receive less in sterling terms. So he might sell Danish currency today for delivery in two month's time, locking in to a known exchange rate.

> ### Exam Tip
> You do not need a detailed knowledge of the precise workings of the foreign currency markets, but you should be aware of the use of such techniques as hedging to counter the risks associated with pricing in an environment of foreign exchange fluctuations.
> This chapter in general contains a considerable amount of detail on pricing which should help you in devising appropriate strategies. The standardisation v adaptation debate is relevant too.

Quotation in own currency

7.13 **Price quotation in own currency** is administratively convenient, an important factor for the small firm or the firm where export revenue is a small proportion of total revenue. Effectively the exchange rate risk of variation is borne by the foreign customer.

Quotation in foreign currency

7.14 Quotation in foreign currency means that the exporter accepts any exchange risk of fluctuating values and has to deal with it. These risks become even greater the 'softer' a currency is (ie the less easy to convert into other currencies). The exporter might be made vulnerable to a severe risk of loss, unless the exporter engages in hedging.

7.15 **Advantages of foreign currency pricing** are as follows.

(a) An exporter can gain a **competitive edge** by quoting in a foreign currency if the importer would prefer his own currency, either to avoid exposure to currency fluctuation or because of exchange control regulations. Foreign currency pricing also makes it easy to relate to retail prices overseas. In addition, constant adjustment to a sterling price list is avoided.

(b) Foreign currency invoicing can sometimes help exporters to borrow at **lower rates of interest** than at home.

(c) The exporter may purchase the foreign currency 'forward' on the exchange markets (ie at a fixed rate some time in the future). The exporter can use that particular rate, which may be better than later 'spot' rates in some cases, or at least the risk of loss is avoided.

Resolving differences between exporter and importer

7.16 Despite the advantages of foreign currency pricing noted above, UK exporters frequently prefer to quote prices in sterling. It makes calculation of profits, cash flows and possibly costs easier and avoids short-term exposure to exchange rate risks. But foreign customers normally prefer to receive price quotations in their own currency since it places the risk of exchange rate fluctuation on the exporter and facilitates comparison of prices from a number of foreign sources.

7.17 Resolution of this potential conflict depends on several factors.

- The relative strengths of the two parties
- The importance of the contract to either party
- The economic situation in both countries (such as balance of payments position)

7.18 Whichever currency is used there are a number of ways of minimising problems caused by foreign currencies.

(a) The simplest way is to have an appropriate clause in the contract to adjust the price if it fluctuates within agreed limits or to renegotiate if these are exceeded.

(b) To purchase (or sell) forward as appropriate whereby a fixed rate is agreed for the given sum at a specified date in the future by a bank. The net sum (after commission) received or paid at the end of the period is at least guaranteed.

(c) In a situation where either or both currencies are unstable a third currency can be quoted, eg the US dollar. A strengthening or weakening in one party's currency would be felt in relation to the dollar and the other party would not be affected. Each party to the transaction thus takes on the risk associated with its own currency. If the dollar changed value, it would be likely to be relative to both currencies and the risk (or benefits) would be shared. The one disadvantage is that there is a double exchange transaction involved. However, this may be more acceptable than other options.

Terms of a price quotation

7.19 Whatever the pricing objectives or the organisation's pricing bases, cost aspects are of vital importance as a guide.

(a) In more ethnocentric export companies, overseas prices are based on domestic prices, plus additional costs of freight etc. Often however the domestic price will include costs not relevant to the export situation, eg domestic advertising, selling, distribution etc.

(b) One of the key tasks of the international marketer involved in pricing decisions is to take into account all the **relevant costs** in order that exports achieve the defined level of profitability or market share.

Over and under invoicing

7.20 Some countries still have price and/or **exchange controls**. Exchange controls prohibit the export of foreign currency or restricting it to certain conditions. In other countries, with high political risk, investors prefer to export currency to 'safe' locations.

7.21 Over-invoicing means that an invoice is made up for an amount greater than what is actually paid. Under invoicing is the opposite.

(a) Overseas customers may be 'under-invoiced' and asked to transfer the balance to an account in a third country.

(b) A supplier may over-invoice, enabling the business to transfer currency out of the country.

Competitive bidding and tendering

7.22 Competitive bidding calls for the preparation of cost data for the purpose of submitting a bid to a potential customer, in the hope of securing his order. There will be three factors in the customer's choice of supplier from among the tenders submitted.

(a) The **price** itself.

(b) **Performance**, especially if the product is new and largely untested in the open market, reliability, service etc.

(c) **Financial matters**, such as inflation (and cost escalation clauses), foreign exchange rates and export credit insurance.

7.23 Co-operation is needed between the accounting and marketing departments of a bidding company because a balance has to be drawn between putting in a bid which is too low to make an adequate profit, but keeping the bid low enough to stand a good chance of winning the contract. Consideration must be given to the following.

(a) The **contribution to profit** that would be obtained from the contract.

(b) The **consequences** for the company if it failed to win the order.

(c) The **probability** of winning the order, which might be assessed on the basis of past experience.

(d) There may be some **non-price product differentiation** in favour of the supplier eg quality of service, reliable delivery times, finance facilities offered etc.

Shipping terms

7.24 In addition to the obvious manufacturing costs of the exporter there may be significant extra costs in getting the goods to a foreign buyer. Generally, the costs of physical movements are as follows.

- Transport from the manufacturer's premises to the docks
- Loading aboard ship
- Freight charges
- Unloading
- Customs duties
- Transport from the docks to the customer's warehouse

As well as these costs of physical movement there are also insurance charges and possibly additional costs for any delays.

7.25 There are a number of internationally accepted standard forms of dividing these costs between buyer and seller. Who pays what, and who is responsible for arranging for the transport, has to be confirmed when the sale contract is agreed. The standard forms are known as **INCOTERMS** and have been designated by the International Chamber of Commerce. You will note that many of the descriptions contain the term 'free'. This indicates the time at which legal title passes from seller to buyer (and thus risk of loss in case of damage, theft and so forth). Among the more common forms of quotation are the following.

7.26 **EXW: Ex-works.** The buyer must take delivery at the exporter's factory and pay all the costs of freight, insurance and other expense items to get the goods transported from the supplier's factory to their destination. This represents the minimum obligations for the seller.

7.27 **FAS: Free Alongside Ship**

(a) The seller arranges the following.

(i) Delivery of the goods alongside the named ship at the port of loading named in the contract

(ii) Payment of all the charges up to delivery of the goods alongside ship, including freight and insurance charges to that point

(b) The buyer is responsible for the following.

(i) Choosing the carrier to transport the goods abroad and paying the cost of freight from the port of shipment including the cost of loading the goods on board ship (if loading costs are separate from freight charges)

(ii) Arranging insurance and paying insurance from arrival at the dockside onwards

(iii) Arranging and paying for any export licence or export taxes

The point of delivery of the goods from the seller to the buyer is alongside the ship.

Action Programme 1

Describe 'FAS Felixstowe' for the export of goods by a UK firm to an overseas buyer.

7.28 **FOB: Free on Board.** FOB means that the buyer does not have to pay for transporting or insuring the goods from the place where they are originally despatched up to the point when they are taken on board ship. The costs up to this point are borne by the seller/exporter. The place of delivery is the ship's rail.

(a) The seller/exporter

(i) Pays for transportation, freight and insurance charges to the named port of shipment (eg 'FOB Los Angeles' would mean that an American supplier would be responsible for sending goods for shipment on board at Los Angeles, and to pay costs up to that point)

(ii) Provides and pays for the export licence

(iii) Pays export taxes

(iv) Delivers the goods on board the ship (or airline flight) that the buyer has specified

(v) Pays for the cost of loading the goods on board ship (if loading costs are separate from freight charges)

(b) The buyer

(i) Nominates the carrier to transport the goods (eg, if the shipping terms for an export consignment from the UK are FOB Stranraer, it is the buyer who specifies the shipping company, sailing date and time)

(ii) Gives the seller the details of the ship and sailing time

     (iii)   Pays for the carriage from this point (ie freight from that point, including costs of unloading at the place of destination)

     (iv)   Arranges and pays for insurance of the goods from this point

7.29   **CFR: Cost and Freight**. With Cost and Freight, the exporter/seller must nominate the carrier to ship the goods abroad, arrange the contract of carriage and pay freight charges. In these respects, CFR differs from FOB. Though the supplier pays the freight charges to the port of destination, the place of **delivery** of the goods is the ship's rail when the goods are taken on board. When they are on board, they are the **responsibility** of the buyer even though the supplier pays freight charges.

   (a)   The seller

     (i)   Nominates the carrier and so makes the contract of carriage

     (ii)   Pays for transportation of the goods to the place of shipment and insures the goods up to this point

     (iii)   Provides and pays for the export licence

     (iv)   Pays export taxes

     (v)   Delivers the goods on board

     (vi)   Pays for the cost of loading the goods if the loading charge is separate from the freight charge

     (vii)   Provides the buyer with a clean on board bill of lading

     (viii)   Pays the cost of freight charges to the named port of destination (eg, 'CFR Rotterdam' would mean that the UK exporter must pay freight charges for delivery to the port of Rotterdam)

     (ix)   Sends to the buyer advice of the carrier and the shipment date

   (b)   The buyer

     (i)   Pays for the insurance of the goods from the time they are taken on board, and so bears the risk of loss or damage to the goods

     (ii)   Pays for unloading costs at the port of destination if these costs are separate from the freight charges

     (iii)   Pays for any import licence required

     (iv)   Accepts delivery of the goods, when the appropriate documents (eg bill of lading, invoice) have been presented, an obligation of great practical importance because the supplier does not want the buyer to refuse the goods after they have been shipped to the buyer's country, the seller already having paid freight charges to get them there

     (v)   Arranges and pays for transportation and insurance from the port of destination to their final destination in the buyer's country

7.30   **CIF: Cost, Insurance and Freight**, Cost, insurance and freight is similar to CFR, with the exception that it is the seller, not the buyer, who must arrange and pay for the **insurance** of the goods to the port of destination.

   (a)   The obligations of the seller are therefore the same as for CFR with some additional responsibilities.

(i) Arranges for insurance of the goods from the port of shipment to the port of destination (the amount of insurance cover is often the CIF value of the goods plus 10%)

(ii) Pays the insurance premium

(iii) Provides the buyer with the insurance policy or certificate

(b) The buyer's obligations are the same as for CFR, with the exception that he does not have to pay for the insurance of the goods between the port of shipment and the port of destination.

7.31 **DDP: Delivered duty paid.** The seller must pay the costs of delivering the goods to the named destination, having paid import duties on the goods. The seller must therefore pay the import duties or taxes, arrange and pay insurance and provide documents that will enable the buyer to take delivery. The buyer's responsibility is to take delivery of the goods at the named destination. This represents the maximum obligation for the seller.

INCOTERMS and the marketing mix

7.32 **Delivery and insurance** are real costs to those firms who incur them. The marketer can use these items as ways of satisfying customer needs, thereby making the export quotation more attractive.

(a) For example, let us assume that shipping insurance is cheaper to arrange in the UK than, say, in South Africa. A UK firm wishing to export to South Africa might wish to arrange the insurance and include it in the export price - the South African importer will benefit from cheaper insurance of goods in transit.

(b) A firm might have its own fleet of delivery lorries. DDP means that the buyer escapes most of the hassle of transportation for a reasonable price.

(c) A firm might be able to offer a menu of export prices. The supplier might agree to a lower price, but on condition that the goods are delivered EXW, in other words that the buyer pays for delivery.

(d) If firms wish to indulge in 'over invoicing' then DDP is a means of maximising the value of the invoice.

8 METHODS OF PAYMENT

8.1 In the context of international marketing there are **three essential elements** in taking pricing decisions.

(a) Determining the **basis of calculating the price** (eg cost plus, transfer price, local market price and so forth).

(b) Agreeing with the seller the **basis of shipping**, insurance etc.

(c) Agreeing with the seller the **method of payment**.

The first two of these have been considered above and this section is devoted to the third.

8.2 There are any number of variations in the methods of payment that may be agreed between the exporting company and its customer but the following provide a series of 'yardsticks'. They are listed in order of **increasing risk for the exporter.**

- Payment in advance   Lowest risk
- Letters of credit (documentary credits)
- Payment on shipment
- Documentary collections
- Open account trading   Highest risk

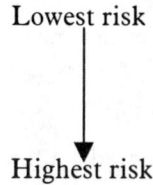

Payment in advance

8.3 The most secure method of payment for an **exporter** is to obtain payment in full in advance of shipping the goods. He will then not have any risk that the foreign buyer will refuse to pay or be unable to pay for goods that have already been shipped to him. Payment in advance also means that the exporter, by not giving the buyer any credit, does not have to finance the sale himself for a credit period.

8.4 Payment in advance gives security to the exporter. The obvious drawback to payment in advance is the risk **for the buyer** that the exporter will not actually despatch the goods, or if he does despatch them, that they will not arrive in the required condition or to the right specification. It also means that the buyer is financing the sale for some time before he takes physical possession of the goods.

8.5 As you may imagine, 100% cash with order is not a common form of payment. However, it is quite common for the overseas buyer to pay a cash deposit in advance, and then to pay the balance by another method.

Letters of credit (documentary credits)

8.6 The documentary credit system is a customary method of payment in international trade.

> **Key Concept**
>
> **Documentary credits** involves banks giving a **guarantee** of payment to the exporter provided that the exporter complies with various terms and conditions (such as providing specified documents to a bank for checking after shipment of the goods and shipping the goods within a certain time).

8.7 In brief, the documentary credit system works as follows.

Stage 1   The buyer and seller (exporter) agree a sales contract that includes payment by a documentary credit.

Stage 2   The foreign buyer requests his own ('foreign') bank to issue a letter of credit in favour of the buyer.

Stage 3   The foreign bank issues a letter of credit in favour of the buyer. By doing so it is guaranteeing payment to the exporter provided that the latter complies with the terms and conditions.

Stage 4   The foreign bank asks a bank in the exporter's country to advise the credit to the exporter. This does not necessarily involve the latter in making any commitment to the exporter to add its own guarantee of payment but if it does so it is then known as a confirmed letter of credit.

Stage 5   After shipping the goods the exporter has to present the documents specified by the letter of credit. These normally include a commercial invoice, bill of lading and insurance certificate.

Stage 6   Provided the documents are in order the exporter arranges for payment to be made (either immediately or on deferred terms) by the buyer's bank.

8.8   These are the two basic types of documentary credit.

(a)   A **revocable** credit allows the foreign buyer to amend the credit (or even cancel it) without giving prior notice to the exporter. In other words, for the exporter this is high risk.

(b)   An **irrevocable** credit can be amended or cancelled only with the agreement of **all** parties to the credit (ie buyer, issuing bank, advising bank and exporter). It therefore gives greater security to the exporter because the issuing bank's guarantee remains in force, even if the buyer changes his mind.

8.9   Although the irrevocable letter of credit gives the exporter the guarantee of a foreign bank, the exporter may not be entirely happy relying on a bank about which the exporter has little information in a country that might, for example, impose exchange controls. This can be overcome by **confirmation** (or additional guarantee of payment) by a bank in the exporter's own country. In the UK an exporter might ask for a credit to be **confirmed** by a first-class London bank (eg one of the clearers). A **confirmed irrevocable letter of credit** thus gives greater security to the exporter because the guarantee is given by a bank in the exporter's own country. It makes little difference to the buyer.

8.10   Not surprisingly, all this international activity costs money. The cost of issuing a letter of credit is usually borne by the buyer, although the buyer may be able to persuade the exporter to bear some or all of the costs and charges. Who pays what costs depends of the relative bargaining strength of the two parties.

Payment upon shipment of the goods

8.11   The exporter and overseas buyer might agree an arrangement whereby the buyer pays for the goods as soon as they are shipped. The exporter would have to notify the buyer of the shipment, giving full details of the shipment, and then expect the buyer to make an immediate payment. The goods will therefore be in transit or at their point of destination when the payment is received.

8.12   Security is provided to the exporter because there are documents of title to the shipped goods, and the exporter can arrange to keep these documents until payment has been received. If the buyer does not make the payment on shipment, or if the funds are not cleared, the exporter will still have title to the goods, because he holds the documents of title. However, the goods would now be in transit and so he would have the problem of deciding what to do with them when they arrive at their destination.

Documentary collections

8.13   **Documentary collections** involve the exporter asking his bank to help with the arrangements for payment, by handling **shipping documents** as well as a bill of exchange or a cheque. They provide some security of payment for the exporter because the banks involved in a collection should act in accordance with the internationally accepted rules that apply to collections.

8.14   A significant feature of a documentary collection is that if a bank is instructed to handle commercial documents which include a **bill of lading,** the exporter can keep control over the goods until the foreign buyer has either paid for them or accepted a bill of exchange.

This is because the bill of lading is a document of title and a full set of the signed originals of this document can be kept by the bank.

Open account trading

8.15 **Open account trading** where payment is received after delivery without any guarantee is the most risky method of trading for exporters, although it accounts for some 70% of UK exports. However, when trading relations between an exporter and buyer are well-established, and risk is considered low or non-existent, then open account trading might be perfectly acceptable without excessive risk for the exporter. Open account trading has developed quite extensively between countries in the EU for these reasons. A further point to bear in mind is that a vast amount of world trade occurs between fellow members of multinational groups (eg a vehicle manufacturer assembling cars in country A with engines and gearboxes bought from its sister companies in countries B and C).

8.16 It is fair to ask why an exporter, who is worried about the risk of non-payment, does not insist on payment in advance, payment on shipment or a letter of credit every time he or she exports goods. The answer is, of course, that it takes two parties to trade, the exporter and the importer. The exporter is often unable to get payment terms which would be desirable in an ideal world, because of the fierce competition in international trade. Another supplier might offer more favourable terms.

Bills of exchange

8.17 The methods of payment described above have focused on the degree of risk incurred by the exporter. As the final item in this chapter we look at the technique of payment known as a **bill of exchange**. This can be coupled with a number of different payment methods but is such an important and established means of payment in international trade that it is worthy of consideration in its own right. It is similar to a cheque. (By writing a cheque, you are asking your bank to pay a sum to the payee whose name is written on the cheque.)

8.18 Thus it is basically a request for payment, normally from the supplier (exporter) to the customer. A bill known as a 'term bill' allows the recipient a period of credit before payment. When such a bill is sent to the customer he is expected to sign it as the 'acceptor' and the bill becomes an 'accepted' bill.

Action Programme 2

What significance do you think changes in the US $ exchange rate has on two competing aircraft manufacturing companies, one of which is based in the US, and the other in Europe?

---

9   COUNTERTRADE AND BARTER

9.1 New phenomena in modern international marketing are **countertrade** and **barter**. They are included here under the broad heading of price since they are mainly concerned with payment. The main distinguishing feature is that countertrade involves some compensation in money, whereas barter does not.

> **Key Concept**
>
> **Countertrade** is the exchange of goods and services for other goods and services (eg oil for fighter aircraft)

9.2 A UN commission defines countertrade as '...commercial transactions in which provisions are made, in one or a series of related contracts, for payment by deliveries of goods and/or services in addition to, or in place of financial settlement.' Countertrade generally takes longer to complete, and is riskier, than barter.

9.3 Countertrade is reaction to adverse developments in the world economy.

   (a) Countries with large external debts can acquire imports which are otherwise denied them for financing reasons.

   (b) Firms facing excess world capacity and slack demand can gain competitive edge by accepting customer's outputs as payment.

   (c) Reciprocal trading can be established between countries endowed with appropriate scarce raw materials goods.

   (d) Countertrade deals can overcome financing difficulties arising from high rates of interest and inflation;

   (e) Countertrade can be used as a form of payment

   (f) Countertrade is better than 'no trade'.

9.4 In simple terms, countertrade is the sale of goods from one party to another subject to a sale in the reverse direction. It can be treated as a modern form of barter. Two separate contracts are normally involved; one for the supply of the goods (or the mix of money and goods) delivered by each party, specifying the quantity, dates and method of payment. There is not normally a legal link between the two contracts and the performance of either is legally independent of the other.

9.5 Countertrade is better than nothing, but most firms prefer cash.

   (a) Countertrade is highly complex, time-consuming and costly.

   (b) The compensation goods are often unattractive and/or difficult to dispose of.

   (i) For firms having an 'in-house' use for the offsets, the problems are concerned with low or inconsistent quality, design and poor delivery.

   (ii) For firms without an 'in-house' use for the offset goods, the problem lies in difficulties in reselling them.

   (iii) The goods taken in compensation might become serious competition in Western firms' own markets.

   (iv) Many factors lead to **pricing** problems in countertrade.

9.6 Barter and countertrade present their own challenges to the international marketer. Barter is sometimes the only way to get into a new market or penetrate an existing one. Barter requires the commitment of fewer resources and so can be a good way of 'testing the water'.

9.7 It is not certain how much room for expansion is offered by barter and countertrade as countries continue to develop, but there are still a large number of countries where economic difficulties mean that barter and countertrade are still seen as attractive arrangements. Exporters from more highly developed countries may find themselves required to take unrelated goods, but they often consider this a price worth paying given the opportunity to crack a new market.

Chapter Roundup

- **Pricing** is the only mix element that generates revenue. There are a number of approaches to pricing. Prices can be based on cost or demand, both of these, what competitors are charging, and so forth.

- **Pricing strategy** (eg the choice between skimming and penetration strategy) can be adapted from country to country. In some organisations, the pricing strategy is determined autonomously by local subsidiaries.

- Traders have to determine who is going to pay for delivery and insurance. This can be used as part of the price.

- **Export pricing** is made complex by the difficulties of finding proper market information. Moreover, the impact of the **currency** chosen can greatly affect profitability, both of the export market and of the firm if it is heavily dependent on export markets. **Hedging techniques** are used to manage this risk. The marketer must decide whether to get the customer bear the risk.

- Techniques of **export finance** include bills of exchange, letters of credit and so forth. Each offers a different risk profile.

- **Countertrade** (eg barter) is the exchange of goods for goods. It is used by countries when access to hard currency is difficult to find. Generally speaking, it is not preferred as a means of trade, owing to its administrative and logistical complexities.

Quick Quiz

1. Why should pricing be flexible? (see para 2.3)
2. What three approaches to pricing can be adopted? (2.5)
3. When is cost-based pricing a sensible approach? (3.2)
4. List nine general approaches to competitive prices? (3.6)
5. When would penetration pricing be used? (3.10)
6. When would skimming pricing be used? (3.11, 3.12)
7. What are the main internal influences on pricing? (4.1)
8. What factors make export pricing more complex than domestic pricing? (5.1)
9. When should a company price its products on the basis of marginal costs? (5.11)
10. Under what conditions will a multinational organisation wish to set a transfer price which is different from the open market price for its products? (6.2)
11. What is the principal problem that has to be resolved when deciding the currency of invoicing? (7.16)
12. What is meant by EXW, FAS, FOB, CFR, CIF, DDP? (7.26 - 7.31)
13. What are documentary credits? (8.6)
14. Why is open account trading widely used? (8.15)
15. What is countertrade? (9.2, 9.4)

Action Programme Review

1. The exporter must:

   (a) deliver the goods free alongside ship at Felixstowe; and

   (b) pay all the costs, including freight and insurance, to bring the goods alongside the ship at Felixstowe.

   The overseas buyer must nominate the carrier(s) to take the goods from Felixstowe to their destination and (a) pay freight from Felixstowe, (b) pay export charges (if any), (c) pay for loading the goods on board ship (if separate from freight charges), and (d) pay for insurance of the goods from their time/point of delivery at Felixstowe.

2   This is not quite a fair question, because many goods are internationally traded in US $. Examples are oil and aircraft. The US plane manufacturer pays its work force and, presumably, most of its US based component suppliers in US$. A falling US $ exchange rate makes its aircraft cheaper internationally, and this may increase the market for aircraft. It has no effect on its production costs or profitability in the US.

On the other hand, a European manufacturer has a double problem. Firstly, a falling US $ exchange rate will mean lower revenues (eg when translated into £ sterling or DM). Secondly, as the firm's **costs** are not in US $, it means that its profits are squeezed very hard.

Now try illustrative question 10 at the end of the Study Text

11 International Marketing Communications

Chapter Topic List	Syllabus Reference
1 Setting the scene	-
2 Issues in international marketing communications	3.3
3 Cultural considerations	3.3
4 Legal considerations	3.3
5 Media considerations	3.3
6 Other market considerations	3.3
7 Designing the international mix	3.3, 3.9
8 Planning the international campaign	3.3
9 International agency selection and management	3.3

Learning Outcomes

Upon completion of this chapter you will have an understanding of international marketing communications issues including:

- cultural considerations

- legal considerations

- choice of media

- the international promotional mix, including personal selling

- planning the campaign and choosing an agency

Key Concepts Introduced

- Media
- Direct mail
- Personal selling
- Sales promotion
- Public relations

BPP PUBLISHING

Examples of Marketing at Work

- Sainsbury
- Frankfurt Book Fair
- Daewoo Cars

- Arts sponsorship
- Standardised advertising messages
- Shell

1 SETTING THE SCENE

1.1 Communications decisions are some of the most sensitive in international marketing. After all, marketing communications are the organisation's public face.

1.2 Not only does the legal environment differ, in that countries have different laws and regulations regarding advertisements, but the advertisements must be in keeping with the culture of the country as well as the aspirations of the market segment within the country that the firm is selling to.

1.3 In international marketing communications, firms face similar dilemmas to other areas of the mix.

- Are messages standardised or adapted for the local market?
- Are worldwide or local advertising campaigns used?
- Does the firm use one advertising agency or several local ones?

1.4 The rise of international advertising agencies reflects the risk of large international businesses, but some firms prefer to use local companies.

2 ISSUES IN INTERNATIONAL MARKETING COMMUNICATIONS

2.1 **Effective communications** are particularly important in international marketing, due to the **geographical and psychological separation** of the producer and its market. Consequently, the international marketer has to rely more on intermediaries and impersonal communication for a major part of the communication process.

2.2 The methods of promotion in any one market will be affected by the following.

- The **promotional objectives** for that market
- **Cultural** constraints
- **Legal** constraints
- **Facilities** available for promotional effort in the market
- **Economic development**
- **Distribution** infrastructure
- **Media** availability
- **Competition**

2.3 **Standardisation** is rare and can only occur when the product and its cultural meaning is more or less identical across a number of countries and cultures. The more normal state of affairs is that of **adaptation of promotional effort** to match the different communication requirements of the market in question.

Promotional objectives

2.4 In **new or developing** markets the promotional objectives may well be to create awareness and encourage trial. In **mature** markets the objectives will be to encourage repeat purchase and remind the customer. The objectives chosen will thus influence the promotional campaign for a market. Thus in a new market the use of 'samples' may be used to encourage trial but in a mature market the use of 'price off next purchase' coupons (if allowed) might be more appropriate.

3 CULTURAL CONSIDERATIONS

3.1 Culture, as we have seen, is a term used to describe the set of values, beliefs, norms and artefacts held in common by a social group. **Marketing communicators** need to be particularly sensitive to culture in promotion if these messages are to work in global markets.

3.2 The following dimensions of culture are of particular relevance to the international marketing communicator.

- Verbal and non verbal communications
- Aesthetics
- Dress and appearance
- Family roles and relationships
- Beliefs and values
- Learning
- Work habits

Language and non verbal communication

Language

3.3 Commonsense dictates that care must be taken when translating copy from one language to another. A literal translation of an advertising slogan would be meaningless in many countries.

(a) The **spirit** of a communication message is preferred to word-for-word translation.

(b) **Which language?** It may be difficult to decide exactly which language to choose for translation purposes. In Canada, although the majority of the population speak English, packaging must include a French translation.

(c) **Brand and product names** must be assessed for their suitability in international markets. For instance Ford's Mondeo name works well in European markets, where the 'world' association comes across powerfully. In the US market however, the car is called the Contour.

Aesthetics

3.4 Attitudes towards different design and colour aesthetics vary around the world.

(a) **Symbols.** A fragrance or toiletries carton decorated with chrysanthemum flowers would not be a success in France, where the flowers are traditionally associated with funerals.

(b) **Visual representation.** The ideal of showing a figure partially out of frame is well known in Europe. In much of Africa by contrast, figures that go over the edge of their frame transgress the cultural rule about how pictures should look.

Dress and appearance

3.5   Advertisers need to be aware of cultural dress codes when deciding if an execution prepared in one market will be acceptable in another.

Family roles and relationships

3.6   Family has always been the dominant agent for transmitting culture.

(a) **Family structure.** In many third world countries, the extended family lives in a tight knit community. This contrasts with the nuclear family, high divorce rates etc, in the West.

(b) **Family roles** can differ greatly from country to country.

Beliefs and values

3.7   Beliefs and values evolve from religious teachings, family structures and the pattern and nature of economic development in that society.

Education and literacy

3.8   The level of education within a culture is an important factor for the international marketing communicator. Low literacy levels will mean that visual methods of communication take precedence over textual ones.

Work habits

3.9   Not all societies conform to the routine common in Northern Europe, even though, with flexible employment patterns, this is fast disappearing.

Advertising culture

3.10 Mary Goodyear suggests that in addition to being sensitive to a country's culture in general, marketers should be aware of the level of a country's **advertising literacy**. She identifies **five levels of advertising development** along a continuum from the unsophisticated to the sophisticated.

(a) **Least sophisticated.** The emphasis of advertising is on the manufacturer's description of the product.

(b) At the next level, **consumer choice is acknowledged** so emphasis switches to the product's superiority over the competition.

(c) **Mid point.** Consumer benefits are emphasised rather than product attributes. Executional devices may include the use of celebrity endorsements; role models may give demonstrations.

(d) At a **more sophisticated** level, brands and their attributes are well known, so need only passing references (perhaps by way of a brief pack shot or logo).

(e) At the **most sophisticated** level, the focus is sometimes on the advertising itself. The brand is referred to only obliquely, perhaps at a symbolic level, (eg Benson & Hedges). Consumers are believed to have a mature understanding of advertising, and are able to think laterally in order to decode messages.

4   LEGAL CONSIDERATIONS

4.1   Laws and regulations governing marketing communications must obviously be observed. Each country will have its own set of restrictions which apply to advertising, packaging, sales promotion or direct marketing.

(a) **Advertising.** In some countries, restrictions apply to the use of non native models and actors. This can mean that advertising has to be reshot for specific countries.

(b) **Packaging regulations** can vary. In a number of European markets, the push towards environmentally friendly packaging has resulted in far more stringent rules than apply in the UK. In Denmark, soft drinks may not be sold in cans, only in glass bottles with refundable deposits.

(c) **Direct marketing.** There are laws requiring that consumers have the choice of opting out of receiving further mailings.

(d) **Promotional methods and claims.** In the UK, although considerable tightening up is in progress, the attitude towards promotional claims is relatively liberal, as is the attitude to what is promoted, when and where. 'Reaching the parts that other beers cannot reach' could only be claimed in the UK, where the diversity of the English language allows irony, overstatement and puns. Legal constraints may exist.

- What can be claimed
- What products may be promoted
- What media may be used
- When they may be promoted
- How much may be spent on promotion

(e) **What can be advertised.** Different countries in the EU have a variety of restrictions on advertisements directed to children. Advertising to children under 12 is banned in Sweden. In the USA, such adverts are normally unlimited.

5   MEDIA CONSIDERATIONS

> **Key Concept**
> The term **media** refers to any non-personal means of communication such as TV and newspapers.

5.1   Media is a complex, highly specialised area within marketing communications. You need to have a grasp of the factors influencing media choice in overseas markets, and some understanding of the practical problems which may be experienced when planning the use of media. Coverage by various media can be limited.

- Localised media organisations
- Circulation/audience limitations
- Legal restrictions

5.2   **Media availability** can vary greatly from country to country.

(a) The UK is a media rich country which offers a great variety of choice to the advertiser. Press is a well segmented sector with over 6,000 consumer, trade and technical magazines, as well as the national and regional newspaper titles. Commercial television includes terrestrial and satellite channels. Radio as a sector is strengthening, with both local and national stations. Cinema and outdoor are mature media.

(b)   In other countries, not all media are available, and the international marketer will have to adapt to unusual media to gain adequate coverage. Sometimes the medium will have to be provided by the advertisers (eg a free advertising sheet, or sponsoring a local radio station).

Press

5.3   **Literacy.** The first point to check when contemplating press as a media option, is the literacy levels prevailing within the country. The majority of European nations have literacy rates of 98% or 99%. In countries with low literacy, newspapers etc may only be read by the educated elite, in which case radio, TV and posters might be better solutions.

5.4   **National and regional newspapers.** In the UK, there are a large number of national newspaper alternatives. Other countries have more of a tradition of reading strong daily regional papers.

5.5   **Trade press.** The UK has one of the world's largest trade and technical press sectors, with business to business advertisers being particularly fortunate in the choice available to them. A strong trade press sector tends to go hand in hand with a strong economic industrial base. Less developed nations may have few, if any, trade media vehicles.

5.6   **'International' journals.** Serious business journals such as Time, Newsweek and the Economist are widely available, as are women's titles with different national editions (eg Marie Claire, Cosmopolitan, Elle). However, such publications are likely to be read by only a niche business and professional or lifestyle group. To reach the less wealthy, less well travelled wider populations, other local media will have to be accessed.

Television

5.7   Before TV can be included on the media options list the market needs to ask: How extensive is television ownership? In the UK, 98% of households have a television. In India by comparison, television penetration to individual households is very low. However, television may be used as a group resource for several families in a village, or be shown in a public place.

5.8   There are a number of developments in television.

(a)   There are **more satellite channels** available.

(b)   **Cable television** has been introduced to many markets, offering greater choice. However, some channels cater for minority interest.

(c)   **Digital television** enables the provision of far larger numbers of channels.

5.9   A problem might be the increasing fragmentation of the audience: however, the opportunity might exist to target audiences more precisely, if discernible customer segments can be related to particular channels.

Outdoor

5.10   Posters and neon hoardings offer a good opportunity to communicate to international target groups, as copy tends to be minimal and visuals are key.

Cinema

5.11 Cinema may not always be experienced in the same way around the world. In some countries, cinema is viewed in outdoor theatres.

Radio

5.12 Whilst the cost of purchasing a television set is prohibitive in some nations, radio ownership seems to be ubiquitous around the world. In most countries, radio plays the role of support medium.

The Internet

5.13 A new medium for marketing communications is the Internet, an interlinked network of computers. The **World Wide Web** enables people to access different sites quite easily, with **hypertext connections** between different documents.

5.14 Connections or sites on the Internet are growing rapidly in number. The advantage to marketers generally is that people who 'visit' Internet sites via computers generally **want** to do so. Hypertext enables advertisers to offer a much greater volume of information in the ad, and to provide pathways where the enquirer can find answers to any questions raised by the ad.

Advertising on the Web

5.15 The multimedia capability of the Web allows advertising to be more colourful and entertaining and to reach many more people for the cost of an advertisement in a magazine. In addition, Web users tend to be from higher socio economic groups.

Public relations

5.16 The Internet can be used for a variety of functions, such as posting of product notices and press releases, sponsorship and on-line publications.

Direct sales

5.17 Concerns about security are being dispelled and there is more and more on-line ordering and product information. Books, music and travel are particularly strongly represented, but there has also been an explosion in on-line share dealing.

Marketing research

5.18 This can be carried out on the Web via opinion surveys, product reviews and focus group activities. Direct marketing benefits from customers giving details such as age, name and household income.

5.19 The limitations of the Internet as an advertising medium are these.

    (a)   For international marketers, whilst Internet use is high in countries such as the US and the UK, in countries with poor telecommunications or a low level of computerisation, the Internet is useless.

    (b)   Anecdotal evidence suggests that many Internet users are youngish and male. Advertisers wishing to reach affluent older people might be wasting their time.

(c)   Designing good websites is a skill in short supply.

5.20   The Internet is valuable in **business to business** marketing, perhaps for small businesses, as it avoids the expense of an international advertising campaign.

5.21   It is increasingly likely though that, in the future, organisations will have to use high speed communications channels in order to stay in touch with their markets and stay competitive. The three areas of organisational knowledge, integration of business processes and use of efficient commerce links are fundamental.

Marketing at Work

The UK retail giant Sainsbury has an e-commerce system linking 1,000 of its smallest suppliers using Internet technology. This replaced an old fax-based ordering system and enables two way communication with suppliers, thus extending the company's supply chain across the world and reducing inaccuracies and delays.

Media planning and buying

5.22   As well as the usual media planning considerations (eg campaign objectives, target markets, media availability, budgets), there may be specific factors which need to be taken into account when planning in international markets. For a food product, media scheduling will need to take account of climatic and seasonal characteristics of individual countries.

5.23   Some international print media may be purchased from the home country market via international media representatives. Other media may have to be bought by a local country agent, acting for the advertiser.

5.24   Media buying practices can vary from country to country. In the UK, published ratecard costs tend to be negotiable downwards. Other countries may be less flexible in negotiations.

6   OTHER MARKET CONSIDERATIONS

Economic development

6.1   The level of economic development will affect the amount and way in which a product is used, affecting the message. It may also be connected with educational and literacy levels, affecting the choice of media.

Distribution infrastructure

6.2   The nature of the trading channels in the market will determine their ability to provide all or even part of the promotional effort in a market.

(a)   Thus a distribution system which consists mainly of small scale market traders cannot be expected to promote the product to any significant degree, but a major distributor such as Cadbury-Schweppes in the UK could be expected to promote Coca Cola as part of the dealership.

(b)   This might affect whether the objectives of the campaign are pull or push.

Competition

6.3 The level of competition will of course affect the promotional programme in a country. The entry of a foreign competitor into a market will normally provoke a response from local operators, be they indigenous or existing international companies. Thus the entrant will have to consider not only the promotional programme but his response to competition.

6.4 The above discussion suggests that promotion in international markets usually needs **adaptation** and benefits from **expert advice**.

7 DESIGNING THE INTERNATIONAL MIX

7.1 Possible media for promotion are as follows.

- Trade and professional journals
- Consumer media (magazines, newspapers, TV, radio, posters etc)
- Direct mail
- Trade fairs and missions
- Personal selling
- Telemarketing
- Sales promotion
- Public relations

Trade and professional journals

7.2 Where they are available these publications have the advantage of providing a targeted audience. Due to the nature of the journals, literacy levels and technical expertise will be high. They provide excellent business to business contact but are unsuitable for consumer marketing because of their restricted circulation and technical content. Many UK professional and trade journals have significant foreign readership.

Consumer media

7.3 Here the directed nature and coverage of the media are open to question. Major media groups with international connections provide reports on readership and reader profiles. In many countries however, the data on consumer media are sparse and the international marketer has to rely heavily on local knowledge. Here are some issues to consider.

- Extent of target market coverage
- Image carried by the medium
- Literacy levels
- Ownership/readership
- Ability to convey the message
- The cost of contact (usually expressed as cost per 1,000 audience)

Direct mail

Key Concept

Direct mail is a means of promotion whereby selected customers are sent advertising material addressed specifically to them.

BPP PUBLISHING

7.4 In most developed countries suitable listings based on company or consumer segmentation profiles (eg TGI or ACORN in the UK) are widely available. For trade contacts, the use of international buyers guides provide adequate contacts. In developing or lesser developed countries the international marketer may find that such information is harder to come by. International direct marketing, however, has been growing slowly over the last decade.

(a) **Factors driving the move to international direct marketing**

(i) The growth in sophistication of computer and database technology

(ii) The increasing availability of suitable consumer or business listings

(iii) The growth of international media which can be used for direct response advertising

(iv) The perceived accountability of direct marketing campaigns compared to other communications campaigns

(v) The ease with which direct marketing campaigns can be pre tested in order to maximise their effectiveness

(vi) The improving skills of direct marketing agencies

(vii) The increasing willingness of the consumer to purchase items directly

(viii) The increasing use of internationally accepted credit cards

(b) **Factors restraining the move to international direct marketing**

(i) Lack of telephone and postal infrastructure.

(ii) Lack of road and rail penetration to facilitate distribution.

(iii) Lack of suitable media to use to target consumers.

(iv) Lack of consumer and business lists in some countries.

(v) The threat of increasingly strict legislation concerning the use of consumer information.

(vi) Consumer backlash against what is seen as junk mail.

7.5 The major problem with using direct mail in an international context is the inability to 'follow up' enquiries generated. Thus it is important that the local sales office, agent or distributor in that country is provided with leads as quickly as possible. In developed markets direct mail can be used in several ways.

- Direct response promotion, that is buying 'off the peg'
- To generate enquiries for more personal contact
- To provide an introduction for personal contact

Generally direct mail tends to be more expensive than advertising in terms of contact costs, and has only slightly more response. However, it can have the advantage of providing a more targeted audience, which can save money significantly.

Action Programme 1

You work for an American cake-making company which sells cakes, generally by mail-order, from Texas to Europe. What would be the advantages and disadvantages for the company's promotion strategy in the UK of:

(a) direct mail?
(b) television advertising?

Trade fairs and missions

7.6 **Trade fairs** are probably one of the most effective methods of initial business to business contact, providing an opportunity for producers, distributors and customers to meet. They allow not only communication with a targeted audience but also the ability to demonstrate and provide trial of the product or service. Although 'fairs' exist in the consumer markets, they are less attractive and effective to the international marketeer.

7.7 For smaller companies, the high cost of a presence at some of the major fairs, and the possibility of being ignored in the presence of major international competitors has led to the development of 'fringe' venues, such as a local hotel, where the company may display its offers without competitor presence. The client is often encouraged to attend by direct mail invitations and the provision of refreshments.

(a) **Advantages of trade fairs**

(i) The ability to let potential customers see demonstrations and trials.

(ii) The ability to make personal contact with existing and potential customers to maintain and develop relationships.

(iii) Allowing direct contact with major decision makers and influencers at a time when they are interested in the product.

(iv) Providing an opportunity for market research, such as competitor activity and buyer response.

(v) Contacting a large number of potential customers in one place.

(b) The **principal disadvantage of trade fairs** is cost, especially for smaller companies forced to compete with large multinational exhibitors. Most trade fairs are by their nature specific to a particular trade such as 'engineering' or 'toys'. Where internationally renowned trade fairs are held in your own country attendance should be considered both from the domestic and international perspective.

Marketing at Work

The Frankfurt Book Fair is an event which brings together publishers, booksellers and customers from all over the world. Firms make new contacts and can exchange ideas.

Personal selling

> ### Key Concept
> **Personal selling** (or direct selling) is the use of sales people to sell and supply goods.

7.8 In international marketing, personal selling will be required one or more times in the trading channel. Personal selling is expensive but effective. Normally advertising and direct mail can be used to generate enquiries, and the expensive resource, the salesperson, can be used to convert the lead to an order.

7.9 The international salesperson cannot work in isolation but needs support.

- Generation of enquiries
- Product literature and samples where relevant
- Information on price, delivery and terms

BPP PUBLISHING

7.10 The international salesperson will require several attributes.

- Knowledge of the product and market
- Language and cultural knowledge specific to the country
- Technical knowledge where necessary
- Contacts, preferably from experience in the market
- Suitable personality
- Selling skills
- Motivation to succeed

7.11 Personal selling tends to be more important in international than domestic markets because face to face contact is often so important when making overseas sales. In many Asian countries personal contact is seen as very important to selling. Sales personnel may be natives of the target market, expatriates (usually used when there is rapid market growth) or 'cosmopolitan personnel' (eg a UK telecommunications manager working for an Italian company in Russia).

7.12 Recruitment of sales personnel can present problems. This again is due to culture. In the USA, for example, sales positions are given fairly high status, whilst in Europe selling is seen as a low status job which will not attract high calibre people.

7.13 The idea of an 'ideal' sales person is probably outdated given the diversity of products and markets. Avon in the Asian market for example, does not cold call door-to-door, but uses personal networks of friends and relatives.

7.14 Direct selling in this way can also be a method of overcoming the cynicism and jaded responses of consumers who are bombarded by a growing number of advertising messages and are becoming immune to sales pitches by less direct means. Research has shown that fact-to-face and word of mouth communication can be a more credible source of product information. On the other hand, direct selling can be seen as an unwelcome personal intrusion.

Business-to-busines

7.15 Selling industrial equipment or business services is very different to selling consumer goods. For an **industrial products,** the use of personal selling at international trade fairs mentioned earlier may be necessary. There are thousands of such shows every year which bring companies and potential customers together. They are costly exercises (almost 25% of most UK manufacturing companies' promotional budget is spent on trade fairs) but they provide valuable contacts and are a good source of market news.

7.16 Personal selling can only be justified where the contribution, that is the combined effect of margin and order size, is sufficient to justify the costs involved. It is an effective tool where the market is concentrated and the product is of a high value and where demonstrating or tailoring to customer needs is required.

(a) It is ideal in **business-to-business** marketing and might be essential in dealing with government purchasing agencies, particularly in major **infrastructure and industrial products.**

(b) It is rarely used in consumer marketing, although it can be seen when selling cars or personal financial services.

Marketing at Work

Daewoo Cars in the UK was established in 1994, and aimed to capture 1% of the UK market by 1997. Previously unknown in the UK, the promotional strategy of dealing directly with customers and discarding traditional dealerships took the market by storm. The company achieved its 1% target by the end of 1996.

Telemarketing

7.17 Telemarketing, that is the use of telephone to sell, is often used domestically.

- To prospect potential customers for personal selling
- To handle repeat purchases not requiring personal visits
- To deal with customer enquiries or complaints

7.18 Whilst widely accepted in business to business trading, the acceptance of telemarketing in consumer markets, especially in prospecting customers, is not so widely accepted.

(a) Thus in the UK there is more resistance to telemarketing than in the USA. In France the existence of MINITEL has allowed the growth of telephone ordering to a considerable degree.

(b) In the international context, the **lack of a telecommunications infrastructure** and cultural inhibitions to telephone selling may limit the attraction of this medium. Telephone ownership varies considerably. In most developed countries there is at least one telephone for every two people, showing widespread telephone access. In the former Eastern block it is one telephone per ten people, in Burma one per 750 people and in Zaire one per 2,100 people.

(c) **'Follow up' calls.** Telemarketing requires the ability to react and thus probably works best from **within** a market rather than on a country to country basis.

7.19 Generally, the **impersonal** methods of communication are less expensive in terms of cost per contact, but **less effective** than personal communication. The order size and potential contribution may well dictate the appropriate medium. Thus high value, high volume sales on a business to business basis warrant trade fair visits, and foreign sales representation, whereas consumer communications are better suited to indirect methods such as advertisements.

Sales promotion

7.20 **Sales promotion** describes a range of techniques appropriate for targeting consumers, for instance via price reductions, free gifts, or competitions. Trade and sales force promotions are also implied under the general heading of sales promotion.

> ### Key Concept
> **Sales promotion** encompasses marketing activities other than personal selling, advertising and publicity, aimed to stimulate purchasing by customers. Examples include money-off coupons, free flights, competitions etc.

7.21 Different countries have their own local restrictions concerning different sales promotional devices. For instance, collector devices are a well used method of encouraging repeat purchase in the UK. However, they are not allowed in West Germany, Luxembourg, Austria, Norway, Sweden and Switzerland.

7.22 Sales promotions that are to run across a number of different countries must tap into common tastes, interests and activities.

Public relations

> ### Key Concept
> **Public relations** is 'the planned and sustained effort to establish and maintain goodwill and mutual understanding between an organisation and its publics'.
> - Customers
> - Shareholders
> - Employees
> - Suppliers
> - Trade intermediaries
> - The local community
> - Media
> - Government
> - Pressure groups

7.23 There is wide disparity in the sophistication of PR from country to country, as well as the usual list of cultural, language, media and legal barriers. The political context of individual countries may also affect the extent to which different public relations techniques can be used.

7.24 **Sponsorship** as a method of international marketing is burgeoning. Nike sponsored the Brazilian football team in the World Cup, and backed this up with poster and television campaigns. Nationwide, the British building society, sponsored the English football team. Every major football club in the UK (and certainly those which have a high international profile) are sponsored by major companies. Formula 1 motor racing, a multi-million pound industry, is heavily sponsored by international tobacco companies, although this is to be phased out.

7.25 Companies are keen that they sponsor events or organisations with a good **public image**. Johnson and Johnson withdrew from sponsoring the 2002 Winter Olympics in Salt Lake City, partly because of the corruption and bribery scandal surrounding the International Olympic Committee.

Marketing at Work

International businesses are sponsoring art exhibitions with increasing frequency. Ernst and Young, the Big Five accountancy and consulting firm, sponsored major exhibitions such as Monet and Cezanne in London and Andersen Consulting recently sponsored the largest showing of Van Gogh's work outside the Netherlands, in Los Angeles. Andersen's campaign is built around getting close to the so-called 'C-suite' - the chief executives, chief financial officers and chief information officers of the world's top 10,000 companies. They want to catch these people 'off duty'. Research shows that interest in the arts among successful business leaders is on the increase, and contacts made though cultural events are often used when choosing consultants from a 'stable' of big names. Top executives are increasingly looking for longer term relationships with their consultants. Buyers feel discussions in non-work settings allow for more visionary thinking.

8 PLANNING THE INTERNATIONAL CAMPAIGN

8.1 The way in which a company handles an international advertising campaign will depend upon a variety of factors.

   (a) The **number of markets** in which the company operates and the relative importance of sales in those markets

   (b) The extent to which the different markets are **similar or dissimilar**

(c)   The way in which the company is currently **organised** to do business internationally

(d)   The corporate **culture** and management style of the organisation

(e)   The degree to which the company has a corporate **world-wide identity**

(f)   The **skills and money** available in the different markets

8.2   In planning an international campaign the international marketer needs to make decisions on the following.

- The marketing communications strategy ('push', 'pull' or 'profile')
- Professional assistance
- The message
- The media
- The promotional budget
- Monitoring and control
- Organisation
- Independent or co-operative promotion

Professional assistance: selecting an agency

8.3   The normal form of assistance is to hire an **advertising agency**. This will be either of the following.

- International agency with local offices
- Local agencies in each market

8.4   Considerations when making the decision

- The agency's **knowledge and coverage** of the relevant market
- The agency's **quality and reputation** within each market
- The additional **services** provided (for example, market research, public relations etc)
- The ability to **liaise** with the agency easily
- Whether the campaign is to be **standardised**
- The value of the promotional **budget**
- The **organisation** of the international marketer's company

Selecting the message

8.5   Whilst commonality of needs is largely recognised worldwide, the way in which these needs are satisfied varies, as does the frequency with which these needs occur in any society. Social and cultural values will almost inevitably mean that selecting the message will require local advice, either from the local office or the local distributor. Further considerations concern the following.

- Localised or standardised campaigns
- Market conditions
- Market segments sought

8.6   The degree to which promotion should be **standardised** is a difficult decision. Where the product or service is perceived or used in a significantly different way, the message has to be adapted. Where the media availability and market coverage is significantly different from the home market, a new and different media campaign will be required. Finally, legal restrictions may force both message and media adaptation.

Marketing at Work

International advertising campaigns: Benetton; British Airways; Pepsi-Cola and Levi jeans are all advertisers who have successfully used standardised campaigns in different markets.

A counter example is provided by the Channel Tunnel. In France, Eurotunnel advertised its services as technological achievement, with the help of Emperor Napoleon I and Queen Victoria. In the UK, on the other hand, the practical benefits of the Channel Tunnel and its ease of use were the basis of the advertising message.

8.7 **Advertising guidelines** dictated centrally may be easy to implement and control, but local agencies can rebel against tightly delineated operating rules. Local staff may feel that a standardised execution is not correct for their particular market.

(a) The 'not invented here syndrome' can be overcome by involving regional subsidiaries at the initial strategic stages of a piece of work, so that everyone has a sense of ownership over the finished campaign.

(b) If advertising is totally adapted to meet the individual circumstances of the local marketplace, regional subsidiaries are likely to have high involvement in the campaign.

(c) **Pattern advertising** is a halfway house between total standardisation and total adaptation.

(i) Here, agency and client head office dictate the strategic direction which the advertising must take. Local subsidiaries interpret this to suit the **specific** characteristics of their market.

(ii) A slight variation to pattern advertising is offered where Head office dictates the strategic direction and produces the bulk of the creative work centrally. However, the advert is finished off with local shots. Patrick (1991) described an American Express pan European television campaign which features two different executions. One was a picturesque country wedding; the other a Paris fashion show. The key wedding and catwalk sequences were common to all countries in which the adverts ran. However, scenes involving card members were shot locally in order that each market could feature authentic backgrounds and nationals playing the main roles.

Exam Tip

Remember that in all questions about campaigns you need to establish the **objective** of the campaign and the strategies needed, for example 'pull or push'. The distribution infrastructure may well affect that decision.

Selecting media

8.8 As suggested in the discussion above, the **availability, cost** and **effectiveness** of media may not be the same as in domestic markets. In considering the use of any media one needs to take into account the following.

- The target market you wish to contact
- Degree of market coverage
- Legal restraints on using the medium
- Physical constraints of medium (eg ability to show colour etc)
- Degree of customer response to the medium
- Cost per enquiry generated

8.9 Generally, unless you are a multinational company operating in a particular country, such information will be difficult to obtain. The advice of either your local distributor or advertising agency should be sought.

Deciding on the promotional budget

8.10 As in domestic markets there are several methods used to decide on international promotional budgets. The first two are the most common. Unfortunately they do not take into account either competition or the requirements to achieve sales objectives.

- What can be afforded
- Percentage of sales
- Competitor parity
- Historical precedent
- Objective funding

8.11 **Objective funding** assumes the following.

- Sales objectives in a particular market can be quantified
- The appropriate level of promotion can be determined
- The necessary funding will be provided

8.12 This is a more appropriate method of deciding on promotional budgets, and has the advantage that when sales are hard to obtain, a case can be made for an appropriate budget. In practice, promotion is often regarded as an 'optional' cost and considerable diplomacy is required by the international marketer to justify increased budget at a time of financial stringency!

Monitoring and control

8.13 Investment of any kind should be related to the return that the investment generates, and this applies equally to promotional campaigns. Costs are usually easy to obtain from the internal records. Typical monitoring measures could include the following.

(a) **Coding advertisements** so that enquiries can be related to a particular medium or advertisement

(b) **Comparing response rates** between media

(c) Comparing against other salesforces, calls and orders per call to establish the **costs of contact and order generation**

As a result of this and similar feedback the mix can be adjusted to improve **promotional productivity**. Modern information technology using **database** and **management information software** has reduced the effort required to monitor programmes.

Organising international promotions

8.14 In most cases the company will rely on the advice and help of both the local distributor and agency for operational and administrative decisions. Strategic decisions will always be the domain of the company.

Independent or co-operative promotion

8.15 Part of the task of a channel of distribution is that of promoting the product. **Trade promotion** is usually undertaken by the producer in most markets with enquiries being direct to the distributor or agent. Where **consumer markets** are involved the main distributor is usually required to provide the promotion. Smaller distributors such as retailers may well be tempted to promote the product locally to the end users, if an incentive is offered. Thus a foreign department store may be tempted to put a special promotion on for a product if the costs can be shared between it, the distributor and the producer.

9 INTERNATIONAL AGENCY SELECTION AND MANAGEMENT

International agencies

9.1 Over the last forty years, as companies have expanded their operations internationally, so too have advertising agencies. Many of the large agencies have developed internationally, either by setting up branch offices in foreign countries or by merging with or acquiring local agencies.

9.2 Some agencies expanding abroad prefer to establish international networks or alliances where local offices are not wholly controlled. The argument is that local partners with a stake in the agency will be motivated to produce superior work.

9.3 **Media independents** have mirrored the pattern of agency development and many belong to international media planning and buying groups.

9.4 The trend amongst clients is towards the centralisation of advertising. Many large companies believe **international brands** are best served by an agency operating internationally.

Selection

9.5 Selecting an international advertising agency will follow a series of well defined stages. Locating suitable agency candidates is the first step in the process.

(a) **Initial search.** Prospective clients will probably be aware of the large multinational agencies based within their own country.

(b) A **shortlist** of agencies will then be drawn up, usually on the basis of their current work and past track record.

(c) The **client will then visit** the local offices of those agencies for a series of credentials presentations. These initial visits will help to form an opinion about which candidates should be requested to formally pitch for the client's business. All agencies involved in the pitch should be given the same written brief to follow.

(d) The **agency's response to the brief** will usually involve a formal presentation backed by a written proposal document with several important features.

- The agency's interpretation of the client's advertising problem
- The creative and media strategy which will ensure objectives are met
- Control mechanisms to be used
- Timing schedules
- Allocation of responsibilities
- Costings

- Terms and conditions of business

(e) The **final selection decision** will have to take into account many client side factors such as the client's organisational structure and management style, the number of brands to be advertised and the degree to which brands penetrate different markets.

9.6 Other criteria for selection would include the following.

(a) The types of advertising and other communications services offered

(b) Level of **expertise** in the client's field of work

(c) The agency's **international creative track record**

(d) The **balance** within the agency of campaigns handled for local clients and those handled for international ones

(e) Whether the agency has **strong local offices** in the client's home and other key markets

(f) The extent to which the agency's **culture and management** style fits with that of the prospective client

(g) The **potential conflict** with existing business handled within the agency network

(h) The **control and co-ordination** procedures in place

Action Programme 2

Your company is about to launch a group of new consumer toiletries products in the Middle East. What sorts of assurance would you want from an advertising agency pitching for this account?

9.7 The **advantages of using an international agency.**

- Less duplication and dilution of effort on the part of agency and client
- Centralised control of all advertising effort
- Speedy response across markets
- Pooling of talent and ideas from the entire agency network
- Specialised resources available
- Standardised working methods by the agency
- Reduced costs due to economies of scale

9.8 Bennett (1993) outlines a number of **criticisms of international agencies.**

- They provide an uneven quality of service in their different branches
- They produce bland campaigns
- Quality control suffers due to handling hundreds of campaigns simultaneously
- Clients have to tailor their campaigns to suit the conventions of the agency
- Small or medium sized clients suffer a lack of attention from senior staff
- High staff turnover rates exist amongst creative employees

Local or international?

9.9 Despite the increasing presence and power of international advertising and media networks, **independent local agencies** exist in the markets of most countries. Some companies prefer to retain country by country agency arrangements, believing local agencies to be **creatively closer** to their own markets.

9.10 Cherry picking **local agencies** is an appropriate strategy for the client who has only a small portfolio of products to be advertised in a limited number of markets.

Management issues

9.11 **External factors,** such as **market diversity,** segmentation and competition affect the type of co-ordination chosen. **Internal factors,** unrelated to the market, can also dictate the management and co-ordination of international promotions.

(a) **Organisation structure**

(i) **Local autonomy.** Each subsidiary of an international agency may act as a separate profit centre, attracting its own clients in the home market. Upon appointment, the subsidiary which has brought in the client takes the role of lead agency office, with overall supervision of the client's account.

(ii) **Central control.** Alternatively, an agency may exert strong central control on regional offices from its headquarters base.

(b) **Organisation culture.** Managers may have different assumptions as to how advertising ought to be done, and it might be a basic hidden assumption that decisions are taken at the top or, on the other hand, by giving local managers their head.

(c) The need for **integrated marketing communications**; firms with worldwide exposure may need central control of marketing communications to ensure they are, in fact, integrated.

Marketing at Work

Shell, the oil company, promoted a 'green' image in the UK, but was wrongfooted by Greenpeace and, later, bad publicity about its Nigerian operations. Where marketing communications are driven off track, centralisation is necessary for PR.

Control

The advertiser

9.12 A number of management and control problems need attention.

(a) **Budgets.** If advertising budgets will be split among the different units, the money might be spent less effectively than if control is centralised.

(b) **Timing.** The local advertising campaigns might need to be co-ordinated so that the production side can cope with demand. This is especially true if the firm is an exporter, with a number of local sales offices and warehouses. Local advertisers may generate demands which cannot be met.

(c) Some central review is necessary so that good ideas can be passed around within the group.

(d) **Expertise.** The person responsible for advertising in a 'small' subsidiary may not have a great deal of expertise and may rely too much on local advertising agencies for ideas, rather than controlling the output directly.

(e) Finally, all advertising campaigns need to be **evaluated** for effectiveness.

(i) Local campaigns may have different objectives, and so appropriate effectiveness measures need to be outlined.

(ii)   It is easier to measure message recall and media buyer efficiency in advanced economies, and there may not be the facilities in less developed countries, even if these promise high growth.

Between client and agency

9.13   Relationships with agencies need to be managed. In many agencies, there will be an 'account manager' responsible for overall liaisons with client. It is in the agency's interests to establish a long-term relationship with the client.

9.14   The agency's account executive is a lynchpin, in communicating the client's needs to the creative team. The agency must also be able to liaise, where necessary, lower down the chain of command, and to communicate to the units of the business, in clear terms, the objectives of the promotion campaign.

Within the agency

9.15   Within the agency, there are the following issues of management and control.

(a)   A general problem of **central direction vs local freedom**. This we have already discussed, in terms of tailoring local advertising campaigns or adopting a standard approach.

(b)   **Conflicts of interest**: how free are local offices to tout for business, if this involves offending a major client?

(c)   How do you co-ordinate the activities of **different creative teams**?.

(d)   There may exist problems of corporate culture, particularly if an agency grows up as the result of a takeover.

(e)   **Performance appraisal** and culture.

(f)   Many human resources issues are relevant (eg corporate culture, details of organisation structure).

Current client/agency issues

9.16   As markets expand, clients are likely to forsake traditional, vertical organisational structures where brands are managed on a country by country basis, in favour of a horizontal structure which cuts across country divides. This implies **brand and product management at a centralised level** and may result in a preference for centralised agencies. Consequences might be as follows.

(a)   **Clients** are likely to become more demanding of their agencies, as clients strive to ensure that their advertising is accountable and effective. In America, the trend is already towards payment by results. Clients are also likely to demand a larger base of expertise in terms of communications and research services provided.

(b)   **Agencies** will continue to expand internationally to meet the needs of their clients. This may lead to a concentration in advertising agency ownership as the large agencies seek to expand still further by way of acquisition and merger.

(c)   Agency expansion will also mean that an increasing number of local agency offices will be established in new markets (eg Russia, Eastern Europe, China). Agencies may need to take a **long term perspective** on emerging markets. Initial resource requirements will be high.

9.17 **Media buying and selling power continues to concentrate.** On the one hand, large international media independents hold consolidated buying power and have the ability to level volume or other discounts. On the other hand there is increasing concentration in global media ownership.

Chapter Roundup

- The **international marketing communicator** needs to decide whether or not it is appropriate to standardise communications across markets.

- Companies operating outside their home markets need to be aware of the implications of **cultural differences** for all aspects of the marketing mix. Verbal and non verbal communications, aesthetics, dress and appearance, family roles and relationships, beliefs, learning and work habits are dimensions of culture of particular relevance to communications.

- **Planning and media buying** across borders can be a complex task. Media availability can vary greatly from country to country. Media conventions which apply in a home market may not apply elsewhere.

- **Laws and regulations** governing marketing communications must obviously be observed. Each country will have its own set of restrictions which apply to advertising, packaging, sales promotion and direct marketing.

- Clients and their **agencies** can choose to handle international advertising campaigns in a number of ways. Although a variety of factors will influence the management of any particular campaign, the organisational structure of the client company will play an important role.

- Some agencies have expanded abroad by setting up their own subsidiaries overseas. Others have established alliances with local agencies already in existence.

- There are arguments both for and against using the services of an **international advertising agency**. The current preference amongst large clients is to centralise advertising with an internationally based agency, rather than choose local agencies on a country by country basis.

- The **standardisation versus adaptation** debate has implications for agency management. If campaigns are totally standardised across markets, the lead market agency office will taken the major role in designing and implementing the global campaign; local agency subsidiaries will have minimal input.

- The **process** of selecting an international advertising agency involves initial search; credentials presentation and shortlist; competitive pitch and final selection. The client will gauge competing agencies against criteria such as response to the brief, types of communication service provided; expertise in handling local and international campaigns; and similarity of management style and culture to that of the client.

Quick Quiz

1   Why might the promotional objectives in a new market be different from those in a mature market? (see para 2.4)

2   What kind of problems can be anticipated when translating copy from one language to another? (3.3)

3   What legal concerns generally affect international marketing communications decisions? (4.1)

4   Describe the factors which influence choice of press as a medium in international markets. (5.3-5.6)

5   What should you consider before using TV? (5.7)

6   What are the limitations of the Internet as an advertising medium? (5.19)

7   Explain the reasons why international direct marketing has experienced growth over the last decade. (7.4(a))

8   Are there advantages to a smaller exporter in using trade fairs in exploring a possible market to enter? (7.6-7.7)

9   What factors would you take into account in selecting a salesperson for a foreign market? (7.10)

10   What would you consider when deciding whether to hire an advertising agency? (8.4)

11   What measures would you use to monitor a promotional campaign? (8.13)

12   What criteria do you use to select an agency? (9.5, 9.6)

13   Name four advantages and four disadvantages of using an international advertising agency. (9.7, 9.8)

Action Programme Review

1   Advertising on television would reach a wide audience, but perhaps could not say too much about the product. Also, it might be faced with mass scepticism, from people not willing to pay more for a cake that was imported when it could be purchased at a supermarket.

Direct mail would have the advantage of targeting. The firm could buy mailing lists of people who might in principle be more receptive to such a product.

2   Ideally, the agency should be able to assure the client of experience in both consumer market generally and the toiletries market in particular. The agency should have local offices in a number of the Middle East states in which the client does business and be used to handling local and international campaigns in those countries.

The agency must demonstrate knowledge concerning cultural, legal, and media difficulties which may be encountered and be able to propose solutions for overcoming these problems. Proof of successful campaign outcomes for other British based clients advertising in related markets would also be reassuring.

Now try illustrative question 11 at the end of the Study Text

12 International Distribution and Logistics

Chapter Topic List	Syllabus Reference
1 Setting the scene	-
2 Strategic importance of distribution	1.2, 3.4
3 Channel design and evaluation	3.4
4 The use of overseas agents and distributors	3.4
5 International physical distribution	3.4, 3.9
6 Trends in distribution	3.4, 3.5
7 Documents used in foreign trade	3.4
8 Financing goods in distribution	2.9, 3.4

Learning Outcomes

After studying this chapter you will have a good understanding of international distribution and logistics strategy.

- foreign channel design and management
- customer service
- new forms of distribution such as e-commerce
- the use of overseas agents and distributors
- documentation and financing.

Key Concepts Introduced

- Distribution channel
- Supply chain management
- Exclusive, selective and intensive distribution
- Overseas sales agent

- Logistics management
- Just-in-time (JIT)
- Bill of lading
- Export Credit Guarantee Department (ECGD)

Examples of Marketing at Work

- Japanese firms
- Li and Fung
- PricewaterhouseCoopers
- Distribution in Japan
- British manufacturers and the Internet
- Royal Mail

- Sony
- Channel Tunnel
- Marks & Spencer and Boots
- Disintermediation
- Customs red tape
- Kenyan horticulture

1 SETTING THE SCENE

1.1 For many manufacturers, distribution is the 'Cinderella' of the marketing mix, less glamorous and 'creative' than promotion, and less involved in the heart of the company than the product. However some firms use distribution as a means of competitive advantage and retailers, of course, take distribution very seriously (section 6).

1.2 As in all aspects of international marketing, distribution abroad increases in complexity, even in a market such as the EU with a fairly modern transport infrastructure. Border controls still exist in many areas within the EU. In less developed markets, poor roads and communications can add significantly to costs. Therefore a selection of the channel (section 3) and any intermediaries (section 4) can be of vital importance.

1.3 The additional complexity of distribution can arise from special documentation (section 7) and the perceived extra risk requires special financing arrangements (section 8).

2 STRATEGIC IMPORTANCE OF DISTRIBUTION

> **Key Concept**
> The **distribution channel** is the means of getting the goods to the customer.

2.1 The distribution channel is of strategic importance.

   (a) It is **hard to change** in the short term, unlike the price or promotion elements in the marketing mix.

   (i) A distribution channel often involves **contractual arrangements** with the distributor which cannot be changed easily.

   (ii) There is a substantial **physical infrastructure** involved, of warehouses, lorry fleets, containers etc.

   (iii) In many respects, **distributors are 'customers'** whose needs should be considered, and with whom a **long-term relationship** should be built.

   (b) A firm's **marketing communications** will be strongly influenced by the extent to which the firm is able to obtain wide distribution.

   (c) In overseas markets most new managers will be inexperienced. At home, the distribution channel will exist already, whereas abroad a new channel will have to be built up from scratch, in very different conditions. Distribution is often **outsourced.** The firm obtains services from logistics firms, banks and insurance companies.

299

(d) Distribution is a competitive battlefield.

(e) Distribution can offer competitive advantage.

2.2 The case example below indicates how distribution has been important.

Marketing at Work

Japanese firms

A little while ago, it was assumed that, following the success of Japanese firms worldwide in motor vehicles (Nissan, Honda, Toyota) and consumer electronics (eg Sony, JVC, Matsushita), no Western companies were safe from Japanese competition. Kao (household goods), Suntory (drinks), Nomura (banking and securities) were seen as successors to firms such as Procter and Gamble, Heineken etc.

This has not happened: for example, Japanese pharmaceutical firms, such as Green Cross, have not achieved the world domination anticipated. US and European firms are still dominant in this industry.

Perhaps cars and consumer electronics are the exception rather than the rule. The reason for this might be distribution. Normally, outsiders do not find it easy to break into established distribution patterns. However distribution channels in cars and consumer electronics offered outsiders an easy way in.

(a) The car industry is vertically integrated, with a network of exclusive dealerships. Given time and money, the Japanese firms could simply build their own dealerships and run them as they liked, with the help of local partners. This barrier to entry was not inherently complex.

(b) Consumer electronics

   (i) In the early years, the consumer electronics market was driven by technology, so innovative firms such as Sony and Matsushita could overcome distribution weaknesses.

   (ii) Falling prices changed the distribution of hifi goods from small specialist shops to large cut-price outlets, such as Comet. Newcomers to a market are the natural allies of such new outlets: existing suppliers prefer to shun 'discount' retailers to protect margins in their current distribution network.

Japanese firms have not established dominant positions

* In healthcare, where national pharmaceuticals wholesalers are active as 'gatekeepers'
* In household products, where there are strong supermarket chains
* In cosmetics, where department stores and specialist shops offer a wide choice

---

2.3 Key issues in distribution are these.

   (a) **Coverage and density,** in other words the number of sales outlets.

      (i) Countries like the UK and US allow large stores.

      (ii) In Japan, there have been restrictions on store size, to protect the livelihoods of small retailers.

   (b) Channel length - the number of intermediaries between producer and consumer.

   (c) **Power and alignment.** The international marketer has to realise that distribution channel power is not equal in each country. Different roles are played by retailers, wholesalers and agents in each country. For example, wholesalers are most important where retailing is fragmented. In the UK, where, in groceries, concentration of retail power has gone furthest, the major supermarket chains are powerful.

   (d) Logistics and physical distribution.

Distribution costs

2.4 The company should remember its basic distribution and logistics strategy is constrained by the distribution cost structure which may be represented by the following function:

$$D = T + W + I + O + P + S$$

where
    D = total distribution cost
    T = total transport costs
    W = warehousing costs
    I = inventory costs
    O = order processing and documentation cost
    P = packaging cost
    S = total cost of lost sales for not meeting standards set

2.5 In international distribution many of these costs will rise.

- Transport: longer distances and the use of several modes will raise costs
- Warehousing: the firm might have a warehouse system for each country
- Stock and inventory will be higher
- Packaging might need to be able to handle long journeys
- Order processing and documentation: customs forms, taxes and excise, insurance etc

2.6 The key here is to remember that as some of these cost functions increase others will decrease. So, for example, larger deliveries to a holding warehouse in your main market may reduce total transport costs through efficiencies or discounts with the freight forwarders or shipping companies, but this may be achieved at the expense of increased warehousing and inventory costs.

The supply chain

2.7 Many multinational enterprises (MNEs) have been getting larger. Some writers are arguing that the trend will continue - so that for many sectors there will be fewer players of world class dominating the field. We have seen this in the automobile industry for example, with many European companies merging to be able to compete effectively with US giants and the Japanese.

2.8 There have been, at the same time, much **closer links** with companies in the supply chain in order to extract best value for money and reduce stockholdings. This has had major consequences on the distribution methods of companies in these supply chains, delivering to their customers on a **just in time** (JIT) basis.

2.9 The change in supply chain linkage is demonstrated in the following model (taken from Monczka).

Supply chain model

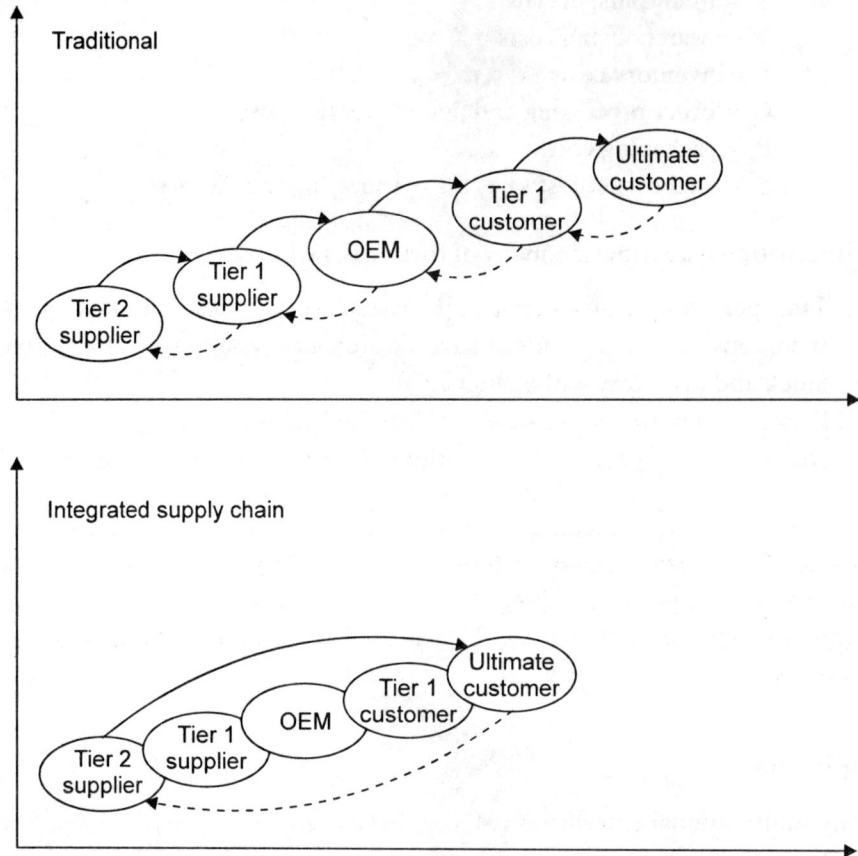

Traditional

```
Ultimate
customer

Tier 1
customer

OEM

Tier 1
supplier

Tier 2
supplier
```

Integrated supply chain

```
Ultimate
customer

Tier 1
customer

OEM

Tier 1
supplier

Tier 2
supplier
```

2.10 Historically, businesses in the supply chain have operated relatively independently of one another to create value for an ultimate customer. Independence was maintained by buffers of material, capacity and lead-times. This is represented in the 'Traditional' model shown above.

2.11 Market and competitive demands are now, however, **compressing lead times** and businesses are reducing inventories and excess capacity. Linkages between businesses in the supply chain must therefore become much tighter. This new condition is shown in the 'Integrated supply chain' model.

2.12 Monczka further claims that there seems to be increasing recognition that, in the future, it will be **whole supply chains** which will compete and not just individual firms. This will continue to have a great impact upon distribution methods.

> **Key Concept**
> **Supply chain management** is about **optimising the activities** of companies working together to produce goods and services.

2.13 The aim is to co-ordinate the whole chain, from raw material suppliers to end customers. The chain should be considered as a **network** rather than a **pipeline** - a network of vendors support a network of customers, with third parties such as transport firms helping to link the companies.

Marketing at Work

The Hong Kong based export trading company, Li and Fung, takes the following approach to its manufacturing supply chain.

'Say we get an order from a European retailer to produce 10,000 garments. It's not a simple matter of our Korean office sourcing Korean products or our Indonesian office sourcing Indonesian products. For the customer we might decide to buy yarn from a Korean producer but have it woven and dyed in Taiwan. So we pick the yarn and ship it to Taiwan. The Japanese have the best zippers and buttons, but they manufacture them mostly in China. Okay, so we go to YKK, a big Japanese zipper manufacturer and we order the right zippers from their Chinese plants. Then we determine that, because of quotas and labour conditions, the best place to make the garments is Thailand. So we ship everything there. And because the customer needs quick delivery, we may divide the order across five factories in Thailand. Effectively, we are customising the value chain to best meet the customer's needs.

'Five weeks after we have received the order, 10,000 garments arrive on the shelves in Europe, all looking like they came from one factory with colours, for example, perfectly matched. Just think about the logistics and the co-ordination.

'This is a new type of value added, a truly global product that has never been seen before. The label may say "Made in Thailand", but it's not a Thai product. We dissect the manufacturing process and look for the best solution to each step. We're not asking which country can do the best job overall. Instead, we're pulling apart the value chain and optimising each step - and we're doing it globally.... . The classic supply-chain manager in retailing is Marks & Spencer. They don't own any factories, but they have a huge team that goes into the factories and works with the management.'   (*Harvard Business Review*, 1998)

2.14 Managing the supply chain varies from company to company. A company such as Unilever will provide the same margarine to both Tesco and Sainsbury. The way in which the product is delivered, transactions are processed and other parts of the relationship are managed will be different since these competing supermarket chains have their own ways of operating. The focus will need to be on customer interaction, account management, after sales service and order processing.

2.15 If the supplier 'knows' what his customers want, it does not have to guess or wait until the customer places an order. It will be able to better plan its own delivery systems. The potential for using the Internet to allow customers and suppliers to acquire up to date information about forecast needs and delivery schedules is a very recent development, but one which is being used by an increasing number of companies.

2.16 The greatest changes in supply chain management during the 1990s have taken place in the implementation of software applications. Managers today have a wider choice of systems with quick implementation times - important in a competitive market where a new supply chain system is required. Supply chains at local, regional and global level are often managed simultaneously, via a standardised infrastructure that nevertheless allows for local adaptation where this is important.

Marketing at Work

- A leading European manufacturer has said: 'We must localise those part of our supply chain that face the customer and regionalise all other parts of our supply chain to lower costs and improve speed of operations'.

- PricewaterhouseCoopers has run full page newspaper advertisements promoting its supply chain consultancy services, which indicates the importance of supply chain management to most companies. The text of one such advertisement reads: 'When it come to supply chain management, there's one universal truth: every customer is unique. What may be right for one, may not be for another.... We're working on some of the toughest supply chain problems all around the world. Reinventing strategy, optimising processes and applying new technologies intelligently. All to help companies improve their ability to operate globally and serve customers locally. With 150,000 people working in 50 different countries, we can make the world seem like a pretty small place'.

This may contain more than its share of buzzwords but it does illustrate the issues involved: the importance of individual customers, strategy and technology, and the ability of a large company to deliver services on a global basis where it has the resources.

> ### Exam Tip
> The December 1997 exam covered distribution in the context of the 'global village'. Whilst physical distances have not shrunk, firms in the supply chain are developing closer relationships, and, as evidenced by the Internet, communication is only restricted by communications infrastructure and time zone.
>
> Amazon Books is a good example of the effect of communications on distribution. Amazon is sited near book wholesalers in the US but takes orders from all over the world.

3   CHANNEL DESIGN AND EVALUATION

Types of trading channels within a market

3.1   The participants in a **trading channel** have to provide certain services to the customer. A good trading channel will provide the following.

- Research and information feedback about the market
- Promotion of the goods and services
- Contact and negotiation with prospective buyers
- Storage, sorting, assembling and processing of orders
- Physical distribution
- Financing operations
- Speculative risk taking

The producer's problem is in ensuring that these activities will be carried out. It can be seen that where a weak distributive infrastructure exists within a country, the duties will fall on the exporter and the selected entry organisation, and thus care must be taken in the selection of any partner in international marketing.

Channel structure

3.2   The series of **trading intermediaries** used to transfer title and physical possession from manufacturer to end user is known as a trading channel. The actual structure of a trading channel is dependent on many factors, which determine the economic viability and efficiency of that form of trading. A key factor is the ability of a trader to solve the 'discrepancy of assortment'.

3.3   The **discrepancy of assortment** refers to the difference between the variety and quantity of goods that are available at the manufacturing level, compared with the requirements at the user level.

(a)   Generally, producers wish to produce a very narrow variety of goods and in bulk.

(b)   End users, on the other hand, prefer to buy a variety of goods in small quantities.

(c)   A further consideration is the cost of handling and servicing an order compared to the margin available. Thus small orders tend to be unprofitable.

Consumer trading channels

3.4 **Consumer trading channels** generally require a variety of goods in small quantities, and progressively the trading channel both accumulates a wider variety of goods and breaks down the trade quantities to smaller units. Thus whilst an importer may import wine in bulk and then sell it by the case to the retailer, the retailer will sell wine by the bottle and other associated goods that will appeal to the consumer, and provide a sufficiently large order to make the cost of trading worthwhile. Because the discrepancy is so large, consumer trading channels tend to be longer, with more intermediaries. In some underdeveloped countries, where the cost of even a standard pack may be prohibitive, the local market traders may even break open consumer packs and sell the contents in smaller units such as cigarettes.

Business trading channels

3.5 Unlike consumer trading channels, trading on a **business to business** basis usually requires a narrow variety of goods from specialist suppliers in larger quantities. Thus the problems of discrepancy of assortment are less and the **trading channels shorter,** often involving only one or two intermediaries between the originator and the end user.

Marketing at Work

The distribution system in Japan has been considered as an impediment to imports, in that planning regulations and trading practices are prejudiced against the sort of independent and powerful retailers which exist in the UK. While there are a few large department stores in Japan, there are far more small 'corner shops' with semi-dependent relationships with either manufacturers directly or wholesalers. As the system is so fragmented, it is costly and difficult to reach customers.

Recent reports have indicated some relaxation to permit the construction of larger stores, enabling imported goods to be distributed more easily.

Design and evaluation

3.6 We have seen above that the channel used to trade with customers in a market needs to fulfil certain functions, and that the design will also be affected by the discrepancy between the assortment provided at market entry and that required by the end user. The international marketeer has to select intermediaries to fulfil all these roles, and to ensure that these duties are carried out within the channel. **Channel design** will be affected by the following.

- Buyer behaviour and culture
- Product features
- Competition and competitive advantage
- Company objectives in the market
- Mode of entry

3.7 The type of product or product service dictates a channel and its management.

Different channels for different types of product

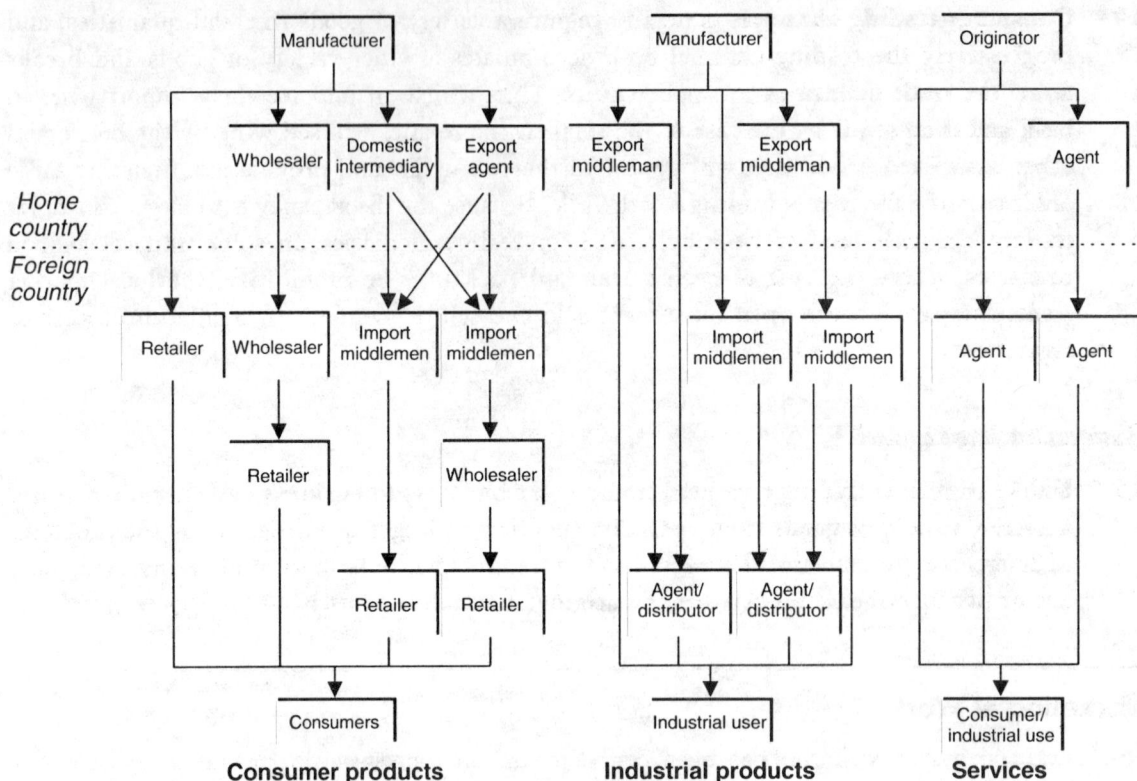

Manufacturer	Manufacturer	Originator

Home country / *Foreign country*

Wholesaler — Domestic intermediary — Export agent | Export middleman — Export middleman | Agent

Retailer — Wholesaler — Import middlemen — Import middlemen | Import middlemen — Import middlemen | Agent — Agent

Retailer — Wholesaler

Retailer — Retailer | Agent/distributor — Agent/distributor

Consumers	Industrial user	Consumer/industrial use
Consumer products	**Industrial products**	**Services**

(*Source:* Chee and Harris, *Global Marketing Strategy*)

3.8 Fresh flowers from Zimbabwe to the UK require different channel management decisions than the export of machinery from Poland to the UK, because the flowers are more perishable and need to reach their destination quickly with little add-on cost.

3.9 A product or service will get different coverage in the market depending on its nature. Intensive distribution is applied to convenience goods such as food. More limited distribution will be given to segments such as clothing, and furniture. Customer shopping habits will also be important. In higher income countries, people expect to find expensive cosmetics and perfumes in general department stores, whereas in developing countries they may only be available to the wealthy elite in specialist outlets.

Buyer behaviour and culture

3.10 The social, demographic and economic profile of the target customer varies from country to country. Each segment exhibits different purchasing habits. A key determinant of this behaviour is the **purchasing culture** prevalent in the target market. This affects the following.

(a) The end user preference as to **where** to buy, **frequency** of purchase and **services** required

(b) The services that the **intermediary** both expects and is capable of providing, and their purchasing patterns

3.11 Thus, whilst UK retailers, through their economic concentration and power, have generally thrust most of the duties outlined above back onto the manufacturer, in other countries stocking and promotion may be regarded as the legitimate activity of the importing wholesaler/ distributor rather than the manufacturer.

3.12 In some countries, local legislation may prohibit the ownership of trading organisations by foreign companies (for example, most developing African countries) and the international marketer is either forced into some form of joint ownership or to select a local intermediary to act on their behalf.

Product features

3.13 As noted above, the nature of the product being sold will affect the choice of channel members in a particular country. Perishable goods need short quick turnover channel systems to retain their value. Some goods require presales surveys, advice, installation, aftersales service, maintenance and local spares and accessory availability. The distribution channel must be able to provide these enhancements efficiently and quickly. In other cases the intermediary will only be required to collect and pass on orders with few other demands or restrictions. Financial services may be required to offer credit in the cases of some high value goods, and the intermediary may be required to provide such a service.

Competition

3.14 **Established competition** in a market will indicate the usual form of trading channel.

(a) Where strong and concentrated competitors exist, this may mean that it will be difficult to attract the better dealers in a trading channel. Typically the competitors will have offered exclusive dealerships in return for an undertaking not to stock competitive goods (eg computers, cars, machine tools etc). Thus the new entrant will find it difficult to attract quality dealers to stock and trade in their goods or services.

(b) The international marketer may then be forced to consider new and innovative approaches to trading in a market where the traditional outlets are blocked.

- Other traders selling to same market
- Catalogue selling
- Direct mail

Company objectives in the market

3.15 The choice of trading channel will also depend on what the company wants to achieve in a particular market. Three types of distribution objective are generally considered: **coverage**, **market share** and **commitment** required from intermediaries.

Coverage

3.16 There are three approaches to coverage.

BPP PUBLISHING

> ### Key Concepts
>
> **Exclusive distribution** involves the selection of high quality intermediaries, who in return for providing local stocks and services are given an exclusive territorial trading right, ensuring that no outlet carrying the same product range will be trading nearby. This approach is used when the international marketeer requires most of the functions to be carried out locally to a high standard, through a reputable dealer. It results in a few, strategically located, main dealers in a country giving wide coverage, service and support. (It applies to most high value goods requiring good pre and post sales support.)
>
> **Selective distribution**. This strategy involves the use of premium quality dealers selected area by area, and whilst not given any 'rights', involves the avoidance of too many competitive dealers in an area. (Luxury consumer goods, designer clothes, perfumes, high quality durables fall into this category.)
>
> **Intensive distribution**. In this situation the goods or services involved require little or no pre or post sales support and have wide appeal (eg most fast moving consumer goods). Sales can be increased by engaging as many dealers as possible in the distributive network, and the exporter seeks to get as high a market coverage as possible.

Market share

3.17 Where a company is content with a **small share** of the market, the use of a **local distributor** in a region of the market may be appropriate. In the UK most trading channels can provide national coverage, but in large countries such as the USA and India, the availability of national coverage through one or two organisations is almost impossible. Region by region dealerships need to be developed to obtain nationwide coverage.

Commitment

3.18 **The degree of commitment desired.** Where an exporter either has little financial resources, or prefers not to invest that resource in a particular country, the preference will be for independent dealers that have no financial tie with the exporter. On the other hand, a greater degree of control in the channel can be exercised if the exporter has some degree of investment in the dealer network.

Mode of entry

3.19 Earlier it was mentioned that one way of entering an overseas market was by purchasing a company. In this respect, the purchaser acquires the ultimate profits from the **acquisition**, and can use the acquisition as a **distribution channel**. An acquisition can be defined as the purchase of a controlling interest in one company by another.

3.20 Channels of distribution for goods which are unprofitable to use should be dealt with.

- **Abandoned** in favour of more profitable channels
- **Made profitable** by cutting costs or increasing minimum order sizes

3.21 Some firms scrutinise the profitability of their products, and/or market segments, but do not have a costing system which measures the costs of distributing the products to their markets. A numerical example might help to illustrate this point. Let us suppose that Biomarket Ltd sells two consumer products, X and Y, in two markets A and B. In both markets, sales are made through the following outlets.

- Direct sales to supermarkets
- Wholesalers

Sales and costs for the most recent quarter have been analysed by product and market as follows.

	Market A			Market B			Both markets		
	X	Y	Total	X	Y	Total	X	Y	Total
	£'000	£'000	£'000	£'000	£'000	£'000	£'000	£'000	£'000
Sales	900	600	1,500	1,000	2,000	3,000	1,900	2,600	4,500
Variable production costs	450	450	900	500	1,500	2,000	950	1,950	2,900
	450	150	600	500	500	1,000	950	650	1,600
Variable sales costs	90	60	150	100	100	200	190	160	350
Contribution	360	90	450	400	400	800	760	490	1,250
Share of fixed costs (production, sales, distribution, administration)	170	80	250	290	170	460	460	250	710
Net profit	190	10	200	110	230	340	300	240	540

3.22 This analysis shows that both products are profitable, and both markets are profitable. But what about the channels of distribution? A further analysis of market A might show the following.

	Market A		
	Supermarkets	Wholesalers	Total
	£'000	£'000	£'000
Sales	1,125	375	1,500
Variable production costs	675	225	900
	450	150	600
Variable selling costs	105	45	150
Contribution	345	105	450
Direct distribution costs	10	80	90
	335	25	360
Share of fixed costs	120	40	160
Net profit/(loss)	215	(15)	200

3.23 This analysis shows that although sales through wholesalers make a contribution after deducting direct distribution costs, the profitability of this channel of distribution is disappointing, and some attention ought perhaps to be given to improving it.

3.24 Different conditions in different countries will affect the distribution channel. (See Paragraph 6.2 for more examples.) The more intermediaries there are, the higher the price. In Japan, there are often several intermediaries who have powerful vested interests. Preferred distribution methods are often deeply rooted in national culture. Direct selling is not acceptable in some Asian counties unless it is done via a network of friends and relatives.

3.25 An important aspect of the distribution channel is **communication**. Good communication is affected by factors such as geographic distance and cultural differences. Religious festivals, for example, in some countries could mean that business cannot happen at all during certain times. Summer holidays in certain countries tend to be taken by a large proportion of the population all at the same time.

E-commerce

3.26 The growing importance of **e-commerce** will revolutionise channel design. Direct access to customers and businesses via the Internet will speed up delivery times and improve communications. A company that wishes to use e-commerce as a channel for business will have to satisfy itself that customers and business partners are sufficiently equipped. Alternatively it may be forced to accept e-commerce as a channel because customers insist on doing business that way.

Marketing at Work

A study by the DTI in Britain has revealed that many British manufacturers are not using the Internet to its full potential for areas such as speeding up design work, selling products and services, forming closer links and even gaining payment. Setting up links with parts suppliers to assist JIT production is another area that could be developed. Lack of technological knowledge and security fears mean that Britain lags behind Germany and the US. The DTI believes use of the internet for business-to-business activity is a key area where competitive edge can be gained.

3.27 Various European Commission targets are being set, for example, on the level of e-commerce that is to be achieved in public contracts in the early years of the new millennium. Companies submitting tenders for such work will be expected to do so electronically.

3.28 E-commerce will facilitate corporate buying and selling when companies post their requirements on a website. Looking through company websites may also help companies seeking distribution channel partners to link up with appropriate contacts.

Marketing at Work

The Royal Mail in the UK has entered the world of e-commerce with the launch of a secure electronic mail system, call Via Code. It is the first time it has offered a service not involving the traditional hard copy letter (*Financial Times*, March 1999).

According to its managing director, the system combines 'Royal Mail's 350 year old reputation for trust in delivering mail with the Internet's global capacity for handling messages, complex documents and commercial transactions. ...'Anyone serious about e-commerce will have to adopt security practices and techniques of this kind to safeguard their business.'

Choosing a distribution channel

3.29 The following checklist can be used to assess the choice of a particular distribution channel.

(a) **Internal factors**

- Cost of ongoing distribution and margins to distributors
- Capital investment required
- Control over the channel
- Coverage of the market
- Character of the distribution: changes in the market
- Continuity in the relationship

(b) **External**

- Customers
- Cultural differences between channel members, expectations of each other
- Competitors: how do they distribute? What influence do they have?
- Company objectives
- Communications

Marketing at Work

Three years ago Sony was a nonentity in the video games market; today it is the market leader. It has achieved this as follows.

(a)   Realising synergies between hardware and software (eg Sony Music Entertainment - SME).

(b)   Some luck, in that the *Sega* 32-bit machine was launched a month before the Playstation.

(c)   Paying attention to distribution, a crucial element of its approach to branding.

The company's technological expertise meant that producing an attractive machine was not the biggest problem. There were other hurdles.

(a)   *Branding.* Although the name Sony is one of the most widely recognised consumer brands in the world, the company did not have any street credibility in video games. The strategy the firm adopted was to underplay the Sony name and emphasise the PlayStation brand in TV advertising.

(b)   *Distribution.* At the same time, it decided not to sell the PlayStation at consumer electronics retailers. Sony's market research in Japan had shown it that consumers do not buy video games machines at consumer electronics retailers but at discount stores and specialist video games stores. The move was unprecedented and triggered protests from shops which normally carried Sony's consumer products.

Sony Computer Entertainment stood its ground, helped by the fact that it was separate from Sony. If the video games business had remained within Sony it would have been more difficult to keep the machines out of its affiliated retailers and so build SCE's image as a video games maker.

4   THE USE OF OVERSEAS AGENTS AND DISTRIBUTORS

4.1   In Chapter 7 the use of overseas agents was outlined as part of the discussion on modes of entry into overseas markets.

4.2   Here we analyse their use in more detail since, despite their limitations (particularly for the large scale exporter), they offer many advantages to the small exporter if selected and motivated carefully.

> **Key Concept**
>
> The **overseas sales agent** is a firm employed to bring about a sale of goods from his principal to a third party. An agent does not take title and is paid by way of commission.

4.3   In practice the terms 'agent' and 'distributor' are often used interchangeably. **Distributors** do take title, they therefore buy and sell goods and are rewarded by way of profits (or losses).

4.4   Agents may be either **commission agents** or **stocking agents**. Commission agents do not hold stocks. They sell from samples or catalogues. They pass on orders received and the producer delivers directly to the customer. Stocking agents do hold stocks, deliver to the customer but nevertheless are remunerated by commission.

4.5   Distributors buy and sell for profit. They hold stocks and are usually given a degree of exclusivity. They often perform after sales services and other duties on behalf of the producer.

4.6   The comments below are intended to refer to agents, although some of them are also relevant in the context of distributors.

Overseas agents

4.7 Vast numbers of firms use overseas agents since they offer the exporter considerable benefits.

- The exporter gains the benefits of the agent's market knowledge and contacts
- It may get rapid results
- The agent usually sells complementary goods
- Investment is minimal
- There is little or no political risk
- The producer gains exporting and market experience

4.8 However, the use of agents also involves various disadvantages.

(a) There are likely to be problems in gaining the agent's **full commitment** since the agent may be selling competing products.

(b) It may be unwilling to invest the necessary **time and effort** in developing the exporter's sales if it does not gain immediate results.

(c) Many agents are **not large enough** to serve an entire national market.

(d) If the exporter achieves significant market penetration, it may become more economic to open a **branch office** there. Agents should be used only if they are best suited to achieving the exporter's objectives.

How to find agents

4.9 Finding satisfactory agents may involve varying degrees of difficulty. The names and addresses of potential agents can be found fairly easily, however, since they are available from many sources including the following.

- DTI (OTS)
- Trade associations
- Agents' associations
- Chambers of Commerce
- Banks
- UK and foreign embassies
- Advertisements in the relevant press

4.10 The next step is to draw an identikit of the 'ideal' agent that would provide the required market coverage, product and market knowledge, stocking and servicing, reputation and so on.

4.11 At this stage, neither the exporter nor the chosen agent is committed to anything. Even so, both parties may wish to explore the details of a potential contract between them.

The agency agreement

4.12 The agreement is a commercially binding contract negotiated in great detail by the two parties. **Such contracts now come under EU law, and are more tightly regulated than before.** Agreements used to vary among firms and between markets. Even so, they normally include all or most of the following features.

(a) Identity of the parties

(b) The purpose of the agreement

(c)   The products that are subject to the agreement and any future changes

(d)   The agent's territory

(e)   Exclusivity

- for the agent
- for the producer

(f)   Duties of the principal, such as promotional support and training of the agent's staff

(g)   Duties of the agent such as minimum turnover required and after sales service

(h)   Agent's commission, dealing with issues such as the percentage rate, any variation across markets and dates payable

(i)   Duration and dates of contract period

(j)   Provision for termination before expiry of contract (for example breach of contract and bankruptcy)

(k)   Arbitration provisions for settling major disputes

(l)   Authentic text (that is evidence of which text is authentic if the agreement is written in two different languages)

(m) Specification of the country whose law governs the contract

4.13   The above list should be treated as a skeleton checklist. Most of the points mentioned should be considered in far greater detail before any specific agency agreement is finalised.

Selecting an agent

4.14   A visit to the market by one or more senior managers is an essential part of selecting an overseas agent. Moreover, it allows the company to have full discussions with agency management, sales staff and service personnel. A visit also enables the exporting company's manager to hold discussions with customers and potential customers so as to gain an impression of how they perceive the potential agent.

4.15   Many companies engaged in international marketing compile a list of selection criteria for use in an agency analysis. Here, each criterion is weighted, candidates are rated on each criterion and the agency with the highest sum of weighted scores becomes the chosen one.

4.16   Typical selection criteria include the following.

- Ownership of the agency
- Career histories of executives
- Past and present success with other firms and other products
- Geographical market coverage
- Types of outlet visited
- Frequency of visits per outlet
- Number and quality of salespersons
- Agent's market knowledge
- Agent's product knowledge
- Agent's marketing competence
- Servicing facilities offered by the agent
- Agent's enthusiasm for the product
- Financial status and business reputation

Motivating agents

4.17 A major problem for exporters is gaining the **motivation and full commitment** of agents and distributors. They usually carry the products of many firms and they are tempted to commit most of their resources to the products which provide the quickest returns.

4.18 There are various methods for motivating overseas agents, of which the following are the most important.

(a) **Regular and fairly frequent personal contact with the agent**. This enables both parties to communicate their needs, problems, philosophies, objectives and mutual responsibilities. Moreover, it allows good personal relationships to be developed among the two sets of personnel. Personal contact can be brought about in several ways.

　(i) Exporters' visits to the market

　(ii) Inviting agents to the exporter's headquarters

　(iii) Agents'/distributors' advisory councils. These can take the form of conferences, holiday breaks and conventions paid for by the producer. They are very successful as motivators and they allow agents to share experiences, complaints and successes

(b) Assuring agents of **long term business relationships** with the exporter

(c) Provision of attractive **commission** and other financial incentives

(d) Attractive credit terms

(e) Provision of cheap development loans

(f) Local advertising, promotions and sales support

(g) Training for the agent's personnel in marketing, finance, stock control

(h) Exclusivity

(i) Effective permanent communications - regular contact by telephone, telex, company newspaper etc, providing up to date product and company news

(j) Threats to discontinue dealings

4.19 **Controlling agents** and distributors can be difficult.

- Realistic expectations of performance are necessary
- Contracts should be clear and mutually understood
- Performance should be analysed in the light of changing environmental conditions
- Attention will need to be paid to the culture of the negotiating situation

5　INTERNATIONAL PHYSICAL DISTRIBUTION　　Specimen paper

5.1 The **cost** of physically transporting goods between countries has been estimated to be as high as 25% of the **landed price** of an item (more typically 15%), and thus represents a significant part of the cost structure of the item involved. But international logistics provide services to the customer in terms of availability, speed of delivery and convenience, which provide significant added value to the goods themselves. Logistics involves the following.

- Order processing
- Transportation
- Stock management
- Warehousing

- Customer services

5.2 In international marketing, the longer distances involved and the problem of dealing with alien cultures mean that the time between order and delivery can be considerable when compared to locally sourced supplies, and the cost significantly higher. A key concept in the management of international logistics is that of **customer service**. Customer service involves defining adequate levels of performance.

- Order cycle time
- Accuracy of order processing
- Delivered quality of goods

It is thus concerned with getting **the right goods to the right person, at the right time, at a reasonable cost.**

Transportation

5.3 **Transport between markets** is often the easier part of the problem, with good transport systems and infrastructure (roads, ports, airports, railheads etc) between nations. Within a particular country however both the transport systems and the infrastructure may vary in quality considerably. As we look to the lesser developed countries, the quality of communications, availability of transport facilities, and the physical infrastructure may pose significant problems.

Modes of transport

5.4 The international marketer has not only to take into account the cost of transport between countries, but also the cost within the country. Temporary storage and handling form a significant part of the overall cost of transport. Thus methods of transport which minimise them tend to be more competitive. The development of **container systems** for road, rail, sea and air has reduced the amount of labour involved in transferring goods between types of transport. The preference is therefore to use a mode of transport which, wherever possible, provides a '**through delivery**' to the customer.

Road transport

5.5 **Road transport** has a major advantage in its ability to deliver directly to the customer's premises. Since other forms of transport (rail, air, water) normally use road transport at the beginning and end of the journey, they require handling on the transfer from one form of transport to another. Per tonne-mile road transport is more expensive than rail due to the upper size limit on vehicle loads in most countries, and is generally slower on long journeys than air, even taking handling transfer into account.

Rail transport

5.6 Where physical conditions permit, the use of **rail transport** has significant advantages over its main inland rival, road, in that it can carry much larger quantities over long distances.

(a) Per tonne-mile, rail is far superior to road in cost over distances exceeding 1500 km. Over shorter distances the advantages of the load capacity are outweighed by the transfer costs on and off the rail network.

(b) The **Channel Tunnel** has transformed rail use, as it provides access to a pan-European rail network.

(c)   The newly privatised rail companies have also expended their freight operations and capacity has been increased at the ports. The volume of traffic in the UK has increased from 150,000 tonnes to 1.5m tonnes.

Water transport

5.7   For bulk transfer of items, water transport has similar advantages to rail, and is widely used where geography allows. Where a suitable network of rivers and canals exists, inland waterways can bring the load nearer to the customer. Again the problem of transfer and handling may make this approach expensive.

Air transport

5.8   Air transport is probably the most expensive of all four options for short journeys. The economics of air transport, together with handling costs, make air uncompetitive both in time and cost over short distances. The advantage of air transport lies in speed rather than cost, and this can be most effective over longer distances. The load carrying capacity and fuel costs do not make sense for bulky, low unit value loads, but where high value, small unit size loads are being considered, air transport may be viable.

5.9   In particular, where early speedy delivery to a market can give significant price advantages (for example early flowers and vegetables can command a 10-fold price advantage over maincrop in many cases) air transport costs can be justified because of the high unit value of the goods. Similarly where the customer is willing to pay a premium for speedy delivery, for example a spare part for a manufacturing plant, air transport can be justified. It is of course widely used for high value, low volume, perishable items such as pharmaceutical drugs.

5.10 The advantage of air transport, speed, can however be lost where delays at the airport in forwarding to the customer erode the time saving.

Location of warehouses

5.11 If a company is seeking to build or acquire a new warehouse, it must seek a general area and then a specific site in that area.

(a)   Selecting the area will depend on the market potential. To minimise costs and improve delivery service (and thus increase sales), the warehouse should be sited in the middle of an area with high market potential. The size of the warehouse (ie the amount invested) is also likely to influence the extent to which the market potential is exploited.

(b)   The choice of site within an area.

- The sites available
- Whether the customer will come to the supplier, or vice versa
- Local transport facilities (road, rail, etc)
- Future development in the area
- Whether a lease or a freehold is required
- Its geographical position within the market area

Logistics management

> **Key Concept**
>
> **Logistics management** includes **physical distribution** and **materials management**. It encompasses the inflow of raw materials and goods together with the outflow of finished products.

5.12   Logistics management has developed.

(a)   **Customer benefits** that can be incorporated into the overall product offering because of efficient logistics management

(b)   The **cost savings** that can be made when a logistics approach is undertaken

(c)   Trends in **industrial purchasing** that necessarily mean closer links between buyers and sellers, for example just-in-time purchasing and computerised purchasing.

5.13   Logistics managers organise inventories, warehouses, purchasing and packaging to produce an efficient and effective overall system. There are benefits to consumers of products that are produced by companies with good logistic management. There is less likelihood of goods being out of stocks, delivery should be efficient and overall service quality should be higher.

The logistics industry

5.14   Contracted-out distribution services require enormous trust, especially in the food business. Sensitive information must be exchanged between the retailer or manufacturer and the distribution company and responsibility for food safety and hygiene must be shared. However, contracting out offers great benefits in terms of **flexibility** and the elimination of the need for **costly capital investment**: hence the success of specialist distribution companies such as NFC, Christian Salvesen and Hays.

> **Action Programme 1**
>
> What factors have influenced the way goods and services are delivered by your own employer? Do you think the choices made are all the right ones?

5.15   Since the advent of the Single European Market, many firms have developed **Europe-wide distribution systems,** and are ceasing to use merely national bases for distribution. The Channel Tunnel has already had a significant impact: rail will become more cost effective for long journeys from the UK. This is partly dependent upon the speed with which the additional infrastructure of goods depots linking in to the Tunnel are put into place. Another factor affecting rail will be the increase in trade with Russia etc whose road network, by Western standards, is poor.

BPP PUBLISHING

Just-in-time (JIT)

> **Key Concept**
>
> **JIT** can be defined as follows: 'A technique for the organisation of work flows, to allow rapid, high quality, flexible production whilst minimising manufacturing waste and stock levels'.

5.16 JIT has two main aspects.

(a) **Just-in-time production,** which is a system which is driven by demand for finished products whereby each component on a production line is produced only when needed for the next stage of a job.

(b) **Just-in-time purchasing,** which involves matching the receipt of material closely with usage so that raw material inventory is reduced to near-zero levels.

5.17 JIT might not even be appropriate in all circumstances.

(a) It is not always easy to predict patterns of demand.

(b) JIT makes the organisation far more vulnerable to disruptions in the supply chain. In February 1997, it was reported that a fire at one of Toyota's suppliers 'not only paralysed Toyota's production system, but also hit production at Toyota's other hundreds of suppliers'.

(c) JIT, originated by Toyota, was 'designed at a time when all of Toyota's manufacturing was done within a 50 km radius of its headquarters. Wide geographical spread, however, makes this difficult.

5.18 Finally, JIT was introduced when customers could enforce it on suppliers. Even in Japan, suppliers to some industries are rebelling against the high administrative and transportation costs. JIT is a feature of markets where customers have high bargaining power. The customer is able to save on inventory costs, but some of these costs are inevitably passed on to suppliers. Suppliers had to build up stocks to ensure flexible delivery.

5.19 It has got to the stage where firms supplying the plastics industry in Japan, hit by the enormous costs of JIT, have collectively decided to reduce their JIT commitment.

- Only delivering once as opposed to three times a day
- Encouraging customers to take larger quantities

Marketing at Work

The Channel Tunnel has the potential to change distribution patterns in the UK and Europe.

(a) It permits swifter deliveries from the UK to France - British firms are delivering freshly made sandwiches to supermarkets in northern France, thanks to the Channel Tunnel.

(b) It might encourage users to switch to rail. In the meantime more lorries are using the drive on drive off service, which appears to be more speedy than waiting at some of the ports to board a ferry.

(c) Fire in the tunnel has brought some second thoughts, however, about safety issues and insurance risks.

Problems in physical distribution

5.20 Distribution costs are affected by the following factors.

(a) **Transport costs**: higher in overseas markets owing to distance and, in poorer countries, low quality physical infrastructure. A greater variety of transport modes are used.

(b) **Warehousing**: more sites might be needed in regional centres.

(c) **Stock levels** will be higher, as distances are longer, from the manufacturer.

(d) **Order processing** might include customs and VAT documentation.

(e) **Packaging**: some adjustment might be needed.

(f) **Failure costs** include lost sales through lack of available time. Customers in some markets (eg Germany) are very unforgiving if time and quality specifications are not met.

5.21 There are **trade-offs** between these items.

(a) Faster delivery (eg by air) might reduce the need to have 'buffer' stocks to satisfy customer orders.

(b) Stronger and more expensive packaging reduces breakage and theft.

(c) More warehouse space saves transport costs. Warehouses can be used to tailor the product precisely to the market.

(d) Investment in IT (eg electronic data interchange) can speed order processing, which might reduce delays, and make ordering easier for the customer, too.

5.22 Finally, distribution can be designed as part of the entire **customer service** package. Elements of customer service include the following.

(a) Speed, punctuality and flexibility of physical delivery.

(b) Speed, efficiency and accuracy of procedures for ordering, invoicing and claims.

(c) Condition of goods when delivered: physical condition and conformance to customer orders.

(d) Flexibility and convenience of order sizes.

(e) Personnel: sales visits, after sales support.

6 TRENDS IN DISTRIBUTION   Specimen paper

6.1 **Place** is one of the Ps of the marketing mix most liable to cause problems in overseas markets, simply because it reflects a lot about the society's economy and culture. Getting goods to the consumer so that they can be bought is not always easy.

6.2 **Retail practices** differ significantly from country to country.

(a) In Germany, opening hours for most shops are still very restricted (including compulsory closure at 6.30pm on weekdays, and limited Saturday opening). In the UK and many other countries, opening hours are more or less at the shopkeeper's discretion, with some restriction on Sunday opening for large stores. The German parliament has recently passed a bill which will partly deregulate opening hours.

(b) In the US (and the UK) retailing is characterised by large chains of supermarkets, which can be **accessed easily by car**. In Japan, there are fewer supermarkets and retailing is concentrated in smaller stores, often with exclusive distribution arrangements with manufacturers. The Japanese retail and distribution structure is held to be a structural impediment to trade.

BPP PUBLISHING

(c) In the UK, supermarkets' **own brands** are often of a comparable quality to branded goods, or consumers regard them as such. The 'own-brand' takeover has not really happened in the US, where their quality is believed to be lower.

(d) In **developing countries**, people may not have **refrigeration equipment** to buy in bulk, or the space. Rather than do a once-weekly visit (by car) to the supermarket to fill up the domestic freezer for a week, consumers may make frequent trips to the shop. In some countries, even cigarettes are sold **individually** - this would not happen in the UK. Many shops are small, with either a limited range or a wide range with a limited choice. There are few supermarket chains and they are family businesses.

6.3 Despite this, there is evidence that retailers are now expanding their operations overseas.

Marketing at Work

(a) Marks and Spencer store in Paris is apparently profitable, both for selling 'English' food, and also for its clothes which do not require trips to expensive boutiques. The store chain has now got over twenty shops in France, has opened its first store in Germany and has announced a £2 billion globalisation plan to become the world's first truly global retailer. In April 2000 it announced expansion into Croatia.

(b) Boots the Chemist, having sold its pharmaceutical manufacturing arm, is expanding its stores rapidly, targeting a number of European countries and former eastern bloc countries. It is now challenging a tradition where European pharmacies are run by independents.

(c) Some of the supermarket chains have purchased retailing subsidiaries.

- For their existing distribution system
- As a strategic investment assuming that liberalisation of retailing laws will continue

It has not always been easy to turn these to profit.

6.4 Internationalised retailing reflects increasing urbanisation, and the ability to communicate to strategically equivalent market segments in different countries. Benetton and Body Shop have followed this approach. In the UK, Aldi and Netto have introduced low cost shopping formats from Denmark and Germany.

6.5 Potential problems with retailing overseas.

(a) 'Country of origin' associations

(b) Cultural differences (apparently Marks and Spencer's French customers were flummoxed by what to do with a Christmas pudding)

(c) An inability to exploit economies of scale if the firm only has a few shops

(d) Manufacturer power in markets where there is a large number of retailers

(e) Local competitors who are imitating Western formats. This is beginning to happen in the Far East. Huge shopping malls are being constructed in Bangkok, for example

6.6 A checklist covering retailing differences between countries is offered below.

- Concentration of retail power
- Site availability, selection and location
- Permissible/feasible outlet size
- Product offering
- Technology (eg EPOS vs handwritten invoices)
- Communications with customers (retailer's or manufacturer's responsibility)

6.7 Activities like customer acquisition and customer service are already encountering threats from electronic commerce. Even more profound challenges are emerging, however, when the whole **value chain** is undermined through the introduction of entirely new delivery systems.

Disintermediation

6.8 This term refers to the process of 'removing the **middleman**', giving the consumer **direct access** to information that would otherwise require an intermediary, such as a salesperson or a retail channel. The new technology of the **Internet and e-commerce** gives consumers the power to find product information directly, either removing the need for the salesperson altogether, or at least changing the relationship between buyer and seller.

6.9 **Customers can increasingly collect information for themselves** by searching the world wide web. This can be advantageous for new entrants into the competitive marketplace, though it may also be a liability if their offerings are unsatisfactory. It is particularly important for new entrants to ensure that their first customers are pleased with what they get, so that positive rumours begin to spread. The position is further complicated by the fact that new entrants inevitably have a very small market share, so opinions about their product reliability can be shaped through the feedback from a very small number of customers (bearing in mind, too, that it is the dissatisfied customers who are more likely to make a noise).

Marketing at Work

The potential of the Internet to serve as a channel for products and services is a real challenge for many brand-name 'bricks and mortar' companies. Traditional bookshops find themselves challenged by companies such as Amazon or BOL. Stockbroking firms are seeing a tidal wave of on-line 'home investors' using vehicles such as Charles Schwab's on-line dealing service. These comparatively young internet ventures have a culture of risk-taking that threatens to leave traditional companies behind. As a result, more and more companies are looking for Internet distribution expertise. For example, The New York Times invested $15 million is TheStreet.com, a financial news service.

6.10 The primary advantage of Internet retailing rests on the fact that Internet retailers do not usually hold **stocks**. For example, a company called Valley Media Inc fulfils CD orders for Amazon in the US. When a customer order comes in, the e-tailer (Amazon) takes the order and the **distributor** (Valley Media) fills it. Distributors such as Valley Media are themselves a new kind of middleman.

6.11 **On-line travel** sites are another manifestation of disintermediation. Internet based search agents can now locate flights and fares and book them on-line. Eventually, the Internet service may even generate the tickets themselves. Many customers 'surf' these sites without actually making a booking. (Nevertheless, airlines have been moved to lower the fees that they pay to travel agencies, in part because customers can now make purchases without using local agents.) Travellers often do their price research on-line and then call an agent to make their purchase. This has been termed 'window-shop-on-line, buy-the-old-fashioned-way'.

6.12 In an article in *The Financial Times* (Value Chain: Exposed links in the established chain', 14 October 1998), Peter Martin discusses the specific case of **electricity supply**. Until recently, electricity was generated, transmitted and distributed by vertically integrated monopolies. Changes in regulation have meant that these monopolies are now split into separate generation, transmission and distribution companies. The next change - which, significantly, could not have occurred without the possibilities implied through electronic commerce - is the further split between distribution and supply. This means that one company may own the cables over which electricity travels, whilst another supplies the electricity to customers, having bought it in the first place from the generators.

6.13 As Martin points out, in this sort of operation, 'the **traditional strengths** of an electricity utility - reliability, technological depth, physical presence - may be **less important than skill in managing customer relationships and spot-marketing trading.**'

6.14 The electricity market is only one example of a development which is **crucially dependent on the presence of highly sophisticated electronic communication and data-management systems,** but what it also shows is the degree to which traditional value chains are being modified or even turned upside down. What could happen, in the final analysis, is that the competitive advantage will ultimately migrate to companies that have particularly strong customer relationships. Already, trusted retailers like Tesco, Marks & Spencer and Sainsbury in the UK are extending their brands into other industries, like energy supply or financial services.

6.15 Another issue concerns the degree to which customers are prepared to **rely on a single supplier** (albeit a trusted one) for a range of apparently unrelated products and services. Many are **reluctant** to do so in case it makes them excessively **dependent**. Others are reluctant because of some vague unease about the consequences of **quasi-monopolistic power.** With this in mind, John Hagel of McKinsey envisages the creation of 'infomediaries', businesses that make money by 'capturing customer information and developing detailed profiles of individual customers for use by selected third-party vendors.' This emphasises yet again how current value chains are jeopardised through electronic commerce and its market consequences.

6.16 These developments reflect the growing importance of **digital information.** Increasing the number of people using it costs nothing, but adds exponentially to its value: this is why crucial pieces of Internet software, like the Netscape browser, have been provided free of charge.

7 DOCUMENTS USED IN FOREIGN TRADE

7.1 There are many documents which are used for one purpose or another in foreign trade. Paperwork is a crucial (and costly) part of exporting. They can be categorised under the following general headings.

(a) **Transport documents.** A transport document is a document that indicates loading on board or dispatch or taking in charge. Its functions are to provide evidence of a contract of carriage, evidence of receipt of the goods (by the carrier) and, in some cases, they are also documents of title, giving the holder of the documents title to the possession of the goods.

(b) **Commercial documents:** the most important of these is the invoice. Some types of product also required export licences, such as antiques, works of art and military equipment.

(c) **Insurance documents.**

(d) **Official documents** required by government regulations.

(e) **Financial documents,** eg the bill of exchange or the promissory note.

Marketing at Work

According to a survey by DHL, 6 out of 10 Western companies experience difficulties with customs red tape, which hampers trade with Central and Eastern Europe. Customs officials at one border insisted on returning a consignment because the computer printout of the shipment details was on the wrong coloured paper, whilst another exporter was asked to provide the Latin name for a consignment of potatoes despite the fact that the Mediterranean growers had no idea themselves.

Despite this, there have been some improvements. Forty two per cent of the companies interviewed said they felt the customs officials in these countries 'at least partially realise what businesses are trying to achieve'

Financial Times, 1999.

Transport documents

Bill of lading

> ## Key Concept
> A maritime or marine **bill of lading** is a transport document for goods shipped by sea.

7.2 In spite of the considerable growth of container transport, the marine bill of lading is still the most common transport document for exporting to Africa, Asia and the Middle East (particularly when payment by the overseas buyer for the goods is arranged through the banking system).

7.3 A bill of lading has three separate functions.

(a) It is evidence of a contract of carriage between the shipping company and either the exporter or the foreign buyer, to transport the goods by sea (as detailed in the bill of lading).

(b) It is a receipt for the goods taken on board ship, and provides some details about the condition of goods received.

(c) A bill of lading, once signed by the exporter, is also a document of title, which means that the holder of the bill of lading has the right to possess the goods. This is very important for the payment arrangements.

Indeed the goods will only be released by the shipping company at the port of destination to someone (the buyer's representative) who presents a signed original of the bill of lading.

Air waybill (also called an air consignment note or air freight note)

7.4 An air waybill is a waybill for goods transported by air. Like a sea waybill, it is a contract of carriage and a receipt by the airline for goods received into custody, and it is not a document of title. The airline will hand the goods to the consignee at the airport of destination without the consignee having to present an original copy of the waybill.

Road consignment note or truck receipt

7.5 A truck receipt or a road consignment note is a receipt issued by a carrier for goods that are to be transported by road. The note also specifies the name and address of the sender and the consignee, the place of delivery and the place and date of taking in charge by the carrier. The note acts as both a receipt and a delivery note. A CMR (**Convention Merchandises Routiers**) consignment note is an internationally approved transport document for the carriage of goods by road through European countries that are party to the CMR. A road consignment note, even a CMR note, is non-negotiable and so is not a document of title. The goods will be delivered to the consignee named in the note at the place of delivery given in the note.

Combined transport bill of lading

7.6 Increasingly nowadays, with the widespread use of containerised transport, goods are transported from a place of 'taking in charge' to a place of 'delivery' in the same container(s), but on different modes of transport. For example, a container lorry might take a container of goods by road to a seaport where the unopened container will be loaded onto a ship. It will then be shipped to a port of destination, unloaded, transferred to another lorry, and taken by road, still unopened, to a place of delivery inland.

7.7 The goods, although carried by two or more modes of transport, are shipped under a single contract of carriage and a carrier or freight forwarder will be responsible for the goods over the entire route. A single bill of lading, known as a combined transport bill of lading will be issued by the freight forwarder to cover the entire route from the place of taking in charge to the place of delivery.

7.8 A FIATA Combined Transport Bill of Lading, approved by the International Chamber of Commerce, is evidence that a freight forwarder is acting as a principal, ie accepting carrier responsibility for performance of the entire contract of carriage and responsibility for loss or damage wherever it may occur.

Standardisation of documents

7.9 In the UK, the government made some efforts to simplify the documentation in international trade by standardising the layout of documents such as bills of lading, waybills and invoice. This is one of the continuing tasks of SITPRO (The Simplification of International Trade Procedures Board), established in 1971.

Commercial documents

7.10 The main commercial documents are invoices. There are four main types of invoice.

(a) A **pro-forma invoice**. This is a price **quotation** by an exporter to a potential overseas buyer. There has been no agreement to buy and sell goods at this stage. A pro-forma invoice has several uses.

    (i)   The overseas buyer might need to present a pro-forma invoice to the government authorities in his country in order to obtain an import licence or the foreign exchange to pay for the goods.

    (ii)   It serves as a price quotation, and might include the terms of sale. If the buyer accepts the quotation, there is a firm contract of sale.

    (iii)   It can be used to tender for an export contract.

    (iv)   It is used when the exporter requires cash with order.

(b) A **commercial invoice**. This is the demand for payment for goods sold.

- Description of goods, quantity, unit price and total sales price
- The terms of delivery (eg CIF Sydney Container Terminal)
- The terms of payment (eg 60 days after date of invoice)

The commercial invoice should be capable of easy reconciliation with the transport documentation.

(c) A **certified invoice** is a commercial invoice which also includes a statement by the exporter about the condition of the goods sent, or their country of origin. Some form of statement might be provided at the request of the buyer or for the benefit of **customs authorities** of the buyer's country.

(d) A **consular invoice** is a commercial invoice which is prepared on a form printed in the exporter's country by the consulate of the buyer's country. It is then stamped by the consulate. The purpose of a consular invoice is to help the government of the buyer's country control imports into the country (eg to prevent 'dumping' of goods). A consular invoice will be used for exports to any country which requires their use.

(e) **Other commercial documents** cover weight, quality and contents (for customs).

Insurance documents

7.11 There are three basic types of insurance document.

(a) A **letter of insurance** or **cover note**. This is issued by an insurance broker to provide notice that steps are being taken to issue an insurance policy or certificate.

(b) A **certificate of insurance** shows the value and details of the shipment, and the risks covered (in an abbreviated form). It is signed by the exporter and the insurance company. Only a certificate of insurance is required when the insurance policy of the exporting company provides 'open cover' for the whole of its export trade.

When an exporter takes out open cover with Lloyd's or an insurance company for the whole of its export trade, a certificate of insurance for each individual shipment will be prepared by the exporter on a certificate provided (and pre-signed) by the insurance company.

In the UK and many other countries, an insured person cannot take legal action against an insurer where the only evidence of a contract of insurance is a certificate of insurance. The legal proof of a contract is provided by the insurance policy itself.

(c) An **insurance policy**. The insurance policy gives full details of the risks covered, and it is evidence of a contract of insurance. A policy which provides open cover will not specify the details of any particular shipment.

Documents required by government departments or agencies

7.12 Some documents in international trade are provided to satisfy the legal or procedural requirements of the government of the country of export or import or transit. The following list gives examples and is not comprehensive.

(a) A **certificate of origin** might be required by the importing country's authorities as evidence of the country from which the goods originated. This may be necessary, for example, if an exporter wishes to claim a preferential level of import duty.

(b) A **certificate of health, quality or inspection** might also be required by the importing country's authorities depending upon the type of product. For example, agricultural and animal products may require a certificate of compliance with health regulations. Horticultural products exported from Kenya require phytosanitary certificates.

Marketing at Work

Phytosanitary certificates are important for horticultural products. Horticulture in Kenya is the third largest foreign exchange earner after tea and tourism. According to the Kenya Flower Council it exported $74 million worth of flowers last year. The main markets are the Netherlands, the UK and Germany.

(c) A **blacklist certificate** provides evidence that the goods did not originate in (and were not transported through) a blacklisted country - ie a country with which the importing country has stopped normal trading relations.

(d) Exports to countries in the EU are subject to EU regulations. The EU is founded on the 'free circulation' of goods between member countries. When goods are carried abroad outside countries governed by EU regulations (and the CT system), but between member countries of the Customs Convention, customs formalities at border posts will be reduced if the goods are transported in customs-approved sealed containers. This is known as the TIR Carnet system. TIR Carnets are issued in the UK by the Road Haulage Association and the Freight Transport Association.

Assistance in compiling documentation

7.13 The completion of the relevant forms can be carried out 'in-house' by the exporter. The purchase of the necessary expertise is justified where frequent export activity is involved. However organisations exporting infrequently, or who are too small to justify permanent export staff, can call on several forms of assistance.

(a) The **export management company** will undertake the total management of export activities, including representation, and ensure that documentation and transport are arranged.

(a) The **freight forwarder** arranges transport to the foreign customer and will review and prepare the necessary documentation for a fee. The additional advantage of freight for-warding agents is that they often act a 'transport brokers' consolidating loads for transport to various destinations, and thereby able to obtain transport at very competitive costs.

(c) The **customs broker** performs a similar service to the freight forwarder, but on the import side of the transaction, arranging for collection, transport, customs clearance and payment.

For detailed requirements as to the documentation required in each country, reference to the relevant embassy or consulate is required. Alternatively, standard reference books include the exporter's encyclopaedia published by Dunn and Bradstreet.

Action Programme 2

Find out from appropriate sources (such as your company's export department) about the essential documentation for various types of product going to a selection of one or two countries.

(Hint: the SITPRO website (www.sitpro.org.uk) has 'country factsheets' which show documentation requirements for selected countries).

8 FINANCING GOODS IN DISTRIBUTION

8.1 When an exporter sells goods to an overseas buyer, and the buyer is allowed a period of credit before having to pay for the goods, the exporter might suffer a **cash shortage**. This is because the exporter has paid out money to make and deliver the goods, but has not yet received anything in return. Export finance is a term used to describe the various ways in which an exporter can obtain cash from a financial institution **in advance of payment by the importer.**

8.2 Banks, in particular, have been inventive in devising approaches to trade finance for exporters. One may distinguish between short and medium term finance and the more common forms of each are described below.

Short term finance

8.3 There are four general types of short term finance.

- Overdrafts
- Advances against collections
- Negotiation or purchase of bills of exchange
- Export factoring and invoice discounting

Overdrafts

8.4 Working capital finance provided by means of an overdraft might be one of the following.

(a) **Sterling overdraft.** The bank will be more favourably disposed towards granting a sterling overdraft facility if the exporter has an export credit insurance policy, to reduce the risk of losses through non-payment by foreign buyers.

(b) **Foreign currency overdraft.** The customer expects to earn foreign currency income to pay off the overdraft.

Advances against collections

8.5 Where the exporter asks his bank to collect payments on his behalf, the bank might be prepared to make an advance to the exporter against the collection.

8.6 This is similar to a bank advancing you money even if a cheque you have paid into your account has not cleared. The bank might only agree to make such advances where the foreign buyer is thought to be reliable (eg a regular customer of the exporter). The bank might therefore try to obtain information (from another bank) about the creditworthiness of the foreign buyer, or insist on insurance.

8.7 Advances against collections might be the most appropriate method of export finance where the bank is asked to make a collection of a bill or cheque etc payable in sterling and **in the UK.** When a bill or cheque is payable **abroad** in a **foreign currency,** 'negotiation' (see below) would be more appropriate.

Negotiation or purchase of bills or cheques by a bank

8.8 In trade finance and banking, 'negotiation' is a special term. In effect, it means that if somebody writes you a cheque, you could effectively sell it to someone else, who could claim the sum or pay it into his account. Bills of exchange and some cheques can be negotiated. (You can no longer negotiate most **personal** cheques.)

8.9 The negotiation of bills of exchange and cheques might be arranged for individual items, but an exporter selling regularly abroad might be able to arrange a negotiation line of credit (**negotiating facility**), with a revolving limit. (In other words, the bank will negotiate all the exporter's bills, up to a maximum credit at any given time.)

8.10   The advantages of a negotiating facility are as follows.

(a)   The exporter receives immediate credit that improves his cash position, and does not have to wait for the cheques to be cleared or a collection to be made and then the funds remitted from abroad.

(b)   The bank's charges for negotiation will be reasonably low, because the bank can handle the negotiated cheques or bills on a 'bulk' basis.

8.11   The disadvantages of a negotiation facility are as follows.

(a)   The bank has right of recourse against the exporter.

(b)   The exporter will not know whether the foreign buyer has paid or not, except when non-payment becomes apparent if the bank takes recourse action.

(c)   Occasionally, obtaining a negotiation facility from the bank might restrict an exporter's capacity to borrow in other ways.

(d)   Where the exporter invoices overseas customers for large amounts, an export factoring service might be a more suitable alternative method of obtaining finance.

Export factoring and invoice discounting

8.12   In the context of obtaining working capital to finance exports, 'factoring' means selling trade debts for immediate cash to an 'export factor' who charges commission. Most factors offer three basic services.

8.13   The services provided by an export factor are as follows.

(a)   An accounting, credit-checking and debt collection service. A commission of about 1-2.25% or even 3% of turnover is charged for this service although in certain circumstances the factoring commission can be as low as 0.5%.

(b)   **Credit insurance** against bad debts, for 'approved' debts.

(c)   **Finance.** The provision of immediate cash against invoices, up to 75-85% of the face value of the invoices and, because of the credit insurance, a guarantee of payment of the remainder within an agreed period of time. Advances may be in sterling or a foreign currency.

(d)   **Exchange risks** can also be covered by an export factor. The factor can offer cover against exchange rate fluctuations, where sales are invoiced in a foreign currency, by itself taking out forward cover or foreign currency borrowings. (If a factor cannot cover the client's exchange risks in full, the client would need to arrange forward exchange contracts himself for the amounts not covered by the factor).

8.14   An export factoring service is particularly suited to a business in the following situation.

•   Which conducts its export trade on open account terms
•   Has cash-flow problems

Typically the exporter will sell consumer goods on short-term credit and open-account terms.

8.15   The usual benefits of export factoring are listed below.

(a) Bad debt losses are eliminated for those debts which are factored.

(b) The services of credit agencies, credit reports etc are not required.

(c) Salary costs are reduced because sales ledger bookkeeping etc will be done by the factor.

(d) Overhead costs of the client's sales ledger department (eg accommodation costs) might be saved.

(e) Foreign exchange risks may be eliminated.

(f) Specialised personnel are more efficient, leading to a lower credit period, lower bad debts, etc.

(g) There is more time for top management to concentrate on production and sales.

(h) There is more opportunity for taking up cash discounts from suppliers.

(i) Cash flow is more secure.

8.16 Thus factoring can result in savings to management as well as providing an extra source of finance if bank overdraft facilities are already fully extended. It is particularly well-suited to exporters who sell on open account, or who wish to expand their volume of trade by selling more on open account.

8.17 **Invoice discounting** is similar to factoring except that only the **financing service** is used; copies of invoices sent to customers are discounted with a financial institution (just like bills receivable). The trading company still collects the debts as agent for the financial institution and remits the cash on receipt. Whereas factoring firms prefer to deal with large organisations with a high turnover, invoice discounting is offered as a service to smaller businesses.

Medium term finance

8.18 The three most important forms of medium term export finance are as follows.

- Finance related to credit insurers
- Forfaiting
- Leasing

Credit insurers

8.19 Export-credit insurance in respect of business on terms of **two years** or more is provided in the UK by the **Export Credit Guarantee Department** (ECGD).

> **Key Concept**
> The **Export Credit Guarantee Department** provides guarantees to banks on behalf of exporters.

8.20 Cover for short-term business (up to 180 days or, subject to individual discussion, up to two years) is provided by private-sector insurers, mostly notably NCM Credit Insurance Ltd, a UK subsidiary of Nederlandsche Credietverzekering Maatschappij. For short, we shall refer to NCM Credit Insurance Ltd as NCM.

8.21 Export finance linked with credit insurance is offered under different guises by a number of banks in the UK.

(a) Smaller exports schemes (for firms whose export turnover is less than about £1m pa).

(b) Finance for exports schemes (for firms whose export turnover is above about £1m pa).

Smaller export schemes

8.22 Many small businesses do not credit-insure because they feel, rightly or wrongly, that there is too much paperwork or too small a volume of exports to justify it. Without credit insurance, however, many companies find it difficult to raise sufficient finance for their exports as they cannot provide adequate security for ordinary bank loans or overdrafts.

8.23 NCM covers only 90 or 95% of the risk. Typically, the bank has its own credit insurance cover (which is actually managed for the bank by a policy-management company). The bank is to take the residential risk of 5 or 10%. The bank therefore checks in advance the creditworthiness of the overseas buyer, and the ability of the exporter to meet the contract terms. The bank gives up right of recourse to the exporter, subject to the exporter complying with its commercial obligations. This lending can therefore be made in addition to any **other** facilities the exporter enjoys with the bank.

8.24 Generally the conditions for finance for exports schemes are similar to those for the smaller export schemes, just described, except as follows.

(a) Finance for exports schemes are for firms (with or without their own credit-insurance cover) with an export volume of about £1m or over.

(b) Finance is provided for up to 90% (not 100%) of invoice value.

8.25 The Export Credits Guarantee Department (ECGD) services help UK firms in the following main ways.

(a) ECGD issues **guarantees to banks.** Against the strength of this security, the bank provides, usually at favourable interest rates, finance to support the export contract. The facility will be a buyer credit or a supplier credit, depending on whether it is the exporter or the importer who borrows from the bank.

    (i) With a **buyer credit,** the buyer draws a loan from the bank in the UK, and the proceeds go direct to the exporter. ECGD guarantees to the bank repayment of the principal and interest.

    (ii) With a **supplier credit,** in contrast, it is the UK exporter who borrows from a bank (in order to be able to sell on deferred-payment terms).

(b) ECGD offers Specific Guarantees to exporters who want to finance sales either out of their own funds or by way of ordinary borrowing.

(c) ECGD supports the issue of third-party guarantees/bonds by indemnifying the bondgiver.

Forfaiting

8.26 Forfaiting is a method of providing finance. Banks buy (and sell) medium term **promissory notes** (normally about five years). **Promissory notes** (like IOUs) are similar to bills of exchange, the main difference being that whereas bills of exchange are requests for payment issued by the **seller** (exporter), promissory notes are written **promises of future payment,** issued by the **buyer.** The system is normally used for export sales involving capital goods (machinery etc) where payment will be made over a number of years. Forfaiting deals average about £1.5 million in value (although the currencies used most often are US dollars, Swiss francs and Deutschemarks).

8.27 Forfaiting works as follows.

(a) An exporter of capital goods finds an overseas buyer who wants medium-term credit to finance the purchase. The buyer must be willing to do the following.

- To pay some of the cost (perhaps 15%) at once
- To pay the balance in regular instalments normally for the next five years

Regular instalments are normally a condition of forfait finance.

(b) The buyer will issue a series of promissory notes with a final maturity date about five years ahead but providing for regular payments over this time. Sometimes these will be guaranteed.

(c) The bank will buy the promissory notes, at a discount and collect the finance.

8.28 By these following arrangements.

- The forfaiting bank forfeits its right of recourse to the exporter
- The buyer obtains credit for up to five or so years
- The exporter obtains immediate cash from the discounted notes or bills
- The forfaiter is repaid gradually as the notes or bills mature

8.29 The advantages of forfaiting to an exporter are as follows.

(a) Cash is received at once from the forfaiter bank.

(b) There is no risk of bad debts or exchange rate fluctuations (since these are borne by the forfaiter bank).

(c) Borrowing capacity is increased (because it has cash in the bank and thus lower debts).

(d) There is no need to take out export credit insurance.

(e) The rate of interest is known from the start.

8.30 Major disadvantages of forfaiting.

(a) Cost (as the discount rate on promissory notes, that have no right of recourse against the buyer, can be high)

(b) The exporter may be unable to find a bank willing to act as a forfaiter, particularly if the buyer has a low credit rating or its government is viewed as likely to restrict overseas payments.

Leasing

8.31 Lease finance can be made available to the foreign buyer, and is used for large items such as aircraft.

(a) For major transactions, lease finance from the **exporter's** country, into the lessee's country ('cross border' leasing) can be arranged. The finance will be in the exporter's currency.

(b) For lower value transactions, firms can arrange the leasing in the **buyer's** own country, through an international contact of a leasing company in the exporter's country, in the lessee's currency.

BPP PUBLISHING

8.32 The type of lease involved in such an arrangement will be a finance lease (as opposed to an operating lease). **Finance leases** are leases in which the lessor (leasing company) attempts to recover the full capital outlay of the asset, together with a satisfactory return, from a single lessee. The lease period will therefore cover most of the useful life of the asset, and the lessee is responsible for maintenance and repairs. The lease cannot be cancelled.

8.33 The distinguishing feature of a finance lease agreement is that one company (the lessee) obtains the use of an asset for a period, whereas the legal ownership of the asset remains with the lessor. (A lease is therefore distinct from a hire purchase agreement.)

8.34 What are the attractions of finance leases to the supplier of the equipment (the exporter), the lessee (the buyer) and the lessor (the finance company)?

 (a) The supplier of the equipment is paid in full **at the beginning**.

 (b) The lessor invests finance by purchasing assets from suppliers and makes a return out of the lease payments from the lessee.

 (c) Leasing might therefore be attractive to the lessee:

 (i) if the lessee does not have enough cash to pay for the asset, and so has to rent it in one way or another if he is to have use of the asset at all; or

 (ii) if leasing is cheaper than outright purchase. One way that a company can purchase an asset is to obtain a loan to pay for it. The cost of payments under the loan might exceed the cost of the lease.

Chapter Roundup

- The system of **distribution** can affect mode of entry, depending on the discrepancy of assortment.

- Firms can choose **exclusive**, **selective** or **intensive** distribution. Distribution is a big help in obtaining market share.

- **Supply chain management** is about optimising the activities that get goods from producer to consumer.

- Many firms employ **agents** who have local market knowledge. The agent's needs have to be taken into account, but agents have to look after other manufacturers' products.

- **Retailing infrastructures** and channel conditions differ from country to country, suggesting that the power of the manufacturer to dictate how products are displayed or sold also differs.

- Modern **logistical approaches** enable companies to respond to customers' demands for rapid just-in-time delivery. Distribution can be contracted out to specialist firms.

- **E-commerce** provides a potential new distribution channel that is direct, fast and inexpensive

- **Transport methods** include road, rail, water and air. Each has different costs and benefits for distances covered and bulk carried.

- International trade is characterised by extensive **documentation**.

- A number of methods of **trade finance** exist. These are important in securing the flow of goods and facilitate international trade.

Quick Quiz

1 Why is distribution of strategic importance? (see para 2.1)
2 What is the difference between the 'traditional' model of the supply chain and the 'integrated supply chain'? (2.10, 2.11)
3 What services does a good trading channel provide? (3.1)
4 Why would an fmcg exporter expect to deal almost directly with a large retailer in a foreign country, but not consider dealing direct with the public? (3.2 - 3.5)
5 How does the trading culture of a country affect the choice of intermediary used by an exporter? (3.10 - 3.12)
6 What factors would govern a choice of distribution channel? (3.15)
7 How can e-commerce affect distribution channels? (3.26)
8 Why do firms use overseas agents? (4.7)
9 How would you select an agent? (4.16)
10 What are the major duties to be carried out in international logistics management? (5.1, 5.2,)
11 Under what circumstances would you consider using air transport to deliver wine to another country, and what would be your normal option? (5.8)
12 Describe just-in-time. (5.16)
13 What might be the marketing impact of distribution in terms of customer service? (5.22)
14 How can retailing practices differ from country to country? (6.2)
15 What types of document are used in overseas trade? (7.1)

Now try illustrative question 12 at the end of the Study Text

13 International Marketing of Services

Chapter Topic List	Syllabus Reference
1　Setting the scene	-
2　Services	3,6, 3.7
3　The extended marketing mix for services	3,6, 3.7, 3.9
4　The importance of people	3.7
5　Service quality	3,6, 3.7
6　Relationship marketing and CRM	3,8

Learning Outcomes

After completing this chapter you will have an appreciation of:

- the extended marketing mix for services

- the role of the relationship marketing approach in underpinning the more traditional marketing mix

Key Concepts Introduced

- Services
- Physical evidence

- Service quality
- Relationship marketing

Examples of Marketing at Work

- Quality and customer care in stockbroking

- The Range Rover launch

- Customer relationship management software

1 SETTING THE SCENE

1.1 Each firm has its own unique formula of people, processes and problems to deal with, and arriving at a marketing mix for services is, in that sense, little different from the process involved for conventional goods.

1.2 Deploying the marketing mix in services is a rather difficult task.

(a) **Poor service quality** (eg lack of punctuality of flights, staff rudeness, a bank's incompetence) in one case is likely to lead to widespread distrust of everything the organisation does.

(b) **If the service is intangible** offering a complicated future benefit, or is consumed 'on the spot', then attracting customers means promoting an attractive image and ensuring that the service lives up to its reputation.

(c) **Pricing** of services is often complicated, especially if large numbers of people are involved in providing the service.

(d) **Human resources management,** not just customer care, is a key ingredient in the services marketing mix, as so many services are produced and consumed in a specific social context. The human element cannot be designed out of a service.

1.3 It has, however, been pointed out that in the marketing of services, four Ps do not adequately describe the importance of mix elements. It has been suggested that an extra three, and perhaps four, Ps should be added to the mix for services.

- Personal selling
- Place of availability
- People and customer service
- Physical evidence

1.4 We will look at each of these after discussing the key characteristics of services and their marketing implications.

1.5 We conclude the chapter with some notes on relationship marketing, and how it provides an alternative to the traditional mix.

2 SERVICES

> **Key Concept**
> **Services** are distinguished from products mainly because they are generally produced at the same time as they are consumed, and cannot be stored or taken away. An enhanced marketing mix needs to be deployed.

The rise of the service economy

2.1 There are a number of reasons why services are more important today than they were in the past. These include the following.

(a) **The growth of service sectors in advanced industrial societies**

In terms of employment, more people now work in the service sector than in all other sectors of the economy. 'Invisible' service earnings from abroad are of increasing significance for Britain's balance of trade. According to recent economic statistics the service sector represents at least two thirds of the global economy.

(b) **Increasingly market-oriented trade within service-providing organisations** (eg 'internal markets', 'market testing' and so on).

The extension of the service sector has made a large number of service providers much more marketing conscious.

2.2 The service sector extends across both the private and public domain. Some make a profit, while others are not-for-profit. Broad distinctions could be made as follows.

	Profit making	*Non-profit-making*
Private sector	• Travel • Law • Finance • Commerce • Insurance • Entertainment • Management	• Arts • Charities • Religious organisations
Public sector	Some areas of public sector provision are increasingly looking to make profits, such as refuse collection by local councils.	• Legal • Communications • Medical • Transport • Educational • Information/advice • Military • Employment

Services: some definitions

2.3 The definitions offered of services are as follows.

'... those separately identifiable but intangible activities that provide want-satisfaction, and that are not, of necessity, tied to, or inextricable from, the sale of a product or another service. To produce a service may or may not require the use of tangible goods or assets. However, where such use is required, there is no transfer of title (permanent ownership) to these tangible goods.'(Donald Cowell, *The Marketing of Services*)

'... any activity of benefit that one party can offer to another that is essentially intangible and does not result in the ownership of anything. Its production may or may not be tied to a physical product.' (P Kotler, *Social Marketing*)

2.4 Services marketing differs from the marketing of other goods in a number of crucial ways. While it is difficult to make a judgement which encompasses the wide variety of service types and situations, there are indeed many service organisations which are highly **market oriented** (for instance, in retailing, transport hire, cleaning and hotel groups) but there are many which remain relatively unaffected by marketing ideas and practices. Marketing ideas are likely to become much more important as **competition** within the service sector intensifies.

Marketing characteristics of services

2.5 **Characteristics** of services which make them distinctive from the marketing of goods have been proposed. There are five major differences.

- **Intangibility**
- **Inseparability**
- **Heterogeneity**
- **Perishability**
- **Ownership**

Intangibility

2.6 **'Intangibility'** refers to the lack of substance which is involved with service delivery. Unlike a good, there is no substantial material of or physical aspects to a service: no taste, feel, visible presence and so on. Clearly this creates difficulties and can inhibit the propensity to consume a service, since customers are not sure what they have.

> 'Ultimately the customer may have no prior experience of a service in which he or she is interested, nor any conception of how it would satisfy the requirements of the purchase context for which it was intended.'
> (Morden, *The Marketing of Services*)

2.7 Shostack has proposed that products/services are combinations of elements which are tangible or intangible. There can be depicted on a diagram called 'The service continuum.'

2.8 For each service the number, complexity and balance of the various elements involved will vary a great deal. What is experienced at the end of the process when the service is delivered remains insubstantial. Although many parts of the process (the machines, buildings and staff of an airline, for instance), are very substantial, the actual service itself can only be experienced, not owned.

2.9 Marketers and consumers need to try to overcome this problem and typically seek to do so in a number of different ways. The consumer needs information to avoid making a mistake. The marketer wishes to make the choice of the product 'safer' and make the consumer feel more comfortable.

The Service Continuum

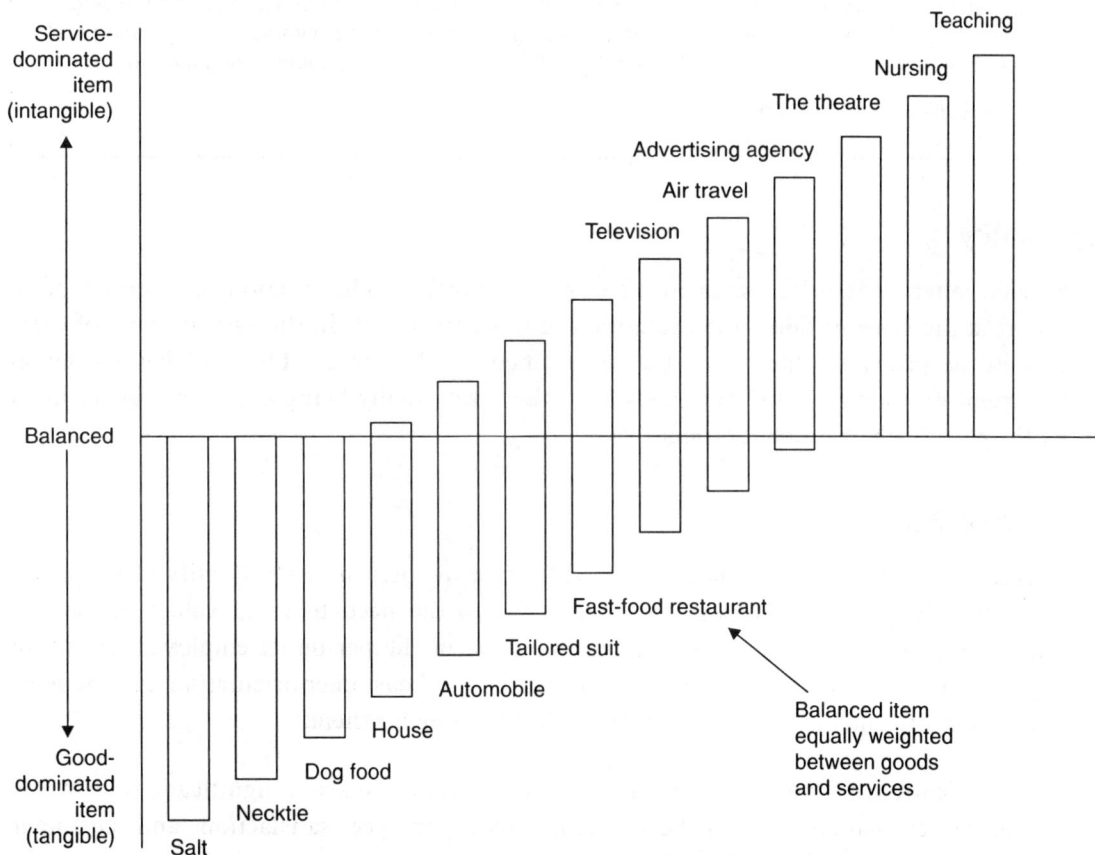

Marketing implications

2.10 Dealing with the problems discussed above may involve the following strategies.

(a) **Increasing the level of tangibility.** When dealing with the customer, staff can use physical or conceptual representations/illustrations to make the customer feel more confident as to what it is that the service is delivering.

(b) **Focusing the attention of the customer on the principal benefits of consumption.** This could take the form of communicating the benefits of purchasing the service so that the customer visualises its appropriateness to the usage requirements within which the principal benefit is sought. Promotion and sales material could provide images or records of previous customers' experience.

(c) **Differentiating the service and reputation-building:** enhancing perceptions of customer service and customer value by offering excellence in the delivery of the service and promoting values of quality, service reliability and value for money. These must be attached as values to brands, which must then be managed to secure and enhance their market position.

Action Programme 1

There may be trouble ahead ...

Insurance is perhaps the least tangible of all the purchases that people commonly make. Insurance adverts create *fears* and then try to sell peace of mind.

Life assurance company Allied Dunbar's Dennis Potter/Nat King Cole style advertisements were part of a £75m campaign to move the company ahead in the market-led 1990s. Part of the research for the campaign aimed to discover how the company was seen by employees and consumers. The message that came back was that the company was both crusading and manipulative, simultaneously caring and aggressive. The next step was to establish what Allied Dunbar's brand or reputation ought to be.

What do you think was the response of consumers?

Inseparability

2.11 Services often cannot be separated off from the provider. The creation of a service often occurs at the same instant on consumption of it occurs. Goods in the vast majority of cases have to be produced, then sold, then consumed, in that order. Think of having dental treatment or a journey. Neither exists until they are actually being experienced/consumed by the person who has bought them.

Marketing implications

2.12 Provision of the service may not be separable from the person or personality of the seller. Consequently increasing importance is attached to the need to instil values of quality, reliability and to generate a customer service ethic in the personnel employed within an organisation. This points up the need for excellence and customer orientation and the need to invest in high quality people and high quality training for them.

2.13 The physical environment of the service delivery system plays a significant role in the customer's evaluation. It has been found that employee satisfaction and customer satisfaction are interrelated.

Heterogeneity

2.14 Many services face the problem of maintaining consistency in the standard of output. Variability of quality in delivery is inevitable because of the number of factors involved. It may be difficult or impossible to attain **precise standardisation of the service offered**. The quality of the service may depend heavily on who it is that delivers the service, or exactly when it takes place. Booking a holiday using standard procedures may well be quite different on a quiet winter afternoon and on a hectic spring weekend, and may well vary according to the person dealing with your case.

2.15 This points up the need to constantly **monitor customer** reactions.

Marketing implications

2.16 In terms of marketing policy, this problem illustrates the need to maintain an attitude and organisational culture which emphasises the following.

- Consistency of **quality control**
- Consistency of **customer service**
- Effective **staff selection, training** and **motivation**

2.17 Also important

- Clear and objective quality measures
- Standardising as much as possible within the service
- Identify and respond most closely to potential 'troublespots'

Perishability

2.18 Services cannot be stored, of course. They are innately **perishable**. Seats on a bus or the services of a chiropodist consist in their availability for periods of time, and if they are not occupied, the service they offer cannot be used 'later'.

2.19 This presents specific marketing problems. Meeting customer needs in these operations depends on staff being available as and when they are needed. This must be balanced against the need for a firm to control expenditure on staff wages. Anticipating and responding to **levels of demand** is, therefore, a key planning priority.

2.20 Risks

- Inadequate level of demand is accompanied by substantial variable and fixed costs
- Excess demand resulting in lost custom through inadequate service provision

Marketing implications

2.21 Policies must seek to smooth supply/demand relationship.

- Price variations which encourage off-peak demand
- Promotions to stimulate off-peak demand

Ownership

2.22 Services suffer from a fundamental difference compared to consumer goods: they do not result in the transfer of property. The purchase of a service only confers on the customer access to or a right to use a **facility**. Often there are tight constraints on the length of time involved in such usage. This may well lessen the perceived customer value of a service and consequently make for unfavourable comparisons with tangible alternatives.

Marketing implications

2.23 (a) **Promote the advantages of non-ownership.** This can be done by emphasising, in promotion, the benefits of paid-for maintenance, and periodic upgrading of the product. Radio Rentals have used this as a major selling proposition with great success.

(b) **Make available a tangible symbol or representation of ownership** (certificate, membership of professional association). This can come to embody the benefits enjoyed.

(c) **Increasing the chances or opportunity of ownership,** for example, time-shares or shares in the organisation for regular customers.

2.24 The issue of how to deal with these problems has occupied many different writers. Some have claimed that the critical factor is the marketing mix which is formulated. Research into the ways in which service quality is evaluated shows that the dimensions of service evaluation are distinctive and quite different criteria are given emphasis when customers are making a judgement.

Marketing at Work

Aspects of quality and customer care in the stockbroking sector are demonstrated in the following table.

Dimension and definition	Examples of specific questions raise by stock brokerage customers
Tangibles: Appearance of physical facilities, equipment, personnel and communication materials	Is my stockbroker dressed appropriately?
Reliability: Ability to perform the promised service dependably and accurately	Does the stockbroker follow exact instructions to buy or sell?
Responsiveness: Willingness to help customers and provide prompt service	Is my stockbroker willing to answer my questions?
Competence: Possession of the required skills and knowledge to perform the service	Does my brokerage firm have the research capabilities to accurately track market developments?
Courtesy: Politeness, respect, consideration and friendliness of contact personnel	Does my broker refrain from acting busy or being rude when I ask questions?
Credibility: Trustworthiness, believability and honesty of the service provider	Does my broker refrain from pressuring me to buy?
Security: Freedom from danger, risk or doubt	Does my brokerage firm know where my stock certificate is?
Access: Approachability and ease of contact	Is it easy to get through to my broker over the telephone?
Dimension and definition	*Examples of specific questions raise by stock brokerage customers*
Communication: Keeping customers informed in language they can understand, and listening to them	Does my broker avoid using technical jargon?

Understanding the customer. Making the effort to know customers and their needs	Does my broker try to determine what my specific financial objectives are?

(Zeithaml, Parasuraman & Berry, *Delivering Quality Service*, 1990)

3 THE EXTENDED MARKETING MIX FOR SERVICES

3.1 Services are provided by **people** for people. If the people providing the service are wrong, the service is spoiled. In the case of a bus service, a cheap fare, a clean vehicle and a frequent service can be spoiled by a surly driver who takes delight in shaking his passengers sick by driving in a series of jolts. People are additionally one of the chief purveyors of **cultural signals**, and so the **human involvement** in services is a significant element in global operations.

3.2 With regard to **process**, services are usually systemised, eg you make an appointment with the hairdresser, you arrive a little before time, you wait, you take the chair, the hairdresser asks you how you would like your hair styled and so on. At any one of these points in the process, right through to brushing you down and taking your money, the service can be spoiled or enhanced by the provider.

3.3 Finally, there is the **physical evidence** or ambience - how are the hairdresser's premises? Are they pleasant and airy or depressing and stuffy? Is the decor tasteful or vulgar? Are the other customers your sort of people or 'aliens'? Again, ambience can be a maker or spoiler of your experience of the service.

3.4 However, here we will expand on the standard approach by identifying **four 'Ps'**. These are as follows (you will see some overlap with the above.) We identified them at the beginning of the chapter.

- Personal selling
- Place of availability (operations management)
- People and customer service
- Physical evidence

Personal selling

3.5 **Personal selling** is more important here because it is harder to sell services than products, for reasons outlined above. The **reputation** of the supplier may be of greater importance. When consumers seek reassurance, personal contact with a competent, effective representative may provide the necessary confidence. In some cases, however, since the quality of the individual salesperson varies, this may not be achieved. This underlines the need to develop standard procedures to minimise customer anxiety. This may not always be possible in cultures where personal 'cold' selling is not acceptable.

Place of availability

3.6 Place of availability is really covered by the **distribution system**, but of course there are special problems for services in the area of **operations management**. The place of availability and the frequency of availability are key service variables, while planning to deal with capacity and making sure that levels of productivity for the assets to be used are optimised, is essential for efficient and profitable operation.

BPP PUBLISHING

3.7 **Process** involves the ways in which the marketer's task is achieved. They include all ordering and customer service features. Efficient processes can become a marketing advantage in their own right. For example, if an airline develops a sophisticated ticketing system, it can encourage customers to take connecting flights offered by allied airlines. Efficient processing of purchase orders received from customers can decrease the time it takes to satisfy them. The following issues can be considered.

- Procedures
- Policies
- Mechanisation
- Queuing

- Information
- Capacity levels
- Speed/timing
- Accessibility

3.8 The level and also the quality of service which is available to the customer is especially sensitive; and in particular, the processes by which services are delivered. Problems with regulating the supply make this a key factor in competitive advantage - a company which gets it right is likely to be clearly differentiated from competitors.

(a) **Capacity utilisation,** matching demand sequences to staff utilisation to avoid unprofitable underprovision and problematic understaffing

(b) **Managing customer contact,** to avoid crowding and customer disruption, meet needs as they arise and increase employee control over interactions

(c) **Establishing objectives within the not for profit sector,** for example, standards for teachers or medical staff

3.9 For marketing service managers, the 'quality control' of the interactions which take place between customers is a key strategic issue. Customers are often, in the course of service delivery, interacting with other customers to gather information. Minimising exposure to negative feedback and promoting the dissemination of positive images about the value of the service are important objectives here.

People   **12/99**

3.10 The **personnel** of the service deliverer are uniquely important in the service marketing process. In the case of some services, the physical presence of people actually performing the service is a vital aspect of customer satisfaction: think of clerks in a bank, or personnel in catering establishments. The staff involved are performing or **producing a service, selling the service** and also liaising with the customer to **promote the service,** gather information and respond to customer needs.

3.11 Managing **front line workers** (eg cabin crew on aircraft) who are the lowest in the organisational hierarchy but whose behaviour has most effect on customers is an important task for senior management. It involves corporate culture, job design and motivational issues. People issues include the following.

- Appearance
- Attitude
- Commitment
- Behaviour

- Professionalism
- Skills
- Numbers
- Discretion

3.12 Thus, another key strategic issue for the service marketing mix is the way in which personnel are involved in implementing the marketing concept, and measures need to be established which will institute a **customer orientation** in all sectors of organisational activity.

3.13 Customers who lack security and confidence in a service will use cues from the demeanour of staff to establish a view about the efficiency of the organisation. The higher the level of customer contact involved in the delivery of a service, the more crucial is the staff role. In many cases the delivery of the service and the physical presence of personnel involved are completely inseparable; technical competence and skill in handling people are of equal importance in effective delivery of a service since, as we have already noted, quality is in the eye of the (consuming) beholder.

Action Programme 2

All levels of staff must be involved in customer service; to achieve this end, it is vital for senior management to consciously promulgate values of customer service constantly to create and build a culture of customer service within the company. How do you think that this might be achieved?

Exam Tip

As a twist on this topic, the December 1999 paper contained a question on keeping a global workforce motivated.

Physical evidence

Key Concept

Physical evidence is the marketing mix element for services denoting the environment in which the service is delivered (eg seating comfort on an aircraft).

3.14 **Physical evidence,** as we have already seen, is an important remedy for the intangibility of the product. This may be **associated with the service itself,** providing cues as to the nature of the service itself (for example, reports of previous work, or credit cards which represent the service available to customers), building up an association with a particular event, person or object, or building up an identification with a specific individual, and transactions with him or her (a 'listening' bank manager).

3.15 Alternatively, the physical evidence may be incorporated into the **design and specification** of the service environment involving the building, location or atmosphere.

- Convey the nature of the service involved
- Transmit messages and information
- Imply aesthetic qualities, moral values or other socio-cultural aspects of a corporate image
- Reinforce an existing image
- Reassure
- Engender an emotional reaction in the customer

3.16 Physical evidence will manifest itself in environment, facilities and tangible items.

   (a) **Environment**

- Colours
- Layout
- Noise levels
- Smells
- Ambience

(b) **Facilities**

- Vans/vehicles/aeroplanes
- Equipment/tools
- Uniforms
- Paperwork

(c) **Tangible evidence**

- Labels
- Tickets
- Logos
- Packaging

4 THE IMPORTANCE OF PEOPLE

4.1 In the overall management picture, this greater emphasis on **people issues** typically involves the management in tight and closely organised practices within the enterprise, in the ways in which personnel are selected and used. Service marketing involves a 'totalitarian' organisational culture.

4.2 As a consequence, **rigorous procedures** are typically applied in the areas of the following.

(a) Selection and training

(b) Internal marketing - promulgating the 'culture' of service within the firm

(c) Ensuring 'conformance' in terms of quality procedures

- behaviour
- dress and appearance
- procedures
- modes of dealing with the public

(d) Mechanising procedures where possible

(e) Constantly auditing personnel performance and behaviour

(f) Being aware of cultural differences

(g) Extending the conscious promotion of image and tangible presentations of the service and its qualities into the design of service environments and the engineering of interactions within and between staff and customers

4.3 If there is one overall message about the essential quality required in successful service marketing, it is that attention to detail, however small, is the key to success.

Action Programme 3

The role of people in services marketing is especially important. What human characteristics improve the quality of client service?

---

5 SERVICE QUALITY

5.1 **Service quality** is one of the most important issues for marketers because it is a significant basis which customers use for differentiating between competing services. Second only to market share **relative quality** is a key contributor to **bottom line profit performance.**

> **Key Concept**
>
> **Service quality** is the totality of features and characteristics of that service which bears on its ability to meet stated or implied needs.

5.2 There are essentially two ways firms can gain from improving their quality of service to customers.

(a) **Higher sales revenues and improved marketing effectiveness** brought about by improved customer retention, positive word of mouth recommendations and the ability to increase prices.

(b) Better quality **improves productivity and reduces costs** because there is less rework, higher employee morale and lower employee turnover.

5.3 Quality is a difficult concept to define in a few words and has been defined in a number of ways. A **market-led definition** of quality is based on the idea that quality can only be **defined by customers** and occurs where a firm supplies products to a specification that satisfies their needs. Consensus exists that customer expectations serve as standards against which subsequent service experiences are compared. Thus when service performance falls short of customer expectations, dissatisfaction occurs.

5.4 Service quality has a number of dimensions.

(a) **Technical quality** of the service encounter (ie what is received by the customer).

(b) **Functional quality** of the service encounter (ie how the service is provided). The dimension relates to the psychological interaction between the buyer and seller and is typically perceived in a very subjective way.

    (i) **Relationships between employees.** For instance, do these relationships appear to be professional? Do they chat to each other whilst serving the customer? Does each appear to know their role in the team and the function of their colleagues? Do they know who to refer the customer to in case of the need for more specialist advice? Are they positive about their colleagues or unduly critical?

    (ii) **Appearance and personality of service personnel.** For instance, do they seem interested in the customer and the customer's needs? Are they smartly presented? Do they convey an attractive and positive image?

    (iii) **Service-mindedness of the personnel.** For instance, do they appear to understand and identify with the needs of the customer? Are they interested in what they are doing? Do they convey competence?

    (iv) **Accessibility of the service to the customer.** For instance, do the service personnel explain the service in language which the customer can understand?

    (v) **Approachability of service personnel.** For instance, do the service personnel appear alert, interested or welcoming? Or are they day-dreaming, yawning or looking at their watches?

5.5 The corporate image dimension of service quality is a result of how consumers perceive the firm. This dimension can be affected by many factors including advertising and past experience with the firm.

5.6 The major determinants of service quality can be seen to fit into a number of dimensions, some of which are more easily measured than others.

(a)	**Tangibles**	The physical evidence, such as the quality of fixtures and fittings of the company's service area, must be consistent with the desired image.
(b)	**Reliability**	Getting it right first time is very important, not only to ensure repeat business, but, in financial services, as a matter of ethics, if the customer is buying a future benefit.
(c)	**Responsiveness**	The staff's willingness to deal with the customer's queries must be apparent.
(d)	**Communication**	Staff should talk to customers in non-technical language which they can understand.
(e)	**Credibility**	The organisation should be perceived as honest, trustworthy and as acting in the best interests of customers.
(f)	**Security**	This is specially relevant to medical and financial services organisations. The customer needs to feel that the conversations with bank service staff are private and confidential. This factor should influence the design of the service area.
(g)	**Competence**	All the service staff need to appear competent in understanding the product range and interpreting the needs of the customers.
(h)	**Courtesy**	Customers (even rude ones) should perceive service staff as polite, respectful and friendly.
(i)	**Understanding customers' needs**	The use of computer-based customer databases can be very impressive in this context. The service personnel can then call up the customer's records and use these data in the service process, thus personalising the process. Service staff need to meet customer needs rather than try to sell products. This is a subtle but important difference.
(j)	**Access**	Minimising queues, having a fair queuing system and speedy service are all factors which can avoid customers' irritation building up. A pleasant relaxing environment is a useful design factor in this context.

Quality gaps

5.7 Parasuraman, Zeithaml and Berry developed the most widely applied **model of service quality** in 1985. The researchers developed their model via interviews with fourteen executives in four service businesses and twelve customer focus groups. The executive interviews resulted in the idea of four gaps which are potential hurdles for a firm in attempting to deliver high quality service.

```
                        ┌─────────────────────┐
                        │    Expectations     │
                        └─────────────────────┘
                  Gap 5           ↕
                        ┌─────────────────────┐
                        │    Perceptions      │
   The Customer         └─────────────────────┘
─────────────────────────────────────────────────────
                  Gap 1
   The Firm       ┌─────────────────────┐      ┌──────────────────────────┐
                  │   Service delivery  │ ◄──► │  External communications │
                  └─────────────────────┘      └──────────────────────────┘
            Gap 3           ↕             Gap 4
                  ┌─────────────────────┐
                  │   Service standards │
                  └─────────────────────┘
            Gap 2           ↕
                  ┌─────────────────────┐
                  │ Management perceptions │
                  └─────────────────────┘
```

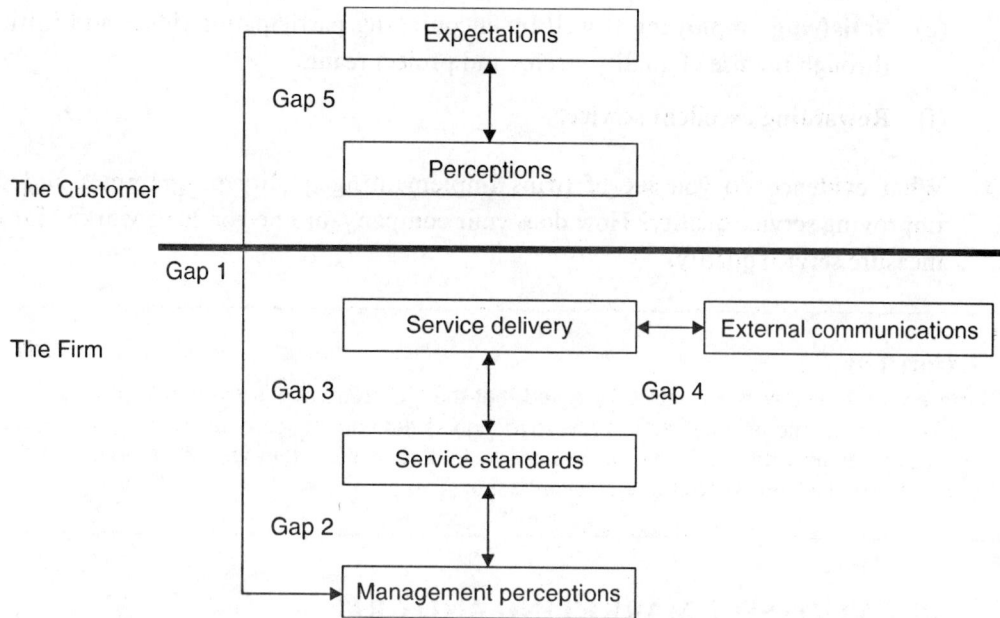

Gap 1: **Consumer expectations and management perceptions gap**

Essentially managers may not know what features connote high quality, what features a service must have or what levels of performance are required by customers.

Gap 2: **Management perceptions and service quality specification gap**

Resource constraints, market conditions and/or management indifference may result in this gap.

Gap 3: **Service quality specifications and service delivery gap**

Guidelines may exist but contact employees may not be willing or able to perform to the specified standards.

Gap 4: **Service delivery and external communications gap**

Exaggerated promises or lack of information will affect both expectations and perceptions.

Gap 5: **Expected service and perceived service gap**

This gap was defined as service quality. The authors argue that gap five is influenced by the preceding four gaps thus if management want to close the gap between performance and expectations it becomes imperative to design procedures for measuring service performance against expectations.

5.8 Once a firm knows how it is **performing** on each of the dimensions of service quality it can use a number of methods to try to **improve** its quality.

(a) Development of customer orientated **mission statement** and clear senior management support for quality improvement initiatives

(b) **Customer satisfaction research** each year which can include regular customer surveys, customer panels, perception surveys, mystery shoppers, analysis of complaints data, employee satisfaction research and similar industry studies for benchmarking purposes.

(c) Results should be **communicated,** and standards set and monitored.

(d) Systems should be established for customers **complaints and feedback.**

BPP PUBLISHING

(e) **Satisfying employees** as well by encouraging participation, ideas and initiative, often through the use of quality circles and project teams.

(f) **Rewarding** excellent service.

5.9 What evidence do you see of firms implementing quality programmes and continually improving service quality? How does your company, or one you have worked for in the past, measure service quality?

Exam Tip

The senior examiner has specifically noted that the '4P' approach is now somewhat limited. Service marketing in an international context has to recognise the importance of physical evidence, people and processes. Expect the marketing of services to feature in the exam, especially as such a significant proportion of the world economy is service-based.

6 RELATIONSHIP MARKETING AND CRM

6.1 Before the evolution of mass markets, the natural approach to marketing was through building a relationship with **individual customers**. The traditional corner shop in the UK, now driven almost to extinction by the power of the big supermarkets, provides an example of a business based on understanding individual customer needs. A good relationship with the customer was essential for repeat business.

6.2 During the twentieth century, **mass media** (television, newspapers, radio) created **mass marketing** and **mass consumption**, aided by production efficiencies. Products became nationally recognisable via distribution and advertising. Technology impacted dramatically on transportation, travel and communications, helping to create a global market. The emphasis on individual customer service became, to an extent, diluted.

6.3 This situation is now changing. For example, long-standardised products such as Coca Cola now have different variants (Diet, Cherry) to appeal to different customer segments. Now that there are more products to promote, companies need to **target the market** more carefully.

6.4 **Relationship marketing** helps them to do this. Again, it is technology which is the key factor. Software developments have made **databases** flexible and powerful enough to hold large amounts of **customer specific data**. While the corner shop of old recognised customers visually, companies today can recognise them electronically.

Key Concept

Relationship marketing can be seen as the successor to mass marketing, and is the process by which information about the customer is consistently applied by the company when developing and delivering products and services. Developments are communicated to the customer, for example via specially targeted promotions and product launches, in order to build a 'partnership' with him and encourage a long term relationship by paying attention to his specific needs.

Marketing at Work

The Range Rover launch, 1995

Ten days before it launched the 1995 Range Rover, Rover let 10,000 of its most privileged customers into its secret. Each one of them received an invitation to a champagne breakfast or candle-lit dinner to see the new car privately - before the rest of the world got to hear about it. Those who came along were not expected to enter into any firm commitments; instead, the aim of the exercise was to turn these 10,000 people into 'brand ambassadors' for Rover. The aim of the preview, said John Russell, Managing Director of Rover International, was 'to achieve the intimacy of a dinner party among friends where our launch messages would be passed on by word of mouth - overheard, not overhyped. We set out not to launch a product but to achieve a breakthrough in the quality of our customer relationships'.

6.5   The underpinning idea behind Rover's approach was relationship marketing, turning 'ordinary' customers into 'brand advocates'. The rewards from effective relationship marketing are potentially impressive (and are linked to the whole exercise of **customer retention**).

(a)   One credit card company calculated that a 5% increase in customer retention would create a 125% increase in profits.

(b)   American Express believes that by extending customer lifecycles by five years, it could treble its profits per customer.

(c)   According to Coca-Cola, a 10% increase in retailer retention should translate to a 20% increase in sales.

6.6   To work, relationship marketing has to operate in three ways.

(a)   **Borrow the idea of customer/supplier partnerships from industry**: by sharing information and supporting each other's shared objectives, marketers and their customers can create real mutual benefit.

(b)   **Recreate the personal feel** that characterised the old-fashioned corner shop or Edwardian department store: make customers feel valued as individuals, and (using modern IT systems) convince them that their individual needs are being recognised and catered for.

(c)   **Continually deepen and improve the relationship** by making sure that everything which impinges on the customer's experience of the brand delights them.

6.7   The value of relationship marketing for the international marketer lies in the fact that customers, consumers, retailers, distributors and agents may be spread all over the world, but they will still look for the familiar features when deciding whether or not to do business: product or service performance, enhancements and reliability of supply. If these business partners are looked after, market share will be of better quality because a greater proportion of sales will be derived from repeat business. Relationship marketing in this way provides an alternative to the traditional marketing mix.

Customer relationship management (CRM)

6.8   The magazine *Business Age* says in its February 2000 issue: "**CRM** will soon be as common a sound to the human ear as any other modern-day computer acronym". Purchasing, distribution, marketing and other activities are all inextricably linked to CRM, as is the Internet. CRM can be built into **e-commerce**, **websites** and **email**, and there is a whole new **CRM software** industry.

6.9   The whole point of CRM is not a new one: "Keeping the customer satisfied". The **call centre** is at the heart of its development. **Data warehousing** and **data mining** techniques are important, but the key for any company interested in CRM is to deliver the **right message and offers** to the **right customers**. Customers can be put off by a deluge of direct mail and hand sell. CRM should aim to target and communicate the following.

- Inform **pre-sales prospects** of the benefits of a relationship
- Sell more and new products to **existing customers**
- **Retain** existing customers

6.10 A CRM system is integrated and covers the entire sales and marketing process, and brings together a number of marketing and customer facing systems within one strategy or homogeneous software application.

Marketing at Work

From *Computer Business Review,* March 1999:

Customer relationship management (CRM) software is an industry in its own right. California-based Siebel Systems is market leader and its chief executive, Tom Siebel, says: 'I think now we have entered an era where the most precious resource is being recognised as the customer relationship. 'A customer in Paris, London or New York ordering on the Internet or by telephone does not care where the supplier is based, he just wants good service and quick delivery. 'There is a huge feeling, even in formerly not-so-service-oriented economies, that companies need to reach, serve and embrace customers. And the game they are playing is absolutely economic survival'.

Another CRM company boss says 'Think of any industry - telecoms, high tech, consumer packaged goods, financial services. There is no time for building relationships ... a system has to be implemented immediately. Loyalty and retention equal revenue ... [and] ... it is the level of service that will keep customers coming back'.

In many industries, mass globalisation has diluted the significance of product features and functionality. Customers are clamouring for a more personalised service, and companies have to satisfy highly individualised markets - ultimately a target market of one customer. Companies like One 2 One, BAT and the Prudential are all using CRM software to build databases and customer information profiles.

Chapter Roundup

- The extension of the **service sector**, and the application of market principles across many public sector and ex-public sector organisations, has made a large number of service providers much more **marketing-conscious**. Services marketing differs from the marketing of other goods in a number of crucial ways, and five specific characteristics of services marketing have been proposed.

- An **extended marketing mix** has been suggested for services marketing. Booms and Bitner suggested an additional 3Ps. Here, we have taken an approach which analyses an additional 4Ps.

- **Service quality** can be defined as the difference between what the customer expects and what he or she perceives him/herself to be receiving. Improved service quality leads to higher profits and is a key task for service marketers.

- **Relationship marketing** focuses on the individual customer and seeks to foster a relationship that will engender increased levels of retention. **Customer relationship management** is emerging as a key discipline in its own right.

Quick Quiz

1   What are the five marketing characteristics of services? (see para 2.5)
2   What are the marketing implications of the intangibility of services? (2.10)
3   What issues arise from the heterogeneity of services being marketed? (2.14 - 2.17)
4   How can the problems of lack of ownership be overcome in service marketing?(2.23)
5   What are the additional 'Ps' in the service marketing mix? (3.1 - 3.4)
6   What factors are bought to bear by people in the marketing of services? (3.11)
7   In what areas should rigorous procedures be applied to take account of the importance of people in services marketing? (4.2)
8   In what two ways can firms gain by improving their quality of service to customers? (5.2)
9   What are the dimensions of service quality? (5.6)
10 What is relationship marketing? (6.4)

Action Programme Review

1   Consumers wanted to know that the company was large, successful and financially secure; they wanted to be treated as individuals and have individually tailored solutions to their financial needs throughout their life; and they wanted to find the company caring, honest, knowledgeable and experienced. They also wanted unpleasant and difficult issues confronted when investments, life assurance and pensions were discussed, and to have a clear idea what provision was being made for which eventualities.

2
- Policies of selection
- Programmes of training
- Standard, consistent operational practices ('McDonaldisation')
- Standardised operational rules
- Effective motivational programmes
- Managerial appointments
- The attractiveness and appropriateness of the service offer
- Effective policies of staff reward and remuneration

3   The following are all dimensions of client service quality.

(a)   *Problem solving creativity:* looking beyond the obvious and not being bound by accepted professional and technical approaches

(b)   *Initiative:* includes anticipating problems and opportunities and not just reacting

(c)   *Efficiency:* keeping client costs down through effective work planning and control

(d)   *Fast response:* responding to enquiries, questions, problems as quickly as possible

(e)   *Timeliness:* starting and finishing service work to agreed deadlines

(f)   *Open-mindedness:* professionals not being 'blinkered' by their technical approach

(g)   *Sound judgement:* clients want business advice not just accounting advice

(h)   *Functional expertise:* need to bring together all the functional skills necessary from whatever sources to work on a client project

(i)   *Industry expertise:* clients expect professionals to be thoroughly familiar with their industry and recent changes in it

(j)   *Managerial effectiveness:* maintaining a focus upon the use of both the firm's and the client's resources

(k)   *Orderly work approach:* clients expect salient issues to be identified early and do not want last minute surprises before deadlines

(l)   *Commitment:* clients evaluate the calibre of the accountant and the individual attention given

(m)   *Long-range focus:* clients prefer long-term relationships rather than 'projects' or 'jobs'

(n)   *Qualitative approach:* accountants should not be seen as simple number crunchers

(o)   *Continuity:* clients do not like firms who constantly change the staff that work with them - they will evaluate staff continuity as part of ongoing relationship

(p)   *Personality:* clients will also evaluate the friendliness, understanding and co-operation of the service provider

---

Now try illustrative question 13 at the end of the Study Text

BPP
PUBLISHING

14 Control Issues in International Marketing

Learning Outcomes

On completion of this chapter you will have an understanding of:

- criteria for the control and evaluation of marketing and other business functions

- traditional and recent developments in evaluation and control including the balanced scorecard and benchmarking

- green marketing and ethical issues.

Key Concepts Introduced

- Control
- The balanced scorecard
- Benchmarking
- Learning organisation

Examples of Marketing at Work

- China and the WTO
- Hoover
- Barings
- Marks and Spencer
- Digital Equipment
- Implementation of the balanced scorecard
- British Airways
- Benchmarking study
- Dell
- Ethical issues
- Copyright
- Shell

1 SETTING THE SCENE

1.1 **Maintaining control** of international marketing is of growing concern to companies, because there is an increasing trend for companies to be global. For most firms, international marketing is an on-going exercise. Ford, for example, has been involved in international activities since the early 20th century.

1.2 Because plans change with the environment, establishing a **control system** is vital. With operations in various countries, this is not an easy task. Two aspects of controlling international activities are:

    (a)   the control of particular marketing plans in the light of **planning and objectives** set for them (sections 2 and 3)

    (b)   the overall control of international marketing strategies to assess how well they are **performing** and identifying their contribution (sections 4 and 5).

1.3 Evaluation and control of business operations is the subject of much debate and there are various **alternative approaches**. We examine some of them in section 6, and conclude with a consideration of **ethics** and **green marketing**.

2 CONTROLLING INTERNATIONAL MARKETING PLANS Specimen paper

> **Key Concept**
>
> **Control** is the process of ensuring that the results of operations (including marketing as well as other business functions) conform to established goals. All planning should have a control element along the following general lines.
>
> (a) Formulation of standards and goals.
>
> (b) Measurement of actual performance against those standards.
>
> (c) Procedures for taking corrective action, either by changing the marketing programme, the personnel involved or even adjusting the standards for the future.

2.1 International marketing presents formidable problems to managers.

    (a)   Each **national market** is different, so it is difficult to deliver the same marketing strategy.

    (b)   Distance, language differences and **cultural variations** create communication problems.

    (c)   There is a greater likelihood of resentment by the subsidiary of **control from headquarters**, and even without this it can be difficult for a large organisation to control the activities of numerous subsidiaries.

2.2 The marketing control system should be designed to minimise international and intercultural differences. Control is closely linked with **planning and organisational structure**, discussed in Chapters 6 and 8.

2.3 Currency values, legal and political systems and cultural factors will influence the development of a **local marketing programme**. In countries where a large proportion of the population is illiterate, such as India or Pakistan, the use of printed media is of limited value. In the Third World, ownership of radio and television sets is becoming more common, so advertising by sound or demonstration is a viable alternative.

BPP PUBLISHING

2.4   The companies involved in international marketing are not the only organisations concerned with evaluating and controlling international activity. The **World Bank**, for example, which supplies capital for developing nations at low rates of interest, will monitor progress on reform programmes (often pledged by the recipient country in return for the loan) and may in some cases suspend loans if progress is unsatisfactory. This will have an effect on companies hoping to export to such countries because imports by the country receiving the loan may be cut back.

Marketing at Work

China needs help in undertaking the schedule of transformation of its regulatory and legal regimes, as well as the economic restructuring that is necessary for WTO membership. The World Bank is reported to be fearful that China would be reluctant to reveal detailed economic information, and this would mean that the proposed reforms could not be monitored properly.

---

3   SETTING OBJECTIVES AND STANDARDS

3.1   The degree of centralisation/decentralisation has important ramifications for the control tasks. For example, a decentralised multinational corporation will not wish to exercise close control, and is likely to find control much harder to implement where it becomes necessary.

3.2   Standards and targets should be **clearly defined**, understood and accepted by those whose activities are being controlled. This introduces some **accountability** and 'reins in' some of the more extravagant ideas and so-called 'blue skies' thinking.

What standards should be adopted?

Corporate objectives

3.3   Corporate objectives include matters of **financial performance**.

- Profit
- Return on capital
- Cash flow
- Earnings per share

Marketing objectives are usually determined to satisfy these corporate concerns and **local marketing activities** will be designed accordingly.

3.4   Where an organisation is decentralised, each subsidiary may be given its own **profit targets**, and **cash flow targets**.

Marketing objectives

3.5   The following are some examples of standards for local marketing activities.

- Market research (number and types of studies)
- Sales volume (by product line/quarter/year etc)
- Market share (by product/quarter/year)
- Product (quality control standards)
- Distribution (market coverage, dealer support)
- Pricing (levels, margins and rigidity or flexibility)
- Branch (volume and nature of local advertising/sales promotion)
- Selling (local sales force standards)

- Customer returns
- Number of complaints
- 'Share of voice' in international promotions
- Consumer awareness

How are standards established?

3.6 Where practical, headquarters should not impose standards arbitrarily but should use local input, because this will be more up to date and will ensure morale and motivation is maintained.

3.7 There are many ways of establishing standards.

(a) **Job specifications** of marketing personnel give the basic performance requirements.

(b) **The annual planning process** will indicate more specific corporate standards

(c) **Communication** (both personal and impersonal) between HQ and subsidiary staff (such as meetings, task forces, internal publications)

Financial performance

3.8 The task of setting financial objectives within a multinational is complex, and several problems must be resolved. The company may decide that a single objective should be applied, so that every subsidiary must earn, for example, a specified return on capital employed or profit margin.

3.9 On the other hand, because of **differing local conditions** (such as government policies, taxation, exchange rate fluctuations) it might be more appropriate to apply a different financial target to each subsidiary. For example, the same product may be at different stages in its life cycle in each country.

International comparisons

3.10 If the firms being compared operate in different countries there will be certain problems for performance measurement.

(a) **Realistic standards** need to be set, taking account of local conditions.

(b) **Controllable cash flows.** Care must be taken to determine which cash flows are controllable.

(c) **Currency conversion.** Care must be exercised to ensure that conversion rates are valid. A firm can lock itself into a particular exchange rate by hedging. Jaguar used this when, as an independent British company, most of its sales were in the US. Hedging instruments were used to protect its profits from any deterioration caused by weakening of its currency receipts.

4 OBTAINING PERFORMANCE INFORMATION

4.1 Monitoring of international marketing performance is difficult since it generally relies more on indirect methods such as reports, as well as direct meetings.

Reports

4.2
- **Standardised** to allow comparative analysis between subsidiaries
- Use an agreed **common language** and currency
- **Frequent** as necessary to allow proper management
- Cover all the **information needs** of headquarters

Meetings

4.3 Gatherings between HQ executives and subsidiary management allow for more intensive information exchange and monitoring; and minimise misunderstandings. They do however take up time and resources, and are generally not as regular as reports.

Information technology

4.4 Information technology makes it much easier for marketing and financial performance to be monitored closely, given the speed of transmission of e-mail and Internet communications.

4.5 Meetings can even be conducted by video-conferencing - this might prove cheaper than flying.

5 MAINTAINING AND ENFORCING CONTROL

5.1 The purpose of measuring performance is to enable senior management to **take action** if the variation between planned and actual performance is unacceptable.

Planning

5.2 If planning is carried out effectively, subsidiary managers will be committed to the goals resulting from the planning process.

Organisation

5.3 The main purpose of organisation as a management function is to facilitate control. Other control methods include the following.

- The budget
- Corporate culture
- Procedures and rules to ensure a standard product or service
- Direct intervention in cases of underperformance

Control of intermediaries

5.4 The problem with controlling 'outsiders' is that there is no control by **ownership**. In the final analysis **negative controls** such as legal pressures or threats to discontinue relationships can be used, resulting perhaps in loss of business. The best control is through good selection and by making it clear to intermediaries that their interests and the company's coincide.

Marketing at Work

Control failures of note in recent years include the following.

(a) *Hoover's* free flight promotion: a failure of control by Maytag, its American parent?

(b) *Barings:* a failure to control basic procedures over an executive's trading activities.

(c) *Marks and Spencer* had to take control action to improve the performance of its Brookes Brothers US subsidiary, which performed less well than hoped, and is likely to be disposed of following the recent management changes at the company.

6 OTHER METHODS OF EVALUATION AND CONTROL

6.1 It has been recognised for a while that there is a need for review of strategic performance, including the success or otherwise of international marketing campaigns, over a whole host of measures rather than just financial. There has been increasing interest in the development of alternative approaches.

- The balanced scorecard
- Benchmarking
- Self assessment
- The learning organisation
- Empowerment
- Investment analysis
- Customer analysis and retention

The balanced scorecard

6.2 Financial measurements do not capture all the strategic realities of a business. A technique which has been developed to integrate the various features of corporate success is the **balanced scorecard**, developed by Robert Kaplan and publicised in the *Harvard Business Review* in 1992.

> **Key Concept**
> The **balanced scorecard** is a way of providing information to management to assist strategic policy decisions. It emphasises the need to provide the user with information addressing all relevant areas of performance. The information may include both financial and non-financial elements, and covers the perspectives outlined below.

Customer perspective

6.3 'How do customers see us?' Given that many company mission statements identify customer satisfaction as a key corporate goal, the balanced scorecard translates this into specific measures.

(a) **Time.** Lead time is the time it takes a firm to meet customer needs from receiving an order to delivering the product.

(b) **Quality.** Quality measures not only include defect levels but accuracy in forecasting.

(c) **Performance** of the product. (How often does the photocopier break down?)

(d) **Service.** How long will it take a problem to be rectified? (If the photocopier breaks down, how long will it take the maintenance engineer to arrive?)

BPP PUBLISHING

Internal business perspective

6.4   Findings from the customer's perspective need to be translated into the actions the firm must take to meet these expectations.

(a)   The **internal business perspective** identifies the business processes that have the greatest impact on customer satisfaction, such as quality and employee skills and behaviour.

(b)   Companies should also attempt to identify and measure their distinctive **competences**. Which processes should they excel at?

(c)   An information system is necessary to enable executives to measure performance. An **executive information system** enables managers to drill down into lower level information.

Innovation and learning perspective

6.5   The question is 'Can we continue to improve and create value?' Whilst the customer and internal process perspectives identify the **current** parameters for competitive success, the company needs to learn and to innovate to satisfy **future** needs. This might be one of the hardest items to measure. Examples of measures might be these.

(a)   **How long does it take to develop and manufacture new products?**

(b)   **What percentage of revenue comes from new products?**

(c)   **How many suggestions are made by staff and are acted upon?**

(d)   **What are staff attitudes?** Some firms believe that employee motivation and successful communication are necessary for organisational learning.

Financial perspective

6.6   Some still consider that financial issues take care of themselves, and that they are only the result of the customer, internal process, and innovation and learning issues discussed above. An extreme example of this approach was the chief executive of a silicon-chip manufacturing firm. At each monthly meeting to review performance, the figures for quality were attended to in great detail, but profit figures did not interest him so he would leave the meeting early.

6.7   This view is rather naive for a number of obvious reasons.

(a)   Money is a **resource** which needs to be properly controlled

(b)   Financial control systems can assist in marketing programmes (eg by identifying where actual results vary from those that were expected).

Marketing at Work

The fall from grace of Digital Equipment, in the past second only to IBM in the world computer rankings, was examined in a *Financial Times* article.

The downfall is blamed on Digital's failure to keep up with the development of the PC, but also on the company's culture. The company was founded on brilliant creativity, but was insufficiently focused on the bottom line. Outside the finance department, monetary issues were considered vulgar and organisational structure was chaotic. Costs were not a core part of important decisions - 'if expenditure was higher than budget, the problem was simply a bad budget'. Ultimately the low-price world of lean competitors took its toll, leading to losses of more than $2 billion in 1992 and 1994.

6.8 An example of how a balanced scorecard might appear is offered below.

Balanced Scorecard

Financial Perspective

GOALS	MEASURES
Survive	Cash flow
Succeed	Monthly sales growth and operating income by division
Prosper	Increase market share and ROI

Customer Perspective

GOALS	MEASURES
New products	Percentage of sales from new products
Responsive supply	On-time delivery (defined by customer)
Preferred supplier	Share of key accounts' purchases
	Ranking by key accounts
Customer partnership	Number of cooperative engineering efforts

Internal Business Perspective

GOALS	MEASURES
Technology capability	Manufacturing configuration vs competition
Manufacturing excellence	Cycle time
	Unit cost
	Yield
Design productivity	Silicon efficiency
	Engineering efficiency
New product introduction	Actual introduction schedule vs plan

Innovation and Learning Perspective

GOALS	MEASURES
Technology leadership	Time to develop next generation of products
Manufacturing learning	Process time to maturity
Product focus	Percentage of products that equal 80% sales
Time to market	New product introduction vs competition

6.9 To apply the scorecard successfully, it must be clearly applicable to the operations involved, and be clearly communicated. A study by the consultants KPMG came up with the conclusion that the balanced scorecard is a very useful tool, as long as the organisation implementing it is very clear as to what it wants to achieve!

Marketing at Work

An oil company (quoted by Kaplan and Norton, *Harvard Business Review*) ties:

(a) 60% of its executives' bonuses to their achievement of ambitious financial targets on ROI, profitability, cash flow and operating cost

(b) 40% on indicators of customer satisfaction, retailer satisfaction, employee satisfaction and environmental responsibility

---

Benchmarking

Key Concept

Benchmarking is a technique by which a company tries to emulate or exceed standards achieved or processes adopted by another company, generally an exemplar organisation.

Marketing at Work

British Airways 'used benchmarking since 1987 to help transform itself from a stodgy, state-controlled enterprise to a leading world airline'. Apparently BA staff analysed their own business processes to identify the weakest elements, and then visited other airlines with checklists and questions. Problems are often found to be shared and competitors are willing to pool information in pursuit of solutions.

6.10 Benchmarking can be divided into stages.

- **Set objectives** and determine the areas to benchmark
- Establish **key performance measures**
- **Select organisations** to study
- **Measure** own and others' performance
- **Compare** performances
- Design and implement **improvement programme**
- **Monitor** improvements

6.11 Benchmarking has the following advantages.

(a) **Position audit**. Benchmarking can assess a firm's existing position, and provide a basis for establishing standards of performance.

(a) The comparisons are **carried out by the managers** who have to live with any changes implemented as a result of the exercise.

(b) Benchmarking **focuses** on improvement in key areas and sets targets which are challenging but evidently 'achievable'.

(c) The sharing of information can be a **spur to innovation**.

6.12 Many companies have gained significant benefits from benchmarking but it is worth pointing out a number of possible dangers.

(a) It implies there is **one best way** of doing business - arguably this boils down to the difference between efficiency and effectiveness. A process can be efficient but its output may not be useful. Other measures (such as amending the value chain) may be a better way of securing competitive advantage.

(b) The benchmark may be **yesterday's solution to tomorrow's problem**. For example, a cross-channel ferry company might benchmark its activities (eg speed of turnround at Dover and Calais, cleanliness on ship) against another ferry company, whereas the real competitor is the Channel Tunnel.

(c) It is a **catching-up exercise** rather than the development of anything distinctive. After the benchmarking exercise, the competitor might improve performance in a different way.

(d) It depends on **accurate** information about comparator companies.

Marketing at Work

An interesting twist on the idea of benchmarking was given by a five year research programme by Insead business school. The study identified the following five companies as likely to still be successful 10 or 20 years from now.

- American International Group (AIG), the US insurer.
- Heineken, the Dutch brewer.
- Hewlett-Packard, the US electronics manufacturer.
- JP Morgan, the US bank.

- SGS Thomson, the Franco-Italian semiconductor maker.

The underlying premise of the study, as reported in the *Financial Times* in June 1998, is that success or failure depends on a complex series of actions. By studying the past history of companies, it should be possible to spot the factors that have made a difference. Companies were compared on 12 capabilities - customer orientation, technical resources, market strategy and so forth. An overall score for effectiveness was calculated.

In general, the study is a means of showing how the best companies go about their business, and allows others to diagnose their shortcomings. To quote the project leader when talking about IBM: 'There was a time when it was the best at customer orientation. If we had had this tool 20 years ago, we could have seen it going wrong.'

Self assessment

6.13   This involves the **regular and systematic review** of processes and results. Doing this allows an organisation to properly assess its weaknesses and strengths, thus highlighting opportunities for improvement and showing what the organisation is doing 'right'.

6.14   In 1991 the Business Excellence Model (BEM) was introduced, based upon the concept that customer satisfaction, employee satisfaction and impact on society are achieved through leadership (of policy and strategy), people, resources and processes. This leads ultimately to business success. A diagram of the model is given below.

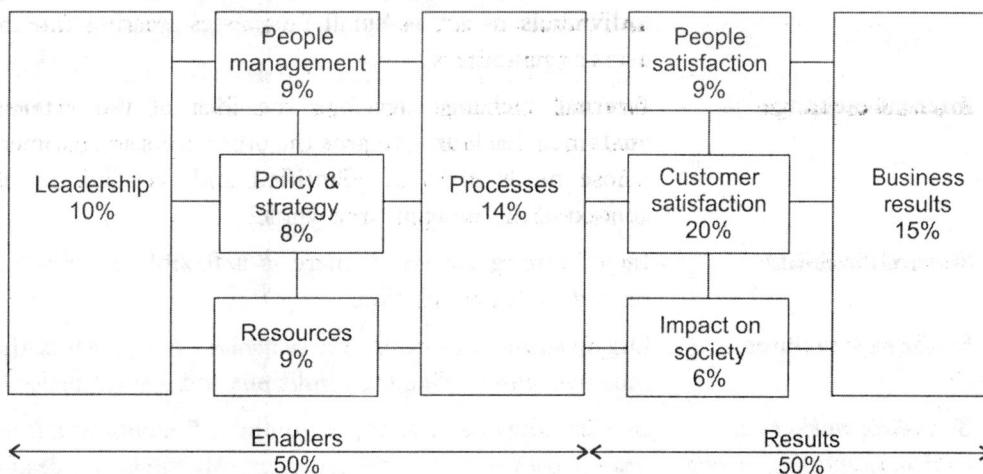

6.15   Many organisations undertaking self assessment compare themselves against these factors (the enablers and the results) using the weightings shown. As can be seen, the model gives a higher priority (20%) to customer satisfaction than to business results. The process of self assessment may include workshop and group discussion or questionnaires. These aim to produce a 'current status' picture of what the organisation is achieving.

6.16   The European Quality Award process has identified role model organisations and leading practitioners of best practice in self assessment. Recent winners include BT plc and TNT.

The learning organisation

6.17   Marketing managers can try to develop the learning organisation.

- Encourages continuous learning and knowledge generation at all levels
- Has the processes to move knowledge around the organisation
- Can transform knowledge into actual behaviour

6.18 Let's start with a definition.

> **Key Concept**
>
> In their book *The Learning Company: A Strategy for Sustainable Development*, Pedler, Burgoyne and Boydell suggest the following might be a good description of a **learning organisation**:
>
> 'An organisation that facilitates the learning of all its members *and* continuously transforms itself'.

6.19 The characteristics of the learning organisation are listed below.

Characteristics	Comments
Learning approach to strategy	Experimentation and feedback built into a system. As much information as possible is brought to bear on a problem.
Participative policy making	All 'members' of a learning company have the chance to participate in the learning process.
Informating	This is the use of information not as a control mechanism, but as a resource for the whole organisation to exploit in order to develop new insights.
Formative accounting	Accounting and budgeting systems should be structured to assist learning. Such systems might encourage individuals to act as 'small businesses treating internal users as **customers**'.
Internal exchange	Internal exchange develops the idea of the **internal customer**. Each unit regards the other units as customers, whose needs must be identified and satisfied, in the context of the company as a whole.
Reward flexibility	In a learning company, there is a flexible approach to reward and remuneration.
Enabling structures	Organisation structures are *temporary* arrangements that must respond to changed conditions and opportunities.
Boundary workers as environmental scanners	In a learning organisation, environmental monitoring is not restricted to specialists or managers. All employees dealing with the boundary should try and monitor the environment.
Inter-company learning	Learn from other firms.
Learning climate	The function of management in a learning organisation is to: • Encourage continuous learning and knowledge around the organisation. • Create processes to move knowledge around the organisation. • Transform knowledge into actual behaviour, products and processes.

Empowerment

6.20 Many large organisations in the late 1980s and early 1990s recognised that their structure was leading to communication problems, overlapping responsibilities and problems with planning and control. The economic recession in this period led many companies to seek ways of cutting costs, and developments in technology meant that the information processing traditionally done by middle managers could be done by computer just as effectively.

6.21 Middle managers thus tended to have too little to do while those lower down the hierarchy were getting frustrated. The trend for some time has therefore been one of **delayering** - removing whole layers of middle management - and **empowerment** of workers lower down.

6.22 An article by Max Hand (*Management Accounting*) refers to the place of **empowerment** in the quality control process: 'the people lower down the organisation possess the knowledge of what is going wrong within a process but lack the authority to make changes. Those further up the structure have the authority to make changes but lack the profound knowledge required to identify the right solutions. The only solution is to change the culture of the organisation so that everyone can become involved in the process of improvement and work together to make the changes'.

6.23 Empowerment has two key aspects.

(a) Allowing workers to have the **freedom** to decide how to do the necessary work, using the skills they possess and acquiring new skills as necessary to be an effective team member.

(b) Making those workers **personally responsible** for achieving production targets and for quality control. Not only will the job be done more effectively but the people who do the job will get more out of it.

Investment analysis

6.24 Levels of marketing expenditure are often significant, and any marketing strategy will have to be evaluated accordingly. However, according to Keith Ward: 'levels of marketing expenditure ... are often subjected to far less rigorous financial evaluations than smaller financial commitments on more tangible assets.'

6.25 In other words, treating marketing expenditure as a cost is appropriate for financial reporting considerations; but for **decision-making** purposes, there is an argument for analysing it, and controlling it, as if it were an **investment**.

6.26 Ward highlights the dilemma: 'for many marketing-led businesses, their most valuable assets are their brands ... yet ... the easiest way ... to improve profitability is to reduce expenditure on marketing or on research and development.'

6.27 Part of the strategic marketing plan therefore should be some form of **quantitative analysis.**

(a) For example, assume the marketing department chooses to spend £10m on re-positioning a product.

(i) How can a link between future sales and the £10m expenditure be established?

(ii) What would happen if the money was not spent? Would market share fall? Or would competitors find an opening?

(iii) Would an alternative use of £10m be more valuable?

(b) The benefits from marketing expenditure might sometimes be much less easy to quantify than, say, the cost savings on new equipment. Markets are an environment, where customers and competitors cannot be controlled. Instability and uncertainty are inherent within them.

Customer analysis and retention

6.28 Many organisations do not evaluate whether their customers and their potential customers are worth the trouble. Many marketing programmes are more concerned with **replacing** the percentage of customers that the company expects to lose every year, rather than trying to stop them **defecting** in the first place.

6.29 Bain and Co, the consultants, have estimated that a 50% cut in customer defections would more than double the average company's growth rate. This is particularly true of markets which are declining or static. So how can companies make sure not only that their customers stay, but also that those who stay are the ones worth having?

6.30 The company must ask itself whether it really knows its customers, what they want and whether they are likely to grow. Successful companies like Dell are offering value for money products to a highly segmented customer base. This success attracts the attention of other customers, as well as potential strategic alliances.

Marketing at Work

Dell has been so successful in its chosen field that in 1999 it was able to attract a $16bn purchasing pact with IBM, whereby IBM will supply Dell with a broad range of components for use in Dell systems. There will also be collaboration in the development of future technology. Early access to IBM technology will give Dell a significant competitive advantage.

6.31 Measuring customer satisfaction is also very important, although this can be very difficult. The company may use surveys, but when translating what the customer says into what he does (and the crucial question as to whether he will remain loyal) there is no direct link.

6.32 Recent research has found that many customers are not profitable at all. It has been held by Cooper and Kaplan at Harvard Business School that there is a 20-225 rule, whereby 20% of customers earn 225% of the profits, while the remaining 80% lose 125%. Profits tend to rise with the length of the relationship with a customer, so retention levels of profitable customers are key.

6.33 **Customer profitability analysis (CPA)** focuses on profits generated by customers. With CPA a company can focus its efforts on customers who promise the highest profit, and rationalise its approach to those who do not. In order to identify which customer groups generate the most profit it may be necessary to structure **accounting information systems** to take account of the many factors by which customers can be analysed. A relational database, whereby information may be structured in many different ways, may be useful.

Action Programme 1

Busqueros Ltd has 1,000 business customers spread fairly evenly over several countries. The sales force is organised into ten regions, each with 100 customers to be serviced. There are sales force offices at the heart of each region. Information is collected on a regional basis. The marketing director has recently carried out an analysis of the major customers by sales revenue. There are five significant customers, who between them account for 20% of the sales revenue of the firm. They do not get special treatment. What does this say about customer profitability analysis in Busqueros Ltd?

6.34 Different customer costs can arise out of the following.

- Order size
- Sales mix
- Order processing
- Transport costs
- Management time
- Cash flow problems (eg increased overdraft interest) caused by slow payers
- Order complexity (eg if the order has to be sent out in several stages)
- Stockholding costs can relate to specify customers
- The customer's negotiating strength.

6.35 Ward suggests the following format for a **statement of customer profitability.**

	£'000
Sales revenue	X
Less direct product cost	(X)
	X
Customer-specific variable costs:	
- distribution	X
- rebates and discounts	X
- promotion etc	X
	(X)
	X
Other costs	
- sales force	X
- customer service	X
- management cost	X
	(X)
	X
Financing cost	
- credit period	X
- customer-specific inventory	X
	(X)
	X

6.36 Such a report can highlight the differences between the cost of servicing different individuals or firms which can then be applied as follows.

(a) **Directing effort to cutting customer specific costs.** Installing an electric data interchange system (EDI) can save the costs of paperwork and data input.

(b) **Identifying those customers who are expensive to service,** thereby suggesting action to increase profitability.

(c) **Using CPA as part of a comparison with competitors' costs.** A firm which services a customer more cheaply than a competitor can use this cost advantage to offer extra benefits to the customer.

(d) Indicating cases where **profitability might be endangered,** for example by servicing customers for whom the firm's core competence is not especially relevant.

6.37 CPA might provide answers to the following questions.(Obviously a firm doing work for one major customer will find it easier to answer these questions than one which works for many customers.)

(a) What **profit/contribution** is the organisation making on sales to the customer, after discounts and selling and delivery costs?

(b) What would be the **financial consequences** of losing the customer?

(c) Is the customer buying in order sizes that are **unprofitable** to supply?

(d) What is **return on investment** on plant used?

(e) What is the level of **inventory** required specifically to supply these customers?

(f) Are there any other **specific costs** involved in supplying this customer, eg technical and test facilities, R & D facilities, special design staff?

(g) What is the ratio of net **contribution per customer to total investment**?

Exam Tip

The examiner has indicated the importance of these new developments in the evaluation and control area. You may get a question that asks for suggestions on some of the less traditional evaluation techniques, and how they might fit into a control system. Customer analysis is a key tool here, and the balanced scorecard reminds us that business performance can be viewed from a variety of perspectives when devising appropriate control measures.

---

7 ETHICAL ISSUES AND GREEN MARKETING

What do we mean by ethics?

7.1 Ethics is about what is right and wrong and how we arrive at such judgements. It deals with questions of absolute values, and their application in the real world. Ethical issues are an important consideration in controlling international marketing strategies.

Marketing at Work

Examples of ethical issues in marketing include the following.

(a) *Product issues.* When the French company Perrier discovered that its mineral water was in danger of contamination, they immediately withdrew all supplies without quibble, involving huge losses. By acting ethically, the company's market was eventually restored and if anything, its reputation was enhanced.

(b) *Promotional issues.* It was because so many companies were acting unethically with regard to marketing communications that the Trade Descriptions Act 1968 came into being. Estate agents were often greatly exaggerating the attributes of properties to the extent that it almost became accepted as a joke and Property Misdescriptions Act 1994 was designed to curtail their worst excesses. Second hand car dealers were not seen as much better. However, the 'angle' on communications can be more subtle, such as the Spiller's Homepride Flour slogan 'Finer grains make finer flour'. The advertisements gave the impression that the flour was made from smaller grains whereas the grains were actually made larger by a process of coagulation. Upon challenge, Spillers claimed they were using the word 'finer' in the dictionary sense of being better.

In the promotional area of personal selling many people think that persuading people to buy something they don't really want is intrinsically unethical, especially if hard sell tactics are used.

(c) *Distribution issues.* Some manufacturers have refused to supply retailers who do not carry out their bidding without question or as a means of manipulating the market.

(d) *Pricing issues.* Petrol companies have been accused of colluding over price increases, deemed to be an unethical practice.

The social climate

7.2 Public attitudes to the ethics of business have been in decline for a number of years. ('Greed is good': Gordon Gekko in the film *Wall Street*.) Surveys in both the UK and the USA show that the majority of members of the public think that business has poor ethical standards, and levels of trust are low. In the USA 90% of respondents in a recent survey thought that white collar crime was 'very common'.

7.3 Possible reasons for this perceived decline in standards are as follows.

(a) Increased pressure on business people to make decisions in a society characterised by **diverse value systems**. This is partly due to greater awareness of such issues, compared to the past, but also because of changes in markets themselves.

(b) **More business decisions are now subject to public judgement and scrutiny**. There are more pressures bringing the behaviour of business to the attention of the public, such as pressure groups, legal requirements and government interest.

(c) Business is now subject to **higher expectations** regarding the ethics of its behaviour. Companies such as the Body Shop have cleverly exploited ecological friendliness as a marketing tool.

7.4 **Cultures** have a strong impact on the kinds of standards which are followed within a particular society. Consequently, we should recognise that such standards tend to be relative to specific societies. Thus restrictions on trade or price fixing are morally wrong according to certain cultural presuppositions (in, say, the USA), but look quite different from the point of view of one which is concerned to protect its institutions from the impact of cultural and economic change (for instance, France), or to maintain extra-legal restrictions on its home markets (such as Japan).

Green pressures on business

7.5 Pressure for better environmental performance is coming from many quarters. Consumers are demanding a better environmental performance from companies - in recent surveys, it has been demonstrated that around three-quarters of the population are applying environmental criteria in many purchase decisions.

(a) **Green pressure groups** have increased their influence dramatically.

Marketing at Work

Greenpeace says it is developing an increasingly constructive relationship with companies (*Financial Times*, April 1999). The focus is now upon *solving* problems rather than merely highlighting them. Greenpeace played a role in the development of chlorine-free paper, a CFC-free fridge and a PVC-free credit card. The organisation vigorously defends itself against charges that it is 'a group of terrorists appealing not to reason but to ignorance and emotional blackmail'. A large number of prominent industrialists, including BP Amoco and Unilever, have appeared at conferences organised by Greenpeace.

(b) **Employees** are increasing pressure on the businesses in which they work for a number of reasons - partly for their own safety, partly in order to improve the public image of the company.

(c) **Legislation** is increasing almost by the day. Growing pressure from the 'green' or green-influenced vote has led to mainstream political parties taking these issues into their programmes, and most countries now have laws to cover land use planning, smoke emission, water pollution and the destruction of animals and natural habitats.

(d) **Environmental risk screening** has become increasingly important. Companies in the future will become responsible for the environmental impact of their activities.

BPP PUBLISHING

Social responsibility and sustainability

7.6 Green marketing is founded on two main ideas; one is a response to and **responsibility for the community**; the other is **sustainability**.

7.7 **Sustainability** involves developing strategies so that the company only uses resources at a rate which allows them to be replenished. At the same time, emissions of waste are confined to levels which do not exceed the capacity of the environment to absorb them. In relation to the development of the world's resources, some policies are based on sustainability.

- Pursue equity in the distribution of resources
- Maintain the integrity of the world's ecosystems
- Increase the capacity of human populations for self-reliance

Green marketing

7.8 As should be clear, there are strong reasons for bringing the environment into the business equation, but the strongest reason is the consumer. The **'green consumer'** must be the driving force behind changes in marketing and business practices.

7.9 Green consumption can be defined as the decisions related to consumer choice which involve **environmentally-related beliefs**. There is increasing evidence of the importance of this market.

- Surveys which indicate increased levels of **environmental awareness and concern**
- Increasing demand for, and availability of, **information** on environmental issues
- Green **product concepts** and green substitute products
- **Value shifts** from consumption to conservation
- Effective **PR and marketing campaigns** by environmental charities and causes

Green marketing contexts

7.10 Manufacturers of **consumer goods** may be seen as 'enemies'.

- Damaging the environment or social institutions to meet consumer demand
- Producing 'dirty' products
- Using up scarce and/or environmentally significant raw materials (eg rare woods)

7.11 Some manufacturers are already making products which contribute environmental improvements (biodegradable packing, for example) while larger manufacturers are under pressures to act in a socially responsible manner because of their size and social prominence.

Marketing at Work

Shell announced in April 1998 that it was pulling out of the so-called Global Climate Coalition of businesses because of irreconcilable differences. The GCC opposes targets for reducing greenhouse gas emissions linked with climate change. Greenpeace was welcoming of the move.

British Petroleum did the same thing over a year ago, and is perceived as being better able to promote its green credentials.

Shell is attempting to clean up its act on environmental and ethical issues following recent PR debacles over its Nigerian operations and the abortive attempt to dispose of the Brent Spar at sea.

The Chairman of Shell Transport and Trading said that an ethically ambitious approach was 'the right way and the most rewarding way to behave' for any company in the 21st century.

Chapter Roundup

- **Control** is the process of ensuring that the results of operations conform to established goals.

- The **marketing control system** will need to overcome international and intercultural differences, and comparing the performance of different countries will be difficult.

- International marketing performance is generally controlled via **reports and meetings**. Information technology has a role to play.

- **Alternative approaches** to evaluation and control include the balance scorecard, benchmarking, self assessment, the learning organisation and customer analysis.

- **Customer profitability analysis** (CPA) enables a company to focus on those customers who generate the highest profit.

- **Ethical issues** are an important consideration in controlling international marketing plans. More business decisions are now subject to public judgement and scrutiny, and pressure groups such as Greenpeace are very influential.

- **Green marketing** is aimed at environmentally aware consumers.

Quick Quiz

1 What problems can international marketing pose? (see para 2.1)
2 What factors may influence the development of a local marketing programme? (2.3)
3 Give some examples of standards for local marketing activities (3.5)
4 Apart from planning and organisation structure, name some other control methods (5.3)
5 What is 'the balanced scorecard?' (6.2)
6 What are the stages of benchmarking. (6.10)
7 Why might it be appropriate to view marketing expenditure as an investment? (6.24, 6.25)
8 What is Cooper and Kaplan's '20-225 rule'? (6.32)
9 What factors can give rise to different customer costs? (6.34)
10 What factors may be cited as evidence of the importance of 'the green market'? (7.9)

Action Programme Review

1 The information reflects sales force administration and convenience. However, it might obscure an analysis of customer profitability, in which case presenting information by customer size might be more important than geography.

Now try illustrative question 14 at the end of the Study Text

Illustrative questions and suggested answers

1   GLOBALISATION   *32 mins*

Many key authors like Levitt, Keegan, Ohmae and others state the necessity to develop a global strategy. State what you consider to be the definition of 'globalisation' and outline the forces driving its development.

(20 marks)

2   WORLD TRADE   *32 mins*

What are the macro factors underpinning the shaping and development of world trade? Making reference to examples, illustrate how these are being reflected in the way companies are planning and implementing their international marketing strategies.

(20 marks)

3   OVERSEAS ENVIRONMENT   *32 mins*

A clothing company based in the United Kingdom believes that its domestic market is limited and is proposing to expand by the manufacture and sale of its products abroad. At this stage, it has not identified where it will locate its manufacturing facility. The company believes that there are major advantages to be gained by setting up a factory in a country with a low-wage economy.

The company recognises the need to understand the marketing environment of the country within which it establishes its manufacturing facility. It appreciates that besides labour, there are other local environmental issues which need to be fully considered before entering negotiations to build a factory.

Required

(a)   Compare and contrast the environmental factors which apply in both the UK and the other country.   (13 marks)

(b)   Explain the possible cultural influences on the effectiveness of the workforce in respect of local education and training, technology, working hours and domestic amenities.   (7 marks)

(20 marks)

4   CULTURE AND IM   *32 mins*

Discuss the view that culture lies at the heart of all the problems connected with international marketing.

(20 marks)

5   MARKET RESEARCH IN DEVELOPING COUNTRIES   *32 mins*

What are the problems encountered by companies carrying out international market research in developing countries? How might these companies deal with the issue of information gaps?

(20 marks)

6   RETAILING DIFFERENCES   *32 mins*

Describe the factors which typically differentiate between retailers in developing and developed countries. Show how the marketing plan would require modification with reference to a product of your choice.

(20 marks)

7   MARKET ENTRY   *32 mins*

Outline the market entry methods and the levels of involvement associated with the development of a company's globalisation process from initial exporting through to becoming a global corporation. Specify what you consider to be the important criteria in deciding the appropriate entry method.

(20 marks)

8   EXPATRIATES   *32 mins*

Your company is considering establishing a new territory outside of its home-base. As International Brand Manager you have been asked to look at the strengths and weaknesses of the use of head office, home-based expatriate sales people, as opposed to using local nationals. What training and familiarisation procedures would you propose for home-based expatriates for them to be effective in sales negotiations in a foreign country with a different language and culture?

(20 marks)

9   STANDARDISATION   *32 mins*

In an ideal world, companies would like to manufacture a standardised product. What are the factors that support the case for a standardised product and what are the circumstances that are likely to prevent its implementation? Support your argument with examples.

(20 marks)

10   EXPORT PRICES   *32 mins*

Examine the advantages and disadvantages of a standard pricing policy in all export markets.

(20 marks)

11   COMMUNICATIONS DECISIONS   *32 mins*

International marketing communications decisions can be taken at a variety of levels: national, world region and global. Explain the reasons for these differences, give examples to illustrate your answer.

(20 marks)

12   DISTRIBUTION DEVELOPMENTS   *32 mins*

Distribution and logistics are increasingly becoming the new battleground in international marketing as companies seek to gain the competitive edge. As International Marketing Manager for a multi-national organisation, write a short report identifying the major developments that are taking place in this important field of international marketing. Making reference to examples, explain what your international organisation should do to stay ahead of the competition.

(20 marks)

13   SERVICE MARKETING   *32 mins*

You have applied for a job with a hotel company which is establishing a formal marketing function for the first time. As part of the interview process, you have been asked to make a short presentation which explains the characteristics of marketing in the service sector. Prepare some notes which detail the areas you intend to cover in your presentation.

(20 marks)

14   CONTROL   *32 mins*

Control is described as one of the major building blocks of planning, providing the foundation on which the future can be constructed. From an international perspective identify the factors which should be taken into account in developing an effective control system. What might affect the degree and effectiveness of such a control system?

(20 marks)

1   GLOBALISATION

Theodore Levitt first put forward the term '**globalisation**' in 1983. The debate as to whether such a thing as a **global company** exists goes on, but there is certainly ancecdotal evidence that world markets are converging. If a **definition** of **globalisation** is accepted as being:

'the process by which the world becomes more homogeneous with regard to the products and services demanded'

then the forces driving its development are as follows.

- Developments in **global telecommunications** using satellite broadcasting are helping to establish English as the international language for interpersonal and business communications.

- Global telecommunications are helping to establish **global brands** that are killing off local brands in certain product categories. The global dominance of Kodak and Fuji in the 35mm film market is an example.

- The emergence of a **global consumer**, particularly amongst young people, is a reality exploited by many multinationals such as Nike and Reebok, who have developed both a global product range and a global brand and image, targeted at a global consumer.

- **Multinational** car companies (GM and Ford) are exploiting developments in transportation systems to source components for their assembly plants in the US and Europe from suppliers all over the world. This is improving the wealth creating (value adding) activities of the developing world, and creating consumers with discretionary money to spend in places where previously no spare money existed.

- Developments in **transportation systems**, particularly air transport, have brought global travel within the reach of increasing numbers of people. Increased travel brings increased demand for goods to be available in places visited by the travellers.

- Increasing **affluence** of consumers, as the global economy grows due to the relaxation of trade barriers through agreements negotiated by WTO and the actions of the multinational companies, encourages spending on travel. This fuels the need for more homogeneous products and services. For instance, airports around the world are beginning to look the same, with similar check-in and baggage processing facilities, retail outlets, and styled restaurants offering food and refreshments from around the world. This reflects the convergence of consumer needs.

- The **convergence of consumer needs** on a global scale re-defines concepts of **economies of scale** and the **competitive** and **absolute advantages** these can generate. The car companies, led by Ford with its Mondeo, are designing and building cars with a global consumer in mind.

- The acquisition and merger activities of companies to ensure profit growth contributes significantly to the process of globalisation, as management teams are forced to abandon their **ethnocentric** 'comfort zones' and adopt **regiocentric, geocentric or polycentric** approaches to managing increasingly global businesses.

For many companies in an increasing number of industries survival will be dependent upon them taking a **global perspective**. There are many ways to achieve the objective of being a global company with the right way for any particular company being the way which achieves the **objectives** set for globalisation.

2   WORLD TRADE

All the 'classical' macro factors of sociological/cultural, economic, legal, political, and technological have a significant impact on world trade, and can be seen to be affecting the way in which companies develop and implement their international marketing strategies.

The **global consumer** is emerging as a focal point for many companies, and identifying these consumers whose needs can be met with a single global product is a major driving force for many companies, eg Kodak and Microsoft. Other companies approach their global consumers with a **global brand**, and adapt the product to suit local tastes and preferences, eg Coca Cola and McDonalds. The '**world youth market**' is an example of a set of global consumers developing out of a **convergence** of the social, cultural, and economic factors aided by the technological developments in global communications.

As the world gets richer due to international companies moving their value adding (wealth creating) activities to the most suitable locations, **world wide travel** has come within the reach of larger segments of the world population. As travel increases so the needs and wants of consumers for their familiar products and brands expands globally. The designer brands and products of North America and the European Union are available in the countries of South East Asia. Similarly, the cuisine and artefacts (so far without strong brand identities) of the countries of South East Asia are widely available in North America and the European Union.

The reduction of tariffs through the continual action of the members of the **World Trade Organisation** (formerly GATT) during the last 50 years has significantly increased the volume of world trade. More recently the formation of **trading blocks** such as the EU, NAFTA and ASEAN is having a significant impact on the structure of world trade, as trade within the blocks becomes easier and trade between the blocks becomes the subject of longer and longer negotiations.

To overcome any difficulties of trading between blocks, companies are setting up facilities to gain access to markets which may otherwise be closed. These developments will significantly reduce the flow of goods around the world between the blocks, but greatly increase the flow of money and information. The emerging **information technologies** will have an increasing impact on the way trade between countries is conducted.

Political developments such as the collapse of the centrally planned economies of Central and Eastern Europe under the influence of the former Soviet Union has created many opportunities for international companies. Car makers have acquired car plants in this area (eg VW bought Skoda), brewers have bought breweries, and more recently retailers have started to acquire businesses in these countries, such as Tesco in Prague.

Information technology is allowing the countries of the world to become more **interconnected and interdependent**. World trade was affected by the fall in the value of the currencies of many of the countries of South East Asia, which created a general lack of **consumer confidence** world wide and increased the threat of a **global recession**.

IT with its ability to provide the world with **real time information** is causing companies to completely rethink their business strategies with respect to what they order, when they order, how much they order, when they pay and in what currency. IT is also providing consumers with information on what is fashionable, and altering their **buying habits** and patterns. **Just in Time** operations (developed through the exploitation of improved transport and distribution infrastructures) are no longer good enough for some products and markets, and this is creating further impetus for companies to change and will influence the way in which world trade develops.

3   **OVERSEAS ENVIRONMENT**

(a) **Environmental factors**

Political and legal factors

(i)   **Political conditions** in the individual overseas markets (eg overall stability) or sources of supply (eg risk of nationalisation).

(ii)   **Relationships between country governments**. If the firm intends to use the plant as a basis for exports to other countries, the country's membership of international trade bodies is important, and political relationships with other states matter.

(iii) In some low wage countries, the **legal framework** is not secure (McDonalds was evicted from a prime leasehold site in Beijing when it was decided to redevelop the property irrespective of the legal agreement).

(iv)   **Political connections**. Where the low wage economy has involved state planning, political connections may be more important than legality, and help might be needed to get round a complex and possibly corrupt bureaucracy.

(v)   **Local labour** law may be different (redundancies are legally hard to achieve in some countries, eg India).

Economic factors

(i)   The overall level of **economic activity** and growth.

(ii)   The relative levels of **inflation** in the domestic and overseas market.

(iii) **Exchange rate**, its level and volatility. This is relevant if the new plant will source some of its raw materials from overseas.

(iv)   **Exchange controls**. Will the firm be allowed to remit profits to its home country?

(v)   The relative **prosperity** of individual overseas markets.

(vi)   The state of the **labour market**. Cheap labour is often unproductive, because it is untrained and perhaps inefficient. While labour costs may be lower, the apparent saving may be reduced by lower productivity.

Social and cultural factors

(i)   The **cultures and practices** of customers and consumers in individual markets.

(ii)   The **media and distribution** systems in overseas markets.

(iii)   The differences in **ways of doing business**.

(iv)   The degree to which **national cultural differences** matter for the product concerned. For clothing, the firm might have to consider different sizes, materials (for ideas as to 'formal' or 'leisure wear' and national stylistic preferences (eg bright colours as opposed to sober hues).

Technological factors

(i)   The degree to which a firm can **imitate** the technology of its competitors.

(ii)   A firm's access to domestic and overseas **patents**.

(iii)   **Intellectual property** protection varies in different countries.

(iv)   **Technology transfer** requirements (some countries regard investments from overseas companies as learning opportunities and require the investing company to share some of its technology).

(v)   The relative **cost of technology** compared to labour.

(vi)   An appropriate **infrastructure** to enable the technology to be used effectively. Some high-tech plants fail in poor countries because there is no supply of spares or trained engineers. More basically, the firm has to rely on public supplies of electricity and water, and in some countries power cuts are frequent and costly. The firm might have to supply its own generators.

(vii)   In some countries **telecommunications** are inefficient and expensive.

Currently, the firm is hoping to exploit low labour costs. How far is this realistic in the long term? If the market is to enjoy overall economic growth, rising prosperity will mean rising incomes and rising wages. If the firm is to make a substantial investment in the local factory, it will have to plan for productivity improvements.

The overall competitive environment

(i)   This relates to the five forces analysis propounded by Michael Porter.

     (1)   **Barriers to entry**. Existing firms might have powerful political connections which they can exploit against the competitor from overseas. Customers may prefer the national products and brands. Also the distribution network may be effectively tied up.

     (2)   **Substitute products**. We are not told what type of clothing is to be made, and who the customers are. In some countries, traditional clothing, made at home, may substitute for factory produced products.

     (3)   **Bargaining power of customers**. No detail is given of distribution, and how the firm intends to sell its products, but distributors might have high power.

     (4)   **Bargaining power of suppliers**. Again, we are not told how the factory will be supplied. Local suppliers might welcome the new business.

     (5)   **Competitive rivalry**. In some countries, local businesses have strong political connections. Whilst overseas investment might be welcome, as official policy, it can all to easily be hindered at local level. Furthermore, in many companies, existing producers are owned by the state, and there may be restrictions on competition. Finally, competitors may have many distribution networks sewn up, and the newcomer may find hurdles greater than expected.

(ii)   We can also use Porter's diamond model of **national competitive advantage** to assess the venture.

     (1)   The **rivalry** between different firms has been discussed above.

(2) **Demand conditions**. The new market might help the firm compete elsewhere, by the demand conditions it possesses, but this seems unlikely.

(3) **Factor conditions**. What is the new market's supply of basic and advanced factors, apart from labour? To what extent is the firm evading other problems by concentrating on low-cost, and low-skill labour, as opposed to improving productivity at home?

(4) **Related and supporting industries**. A country in which there is a cluster of textile and clothing related industries? History often shows that industrialising countries often start off with textiles.

It is also worth mentioning the physical environment. (Shell has received bad publicity about environmental degradation in Ogoniland.)

(b) **Cultural issues and the workforce**

Culture is a shared body of beliefs, values and assumptions, even a way of interpreting the world, which guide the behaviour of individuals. Most organisations have a culture, but this is part of the wider culture of the society in which they exist. The firm will have to deal with the national culture in a number of areas.

(i) **Local education and training**

If low labour costs are a reason for the move, this implies that the processes are fairly labour intensive, as labour costs must be a significant proportion of total costs. The influence of **local education** will make itself felt in a number of areas.

(1) **Basic literacy and numeracy**. Many relatively poor countries, such as Sri Lanka, have high literacy rates in the local language. Sadly, in other poor countries, this is not the case. If this is needed for the factory, the actual supply of labour might be smaller than appears.

(2) **Knowledge of English**. In order to ensure that the factory is properly run, at least some of the local managers and staff need a good working knowledge of business English. In some countries (eg in eastern Europe where Russian was the first foreign language taught) English speakers might be in short supply.

(3) **Technology**. Education and training implications are discussed in (ii) below.

(4) **Attitudes to work**. The firm will have to train its employees, in part to acclimatise them to the corporate culture of the firm. Professor Hofstede contrasted attitudes to work in different countries.

- In some countries, disagreeing with the boss is not acceptable behaviour, whereas a boss from the UK may be touting for new ideas.

- Continuous improvement programmes require people to show more initiative than a culture based on deference to authority might accept.

- Many cultures have a high power-distance, whereas a UK firm might have a low power-distance and a lower group orientation than some Asian countries.

(ii) **Technology**

(1) The firm will have to train its workers how to use the machines and how to maintain them properly, so that their useful life is not shortened through poor management.

(2) If the plant is to develop further and develop new materials, personnel with an appropriate technical knowledge will need to be recruited. Again, some poor countries have quite good universities, so there may be a pool of qualified engineers available for recruitment. It is unlikely, according to Porter, that firms can compete on low labour costs alone, and the firm will invest to enhance the productivity of the labour force.

(3) As is mentioned above, cultural attitudes to technology and the work processes are important. Some labour disciplines regarding machinery need to be enforced, particularly with regard to health and safety.

(4) It is possible that many will welcome the opportunity to raise their skills.

(iii) **Working hours**

Even within Europe, different national cultures suggest different attitudes to time, timekeeping and punctuality. Clearly, the factory has to be operated efficiently, and this might require a greater degree of labour discipline than the people might have expected.

However the firm will be able to offer perhaps better wages than local firms, and will be able to choose employees for which this is not a problem.

Even poor countries have **labour regulations**, and a large factory would be more subject to regulation in this respect than local family businesses or sweatshops. Indeed, there might be legal restrictions on shifts and working hours which have to be respected.

(iv) **Domestic amenities**

In some countries in the past, firms were expected to take a paternalistic approach to employees, and to supply them with **housing**, to ensure **lifetime loyalty**, or other accommodation if the plant is far away from convenient transport. Sometimes such accommodation is restricted to a dormitory arrangement. Few people in wealthier countries would tolerate such an arrangement, but it might be acceptable in poorer countries, especially if transport is expensive or hazardous.

Other amenities can include subsiding the education of workers' children, a good canteen, and health services in the factory. The firm can prove itself a good corporate citizen and earn the respect of the workforce.

4 CULTURE AND IM

The extent to which culture lies at the heart of all problems connected with International Marketing depends much on one's definition of culture. There is no universally accepted definition but it is commonly held to centre on the **value systems** used in a particular society. Those value systems apply obviously in areas such as religion and the arts, but if one's definition of culture is wide enough, can also extend into the economic sphere.

It is probably untrue to assert that all the problems connected with International Marketing can be ascribed to cultural differences but certainly they represent a major, and probably the major, influence on International Marketing. The precise extent of the influence depends on the nature of the goods in question. For example, foodstuffs are well known as highly **culturally dependent** whereas building excavators are not! Thus a manager engaged in marketing food would be much more likely to agree with the assertion than one in the construction industry.

The principal impact of culture in International Marketing lies in its influence on the **environment in which the sales/purchase transaction takes place**. It affects the way in which the seller offers his product to the market , the benefits perceived in that offer by the potential customer (and thus the suitability of the goods for their intended purpose) and, particularly, the communications mix by which the seller entices the potential purchaser.

Culture also has a marked influence on **market research and analysis**. The very fact that cultural differences exist requires market research to be much more extensive and thorough than in the domestic market (where the manager's own cultural values will provide a good deal of secondary information). Consequently it also makes market analysis much more expensive and difficult to perform. And since the market research work may itself be culturally bound it is sometimes in itself of questionable validity.

If one confines one's definition of culture to the impact on buyers and sellers as individuals, culture although important is limited to the types of influence noted above and therefore cannot be said to lie at the heart of all international marketing problems.

If the definition of culture is extended to include the influence of individuals' attitudes on the way society as a whole is organised, a whole new range of international marketing problems comes within its ambit. For example the **political and legal structure** of a nation has a major impact on the way any enterprise markets its products within it. This influence extends over the whole marketing mix.

(i) **Product design and quality** is affected by national standards

(ii) The **structure of business** is influenced by national norms

(iii) The **price** that customers are willing to pay is limited by the benefits perceived in the goods by that culture

(iv)   the **methods of promotion** may be constrained by a range of political, legal and social constraints and attitudes

All this occurs within the context of any one nation. The culture of a country may even dictate whether a foreign marketer is welcome at all. Mars encountered some hostility in Russia when the population became tired of its relentless promotion of the carefree American life in its advertising. Mars is still a strong force in the country, but marketers had to recognise that local advertising had to be adapted to reflect Russian preoccupations and traditions.

Many countries in fact have **sub-cultures** within them, which multiplies the problems faced by the international marketer. When viewed from the perspective of a multinational enterprise cultural differences become a major factor in the assessment of whether to offer a **standardised** product range or a range **adapted** to meet perceived local needs.

Although there are problems in international marketing that cannot be ascribed to cultural differences (such as the method a business chooses for pricing its products) it is certainly possible to assert confidently that culture lies at the heart of most, if not all, problems in the field.

5   MARKET RESEARCH IN DEVELOPING COUNTRIES

Typical problems encountered in conducting **market research** in developing countries are as follows:

- Lack of reliable basic demographic and **economic statistics** upon which to develop a workable database.

- A general lack of up to date **secondary market intelligence** information, including that which is provided by organisations such as the Economist Intelligence Unit.

- When data, or information, is found it may be **out of date**, **inaccurate** or **irrelevant** for the purpose for which is required.

- The **units of measurement** may differ from what is usually expected in the developed world.

- Primary data can be difficult to obtain due to **cultural differences**, which in many developing countries do not encourage the disclosure of personal information.

- There is a lack of **marketing research agencies** in developing countries

- Lack of telephones, poor transport **infrastructure** and problems of accessibility to respondents all hinder the primary research process.

The absence of reliable and appropriate secondary data presents significant management problems regarding the obtaining of primary data. The problems extend to all aspects of collection, analysis, and interpretation of data, as well as the training and supervision of interviewers.

Information gaps may be filled by the following analytical techniques:

- Analysis of **international trade statistics** between the developed world and the target developing countries can be used as a **proxy measure** to establish the pattern of trade, and give a first order approximation of market size

- Multiple factor indices using **proxy measures**, for example, estimating literacy levels from the number of schools, or government estimates of the number of school age children

- **Cross-country comparisons** in which the trade development patterns of an existing developing country are used to estimate the likely development of the target country

- **Time series** approaches with estimates of the rate of product (or service) demand growth, based on the stage of development of the target developing country

- **Regression analysis** looking for relationships between major variables, for example, examining the relationship between the vehicle population, estimates of GDP per head of population and population of a country to estimate annual demand for cars.

If these analytical techniques do not produce meaningful results then a visit to the target developing countries and gathering information from first hand investigation is the remaining option.

6   RETAILING DIFFERENCES

The factors that differentiate between retailers in developed and developing countries can be classified as either **environmental** (which affects the way the retailers are structured), or **logistic** (which affects the process by which they satisfy the needs of their customers).

Factors which differentiate the structure of retailing are as follows.

- **Shopping and buying habits** will influence the development of a retailing sector. In the developed world, shopping is not a daily necessity and the retailing sector is continually responding to changing buying habits. In the developing world shopping is a daily ritual and buying habits are relatively static.

- The stage of **economic and market development** will determine income levels and the spending power of customers within a given market. It will also influence the concentration of retailing and the development of distribution channels.

- The **location of customers** will range from the large, established conurbations in the developed world to the widely dispersed populations in the developing world (complemented by scattered large conurbations).

- The availability of, and access to, **technology** by both retailers and consumers will influence the manner by which transactions occur - 'electronic money' either by EFTPOS or credit/debit card is common in the developed world, whereas transactions are principally for cash in the developing world.

- **Cultural differences** will influence the product and services offered.

The factors which will influence the **logistics** are as follows.

- **Technology** that is available for transporting and storing products to the retail premises will vary. For example, frozen food is accepted in the developed world, with householders having freezers to store frozen food supplied from cold stores operated by both the retailers and food processors. This pattern is unlikely to be encountered in the developing countries with little or no freezing facilities at any stage of the distribution channel. Thus, customers' needs in the developing world are satisfied by what is available rather than what can be made available using technology.

- The **transport infrastructure** will have a significant impact on the development of retailing. The US and the UK, together with an increasing number of EU countries, have developed out of town 'retail parks', allegedly in response to consumers' changing buying habits. These developments have yet to be implemented in the developing world. Good road systems and car ownership are key environmental factors which will affect this.

- The **size and dispersion of the market** will significantly affect the development of retailing, particularly with respect to the service level offered and the service level expected. Consumers in the developed world expect instant satisfaction and are highly critical when this cannot be provided. This puts high pressure on the supply chain to perform to high standards. For example, in the UK the major food retailers who account for around 80% of all food purchases expect at least a 99% accurate delivery performance from their food processing suppliers. As yet there is no evidence of these performance levels being expected in the developing world.

It is evident from the above that the marketing plans of retailers in the developed world will need significant modification to be operated effectively in the developing world.

The main modifications will include:

- Interpreting and assessing the SLEPT factors very critically to establish the impact they will have on the marketing plan, and acting accordingly. See the example of frozen food given above.

- Taking account of the context of the market place will invariably involve all aspects of the marketing mix, as well as the environment in which the consumers live. The Self Reference Criterion can have no place in a marketing plan for a retailer in the developing world, although, in the future, they may achieve the level of the developed world as their economies grow.

- Critically assessing the costs and risks of the significantly different distribution channels and the impact on pricing strategies and hence competitiveness.

It is highly unlikely that a marketing plan prepared for the retailing sector of the developed world could be used in the developing world without significant modification. The most appropriate and effective modifications are likely to be made after a detailed fact finding visit has been made to gain experience and understanding of being a consumer in the urban and rural developing world.

7   MARKET ENTRY

The principle methods of market entry are **indirect exporting, direct exporting, direct inward investment** and **co-operation** through the formation of alliances, partnerships and joint ventures.

Indirect exporting involves the company in very **low risk** since it will be selling its products to a domestic organisation who will then export the product to the final destination. These domestic intermediaries are either classified as **export houses/trading companies** or export management companies.

Piggy-backing is another indirect exporting method which involves another company acting as the carrier for the product.

Indirect exporting offers the exporter little or no control over market development, and although it is often used by many small companies to get started in the international market place it will not lead to a global corporation.

Direct exporting involves a higher level of risk and can result in a company having a global presence if properly managed. Direct exporting is relatively low cost and, subject to no entry barriers being present and the company having adequate resources, it can allow a rapid entry into many markets. The most usual form of direct exporting is either through the appointment of agents who will be paid a commission, or by appointing **distributors** who will hold stock but may or may not own it, depending on the terms of the distributorship.

For certain types of business, **franchising** is the equivalent of direct exporting. An overseas organisation will pay for the rights to use the business concept. As with direct exporting through agents or distributors, franchising would allow a company to operate globally in a very short space of time, providing it had the necessary human resources to support it.

An arrangement whereby a company has its products **manufactured under license** could be seen as similar to franchising. The issuing of licenses to have products made on a global scale will be constrained by human resources of the organisation.

Direct inward investment is a high risk strategy since it is subject to the acceptance of the host government. Examples of direct inward investment are the setting up of own facilities, or the acquisition of or merger with existing businesses in the host country. The advantages of direct inward investment are **total control** of market development and (because of the higher risks) greater profits can be expected. Due to the investment required, direct inward investment as a means of becoming global is **expensive** and usually takes a long time. It took Nissan 30 years to establish 24 plants in 18 countries. It took Ford and General Motors up to 40 years to establish their global presence.

Co-operation strategies can either involve direct inward investment such as the formation of joint ventures (which usually require the incoming partner to share the costs of establishing the new entity), or no inward investment as with strategic alliances. Globalisation via joint ventures can be expensive and slow due to the constraints of limited financial resources and possibly limited targets, whereas strategic alliances can lead to a fairly rapid global presence.

Decision Criteria

These are likely to be based on any or all of the following.

- Company resources
- Company expectations and objectives
- Management expertise and attitude towards international expansion and development
- Existing involvement overseas
- The nature and features of the product
- Nature of the target markets
- Nature and size of competition in the target markets
- Barriers to entry

8   EXPATRIATES

The choice between using **expatriates** and **local sales staff** highlights the inherent dilemma in the **personal selling** element of the promotion mix in international marketing.

Comparing expatriate with local sales staff

The strength of using expatriates is that these are people with a thorough knowledge of the company and its organisation structure and management, its culture, brands, and products and how they are used. These people will fully understand the objectives and performance criteria set and the performance measures used. In short they are the company. However, unless they have had considerable exposure to a given region or country they are unlikely to fully understand the local culture and language, and as such may not be operating optimally. This could have a detrimental impact on the development of sales in the region or country.

The strengths of using local sales people is that they fully understand the culture and language of the country/market in which they operate and should be able, in principle, to generate optimum levels of sales. However, the local sales person may see the position as a job being done for a distant management which works to totally different principles and which uses motivational techniques which appear totally inappropriate. This lack of understanding and empathy with the overseas principal could have a detrimental impact on the development of sales in the region or country.

Expatriate Sales Training Programme

The following training programme is proposed.

- Six months before confirming the appointment of the expatriate start language training in both everyday conversational language and technical and commercial language.

- Three months before confirmation, and whilst continuing with the general language training, start developing the expatriates' skill in the idiomatic language.

- Two months before departure send the expatriate for a one week pre-appointment acclimatisation visit to the target country to gain a first hand impression of the local culture.

- Following this visit, and with the language training continuing, commence a detailed culture awareness programme in which the expatriate can develop the necessary social skills to operate effectively in the target market.

- One month before appointment send the expatriate to the target country for a two week sales development period to enable him/her to test out the skills and knowledge in the field and for him/her to establish their personal 'comfort zone' for operating in that market.

Conclusion

An organisation may consider it appropriate to train 2 or 3 sales people as home based expatriate sales staff, to allow exposure of a larger number of interested sales staff as part of a company wide sales staff development programme. A benefit of this approach is that the company always has appropriately trained and experienced staff available for sales development in regions with common languages and similar cultures.

9 STANDARDISATION

The factors encouraging and supporting **standardisation** of products are, principally, **economies of scale** in production, **research and development** and **marketing communications**. With standardised products, and a belief that an ethnocentric approach to the markets of the world is appropriate, then standardised marketing plans can be used in all markets.

Standardised marketing communications enable single images to be created, and for some products competitive advantage can be extracted from country of origin effect. With standardised products produced in a number of plants around the world, production can be shared amongst the plants and markets supplied from any or all of the plants to take advantage of prevailing favourable conditions.

The use of satellite broadcasting by advertisers encourages the use of standardised advertising due to the very large footprints of the satellite transmissions. Thus, in the medium term developments in global communications technology could give greater impetus to standardisation. In the recent past Ford have announced that the Mondeo is to be their first 'world car', and historically a number of product such as 35mm film, blank VHS tapes and certain designer goods have become standardised throughout the world.

The circumstances that prevent or hinder standardisation are legion. Differing **usage conditions** for example due to differing climates make standardisation of some products difficult. Differences in **taste, income and level of sophistication** will also impact on standardisation.

Intervention by government in the form of tariffs and non-tariff barriers together with pressure from **regulatory bodies** can prevent a standardisation strategy being effective. Markets will vary dramatically in their **development cycles**, and correspondingly, products will be at a different stage of

BPP PUBLISHING

their life cycles in differing markets. For instance, bicycles are leisure products in the developed world but vital transport products in the developing world. This demonstrates that the global standardisation of bicycles will be difficult, but regional standardisation may be practical.

Technology differences will also hinder standardisation. Computer users in the developed world are more likely to operate with the latest versions of micro processors in their PC's. Users in the developing world will invariably use the older technology. It is in the interests of both the micro processor manufacturers and the PC manufacturers to maintain these differentials, in order to re-coup the investments in the respective technologies.

The standardisation of **global brands** is a far more frequently encountered phenomenon with many brands being targeted at the emerging **world youth culture**, for instance Nike and Reebok. These companies appear to be exploiting the global communication of sport and the desire of young people world-wide to be associated with the brands worn by their sporting heroes.

10   EXPORT PRICES

Standardised pricing is a system under which an exporter sells his products with the intention of them having the same selling price in every market. Even if desirable, it is hard to achieve in international markets, due principally to fluctuation in exchange rates and cost differences created by product variation and government regulations and tariffs. Nevertheless it can be aimed for and the following advantages are normally identified with the policy.

(a)   It is **easy to put in place** and is cheap (in terms of management resources) to maintain.

(b)   Because it is so straightforward the international price list can be **updated quickly**.

(c)   If a standardised policy is not adopted, managers in different markets around the world will seek to negotiate a buying price (or **transfer price** if the business is divisionalised) that enables them to maximise the profit of the part of the organisation for which they have responsibility. Such an objective may conflict with the organisation's overall objectives and is a waste of **managerial resource**.

(d)   With increased **personal mobility** customers are purchasing the same product in different markets more frequently. A standardised pricing policy allows them to identify closely with the product when they purchase it abroad.

(e)   The danger of **parallel exporting** is avoided. Parallel exporting is a system by which official distribution channels are circumvented, normally by a wholesaler in one market exporting to another wholesaler, or a retailer, in another market. It occurs because the retailer in the 'cheaper' market notices that he can earn a better return by exporting goods into the distribution channel of another more 'expensive' market than selling the product on in the normal way in his own market. A standardised pricing policy removes this opportunity by **removing the price differential** between markets.

(f)   In the case of a company new to exporting a standardised pricing policy can be a **useful starting point**. It is unlikely to have sufficient experience of its planned export markets to permit it to set accurate alternative prices in each market. Later, if it wishes to, it can move away from standardised pricing.

It can be readily foreseen, however, that standardised pricing also has significant disadvantages. These mostly reflect the **rigidity** that such a system imposes.

(a)   There is no scope for **flexibility in pricing** to take account of the differing competitive conditions across markets.

(b)   According to the marketing concept, pricing is an integral part of the marketing mix. Standardised pricing takes this element of **decision** away from marketing managers.

(c)   A standardised price will almost always be either **too high or too low**. Consequently the enterprise loses potential profit (in markets where the price is too low) and normally prices itself out of markets in which its standardised price is too high.

(d)   **Agents, distributors and dealerships** cannot be motivated to the enterprise's best advantage. Where the standard price is too low agents will be hard to motivate because they are likely to earn an insufficient return from their business. In contrast, where it is too high agents may earn excessive returns - at the expense of the exporter.

(e) Most countries have **anti-dumping regulations** by which they protect their domestic markets from exporters disposing of excess stocks at below cost price. A standard price that is too low may contravene the regulations of some markets.

(f) A further feature of setting a standard price that is too low is that it may be **below marginal cost** in some markets, particularly those where the product incorporates **expensive local adaptations** or where **distribution costs** are particularly high. If this occurs the enterprise actually loses money (rather than failing to make an adequate return).

(g) An exporter with a standard price has two alternatives open to it. It may either invoice in one currency or translate its price list into local currencies. Either course of action has disadvantages. Since, for a variety of reasons, the **purchasing power parity theory** of exchange rates often fails to work in practice, the enterprise's price will vary in an uncontrolled way if it prices only in one currency. This occurs most notably in countries with very high rates of inflation. On the other hand, if the company translates its price list into each local currency it either loses the essential simplicity of standardised pricing (by having to retranslate for exchange rate movements) or again suffers from uncontrolled price movements if it fails to update local prices regularly.

11 COMMUNICATIONS DECISIONS

There are many communications decisions in any promotional campaign, and in the international marketing context, there are a number of added dimensions, caused by cultural and other differences in the international markets.

The **methods of promotion** in any one market will be affected by the following.

- The promotional objectives for that market
- Cultural and other social constraints
- Facilities available for promotional effort in the market
- Economic and development
- Distribution infrastructure
- Media availability

The **communication decisions** will be taken at global, regional or national level will vary according to the type of product, of course. The design of the promotional mix will vary according to the product. **Business to business** marketing will take on a different dimension to consumer marketing. **Consumer goods** will be promoted by a balance of direct mail, media advertising and in some cultures, **personal selling**: the most suitable mix will vary from country to country, depending on the cost of the medium and the audience reach. Newspaper advertising may be inappropriate for countries where newspaper readership or even literacy is low; roadside hoardings might be more suitable in some countries.

At global level, a company might decide the overall budget for advertising and promotion generally, and issue **broad guidelines**. Coca-Cola for example is a global product, widely distributed; in its competition against Pepsi, and perhaps other local soft drinks, it relies heavily on advertising. In this case the broad outlines of the promotional decision - that the product should be supported heavily by promotional activity - should be made clear.

That said, it is not always the case that an identical promotional campaign will be successful in each country. There might be **legal constraints**: cigarette advertising is completely banned in some countries and sales promotion techniques are often tightly controlled. Marketing history is full of examples of linguistic gaffes cause by **mistranslation**, and it may be the case that something as basic as a brand name has to be changed to avoid misunderstanding. **Specialisation** however can be expensive. TV commercials can cost hundreds of thousands of pounds, and there are inevitable virtues in economies of scale.

Another issue is the extent to which promotional campaigns support brands which are already strong (such as Coca-Cola) or brands which are new (eg Snapple iced tea in the UK, or Vimto in Russia) in the particular markets.

In the latter case, key promotional decisions will probably have to be taken at national level, as the product will be in a different stage of its **life cycle** (eg introduction as opposed to maturity) and its **portfolio characteristics** will differ (ie it will be a star or question mark, awaiting metamorphosis into a cash cow). Regional and national managers will be able to offer useful advice, if they have had experience of introducing the product elsewhere. While slightly different life cycle patterns may be seen if different markets, the overall shape might be similar in each of them. Lessons learned in some markets might be applied usefully in others, providing those markets have enough in common.

Finally, a degree of enthusiasm in the promotional team is to be encouraged, and there are motivational advantages in their involvement, as well as the advantage of their local knowledge and expertise.

12   DISTRIBUTION DEVELOPMENTS

Introduction

With the increase in competitive forces and the trend towards global business, **distribution and logistics** are developing as one of the major sources of competitive advantage for multi-national companies. This report looks at recent developments and what is being done to take advantage of the changes and stay ahead of the competition.

Key Driving Forces

There are several key changes in the global economy which are changing distribution and logistics. These are as follows.

- The growth of the **global consumer** has meant that many consumers recognise and buy products which originate from many different parts of the world. More and more brands are global eg Nike, Kodak, Microsoft, Reebok etc.

- Companies are becoming more international and operate in several countries.

- New telecommunications **technology**, including the continual expansion and development of the Internet, has contributed to the speeding up of all forms of communications and has contributed significantly to the development in distribution and logistics.

- **Transport communications** are shrinking the world. Air travel has made moving people and goods around the world faster and cheaper.

- Certain types of product are becoming standardised across the world, and concentrated on particular brands eg Kodak and Fuji 35mm film, Sony Walkman, Intel Micro-Processors.

- The desire to hold less **inventory** by manufacturers and retailers has arisen due to uncertainty about the length of time consumers will demand particular products.

- Changes in the **pattern of retailing** have seen greater concentration of retailer power in the developed world.

- Developments in **home shopping** using dedicated TV channels or the Internet have completely changed the distribution of some goods on a global scale.

- **E-commerce** is having a significant effect on the distribution channel in some areas. Business-to-business trading and government procurement are two areas where customer and supplier can communicate their orders, design specifications etc and have them satisfied by electronic communication.

Changes in the activities of multinationals

Multinationals in general, and the vehicle manufacturers in particular, are developing **integrated supply chain management systems** to gain competitive advantage and improve profitability.

For instance, companies such as General Motors already manufacture different parts of their cars for assembly in different parts of the world, with the final product being sold world-wide. These activities are driven by the cost savings that can be made through concentrating production of particular parts at specific locations, and exploiting transport systems to ship the parts cost effectively to where they are needed for final assembly. This allows significant economies of scale to be achieved, resulting in standardised parts being produced at the lowest possible cost.

Lowest cost component production facilities operating to zero defect standards, complemented by the exploitation of cost effective transport systems, enable significant **competitive advantage** to be derived from waste free final assembly operations producing finished goods that exactly meet the customers requirements. This is the Toyota formula for both the supply of new vehicle and parts for the vehicle after-market world-wide.

The impact of the emergence of Global Consumers - Grey Markets

Levi's is a **global brand** targeted at a **global consumer** and priced differently in different parts of the world. Without an integrated and logistic system grey markets would emerge which would undermine Levi's pricing policies. Therefore, Levis must exploit all the advantages offered by modern distribution and logistic systems to ensure that there is minimum stock in the supply chain to avoid grey markets emerging. The supermarkets in the UK try to exploit this grey market (for example Tesco at one time stocked Adidas products).

Information Systems and Management

All of the developments in distribution and logistics have been made practical through the use of information technology, enabling continual improvements to be made to the information in the control systems.

13   SERVICE MARKETING

Presentation Notes on Services Marketing

By: A. Candidate
Audience: Interview Panel
Equipment needed: Slides, Handout

1   Introduction

This presentation outlines a number of key characteristics of marketing any service and then relate these to the particular task of marketing an international hotel.

2   Aims of presentation

(a)   To outline the distinctive characteristics of marketing an hotel service

(b)   To consider in what ways the marketing mix should be extended when marketing the services of an hotel

3   The characteristics of services

Services are harder to trade than goods, but many services are produced and marketed on a global scale, such as airline transport, legal services, media, retailing, fast food and, of course, hotels. Services have the following characteristics.

Intangibility

A significant characteristic of services is the relative dominance of intangible attributes in the make-up of the service product. A service is a deed, performance or effort not a product which can be seen, touched and taken away. This makes it difficult to evaluate before purchase and means that customers do not own the service.

How can the hotel manage this intangibility?

We need to use tangible cues to service quality and manage 'physical evidence'. For example, our staff should look professional which includes a hotel uniform and attention to personal grooming. The decor in the rooms should be spotless and follow the hotel's overall decorative identity. The food we serve should be of a high standard and offer our guest variety.

Inseparability

Services have simultaneous production and consumption which emphasises the importance of the service provider and therefore the role of our contact personnel. The conference organiser and the waiter, in our customers' eyes, is the hotel.

Consequently, selection, training and rewarding staff for excellent service quality is very important. The consumption of the service often takes place in the presence of other customers, as in the restaurant, therefore enjoyment is not only dependent on the service provider but other guests as well. It is important to identify and reduce the risk of possible sources of conflict. For example our restaurant layout should provide reasonable space between tables and smoking areas.

Heterogeneity

This characteristic can also be referred to as variability, this means that it is very difficult to standardise the service our guests receive. The receptionist may not always be courteous and helpful, the maids may not remember to change all the towels and so on. Due to inseparability a fault such as rudeness cannot be quality checked and corrected between production and consumption.

This again emphasises the need for rigorous selection, training and rewarding of staff. Evaluation systems should be established which give our customers the opportunity to report on their experiences with our staff. In addition we must ensure that our processes are reliable. For example, the way we book in guests, organise their keys and deal with checking-out. No hotel is perfect, however it is important for any service delivery failures to be responded to immediately.

Perishability

Consumption can not be stored for the future, once a hotel room is left empty for the night that potential revenue is lost.

This makes occupancy levels very important and it is necessary to match supply with demand. For example if our hotel is busy in the week but not at weekends, a key marketing task is to provide incentives for weekend use. To cater for peak demand we can employ part-time staff and multi-skill full time staff. We can also use reservation systems in the restaurant and beauty salon to smooth out demand and ensure that if our customers have to wait that comfortable seating in the reception is provided.

4 The extended marketing mix

The marketing mix for products is the well known 4Ps of product, price, place and promotion. For service marketing we add three additional Ps to our tool kit: physical evidence, process and people.

Physical evidence is used to manage the essentially intangible nature of the hotel service. As previously stated, smart staff, an impressive lobby and interior design for all areas of the hotel is important to establish an appropriate position and signal this to customers.

Some service ideas transport easily from one country to another (look at McDonalds) and it is often claimed by frequent travellers that a hotel room of an international operator such as Marriott or Hilton looks the same wherever you are in the world. The hotel will need to have a coherent branding strategy, evidenced by staff uniforms for example.

Managing **processes** helps to deal with the inseparability and heterogeneity characteristics. If standards and processes are adhered to a consistent level of service can be delivered. For example receptionists need to be trained to deal consistently with demanding business people and cleaning staff need to prepare rooms to a consistent standard. Airline companies have been aware for many years of the importance of staff giving their best.

Probably the most important element of the services marketing mix is **people**. Hotel staff occupy a key position in influencing customer perceptions of service quality. Without training and control, employees tend to be variable in their performance which in turn leads to variable service quality and customer satisfaction.

5 Conclusions

Key authorities in the field of services marketing all suggest that there are three key jobs for service marketers; managing **differentiation**, managing **productivity** and managing **service quality**. Should I be successful in my application today, I too would make these three issues my top priority for the hotel.

14 CONTROL

There is a close correlation between effective **control systems** and successful organisations. The degree to which control systems are adhered to enables companies to distinguish themselves from the competition. However, continuously analysing and identifying better methods of working and control leads to sustained competitive advantage.

Management commitment

The development and maintenance of effective control systems requires total commitment from management. This commitment needs to permeate to all levels of the organisation. Active involvement from management in the design, development, implementation and evaluation of control systems, taking into account the views of those to be controlled, will encourage widespread ownership of the procedures. Control needs to be positioned as a method of identifying opportunities as well as a means of ensuring performance.

Organisational structure

The level of involvement of subsidiaries in the strategic, operational and tactical management of the organisation will have an impact on the effectiveness of a control system. A **centralised structure** with little involvement of subsidiaries, with control perceived to be handed down on tablets of stone, is unlikely to be as effective as a control system within a **decentralised structure**.

There are fads regarding preference for centralised or decentralised structures. At present the trend appears to be for centralised structures to extract as much cost saving as possible due to no duplication of effort. If other objectives, such as profit or market share, are not achieved with centralised structures then a period of decentralisation will occur, and costs of duplication will be of lesser importance than the achievement of market share and profit.

Financial controls

These are present in any organisation and invariably start with the requirements of the annual budget, whose estimated numbers for sales, cost of sales, gross profit, level of overheads and net profit form the control parameters for the coming year. Comparisons of actual performance against budget are familiar features of late 20th century commercial life.

It is increasingly being recognised that there must be other more effective and more responsive performance measures in the largely computerised world of work. As the world changes so quickly should control systems be developed that operate in real time? No one would expect an oil company to operate an oil refinery based on performance measures established between 12 and 18 months previously, so why should organisations work to such budgets?

Information technology should enable companies to set much shorter term **performance indicators** that are more responsive to market movements than annual budgets. Performance criteria that are set using current data are more likely to be accepted and responded to than criteria set in a different time frame.

Alternative methods of performance assessment and control are being propounded regularly in management literature and it is often recognised that reliance on financial (ie quantitative) measures alone can miss the importance of more qualitative measures, such as customer satisfaction. For this reason the **balanced scorecard** was developed and put forward in 1992 as a means of measuring business performance from both financial and non financial perspectives.

Market research and marketing management information systems (MkMIS)

The maintenance of an effective **MkMIS** is crucial to the control system of any business. All the performance criteria in a control system should be related to the up to date information stored in the MkMIS. No environmental change that has an impact on the business should escape recognition in the MkMIS, and, correspondingly no performance criteria should be set without reference to the MkMIS.

It is recognised that the above is an ideal and such detailed information is not available in many parts of the world. However, the trading records of the company can act as sound **proxy measures** and avoid performance criteria being set which are impossible to deliver. It is impossibilities generated from a lack of understanding of local details that demotivates the people the **performance criteria** are supposed to motivate.

Conclusion

Effective control systems must be based on realistic and timely performance criteria. All personnel must feel that they have contributed to and have ownership of these. Organisations should be in a position to use the real time data that they have in their IT systems to create more effective control systems.

List of Key Concepts and Index

These are the terms which we have identified throughout the text as being KEY CONCEPTS. You should make sure that you can define what these terms mean. Go back to the page highlighted here if you need to check.

BPP
PUBLISHING

BPP PUBLISHING

BPP
PUBLISHING

BPP
PUBLISHING

CIM Order

To BPP Publishing Ltd, Aldine Place, London W12 8AA

Tel: 020 8740 2211. Fax: 020 8740 1184

Mr/Mrs/Ms (Full name)

Daytime delivery address

Postcode

Daytime Tel

Date of exam (month/year)

	5/00 Texts	9/00 Kits	9/99 Tapes
CERTIFICATE			
1 Marketing Environment	£17.95 ☐	£8.95 ☐	£12.95 ☐
2 Customer Communications in Marketing	£17.95 ☐	£8.95 ☐	£12.95 ☐
3 Marketing in Practice	£17.95 ☐	£8.95 ☐	£12.95 ☐
4 Marketing Fundamentals	£17.95 ☐	£8.95 ☐	£12.95 ☐
ADVANCED CERTIFICATE			
5 The Marketing Customer Interface	£17.95 ☐	£8.95 ☐	£12.95 ☐
6 Management Information for Marketing Decisions	£17.95 ☐	£8.95 ☐	£12.95 ☐
7 Effective Management for Marketing	£17.95 ☐	£8.95 ☐	£12.95 ☐
8 Marketing Operations	£17.95 ☐	£8.95 ☐	£12.95 ☐
DIPLOMA			
9 Integrated Marketing Communications	£17.95 ☐	£8.95 ☐	£12.95 ☐
10 International Marketing Strategy	£17.95 ☐	£8.95 ☐	£12.95 ☐
11 Strategic Marketing Management: Planning and Control	£17.95 ☐	£8.95 ☐	£12.95 ☐
12 Strategic Marketing Management: Analysis and Decision (9/00)	£24.95 ☐		

SUBTOLL ☐

SUBTOTAL £ ☐

POSTAGE & PACKING

Study Texts

	First	Each extra	
UK	£3.00	£2.00	£
Europe*	£5.00	£4.00	£
Rest of world	£20.00	£10.00	£

Kits/Passcards/Success Tapes

	First	Each extra	
UK	£2.00	£1.00	£
Europe*	£2.50	£1.00	£
Rest of world	£15.00	£8.00	£

Grand Total (Cheques to *BPP Publishing*) I enclose a cheque for (incl. Postage) £ ☐

Or charge to Access/Visa/Switch

Card Number

Expiry date   Start Date

Issue Number (Switch Only)

Signature

We aim to deliver to all UK addresses inside 5 working days. A signature will be required. Orders to all EU addresses should be delivered within 6 working days.

All other orders to overseas addresses should be delivered within 8 working days.

* Europe includes the Republic of Ireland and the Channel Islands.

REVIEW FORM & FREE PRIZE DRAW

All original review forms from the entire BPP range, completed with genuine comments, will be entered into one of two draws on 31 July 2000 and 31 January 2001. The names on the first four forms picked out on each occasion will be sent a cheque for £50.

Name: _____   Address: _____

_____

_____

How have you used this Text?
(Tick one box only)

☐ Home study (book only)

☐ On a course: college _____

☐ With 'correspondence' package

☐ Other _____

Why did you decide to purchase this Text?
(Tick one box only)

☐ Have used companion Kit

☐ Have used BPP Texts in the past

☐ Recommendation by friend/colleague

☐ Recommendation by a lecturer at college

☐ Saw advertising

☐ Other _____

During the past six months do you recall seeing/receiving any of the following?
(Tick as many boxes as are relevant)

☐ Our advertisement in the *Marketing Success*

☐ Our advertisement in *Marketing Business*

☐ Our brochure with a letter through the post

☐ Our brochure with *Marketing Business*

Which (if any) aspects of our advertising do you find useful?
(Tick as many boxes as are relevant)

☐ Prices and publication dates of new editions

☐ Information on Text content

☐ Facility to order books off-the-page

☐ None of the above

Have you used the companion Practice & Revision Kit for this subject?   ☐ Yes   ☐ No

Your ratings, comments and suggestions would be appreciated on the following areas.

	Very useful	Useful	Not useful
Introductory section (How to use this text, study checklist, etc)	☐	☐	☐
Setting the Scene	☐	☐	☐
Syllabus coverage	☐	☐	☐
Action Programmes and Marketing at Work examples	☐	☐	☐
Chapter roundups	☐	☐	☐
Quick quizzes	☐	☐	☐
Illustrative questions	☐	☐	☐
Content of suggested answers	☐	☐	☐
Index	☐	☐	☐
Structure and presentation	☐	☐	☐

	Excellent	Good	Adequate	Poor
Overall opinion of this Text	☐	☐	☐	☐

Do you intend to continue using BPP Study Texts/Kits?   ☐ Yes   ☐ No

Please note any further comments and suggestions/errors on the reverse of this page.

Please return to: Kate Machattie, BPP Publishing Ltd, FREEPOST, London, W12 8BR

REVIEW FORM & FREE PRIZE DRAW (continued)

Please note any further comments and suggestions/errors below.

FREE PRIZE DRAW RULES

1   Closing date for 31 July 2000 draw is 30 June 2000. Closing date for 31 January 2001 draw is 31 December 2000.

2   Restricted to entries with UK and Eire addresses only. BPP employees, their families and business associates are excluded.

3   No purchase necessary. Entry forms are available upon request from BPP Publishing. No more than one entry per title, per person. Draw restricted to persons aged 16 and over.

4   Winners will be notified by post and receive their cheques not later than 6 weeks after the relevant draw date. Lists of winners will be published in BPP's *focus* newsletter following the relevant draw.

5   The decision of the promoter in all matters is final and binding. No correspondence will be entered into.